Wendy Morgan

Thanks for organizing [illegible]
at the N.Y. Law School [illegible]
your creative input [illegible]
forward to seeing you [illegible] and think
I will because we are both struggling
for equality, justice and real freedom

Dave Dellinger
March 26, 1993

From Yale to Jail

Also by David Dellinger

Cuba, America, Lost Plantations

Revolutionary Non-Violence

More Power Than We Know: The People's Movement Toward Democracy

Beyond Survival: New Directions for the Disarmament Movement
(with Michael Albert)

Vietnam Revisited: Covert Action to Invasion to Reconstruction

David Dellinger

From Yale to Jail

The Life Story of a Moral Dissenter

Pantheon Books
New York

 Published in the United States by Pantheon Books, a division of Random House, Inc., New York, and simultaneously in Canada by Random House of Canada Limited, Toronto.

Library of Congress Cataloging-in-Publication Data
Dellinger, David T., 1915–
From Yale to jail : a memoir / David Dellinger.
p. cm.
Includes bibliographical references and index.
ISBN 0-679-40591-7
1. Dellinger, David T., 1915– . 2. Radicals—United States—Biography. 3. United States—Social conditions—1960–1980. 4. Nonviolence. I. Title.
HN90.R3D46 1993
303.48'4—dc20 92–50473

BOOK DESIGN BY LAURA HOUGH
Manufactured in the United States of America
FIRST EDITION

To Elizabeth

For her life, for fifty years of inspiration and challenge, and for the new insights I have gained from reading the first chapter she has written for her own life story.

And to everyone who has decided—or is thinking of deciding—to live in accord with her or his own feelings of human solidarity and love, rather than by the selfish competitiveness that is enshrined in the present society.

Contents

With a Lot of Help from My Friends

Since I did early drafts of some chapters several years ago, and since so many people read a chapter or more (or heard me read aloud), there is no way I can adequately acknowledge the help I received, let alone remember or list everyone who helped.

My wife, Elizabeth Peterson, my son Dan Dellinger and my friend Dan Weiner read drafts of the entire book and responded with words of great insight and value. Others who gave important help with a particular section or a few chapters were Frederica Matera, Michael Ferber, Noam Chomsky, Howard Zinn, Marv Davidov, David Rome, Jay Craven, Eileen Willenborg, Jane Melnick, Lynn Bonfield, Karen Lewis, Nikko Bowen, Allen Ginsberg, Steve Sato, William Langley, Howard and Betty Douglas, my daughters, Tasha Singer and Michele McDonough, my daughter-in-love Cathy Dellinger, and my grandson Shenandoah Sundance.

My editor at Pantheon, Fred Jordan, gave me outstanding advice and help, even though there were a couple of places (which I won't identify) where I didn't follow it.

From Yale to Jail

Prologue

IN THE UNITED STATES DISTRICT COURT
NORTHERN DISTRICT OF ILLINOIS
EASTERN DIVISION

JUDGE JULIUS J. HOFFMAN, presiding

No. 69 CR-180
UNITED STATES OF AMERICA
Plaintiff
vs.
DAVID T. DELLINGER et al.
Defendants

THE COURT: The court now has the responsibility of dealing appropriately with the contemptous conduct that has pervaded this trial from the very beginning . . .

I will first consider the conduct of the defendant David Dellinger.

[He reads thirty-two charges of contempt of court.]

. . . Mr. Dellinger, do you care to say anything? Only in respect to punishment.

MR. DELLINGER: Yes . . . and I hope you will do me the courtesy not to interrupt me while I am talking.

THE COURT: I won't interrupt you as long as you are respectful.

MR. DELLINGER: Well. I will talk about the facts and the facts don't always encourage false respect.

Now I want to point out . . . that the first two contempts

cited against me concerned one, the Moratorium Action and, secondly, support of Bobby Seale—the war against Vietnam and racism in this country, the two issues this country refuses to solve, refuses to take seriously.

THE COURT: I hope you will excuse me, sir. I ask you to say what you want to say in respect to punishment. I don't want you to talk politics.

MR. DELLINGER: You see, that's one of the reasons I have needed to stand up and speak anyway, because you have tried to keep what you call politics, which means the truth, out of this courtroom, just as the prosecution has.

THE COURT: I will ask you to sit down.

MR. DELLINGER: Therefore it is necessary—

THE COURT: I won't let you go on any further.

MR. DELLINGER: You wanted us to be like good Germans supporting the evils of our decade and then when we refused to be good Germans and came to Chicago and demonstrated, now you want us to be like good Jews, going quietly and politely to the concentration camps while you and the court suppress freedom and the truth. And the fact is that I am not prepared to do that. You want us to stay in our place like Black people were supposed to stay in their place—

THE COURT: Mr. Marshal, I will ask you to have Mr. Dellinger sit down.

MR. DELLINGER: Like poor people were supposed to stay in their place, like people without formal education are supposed to stay in their place, like women are supposed to stay in their place—

THE COURT: I will ask you to sit down.

MR. DELLINGER: Like children are supposed to stay in their place, like lawyers—thank you [motions toward Bill Kunstler and Lennie Weinglass]—are supposed to stay in their places. It is a travesty of justice and if you had any sense at all you would know that the record you read condemns you and not us.

THE COURT: All right.

MR. DELLINGER: And it will be one of thousands and thousands of rallying points for a new generation of Americans who will not put up with tyranny, will not put up with a façade of democracy without the reality.

THE COURT: Mr. Marshal, will you please ask him to keep quiet?
MR. DELLINGER: I sat here and heard that man, Mr. Foran [the prosecutor], say evil, terrible, dishonest things that even he could not believe in—I heard him say that and you expect me to be quiet and accept that without speaking up. People no longer will be quiet. People are going to speak up. I am an old man and I am speaking feebly and not too well, but I reflect the spirit that will echo—
THE COURT: TAKE HIM OUT!
MR. DELLINGER: Throughout the world. [Applause.] [And it] comes from my children, who came yesterday . . . [Marshals grab Dellinger's daughters, twisting their arms behind their backs to force them out of the courtroom.] Leave my daughters alone. Leave my daughters alone.

My sentence on the contempt charges was two years, five months and sixteen days. I was already spending my noncourt hours in the Cook County jail, my bail having been revoked when a Chicago policeman whom I had known earlier as "an honest cop" made up lies about me in his testimony and I responded by speaking up in a way that the judge found offensive. Perhaps it was the effect of that overcrowded and repressive jail (see Chapter 56) that caused me to say "I am an old man . . . speaking feebly." I was only fifty-four at the time but in some ways felt older than I do now at seventy-seven.

The trial began with eight defendants: Bobby Seale (chairman of the Black Panther Party), Abbie Hoffman, Jerry Rubin, Rennie Davis, Tom Hayden, Lee Weiner, John Froines and myself—the so-called Chicago Eight. We were charged with "conspiracy to incite a riot" at the 1968 National Democratic Convention in Chicago and "crossing state lines to incite a riot." But months before our indictment a presidential commission had investigated the disorders and ruled that they had been primarily "a police riot."

Long before the contempt sentencing, Bobby Seale's case had been severed from those of the other defendants and the rest of us had become known as the Chicago Seven. As I will show, the severance was caused by a series of gradually intensifying conflicts in response to governmental maneuvers that first deprived Seale of his right to be defended by the lawyer of his choice and then, in the absence of his lawyer, of the right to defend himself. His last few days in court he was bound, gagged and chained to his chair. It was only after his rights had been denied and he had been physically assaulted by the marshals, even before the bindings and gagging, that I had begun to speak up in court myself. The Moratorium Action that led to my first contempt charge began in the courtroom one morning before the court was in session.

One of the reasons we had demonstrated at the 1968 Democratic Convention was to stop the Vietnam War: "Bring the Troops Home Now!" But we had other goals that have been largely forgotten by most latter-day commentators. Some are indicated by my references to Black people, people without formal education, women, children, a "justice" system that too often keeps the larger truth out of the courtroom and to the existence of "a façade of democracy without the reality." We wanted political changes that would permit *all* the people of the country to participate as equals in the decisions that affect their daily lives, something akin to what Abraham Lincoln called "government of the people, by the people and for the people." We called it "participatory democracy."

By the time of the scene that opens this prologue the trial had gone on for more than four and a half months, and the jury was out deliberating. After four days they found Rubin, Hoffman, Davis, Hayden and myself guilty of having crossed state lines to incite a riot but not guilty of having conspired to do so. Froines and Weiner were acquitted of both charges. All the "guilty" ones were sentenced to five years in jail and fined $5,000 *plus* the "costs of prosecution, *the defendant to stand committed until the fine and costs have been paid.*" Can you imagine what the "costs of prosecution" would have been after nearly five months of trial? But, given the government's aim of using our case to intimidate and discourage a growing and increasingly insurgent movement for justice and peace, I wouldn't have been surprised if the judge had added to our bill the government's costs of lodging and feeding us for five years.

When our attorneys applied for bail, pending appeal, Judge Hoffman's response was "I find they are dangerous men to be at large and I deny your motion for bail."

I have more to say about the Chicago demonstrations and trial, and about my participation in a variety of nonviolent activities that form the personal and political background. But since "The child is father to the man" (Wordsworth)—and mother of the woman—and since "The childhood shows the man as morning shows the day" (Milton), first I will tell you a little about my childhood and early youth. I'll make it brief for now—and return to it at the end of the book, so that you can see the connections from both perspectives.

I

Beginnings

1

My most vivid early memory comes from November 1918, when I was barely three years old. I was playing on a neighbor's big front lawn when the woman of the house, Mrs. Fuller, came running out shouting "Hallelujah, Hallelujah, THE WAR IS OVER! THE WAR IS OVER!" Excited, I ran home to tell my mother, with my nursemaid trailing behind me. My mother didn't believe it, but I was so anxious to believe that the terrible war that everyone worried and talked about had ended that I argued with her. Exasperated, she finally said that my father would tell me the truth when he got home. When he did, he said that Mrs. Fuller was wrong, the war was not over. Two days later, the bells rang and everyone hugged and shouted or cried for joy. This time the war really had ended. It wasn't until years later that I learned the explanation. On November 9, 1918, the German Kaiser abdicated, causing a premature announcement that the war was over. Two days later, the armistice was signed.

We lived in Wakefield, Massachusetts, a suburb of Boston that was still quite rural. When I was in the fifth or sixth grade a German pilot from that war spoke in the Town Hall on the subject of putting an end to old enmities and working for a warless world. A lot of people objected to letting a former enemy speak, but my father took me to hear him and I was moved by his plea for the people of the world to work together to solve their problems rather than going to war and doing terrible things, such as the bombing of cities that he had done.

Earlier, almost as soon as I could talk, people had started asking me what I was going to be when I grew up. But they never asked my sisters. To them they would say, "My, how pretty you are. You'll make someone a lovely wife someday." I was already somebody and so were my sisters, but to adults we weren't people yet. We wouldn't be until we grew up enough for me to become—or be on my way to becoming—a lawyer, businessman or banker and they had become wives. By then we might be as peculiar as they were—and only half alive.

But my Aunt Neva was different. From as early as I can remember she treated me as a person. From her I learned that to be equals you don't have to be the same age or have the same strength, skills, "intelligence" (whatever that is) or anything else. All you have to be is a person, from the moment you are born until you die. Is it intelligent to know how to build a bridge where river, sky, land and sea all meet but not know enough to include a path for people to walk or to ride bicycles on?

When I was growing up, grown-ups said things like "Oh, isn't he smart?"—as if I wasn't supposed to be and wasn't compared to them. They usually meant that I had just said or done something like what grown-ups did, that "I was learning." Too bad. If I kept on learning I might bomb a city someday. Or figure out a way to make a living without working while other people worked for me without making a living. And not give my money or food to people who need it today because I might need it tomorrow—and they wouldn't give it to me then because I didn't give it to them now. It was called being practical, or looking out for the old Number One, as our neighbor the bank president used to say to me. It's the way things work—or don't work, if you are too young to believe that there have to be rich people who are unhappy and die early from consuming too much and not doing enough work, and poor people who are unhappy and die early from not consuming enough and doing too much work.

It's all because of something grown-ups called human nature, but children weren't human nature yet. Indians weren't either. In one of the books my Aunt Neva gave me, Walking Buffalo said,

> Did you know that trees talk? Well, they do. They talk to each other, and they'll talk to you if you listen. Trouble is, white people don't listen. They never learned to listen to the Indians, so I don't suppose they'll listen to other voices in nature. I have learned a lot from trees, sometimes about the weather, sometimes about animals, sometimes about the Great Spirit.

Grown-ups knew a lot of things I didn't, but I could lie on my back in the grass and see things in the sky that they couldn't. They didn't have time. Even if they did, there were a lot of things they didn't see anymore. They even had to go indoors to find out whether it was going to rain, by listening to the radio.

Kids could be friends with trees and clouds, the milkman and their father's friends. One of my father's friends was Calvin Coolidge, when Coolidge was governor of Massachusetts and when he was president. One time when our family was driving through Virginia, on our way back from visiting my grandparents in North Carolina, my mother said, "You shouldn't bother him, Raymond, he's busy. What if everyone who passed through Washington wanted to see him?" But my father said it would be okay, and it was. In the White House, Coolidge said, "This is the boy who asked why I didn't have any hair on my head when I was having dinner at your house. You tried to quiet him, but he was right, just being natural. We should all be more natural like that." When we were leaving, he put his hand on my shoulder and said, "He's a smart one. He'll go places." I liked Mr. Coolidge, but I didn't like the way my father kept telling the story for years. And wanting me to "go places."

My father was a Boston lawyer, chairman of the Town Republican Committee, a tireless fund-raiser for the local Congregational church, the YMCA and other "good causes," and he taught a popular Sunday school class for teenage boys. My mother managed the household, supervised the children, and "entertained"—at afternoon teas, open houses and dinner parties, and as a frequent hostess for the Ladies Bridge Club and the Cosmos Society, a garden club. She attended afternoon concerts and theater matinees with her women friends.

My grandmother on my mother's side was a leader in the Daughters of the American Revolution (DAR), but my mother never joined. The reasons were never explained, but later this reassured me that children don't always have to be just like their parents, even though my parents sometimes seemed to think so.

My father's ancestors were also pre-Revolutionary Americans, but they lived in the mountains of North Carolina instead of in a suburb of Boston. Boston was the Fountainhead of the American Revolution and the Center of Modern Enlightenment. The leading Boston paper called it the "Athens of America" and the "Hub of the Universe." Among their shortcomings, my father's parents were thought to be "poor farmers." So my father was a "self-made man," a shining example of what is possible in our country for people who are willing to work hard, no matter how humble their origins.

When my family visited my father's North Carolina relatives, and I was old enough to notice, I was surprised to find that they had spacious, comfortable houses, served bountiful meals and enjoyed a wide circle of friends by whom they were held in high esteem. Besides the family farm, which was run by my grandparents and one of my uncles, a second uncle owned his own large farm, another was postmaster of a good-sized town and two first cousins owned a thriving nursery business for trees, shrubs and flowering plants. Warm and lovable like my father, they seemed as successful and happy as he was.

My father was the best grown-up I knew at being friends with everyone, rich or poor, milkmen and company presidents. He even defended Catholics, against whom there was a lot of prejudice in our neighborhood. My father would do anything he could to help anyone he knew who was poor or was suffering in any way. But when I think of him now, I think of something Father Helder Camera of Brazil said:

> When I took bread to the poor, people said that I was a saint. But when I asked why they were poor, people said I was a Communist.

A lot of people called my father a saint but no one ever said that he was a Communist. He never asked why people were poor, not if it meant criticizing the economic system that had been so good to him. And he got upset if anyone else did. Especially me when I got older.

The only people he had trouble with were atheists and labor leaders, anarchists like Sacco and Vanzetti, women who smoked and anyone who drank—and that was only if he didn't know them. If he did, he would make excuses for them. They were "different" from the other atheists, labor leaders, drinkers and so on. But even he knew enough not to invite the wrong people to mix with the right people at an open house or dinner party. You could talk with them in a store, on a sidewalk or in your kitchen, but you didn't invite them to come into the front part of the house and sit down, whether anyone else was there or not. Once my father sat down in the front room with someone he shouldn't have. My mother scolded him. "Not in the living room, Raymond. That's for us and our friends. You know how nice I try to keep it."

When the milkman came on Saturday, my father would give him a bear hug from behind until the milkman said "uncle" or broke loose. But my mother always said he shouldn't. She said it was all right to do things like that once in a while with Mr. Beebe, a family friend, but not with milkmen.

One day when the milkman came, my mother said, "You're late, Charlie, I had to wait for you." That puzzled me, because I knew that when she had to go somewhere, she left him a note to tell him what she wanted.

"I'm sorry, ma'am, right away, ma'am. The horses gave me a lot of trouble today, ma'am. First there was lightning and now it's beginning to rain."

"Oh no! It will ruin my plans."

Grown-ups made too many plans, as if they ran the universe. They got angry when a Greater Plan interfered. Or was it just life unfolding naturally without needing a Plan or a Planner? If the rain is your friend, you're glad when she comes, unexpectedly or not, just as you're glad when your other friends, the blue sky and the sun, pay you a visit.

I was going to say that the trouble with grown-ups was that they didn't treat trees and rain the way they treated people, but I guess the trouble was that they did. Something they used to get ahead with or to forget their problems, the ones that gave them so many headaches that they had to carry aspirin everywhere they went. "Damn, I forgot my aspirin." "Here, take mine."

Grown-ups made plans and expected everyone else to fit into them, especially kids and the weather, waitresses and people in the car in front of them. They honked their horns to pass, driving down the mountain or on the bridge by the waterfall, so that they could get somewhere faster. I wondered what they did when they got there.

One of the most important influences in my life was the way my father treated waitresses. He always made excuses for them when they brought the wrong order or did something else that people complained about: "It's okay, miss, that's what I ordered and he can take this one," even though everyone knew he hadn't ordered it and didn't even like the thing he took. Once a waitress spilled some tomato sauce on my mother's new dress. "It was my fault," he said, "I bumped her arm." Everyone knew he hadn't but he knew they wouldn't yell at him the way they yelled at waitresses and other supposedly inferior beings. If they did a little, he could handle it and the waitresses didn't have to. It wasn't just that he did things like that but that our eyes would meet and something very important happened—between us, and inside me.

When I was growing up and until he died, my mother was always teaching my father how to behave. The right way was the way people from "good families" in New England behaved. My father grew up in the Blue Ridge Mountains, so there were a lot of things he didn't understand, even if he had gone to Yale Law School and had played a leading role in the Massachusetts Constitutional Convention. That's where he got to know Cal Coolidge so well, there and during the Boston Police Strike. My father helped patrol the streets and break the strike. When I was in the fifth grade, the Police Strike came up in class and afterwards I hurt my father's feelings by asking if he shouldn't have supported the policemen. I was careful not to use the word "scab," which someone had used in class, but I hurt him anyway. I never brought up the subject again, not even when I was in college and we had lots of arguments about the way things are. I didn't want to hurt him again about something in the past that he had always been proud of.

The case of Sacco and Vanzetti was different, because it was still happening and my father had a choice. They were arrested when I was five and executed on my twelfth birthday. At first I believed that they were bad men but little by little I switched to their side. I hurt his feelings again, but Sacco and Vanzetti were in the death house and my father knew Governor A. T. Fuller, who could have pardoned them. My father kept telling everyone about the latest conversation he and the governor had just had about the case. I was the one whose feelings were hurt, at a very deep level, when he wouldn't ask the governor to pardon them and refused to take me to see the governor so I could.

The Boston Police Strike, Sacco and Vanzetti and the way my father chased my older sister around the house after he caught her smoking all helped me to become independent, even in opposition to my father, who was usually the most loving and compassionate person I knew.

In the section of town where I lived nobody asked the girls what they wanted to be. Everyone knew—wives and mothers. On the other side of town I don't think they asked the girls either. Everyone knew that they would work in the shoe factory, the textile mill or Woolworth's *and* be wives and mothers. Imagine asking someone whether it was her ambition to work in the shoe factory, the textile mill or Woolworth's! Or to clean other people's houses for them.

Of course, some girls would become like Aunt Neva, who wasn't really my aunt at all. She was my grandmother's second cousin but everyone felt sorry for her because she never got married. We called her Aunt Neva so she would feel better. She was an old maid, beginning when she was about thirty. No one asked you to marry him after you were thirty, unless you had lots of money, and my Aunt Neva didn't. Women never asked men.

Everyone loved Neva and she loved them. She seemed a lot happier than my mother or any of the other women I knew, even if she wasn't supposed to be. She gave me books by Charles Dickens, Henry David Thoreau and Emily Dickinson, and she treated me as an equal.

Greg Tuttle's Aunt Patience wasn't married either, but she had more money than my Aunt Neva and didn't have to teach school, so she was a spinster. It wasn't as bad to be a spinster as an old maid. When she left the room everyone lowered their voices and said, "What a shame, too bad—she would have made someone a lovely wife but something went wrong. Too independent, I guess—she always did have a mind of her own."

2

I went to Yale without a lot of questions about its class composition, even though that concern had led me to refuse to spend a year at an exclusive prep school between high school and college. My parents hit me at a potentially weak point when they said that since I was graduating from high school at age sixteen, the extra year would help me to compete in sports with athletes who were closer to my own age. I loved sports and was good at them, so when I resisted this enticement I made one of the most important decisions of my life—that there are more important things than the glory of being a star, in sports or anything else.

But I didn't always live up to that decision in the years ahead, particularly when I was captain of the Yale cross-country team. Our track and cross-country coach thought I had a chance of winning a place on the 1936 Olympic team. But I ruptured a calf muscle, was unable to run as cross-country captain, and reinjured the leg in the first track meet of the spring season when I foolishly ran (and won) the 800-, 1,500- and 3,000-meter runs. It was after this performance that my coach predicted I would make the Olympics, but running the three races had strained the leg, and it never recovered enough for me to run in the Olympic tryouts. By then I think I had finally regained my earlier perspective on the spiritual dangers of being a star, but in between I had intermittently won and lost that battle.

When I first arrived at Yale—and for a long time afterwards—I felt like a young, inexperienced small-town boy (which I was) who had suddenly stepped into a new and exciting world. Yale provided me with friendships, information, activities and courses that opened up a range of problems and struggles that went far beyond my previous knowledge and experience. Step by step, this added a more directly political attitude and involvement to my life, filling in a crucial middle ground between my mystical overview of human unity and my instinctive support of a few aggrieved individuals whom I knew personally—or who, like Sacco and Vanzetti, had been brought to my attention by the intensity of the public controversy about them. In addition, there was a wealth of other excitements: big-time sports, outstanding concerts, trips to nearby New York, visiting speakers and poets. I especially remember Edna St. Vincent Millay and Robert Maynard Hutchins. I had gotten to love Millay's poetry in high school, and now I fell in love with her and her overflowing sexuality. Hutchins presented a view of education that appealed to me and that I eventually concluded Yale didn't live up to, for all the brilliance of some of its faculty.

My first economics instructor, R. R. R. Brooks, took special delight in shocking his students with carefully documented exposés of the hypocrisies and injustices of the U.S. economic system. Later I worked in economics with Irston R. Barnes, a disciple of J. R. Commons, the founder of this country's school of Institutional Economics. Barnes was less fiery than "Triple R" Brooks (as we called him), but systematic analysis of the injustices that are built into our existing institutions and go beyond individual corruption was just what I needed. And Barnes's teaching methods provided an ideal context for searching exploration and discovery, working as we did within the newly instituted Honors Program that emphasized independent research, seminars and private sessions with a tutor.

With Barnes, we conversed more than he lectured, and although he always expressed his own ideas forthrightly, he encouraged us to express ours and to challenge him if we disagreed with him at any point. Even more impressive, he urged us to bring any notes, books and other materials we wished to the examinations. As he put it, the ability to memorize texts, statistics or someone else's ideas is of no great importance. In the real world for which our education should be preparing us, we would have the materials we needed at our elbows, know how and where to get them or have an assistant to look them up for us. What counts, he used to say, is the ability to observe accurately, analyze soundly and think creatively.

The only part that bothered me was having an assistant (an inferior) to look things up for me. Years later, after a conversation with Paul Goodman, I decided that the solution was for the assistant to be an apprentice who was learning a vocation or field of work but was treated as a friend and social equal who was encouraged to contribute freely of her or his insights and abilities. That is the way I tried to approach it in the sixties when my associate, the venerable A. J. Muste, insisted on having a secretary hired to help with the overload of work that was coming in to me. The first one was Ellen Maslow, and in 1991 she embarrassed me—briefly—when I went to Boulder, Colorado, to speak against the Gulf War. In the course of introducing me she said that she had first met me when she had been my secretary. Before I could explain that I always thought of her as a friend and equal who was working for the same causes that I was rather than *for me*, she went on to make the same point. She said that one time she fell seriously behind in her work because of a crisis in the Poor People's Corporation—an organization that she and Abbie Hoffman had founded to market crafts produced by poor people they had worked with in Mississippi—whereupon I told her that her work for the organization was more important than what I was doing and did the work she was behind on myself.

Finally, Ellen found that it made more sense for her to work full time with the Poor People's Corporation, and Barbara Webster took her place. Together we tried to keep up with a myriad of duties and responsibilities associated with publishing *Liberation* magazine and doing civil rights and anti–Vietnam War work. Her insights and knowledge were invaluable and I considered her an equal, whatever the diverse nature of our individual skills, strengths, weaknesses and contributions to our joint work. When people called her my secretary or assistant, I corrected them by saying she was my partner. I can't judge how well I lived up to the term, but we have been close friends ever since, perhaps because of her forgiving nature as well as the many things we have in common.

I always try to encourage anyone who is an apprentice to write letters of his or her own in response to letters originally addressed to me: "In response to your recent letter to Dave Dellinger, with whom I work, my thoughts are . . ." This helps them develop their own creative powers and avoids one of the serious problems in the Peace Movement, which is that some people take credit for mountains of work that someone else does. This aggravates the tendency of the Movement to be identified with a few "leaders" and to be less of an egalitarian community than is healthy and fundamental to its goals. In my experience, some of the failings of the bureaucratic national peace organizations, which I will discuss in Chapter 31 when I come to the Sixties, began when their officials fell into that trap.

At Yale my biggest disillusionment with its academics came from the philosophy department. My instructor in the introductory course was as mechanical and unimaginative as Barnes was exploratory and creative. All semester he gave me "A plus," literally, on every paper and exam until I did a major paper on Plato's *Republic*. I had approached the project with great enthusiasm because of my readings in some of Plato's dialogues and in an excerpt or two from the *Republic*. To my surprise, I was let down by a careful reading of the complete text, and I produced an essay that was severely critical of it. It was only a short undergraduate paper, but it scratched here and there beneath the surface of territory that my friend I. F. Stone would mine comprehensively more than fifty years later, in his book *The Trial of Socrates.** Back came the paper with a "60" on it. Shocked, I read it over carefully and reaffirmed my opinion that it was one of my most thoughtful products. When I discussed the matter with the instructor, I discovered that my offense had been to challenge Plato, whom he worshiped as the primary source of what he thought of as his own enlightenment. Far from appreciating the independence of my thought or the quality of my analysis (which couldn't have been that inferior to my work in earlier papers), he let it be known that it was presumptuous of me to disagree with "experts" who knew more about the subject matter than I did.

Despite this experience, I thrilled to many of my readings in philosophy and enrolled to do honors work in the subject. To do this, I had to be interviewed by the head of the department. I passed the interview, but he didn't. I was appalled by the dry, abstract way in which he approached philosophy. So I interviewed another academically distinguished member of the department, hoping that he would be different and that I might have him for my tutor. He turned out to be no better. The way these two professors approached the subject, philosophy had almost nothing to do with real life or real people—except an in-group of academic experts. There was no dynamic relationship to human beings who are moved by birth and death, loves and hates, hopes and fears, awe and wonder. Instinctively, I felt what the German philosopher Ludwig Wittgenstein expressed in words that I was not to read until years later: "What is the use of studying philosophy if all that it does for you is to enable you to talk . . . about some abstruse questions of logic . . . if it does not improve your thinking about the important questions of everyday life?"

I went home for the summer vacation of 1934 enrolled in philosophy

**The Trial of Socrates* (Boston and Toronto: Little, Brown, 1988). I disagree with some of Stone's interpretations but consider the book an important contribution to understanding Plato, Socrates and the historical and philosophical context in which they lived and to which they responded.

but with a heavy heart and confused mind. For all that I was learning from radical Christians at Yale's Dwight Hall (the University Christian Association) and from some of the antireligious radicals I knew, with both groups sharing my concern for "the small, the variant, the unprecedented, the weak,"* it was not enough. I felt a need for some outside philosophical grounding for holding to the independence I wanted, independence not just from conventional society but also from the religious and secular movements for justice and peace that I worked with. Among other things, I was troubled by their tendency to think that everyone should become like them—whether that meant becoming a Christian or an atheist, an anarchist or a Marxist—and to look down on anyone who didn't. Part of me still clung to the option that the study of philosophy would help me in my search for a sound intellectual center for my spiritual and political impulses and activities, but the evidence to the contrary frightened me.

For the next two months, I sorted things out and gradually came to feel cleansed and energized by the activities that I engaged in. One was my old standby of spending time alone in the midst of Nature's exciting exuberance—looking at the sky, walking in the woods, sitting on a rock by the ocean. Another was sharing with friends from high school (including some who didn't go to college) things that they and I had experienced during the past year, together with the joy, pain, insights and concerns that we had derived from them. Do I need to say that the language of our sharing was not abstract or highfalutin, decidely not the abstruse academese of Yale's philosophy department? Additionally, my summer job was to work from midnight to three in the morning in a factory in Portland, Maine, and then to drive a huge truck until nine, ten or eleven in the morning. This led to some fascinating discussions with my fellow workers in the factory and in the plants where I made deliveries, and to some solitary meditation while driving along the Maine coast. Thanks to all these experiences, I gained the perspective and self-confidence to switch

*The words are from an article about one of the philosophers whom I was most anxious to study, William James, who had thrilled me with his call for "a moral equivalent to war": "James lived his philosophy. . . . It made him an anti-imperialist, a defender of the small, the variant, the unprecedented, the weak, wherever and whenever they appeared" (*Encyclopaedia Britannica*, Fifteenth Edition, 1985).

my honors work from philosophy to economics. Economics was a subject that concerned me deeply, given the human costs of the existing economic system even when it was "successful," and the intensification of those costs when it broke down, as it had in the current Depression. I quickly secured the approval of the economics department and college administration and never took another philosophy course at Yale.

When I got to Oxford three years later, on a graduate fellowship that was largely a reward for my work in economics, I found that my assigned economics tutor reminded me of the philosophy faculty at Yale. Lost in a haze of mathematical abstractions, he showed no real concern for the widespread injustices and human suffering of the time. By contrast, a number of tutors and lecturers in the philosophy department were alive in a human world. This time, I had no hesitations about switching my major study to philosophy, while doing some minor work in economics that I thought would be useful. I also tried to fill in some of the other gaps in my education by attending lectures on a range of subjects—what in the United States is called "auditing" courses: listening and learning but not taking them for credit.

Making these decisions meant deciding not to receive an advanced degree from Oxford, but by then I had no interest in the conventional credentials that tell so little about the real quality of one's education or its value to oneself and one's fellows. Instead, I wanted to improve my understanding of life, as it is and as it might be. Years later, I taught in an adult degree program for B.A. students, first at Goddard College and then at Vermont College. I was asked at Goddard to act as an adviser to Ph.D. students and at Vermont College to M.A. students. I turned down the first invitation for lack of time and accepted the second one. In both cases, the heads of the department were surprised when I said that I lacked both an M.A. and a Ph.D., but both still considered me qualified for the job. And after some thought, I did too.

3

During the first week of my freshman year at Yale, I saw a sign in Dwight Hall inviting students to join a campaign to help the nonacademic employees improve their wages and working conditions by joining a union. I enlisted, but neither my Irish maid nor my Black janitor would talk with me about it. But the Dean did, by calling me into his office.

After telling me what a fine record I had and what a brilliant future lay ahead for me, he said that my janitor had reported me for bothering him by trying to talk to him about a union. The Dean said that the campaign was organized by Communists and that, once I knew this, he was sure that I wouldn't have anything to do with it because it would give me a bad reputation and interfere with my career.

I was so nonplussed that I didn't say much, mostly listening and asking a few questions. But afterwards I decided it was more important to do what I could to help the employees than to worry about what some narrow-minded people might do to prevent me from achieving the kind of success they had achieved. Meanwhile I was curious to find out what Communists were like and kept my eyes open to find out. So far as I knew, I had never met one. Soon I became impressed with the sincere, unconventional Christianity of the graduate secretary of Dwight Hall, the Reverend E. Fay Campbell, and of the Hall's student president, Al Lovejoy, and told them what the Dean had said. They laughed and said that it was a campaign fashioned on Christian principles and if a few Communists joined, so much the better.

No one in the campaign tried to recruit me to the Communist Party, but since this and every other conscientious activity that I supported in the interests of justice, fair play and genuine democracy was called "Communist," I began to think of Communists as people who worked for causes

I believed in. On the other hand, I had found a strong center in Dwight Hall's type of Christianity, with its espousal of issues and attitudes similar to those that I identify today with Liberation Theology. So I had no need, as some people did, to think that if everything good is "Communist," then maybe I am a Communist and should join the Communist Party.

However, I had many spirited discussions concerning communism with my classmate W. W. (Walt) Rostow. We lived in the same entryway during our freshman year and in the same small residential college, Pierson, for the next three years. We were two of the three youngest students in our class and among its top scholars,* so we were often invited to the same small dinners and discussions with visiting dignitaries, people like the poet Robert Frost and New Dealers such as Henry A. Wallace, the secretary of agriculture.† Later, after we had graduated from Yale, Walt and I both went to Oxford, he as a Rhodes Scholar and I as a Henry Fellow. We were in different residential colleges there but met once a week for dinner.

Rostow used to give me books and articles that advocated the basic communist philosophy, including *The Coming Struggle for Power* and *The Rise of Fascism*. The books helped me understand why even the reformed, New Deal version of capitalism was inadequate to the needs of the country and its people, leaving intact the divisions into rich and poor, privileged and underprivileged. But they lacked my spiritual emphasis and took for granted methods that were offensive to me and to my commitment to nonviolent forms of action. That commitment had been strengthened by my association with the people in Dwight Hall, by the campaigns of Mohandas Gandhi and his associates in India, which were

*According to our senior yearbook, we were two of our class's fifteen Scholars of the First Rank.

†I loved Frost's poetry but found him obsessed with his own importance. In the course of at least four dinners together, he always orated endlessly and was never able to listen to and exchange ideas with any of the four or five students present, with the master of Pierson, in whose house we dined, or with the master's wife. Henry Wallace and I became close friends and for years he tried to recruit me to work with him in Washington. By the time he ran for president in 1948, I had been sufficiently disillusioned with him not to support his campaign.

much in the news, and by *The Power of Nonviolence*, a book by Richard Gregg.*

Unlike some people whom I knew in the thirties who seemed sympathetic to the communist philosophy, Rostow didn't seem to have strong emotions about any human beings, not love and not hatred. Disdain for the unenlightened was more his style. Human beings seemed to be as abstract to him as they were for the distinguished professors of the philosophy department. To him, politics seemed to be a geopolitical chess game in which the people were pawns and enlightened people like him and me were destined to move them around—always with the aim of making progress toward an eventual society that would be more just. So, years later, I was not particularly surprised when Rostow changed views and worked with presidents Kennedy and Johnson to help plan the "armed struggle" in Vietnam, Laos, Cambodia and Thailand, using U.S. GIs and the peoples of those countries as pawns in the effort to gain U.S. domination of Indochina. "To save them from Communism" is the way he put it.

In contrast to those who supported the communist philosophy, I couldn't believe that armed struggle, with the bloodshed and hatred it would generate, was the way to build a better world. And, equally important to me, as I grew to know Communists, I found that often their attitudes ran counter to my beliefs that people who wanted to create a better world should live *now* as much as possible in the kind of human relationships they were supposedly working for instead of waiting until "after the revolution" to start doing so. When they showed compassion for the victims of injustice and sacrificed their own material comfort or chances of worldly success to aid them, as many of them did, I felt close to them. But when they lived extravagantly expressed bitter, unforgiving hatred of racists, exploiters, opposing politicians, policemen and the Yale students who ignored or condemned their activities, I drew back from them. I preferred the injunction of Jesus that we should love our "enemies" and pray for those who despitefully use us (or others!). And

*Gregg spent four years in India working with Gandhi and drew on his own firsthand experience to make a convincing case for the dynamic power of nonviolent action.

Gandhi's teaching that our opponents should never even be thought of as enemies.

Meanwhile, there were reports of politically motivated phony trials, executions and concentration camps in the Soviet Union. It took me some time to read everything I could that attempted to prove or disprove the charges, and finally to decide that they were at least partly true. By contrast, Walt Rostow didn't seem particularly concerned either way. Mostly he seemed to think it was all part of the dialectical process of history that was leading to progress—from feudalism to capitalism to the dictatorship of the proletariat to classless Communism.

While Rostow and I were at Oxford, a Yale classmate by the name of Bernie Rankin, a former football star and a fellow officer of Phi Beta Kappa, was studying at Cambridge University, also on a prestigious fellowship. He visited us from time to time, and once he arrived with a plan for signing up the best and brightest of our Yale associates to enter government service. The three of us were to head up a committee to do this, and the effort was to extend to current and recent students of Princeton and Harvard as well as Americans we knew at Oxford and Cambridge. The idea stemmed from a visit to Cambridge by the New Deal economist James Gamble Rogers, who offered me a job and sold Rankin on the plan. When the three of us discussed it, Rostow seemed attracted to it, but I argued that it was too cut off from the grass roots, too "brain-trusty," too noblesse oblige.

Around the same time, I decided to forgo the second year of my fellowship at Oxford in favor of returning to my own country. After several visits to Nazi Germany, I was impatient to work at home against the continuing alliance of the U.S. corporations and government with the Nazis and against the immigration quotas that were turning away Jewish refugees. Also, racism was on the rise, with a spate of lynchings, and the ravages of the Depression were continuing. Hardly had I made this decision known to friends at Yale than I received a job offer from the Dean of Yale College, Norman Sidney Buck, asking me to help inaugurate a program that would encourage a "more positive relationship" between students and the Yale establishment. He wanted me to act as the College's official counselor to freshmen.

I turned down the invitation, choosing instead to work for Dwight

Hall, also as a freshman counselor. In that job I could be freer to encourage a different type of positive relationship with the university than the Dean had in mind, likeable as he was within his own commitment to noblesse oblige. And freer to encourage a vital relationship between students and the disestablished members of our society.

For the next two years I worked more closely with off-campus poor people, a range of union organizers and a variety of outside radicals than I had as a student. I helped organize a free, working-class university that met in a Yale building and had both Yale professors and people from the wider New Haven community on its faculty. I spent one vacation working at some personal risk in a south Jersey company town (Florence) with the Steel Workers Organizing Committee, founder of the United Steel Workers of America. And I began taking trips "on the road" among the unemployed, and worked once again in a union-organizing campaign for Yale's nonacademic employees. To the excitement of these activities was added the thrill of working with students who, at a turning point in their lives, were examining what they really thought about most everything, including what kind of life they wanted to live—at Yale and afterwards.

The union campaign failed, once again, to gain more than minimal benefits for the university's nonprofessionals, and little did I know that forty years later it would still be going on and that I would be involved in it a third time. I will say a few words about the third try now, to complete that part of my history at Yale.

In 1977 I was asked to teach a seminar at Yale. The invitation came because the agitations of the Sixties and Seventies had resulted in a program where students could request an outsider to conduct a seminar. The request had to be approved by the head of one of the departments, and I was approved by the head of the history department, Gaddis Smith, to teach "Radical Dissent and American Politics." Once a week I journeyed to Yale from my home and job in New York City to spend a day and evening with the students.

When I arrived for my first class, the nonacademic employees had announced a strike that would have begun by the time of my next week's class. Weighing my interest in my students and in the people who worked as their servants, I told the students that their assignment for the next class was to investigate the situation and prepare to argue the pros or cons of the strike, together with proposals for what we as a class should do. My own assignment, I said, would be the same.

By the following week, I had decided that my hope was to hold the seminar off campus, as a method of continuing the study while supporting the striking employees. But I didn't say this until after we had gone around the circle of students. After considerable discussion, we arrived at a consensus to do this. I particularly remember that the student who initially argued most forcefully against any support for the strike was a Black man. Obviously, he hoped to use his Yale education as a method of rising higher than most Blacks are allowed to rise in our society and didn't want any blots on his Yale record similar to the one that Dean Warren had warned me against forty-five years earlier.

The strike took place while Yale was choosing a new president, A. Bartlett Giamatti. Shortly after he was selected, Giamatti announced that he planned to tighten up the requirements for the seminar program so that its future faculty would have "better academic qualifications than Howard Cosell and Dave Dellinger." I hadn't known that Cosell was teaching a seminar and knew nothing about his academic qualifications, but I felt sure that it wasn't my lack of them that bothered Giamatti as much as my support for the strike and my past and current political activities. If there had been any question in my mind, it disappeared when I was speaking at Yale a year or two later and students showed me an article by Giamatti that criticized the New York Mets pitcher, Tom Seaver, for having spoken out against the Vietnam War. According to Giamatti, Seaver's job was to throw the ball with the speed and accuracy that made it beautiful for the spectators to watch and hard for the batter to hit, not to interject himself into political matters that didn't concern him.

Ironically, Giamatti was the son-in-law of my childhood and high school friend Peggy Walton.

4

While I was still a student at Yale, I gradually discovered that most of the professors whose teaching had contributed to my political radicalization were not ready to act in accord with the conclusions that followed logically from their analyses. They were sufficiently influenced by the Yale ethos and pressures to hold back from calling publicly for societal solutions more basic than the Band-Aids of the New Deal. Even my economics teachers who spoke to their students of the need for a strong union movement stayed aloof from the campaigns to help the nonacademic employees form a union. A few of the younger teachers were more principled, failed to get tenure and were soon gone, whereas most of those on the faculty who played the game and got tenure seemed, in the process, to lose sight of the presumed purpose for which they had played it—to get to a position of security from which they could operate freely as open persons, following the truth wherever it led them.

Meanwhile, similar pressures were exerted on the students: they might be scholarship students who were not high in the ruling classes when they entered or students who came more obviously from the ruling classes and who followed their youthful consciences for a time to challenge the country's race and class prejudices. But Yale did its utmost to train and condition them either to become or remain members of the ruling classes.

Yale's role for scholarship students seemed to be similar, in its way, to the historic context in which European royalty were periodically allowed (or encouraged) to strengthen bloodlines by marrying commoners—according to a well-established theory, royal blood sometimes ran thin from too much inbreeding, resulting in visibly weakened offspring.*

Similarly, Yale's function in the supposedly democratic United States was to reach out to a few of the "most promising" of each year's white middle-class high school seniors and provide scholarships for them to attend Yale. Then the economic royalists among its faculty, administration and alumni guided them into prestigious careers. In the United States, whatever happened or didn't happen to the bloodlines, the corporate boardrooms and top management clearly gained—but not to the benefit of the bulk of the country's "commoners."†

Perhaps I thought this not just because I observed the way so many of the students from a poorer background were gradually corrupted morally by the Yale way of life and incorporated into ruling circles, but because scattered through the student body were a number of young men from the country's richest and most powerful families who did not seem qualified by normal academic standards to be there. It was hard to believe that they would have been admitted if they had come from less prestigious or less affluent families. Of course, there were many others from similar families who possessed outstanding qualities, but even so it was clear that personally ambitious recruits from other strata were needed if the selfish interests of the country's economic royalty were to be maintained.

In coming to this conclusion, I was undoubtedly influenced by the way I myself was flooded with offers to become a member of one layer or another of that elite, whether by working in the New Deal administration or as an executive in Continental Can, Weyerhaeuser Industries,

*In the words of my historian friend and fellow activist Harvey Wasserman, "Through most of the 1700's the British throne belonged to the house of Hanover, an inbred line plagued by mental illness. George II . . . was notorious for his habit of running through London streets at night, breaking windows. His own father described him as 'a half-witted coxcomb.' A wife was chosen for him chiefly for her relative sanity, but the royal heir was nonetheless born retarded. George III [the king when the U.S. colonies declared their independence] was unable to read before age eleven" (*America Born and Reborn* [New York: Macmillan, 1983]).

†I am, of course, speaking of the Yale of my day, when there were no Black students. Later, the process was extended to Blacks. Naturally, not all of them turned out to be like Clarence Thomas, a graduate of Yale Law School.

IBM, the J. Walter Thompson advertising agency or Colgate, Palmolive, Peat—to mention a few corporations that come readily to mind. In all honesty, I have to say that these unsolicited job offers were usually made by adults who were convinced that they were genuinely concerned for the best interests of the students, the college, their business or governmental department and the country. In their own minds, they were acting out the Yale slogan of "For God, for Country and for Yale." And on a personal level I liked most of the individuals who made the offers.

By coincidence, one of the pressures on me to accept one of the jobs came during the the coronation of George VI in December 1936, while I was studying at Oxford. That undoubtedly helped confirm my hypothesis that Yale served a function for the "democratic" United States similar to that of the matchmakers who arranged for marriages between England's personally enfeebled royalty and genetically healthy commoners. It happened that Carle C. Conway, the president of Continental Can Company and a graduate member of my Senior Society at Yale, came to London with his wife to attend the coronation and they invited me to stay with them at one of London's most prestigious and expensive hotels. We had a wonderful time together, but I couldn't help being embarrassed when we got up in the morning and went to the balcony of our second-floor suite. It overlooked the coronation route and the sidewalks and gutters that had been jam-packed for twenty-four hours or more with commoners waiting to see the new king driven by. It had been awkward enough the night before to be ushered through them into the hotel. Now, as I sipped the champagne from our champagne breakfast, clothed in the silk pajamas and dressing gown that had been supplied me (whether by Carle or the hotel I can't remember), I was mortified. It didn't make me feel any better when Carle tried once again to convince me to accept the top-level job that he was "saving" for me. It was like something I had written earlier about one of my Wakefield neighbors, the president of the National Casket Company, when he had offered me a job: "How could I fail to like him? At the same time, how could I fail to see that his way of life . . . was contrary to the ideas and feelings that were moving inside me and beginning to shape my life?"

5

When I worked at Dwight Hall from September 1937 through May 1939, the U.S. Communist Party had made a temporary turn toward emphasizing its patriotic Americanism. Earl Browder, the head of the Party, called Communism "Twentieth-Century Americanism," and the Party organizer in New Haven talked about Thomas Paine, Samuel Adams, Thomas Jefferson and "the glorious American Revolution" more than about Lenin, Stalin and the Soviet Union. I liked Paine, Adams and Jefferson more than I liked Lenin or Stalin, but this newly found pro-Americanism bothered me—in part because it didn't seem sincere, in part because it led them to speak as if the country's founding fathers were flawless models for a Twentieth-Century movement. They never mentioned that both Washington and Jefferson were slave owners and, along with the other founders, advocates of the private-profit capitalism that neither I nor the Communists believed in. Moreover, I had recently read two books by Charles A. Beard that made clear that the egalitarian promise of the Declaration of Independence had been abrogated (even for whites) when the country's wealthy landowners combined to draft a constitution that enshrined property rights over human rights.

Writing about the Constitutional Convention in *The Rise of American Civilization*,* Beard emphasized that

> "none of the fiery radicals . . . was present. Jefferson . . . was out of the country; Patrick Henry was elected but refused to attend because he "smelt a rat"; Samuel Adams was not chosen; Thomas

*New York: MacMillan, 1927.

> Paine left for Europe that very year. . . . So the Philadelphia assembly . . . was made up of practical men of affairs—holders of state and Continental bonds, money lenders, merchants, lawyers and speculators in the public land. . . . More than half the delegates were either investors or speculators in public securities which were buoyed up by the new Constitution, all knew by experience the relations of property to government.

In the *Economic Interpretation of the Constitution** Beard wrote,

> The [new] system consisted of two fundamental parts. . . . I. A government so constructed as to break the force of majority rule and prevent invasions of the property rights of minorities. II. Restrictions on the state legislatures which had been so vigorous in their attacks on capital. . . . Indeed, most property owners have as much to fear from positive governmental action as from their inability to secure advantageous legislation. Particularly is this true where the field of property is already extended to cover every form of tangible and intangible wealth.

But the Communists never mentioned such realities and steered the conversation away from them when I brought them up on occasions when they were present. That told me that they were playing games with the public instead of dealing straight with them.

Even so, Communists were by far the most energetic organizers of many of the struggles I supported, for racial and economic justice, industrial unionism and even civil liberties. So, despite my worries about the manipulative aspects of their new line, my distrust of the Soviet Union and some disappointments I had experienced with Communists in civil war Spain (see Chapter 14) and in England, I reached a point where for a few short weeks I gave some thought to the possibility of joining the Party. I think I must have been looking rather needfully for a secular political home to supplement the alliance I had with radical religionists. In a way it was similar to my earlier attempt to major in philosophy in

*New York: MacMillan, 1935.

order to find an intellectual base to supplement my involvement in Christian radicalism. This time my thoughts about possibly joining the Communists came shortly after a disappointment I experienced with another political party, the Socialist Party of Norman Thomas. Thomas's sermons at Battell Chapel and his other talks had inspired me, and I was further influenced by visits to Yale of two outstanding women approximately of my age, Fay Bennett and Robin Myers. Neither was religious in the sense that I was, but I had felt an immediate spiritual as well as political connection with each woman, and both were members of the Socialist Party. But when I was invited to a dinner party in Thomas's New York City apartment, my disappointments were twofold. First, the setting was distinctly upper class. We were attended by a white-coated Puerto Rican servant who catered to us as if we were guests in one of the upper-class English castles at which I had been an uncomfortable guest a few months earlier. To my even greater dismay, Norman treated him more like the parents of my upper-class Oxford friends had treated their servants than as a friend and equal. Second, although Norman was not nearly as offensive as Robert Frost had been during my dinners with him at Yale, he clearly acted, somewhat like Frost, as if everyone was there to listen to him and absorb his wisdom rather than to express thoughts of our own and participate in a genuine exchange of ideas. I didn't know A. J. Muste at the time, but looking back now I contrast the way he always questioned and listened to others and incorporated something of what they thought and said into his own thinking, even when he offered his own modifications or disagreements. And I look back and contrast Norman's manner in such a setting with that of his brother, Evan Thomas, a medical doctor and a more persistent antiwar activist than Norman, who became one of my closest friends and supporters from 1941 on. Evan held strong opinions and didn't change them easily, but he knew how to listen seriously with the respect we all owe to one another.

Whatever the background that led to my exploration of the Communist Party as a possible secular political home, the turning point came when I was invited to attend a state convention of the Connecticut Communist Party. The tone of the debates and the subservience of the delegates to their top, out-of-state leadership were such that I knew I could never join such a party. It bore no resemblance to the "beloved community" of warm-hearted democratically functioning, egalitarian revolutionaries that I wanted to be part of. In the early debates the spokespersons for the different "tendencies" treated one another with a contempt exceeded only by their greater contempt for their rivals in several Trotskyist groups and in the Socialist Party. Then a member of the Party's Central Committee arrived from New York, went to the platform and announced a new line that had nothing to do with the preceding debates and reversed a key point in the position that the Party had been taking for months. It had to do with how to apply in the United States the call that Georgi Dimitrov had made in 1936, at the Seventh World Congress of the Comintern, for a worldwide Popular Front.

Until then, working for a Popular Front had been interpreted to mean building an alliance of progressives of all kinds *outside the Republican and Democratic Parties*, looking toward the building of what they called a "mass party of the people." Now, the message from the top was to work inside the "progressive Democratic Party" of Franklin Roosevelt. I heard a few private grumbles, but no one challenged the announcement or raised any serious questions. The speaker talked about how to carry out the new line and the members went home to do it. I was doubly offended: first, by the manner in which the directive was issued and accepted, and second, by the idea of working within the Democratic Party to achieve basic social change. Later, my Party-organizer friend explained to me privately that it was necessary to work inside the Democratic Party in order to counter Roosevelt's tendency to play ball with Nazi Germany and isolate the Soviet Union. Since they and their allies had failed to achieve this through independent activities and pressures from outside the Democratic Party, as was notoriously the case in the U.S.'s de facto support to the Nazi-supported Franco, they must change their tactics. (Officially the United States used the Neutrality Act to prevent the shipment of arms to either side in the Spanish Civil War, but sub rosa it permitted, even encouraged, the shipment of arms to Franco.)

I was never tempted by Communist politics again and, despite my disappointing dinner with Norman Thomas, joined the Socialist Party, becoming, in fairly short order, a member of the executive committees of both its youth and adult sections. And I had some more positive experiences with Norman than the one I have reported, even though something similar to my earlier experience came back to haunt me a few years later, when the Party was debating the stand it should take on World War II. Norman, acting a little like the out-of-state leader had acted at the Connecticut convention, forced a reluctant national convention to adopt a pro-war stance that was contrary to its previous position and clearly contrary to the private views of a majority of the delegates.

6

My last fistfight took place at Yale, after my return from Oxford. I blush to recall the circumstances.

One Saturday afternoon, Yale played Georgia in football and Georgia won. There were very few Georgians there to savor the victory, but in the closing minutes of the game there was a surge of jubilant "townies" onto the field to tear down the goal posts. They were immediately followed by a rush of Yale students to thwart them.

At first, my companions and I stayed aloof and watched the battle from our seats. But when the goalposts fell, it was more than my friends could stand. If students from Georgia had pulled them down, they would have made a few condescending remarks and let the matter rest. Georgia students may have been our "inferiors," but they were like second cousins from less prestigious branches of the family, looked down on but tolerated on brief special occasions such as this one. They did not constitute a rebuke to Yale's way of life or represent a shadowy threat that might emerge some day as a real and present danger.

Townies were another matter. They represented an alien and hostile world whose lurking dangers had been brought close to the surface by the Depression. Their interference now in matters that did not concern them symbolized the underlying threat "civilized" people always feel from restless natives. They were the visible presence of all the "unwashed peoples" (a common phrase at Yale those days*) who challenged the legitimacy of the way of life and adult glories for which Yale was preparing its students. Their general "uncouthness" (lower-class manners) was joined to an "irrational" hatred of Yale. All during the game, whenever cheers for Georgia had gone up, there had been sneering comments in the Yale section about people who, knowing that Georgia was one of the best teams in the country, had gone without lunch for weeks in order to buy a cheap seat in the end zone and gloat over Yale's expected defeat. I was disgusted by these comments and had gotten into a little trouble with two loudmouths behind me by asking when the last time was that they had gone without a meal for any reason. My feeling was that if some townies had done so, it was a compliment to their desire to do something about the daily humiliations they were expected to endure with a smile.

This was the context in which my companions rushed onto the field to reclaim the captured goalposts, and in which I followed them. I went not to enter the fray but to wait nearby for the time when we could join up again and return to the college.

About an hour later, we finally got back to the edge of the campus, riding on the outer steps of one of the open trolley cars (San Francisco cable-car style) that were used on football weekends. My friends were triumphantly carrying a section of the goal posts as evidence of Yale's victory over the barbarians. By then, success in this engagement had become more important to them than the defeat by Georgia in the game. But suddenly, a swarm of townies descended upon us in a last effort to recapture the spoils of victory. In the course of the attack, I was blindsided by one of them. Quite understandably, he viewed me as one of the Yalie enemies rather than as the innocent bystander I had told myself I was, a noncombatant accompanying my combative friends back to school.†

*Do I need to say that the phrase did not refer to hippies, as it would have in the Sixties? The hippies were in revolt against the same artificial and overprivileged way of life that offended the townies, but most of them had been born into it, while the circumstances into which the townies had been born excluded them from it.

†The logic of his belief and the virtual inevitability of my response taught me a lesson that stood me in good stead a few years later when well-meaning friends were urging me to express my nonviolent convictions in a "positive way" by doing "noncombatant"

The sharp pain from the blow, the affront to my neutrality, and my personal loyalty to my hard-pressed friends combined to transform me into an active combatant. I joined the fight, chased down the one who I thought had clobbered me, and, after a few harmless exchanges, landed a haymaker on his chin. He slumped to the pavement, out cold.

I shall never forget the horror I felt the instant my fist struck solid flesh. It was the exact opposite of what Robert Frost speaks of as hearing "the clean sound of the axe striking good wood."

I had never experienced anything like this before. Like most boys, I had engaged in occasional fights when growing up. In most of them I had bloodied my opponents or whipped them into submission, without feeling good about it. The only fight I remember feeling good about was one I lost in the fifth grade defending a little kid against Jimmie Dean, an older bully. Very early I had come to feel that I did not enjoy fighting and that it was senseless. Fisticuffs was a silly, prideful way of settling disputes by evading the issue under contention and focusing on the irrelevant issue of who could win a physical battle. If I had enough good will, imagination and a certain kind of courage, fighting was seldom, if ever, necessary. So, from seventh or eighth grade on I had usually talked off an opponent, holding him at bay—physically if necessary—until I could neutralize him through laughter at the ridiculousness of the situation or disarm him by convincing him of the genuineness of my desire to work out our differences and be friends. I had not read Gandhi yet, but I was operating intuitively on the Gandhian principle of refusing to let one's opponent choose the weapons with which one fights.

Now my feelings went far beyond those early experiments. The lesson I learned was as simple, direct and unarguable as the lesson a child learns the first time it puts its hand on a red-hot stove: *Don't ever do it again!* But the pain I felt was a spiritual pain, as if I had suddenly emerged from a fit of anger and realized that I had pressed a child's hand onto the stove. I knew that I would never be able to strike another human being again.

---

service in the U.S. Army. Of course, I had other reasons as well for not taking this position.

When my victim fell, I dropped to my knees, lifted his head and inert upper body and cradled him until he came to. By then both his friends and mine had been long gone, the mobility of the fighting and chasing having carried them away. I walked him home—to be sure that he was all right and to convey more meaningfully my sadness, shame and love.

Sadness, shame *and love*? In line with the conditioning I have never completely outgrown to underexpress (and underlive) my true emotions, I first wrote "to convey more meaningfully my regrets and apologies." But from reliving that afternoon by writing about it, I have been reexperiencing the emotions I felt at the time and know that the shock I experienced had stripped away a layer of my conventional defenses. Sadness, shame and love were what I felt and wanted to communicate.

When we got to my new friend's neighborhood, he thanked me for my help and said, somewhat wistfully, I thought, that he was all right and didn't want me to go any farther with him. For a moment, I wondered whether he was afraid for my safety on that day of battle; but perhaps he would have been worried on any day to be seen in his neighborhood with a Yalie. Yet his manner indicated that something deeper was at work and that he felt the power of our unexpected and unusual bonding. And then he proved it by giving me a quick, shy hug and walking rapidly away.

I never saw my "enemy" again, but the impact of our encounter has never left me. I will always remember the spontaneous feeling of horror at striking human flesh and the absolute nature of my knowledge that I would never again be able to hit anyone. But later I'll tell you how I wavered, in prison, when I thought it might be necessary to hit someone in order to protect someone else. As Rabbi Abraham Hertzberg has said in a different context, "Our truths are not absolute. They are biographical."

7

The second winter after the 1929 stock market crash, my parents took my sister Lib and me to New York for a week of shows and sightseeing. I was fifteen at the time. We stayed at a fancy new hotel near Pennsylvania Station. Around the corner from the main entrance, there was a long line of men in shabby clothes, a "breadline" of people waiting for a free meal. The line stretched down the block and out of sight around a distant corner. For days we never left or returned to the hotel without seeing these people. And when I looked obsessively out my window from ten or fifteen stories up, there they were, tiny figures huddled together against the cold.

The first chance I got, I walked down the block looking at the faces of the men, wondering what it was like for them, wondering where they went after their hours of standing in line for a meager supper. I wondered why there weren't any children there and only a few women. What happened to them? How did they get fed? Did the men bring home to them whatever they could slip into their pockets? Could it be true that the men and their families preferred this kind of life to working?

I never forget that breadline, but it wasn't until a few years later that I found out for sure whether most of them wanted to work or not, whatever I had thought and argued in the meantime. I found out by leaving Yale one afternoon in my oldest clothes and without any money, hitching rides and riding freight trains for a couple of weeks, staying at missions and in hobo jungles, standing in breadlines myself.

It was an artificial attempt to get to know in a natural way some of the people who a lot of my Wakefield neighbors and Yale associates said were lazy. And it worked. My experiences on the road and the personal relationships I shared were less artificial than the privileged life I had been living. They broke the mold of the abstract and intellectual arguments I had been involved in. They had a profound effect on the rest of my life.

I might not have gone on the road that time except for some other things that happened in the years that followed my first unsettling glimpse of a breadline. The first of them occurred outside Dwight Hall, the University Christian Association, during my freshman year. Inside, the graduate secretary was leading a small group of us in a discussion of what it meant to be a Christian in an un-Christian world. Suddenly we heard through the open window some excited shouts and the sounds of a policeman's whistle. We rushed to the window but could not see what was happening. A few minutes later a late arrival informed us that a "bum" had collapsed on the campus and the university police had summoned an ambulance. The rest of the discussion ignored what had happened, but for some reason I brooded on it.

Back in my room trying to go to sleep, I couldn't get the incident out of my mind. Finally I got up, dressed, went to the office of the campus police and asked some questions. The man on duty was annoyed that "a bum" had slipped through their security precautions and gotten onto campus. Usually such people had to hang around on the streets just outside the university grounds if they wanted to solicit the students for funds. In the end, the officer told me which hospital he had called for the ambulance. By then it was after midnight, but I walked to the hospital.

"Who are you? Why do you want to know?"

"Was he a relative? What business is it of yours?"

"We're busy. Come back tomorrow, during visiting hours."

Eventually I worked my way through to a sympathetic intern who told me that the man had died. "Of malnutrition," he said. I asked some more questions and finally, after looking me up and down and obviously taking in my Yale clothes and Yale look, he said in the manner of an older, wiser brother: "If you really want to know, he died of starvation."

"Had he been drinking?"

"There were no signs of alcohol at all."

I asked this question because the conventional wisdom at Yale was "Don't give them money; they'll just spend it on liquor."

From then on, still nervous about liquor but anxious to help some of those whose plight had been brought home to me—and wishing both to establish human contact and to learn more—I ate more meals than I otherwise would have in the nearest off-campus cafeteria.

"I'm just on my way to get a bite myself," I used to say. "Would you like to join me?"

So they had to pay for their meal by submitting themselves to my questions and conversation, though I tried to be sensitive to their pride and to act as a friend rather than an interrogator.

At least it probably wasn't as bad for them as it would have been at the Yale Hope Mission, located a few blocks off campus, which received some financial and other assistance from Dwight Hall. There, they were lectured for their sins, exhorted to repent, and allowed to stay longer if they accepted Jesus Christ as their Lord and Savior. The nightly sermons were usually preached by Mac, the superintendent of the Mission, but one night a week a Yale student held forth. Mac, a good-hearted Irishman with a heavy brogue, was a reformed alcoholic who attributed all his own past sufferings to drink and defiance of the Lord.

For a long time I said no when asked to preach there, because I had attended one of the services and had been offended by the way the men were attacked for their plight. Finally I yielded, strengthened by some of the real (if temporary) friendships that had developed during a few of the cafeteria meals and determined to carry the spirit of those meetings into my selection of the scripture reading and talks. That meant, among other things, that I would speak humbly, which wasn't hard, given the things I had learned from the men I had eaten with. And I would make clear that in my view Christianity was a loving, not blaming, religion, one in which no one was without sin and no one was entitled to throw any stones. It was my first sermon and I remember parts of it better than almost any of the thousands of talks of one kind or another that I have given since.

The words I chose from the Scriptures were:

> For I was an hungered and ye gave me meat; I was thirsty and ye gave me drink; I was a stranger and ye took me in; naked and ye clothed me; I was sick and ye visited me; I was in prison and ye visited me.
>
> Then shall the righteous answer him, saying, Lord, when saw we thee an hungered and fed thee? Or thirsty and gave thee

> drink? When saw we thee a stranger and took thee in? Or naked and clothed thee? Or when saw we thee sick or in prison and came unto thee?
>
> And the King shall answer and say unto them. Verily, I say unto you, inasmuch as ye have done it to the least of these my brethren, ye have done it unto me.*

Sitting on the platform before the talk, I tried to establish eye contact with some of the more alert men in the pathetic huddle in the pews and to give them a friendly, if timid, smile. I wanted them to know from the beginning that I was their friend, not a lofty moralist from a world of superior virtue. To provide verbal substance for this message, I began my talk by saying that they had far more experience in life than I did and that it would be presumptuous of me to do more than tell them of some of my own experiences and the thoughts and feelings that came from them. Fairly quickly, I could see that some of them were responding to this unexpected approach—and that Mac was too. I remember being surprised by the nods of approval from a few of the men in the front rows, and even some mutters of agreement. But then I glanced over at Mac. Probably I was nervous about what he would think or do, but I also hoped that he had noticed the response I was getting. "Get to the message, lad" was his anguished murmur. "Jesus, lad, tell them about Jesus."

I did admire Jesus and had learned a lot from reading about him, at least in my way if not exactly in Mac's, and I did get to that after a while. But I am sure that I did so in a less natural way than would have been possible if I had not felt the pressures that came from being caught between my desire to be straight with the men and my feeling that I was an interloper on Mac's turf, violating the rules of the house.

After I had finished and sat through the agony of having Mac call them to repentance, call them to come forward and accept the Lord as their Savior, I was immensely pleased that a few of the men came up and talked with me, some who had come forward earlier to be saved and some who had not. But our conversation lasted only a few moments before Mac

*Matthew 25:35–40 (King James Version).

shushed them upstairs to the dormitory. As soon as they were gone, he ushered me into his office and talked to me, moving rather quickly from the men, their sins and their need to be saved to whether I was truly saved.

I never went back to the Mission again, not even after I returned from my year at Oxford and worked for Dwight Hall for two years. The next time I saw the inside of a mission was in the first of those years, late in the fall of 1937. It was in Bridgeport, Connecticut, twenty-five miles from Yale, my first night on the road.

8

Leaving Yale, dressed in my oldest clothes and carrying no money, I walked to the outskirts of town. On the way, I talked with a hobo who was hanging out on a street corner. He didn't seem to think it was odd for me to be on the road. That made me feel better since I was pretty self-conscious, worried that I might be spotted as a slumming Yalie. He told me that everything filled up early and I had better head for the Yale Hope Mission or I might end up stranded for the night in the bitter cold. "The grub's not bad there," he said, "but they'll only let you stay one night unless you get saved. If you do, you can stay two nights, sometimes three, and then you have to move on." I told him I had to make tracks and he told me that the next place for a free lodging was Bridgeport, at the Sally (Salvation Army), but that I didn't have a lot of time before they closed their doors. As we talked, he shared a "roll your own" with me and I felt that I was beginning to experience the comradeship of the road.

I got a couple of rides fairly soon and managed to get to Bridgeport and find the Sally in time to get admitted. The man at the desk asked me for my name and address and where I had stayed the previous night. For reasons it is hard to explain, this was my first crisis. Probably it shouldn't have been hard for me to give a fictitious name and address but for some reason I couldn't bring myself to do it. Don't ask me all the considerations that went into my reaction, but after stumbling around for a while I gave my correct name and my home address in Massachusetts. At the man's request, I gave my father's name as well. I was so scared that the words practically stuck in my throat. He had to ask two or three times before he could hear them.

I was particularly scared that he would call my father on the phone. Or if he didn't call him, he would routinely send the information to the Wakefield police and my parents would be humiliated by a visit from them. But as I remember it, I had begun by deciding that I couldn't say I came from Yale and had stayed there last night or I would get the kind of attention I didn't want. Perhaps he would throw me out. Suddenly I was in deeper than I had expected, particularly after he asked for my father's name. At that point I think I decided that if worse came to worst, it might be good for my father to know that I was on the road and why. In all our arguments about the Depression and the sufferings of the poor, he argued that I didn't know what life was really like. All my ideas came from books, he would say. Now I was trying to find out first hand a little of what life was like for some of the people we had argued about. Although I hated for my father to be embarrassed, and hoped that the man wouldn't contact him, I was in a sense doing something my father ought to appreciate in the end.

The man seemed to sense my embarrassment and very gently told me to sit in the waiting room, which was just outside the office and in full view of it. It would be a while, he said, until time for the service, followed by supper and bed. But already the benches were nearly filled.

After a while I saw the man at the desk talking on the phone and shortly afterwards he called my name and motioned for me to come back into the office. My heart sank, thinking that he had called my father.

"Those men are pretty rough," he said. "I can see that you're different, so you better be careful, particularly when you go upstairs tonight. For now, you can wait in this little room behind my office." My heart sank again, but not for the reason I had originally feared—and not because of his fears for my safety, which I appreciated but didn't share. I thanked him but told him I'd be all right, and turned down the offer. I didn't want to be treated differently than the others, as I had always been treated differently than poor people.

After twenty-four hours on the road, nobody ever suggested that I looked any different, or was any different, than the rest of the vagrants. In fact, one of my vivid memories comes from early in my travels, when I was treated first with ridicule and then with scorn, as a bum.

I was in New York's Central Park and exhausted, having walked for miles after having been let off in the Bronx by a truck driver. In return for the ride I had helped him unload his heavy cargo before making the long trek to mid-Manhattan. I hadn't eaten since supper at a mission the night before, the standard one-meal-a-day routine that I soon became accustomed to. My head was swimming and I itched all over, either from lice or bedbug bites—or both. I rested for a while on a park bench, dozed off, woke up enough to stretch out full-length and fell sound asleep. I woke to the sounds of two children who were jumping up and down in front of the bench and pointing at me: "Look, Mommy, look at the funny man."

"Get away from there! Come here at once. It's a bum. I told you to stay away from them."

It probably doesn't sound like much, but it was the low point of my trip. "Suffer the little children to come to me, for of such is the kingdom of heaven." But what if you have become so ugly and confused that you scare them away? If I had felt right inside, I probably wouldn't have minded looking unattractive on the outside, even to little children. But before I fell asleep and when I woke up, I hadn't been able to figure out what I was doing there or why. All my good intentions and all the benefits I had looked forward to—and even experienced—had dissipated. My flesh was weak and so was my spirit. I sat there for a long time getting hold of myself, thinking of what I had already learned from the comradeship of the men I had hung out with in the missions and on the streets. I reflected on their courage and fortitude in the face of adversities they had not chosen, and which they could not leave behind by hitchhiking back to Yale.

My headache didn't leave me and I felt dizzy when I stood up and tried to walk, but gradually my spirit recovered. At last I was ready to make a move. I decided that the only realistic thing to do was to ask a passerby for a few cents to buy some food. First, though, I staggered over to the nearby Central Park Zoo to gain some strength from the animals. Before I realized what was happening, someone approached me with an offer of help.

He was a well-dressed man in a business suit and he started a conversation with me. After a few preliminaries, he asked me if I was hungry. When I said "sort of," he invited me to go to his place, where there was plenty of food and drink and, putting his hand on my shoulder, "where we could have some fun." After wrestling with the matter a moment, I decided that it wouldn't be fair to accept his invitation, partake of his food and then tell him that I wasn't open to that kind of fun. So I thanked him and moved to the next cage.

Asking for money was one of the hardest things I ever did in my life. In part I did it because I saw no alternative. I didn't think that in my current condition I could make it downtown to the Bowery, where the missions and the Municipal Lodging House were. But there was another element as well.

For years I had been infatuated with Christian communism, the early disciples' way of life, in which, as I understood it, everyone shared their wordly goods and no one was allowed to go hungry or suffer other privations that could be remedied through sharing. Up to a point, I had tried my best to live that way, but of course I had never succeeded, both because of my own shortcomings and because of the complications involved in trying to do so. In addition to my other confusions and failings, a lot of my attention and energies got diverted into other pursuits and pleasures to which I was also attracted. When I did succeed in being part of a sharing process, it tended to be one-sided in respect to material things. It seemed that I was always more well-off than anyone I knew who was willing to share materially as well as spiritually. With the exception of my traditional relationship with my parents, almost always I had been in the position of giving, not having to receive.

Now I was finding out how much easier it is to give than to receive, how different it is to be asked for help than to have to ask for it. So besides my physical need, I felt a spiritual need to overcome my pride and to ask straightforwardly for what I needed.

The first person walked past me without answering. I can see him now, more than fifty years later, a man in his late twenties or early thirties, with glasses, wearing a dark suit, pinstriped shirt and a tie, and with a little lilt to his walk. He hesitated for a moment, looking at me in a questioning manner, probably because he couldn't hear what I had tried to say. Unable to find my voice, I opened my hand and he moved on. The second man said something like "Get away from me, you bum!" Several more turned me down, with or without words. But by then I didn't care. Already I had received more than I had asked for. With my first request I felt a miraculous release of tension inside me. As I continued, I experienced continually expanding feelings of freedom and joy.

Undoubtedly those feelings had a lot to do with the deeper reason I had gone on the trip in the first place. For my reasons went beyond any lingering need to find out whether the men on the road were shiftless and lazy. I had seen enough in my New Haven years, in the cities of Europe and on a vacation from Oxford, when I had lived with an unemployed miner's family in Wales, not to have any serious ambivalence about that question, despite the prevalence of the idea in most of the worlds I inhabited. Also, I knew that even if I found some of the men to be shiftless and lazy, it wouldn't cause me to think that they should be abandoned. Nor would it have led me to accept our private-profit, rich-and-poor, order-issuing and order-obeying economic system. I would have taken their "irresponsibility" as an indication of the psychological as well as physical harm inflicted on them by that system.

The deeper reason for my being where I was had to do with feelings that were associated in my mind with reading and thinking about Francis of Assisi. Even more than the early Christians, some of whom seemed to have lapsed rather quickly into self-righteousness, theological rigidity, contempt for nonbelievers and prejudice against women, I had for years admired and been influenced by Francis. While traveling in Europe on my roundabout way to Oxford, I had traced his route on one of his journeys through southern Italy, stopping to spend solitary time in each of the little chapels that was identified with him and which usually contained a painting by Giotto of a scene from his life. In a way, my whole trip now was a first experimental step down the road Francis had traveled, rejecting his heritage as the son of a rich Florentine merchant, living the life of the poor, even kissing the leper. Now as I felt a wonderful new sense of freedom, it was Francis who filled my thoughts.

Oddly, the image that came to mind was not of Francis doing what

I was doing and what the poor often have to do, asking for help from those who consider themselves superior. Rather it was the image of Francis kissing the leper. I didn't kiss anyone and no one kissed me, but I couldn't get the image out of my mind. Finally I concluded, perhaps because the incident on the park bench was still fresh in my mind and because of the ugly welts on my skin from the lice or bedbugs, that I had become the leper. By unashamedly approaching the healthy and asking for food, I was affirming the rights of society's lepers. And I was asking the people I approached for more than money or food. I was asking them to come a little closer to being Saint Francis, who gave as freely as he received, moved only by need and not by the supposed virtues or attractiveness of the recipient.

Eventually, someone did give me money, a middle-aged woman. Possibly it was because of the effect the cleansing feelings that flooded over me had on the way I approached her. Or perhaps she would have given anyway. In any event, she gave and I used it not to buy food but to take a subway downtown to the Municipal Lodging House, where I hoped to spend the night.

9

Any doubts I may have had about the attitude of the majority of the men on the road were permanently dissipated by my first night in "the Muni." It seemed as if I had just gotten to sleep when I was awakened by a low roar. Everyone was getting out of bed, grabbing their things and heading for the exit. My first thought was of fire. Jumping up, I was relieved not to smell smoke or see any other danger signs. Puzzled, but fully awake and still a little apprehensive, I followed the others. In the dim light I could barely see a clock on the wall. It said four-thirty! "Where's everyone going?" I asked a man who was rushing by me. "To look for work, you dope." Four-thirty was the time the staff opened the doors, which had been locked the night before to keep out late arrivals.

I talked with someone else on the way out. He explained that everyone was hurrying to get a good place in line on certain street corners. Middlemen customarily came to them in pickups or stake-body trucks, loaded people on the back and took them to outlying districts to be rented out for a day's work on farms or country estates. Others would be taken to one of the boroughs or suburbs to distribute phonebooks or circulars. I felt surprisingly good and decided to follow. But I didn't want to take a job away from anyone as needy and ambitious as the men I had talked with, so I walked at a normal pace and ended up toward the end of the line. There I watched the scene and talked with my neighbors. A couple hours later, about two-thirds of the men were still there; gradually they began to drift away.

At the time, homeless men were allowed three nights at the Muni, but I left after my second night. A new friend who had stayed his three nights was leaving and had offered to show me where and how to ride the freights.

The first thing I learned was that almost no one "rode the rods," the phrase that I had always read in adventure stories. Perhaps some of the authors had never jumped a freight. Or perhaps they had and knew better, but wanted to add color and seeming authenticity by using an esoteric phrase from the lingo. Anyway, riding the rods means to ride on narrow steel rods that undergird the cars. It is extremely dangerous and I never rode there—except experimentally once, for kicks. At the time, I was still new in the business, the train was doing some yard maneuvers, and I climbed on when it was stopped. When it started again, it began to pick up speed rather rapidly and I was terrified, thinking it was taking off. Fortunately it stopped inside the yards, but not before I had learned why my friend had warned me against traveling that way. Some people did it of necessity when they couldn't find a place anywhere else, but they risked getting injured or killed.

On my first trip, my friend and I traveled the first leg on top of a boxcar. That is not a particularly relaxing way to travel either, and was made less so in those days by hot cinders from the engine, particularly if the train went through any tunnels. Luckily, ours didn't. But the greatest danger was that a railroad dick, as the company police are derisively called, would spot us and use his club to force us to jump while the train was going at a relatively high speed. I heard many stories of incidents of this kind, mostly from men who were explaining why they walked with a limp, were nursing broken ribs or carrying a broken arm in a crude sling. We rode that way this time because the boxcars were all locked and the run from the railroad yards on the West Side of mid-Manhattan to the yards in Croton-on-Hudson is slow and relatively safe.

At Croton, we changed trains and managed to get comfortably—and safely—inside a boxcar, but not before my friend had taught me about finding an unlocked, empty car and hiding out in the bushes or wherever else one could until the dicks did a check for riders. Then, if you were lucky, you could get in while the train was stationary or just beginning to move. Otherwise, you had to run alongside, at or near the end of the yards, and hope that you could get the door open and pull yourself in before the train got going too fast. In those days, some friendly railroad workers made a point of leaving a car or two unlocked and slightly ajar so that the hobos could do this. Solidarity forever!

My friend and I separated at Troy, New York; he waited for a through-train to Canada, where I didn't want to go because it was outside the areas I had chosen to research. With his help I boarded a train for the Midwest. I still remember how I felt when we separated and I started off into the unknown again on my own. When the train pulled out, with me the sole occupant of my car, I felt far more lonely and vulnerable than I had when I set out from New Haven on the first afternoon of my journey.

By now I have a blur of memories from the series of trips that I took, off and on, during the next three years, but two things have never left me from that first journey. One is a story I heard somewhere in Ohio. The second is staying for several nights in a hobo jungle in the swamplands outside Newark and Jersey City on my way home.

The story came from a husky fellow close to my own age. He had just finished spending thirty days in jail. One day, after he had walked for miles and was weak from hunger, he came to a house and knocked to ask if there was any work he could do for something to eat. The door was opened by a nun. She greeted him sympathetically and invited him in for some food. He offered to do any odd jobs to pay for it, but she said that it wasn't necessary and began preparing a meal. Soon an older nun came into the kitchen, scolded the first woman for being behind in her work, and left the room. When the food was ready, the first nun, still friendly, set it before him. Before he took a bite, he said, he stood up, thanked the woman for her kindness, and got ready to leave. He stopped talking at this point and I was completely baffled.

"Why?" I demanded. "Why did you leave?" I can still remember how hard it was for him to speak, so choked up was he with emotion.

After a long silence he said that as he had looked up at the woman approaching with the food, he saw through the window behind her two men in uniform coming to the door. Apparently the older nun had called the police. That is why he had spent the thirty days in jail. With my own recent hunger pangs still much in my consciousness, I asked him why he had not taken a few quick mouthfuls before the cops had been admitted and had gotten to him. Again a long silence. "I didn't feel like eating," he finally said, "not after what a woman in a religious order of my church had just done." After that, he and I and another man at the mission talked long into the night. Our conversation had all the earnestness and excitement that I was familiar with from late-night bull sessions in college dorms, but with a perspective and elements of realism that we in the dorms had lacked.

The hobo jungle in the New Jersey marshes was actually a hobo city, with paths worn through the tall grass and leading to little clearings and campfires. Pieces of corrugated metal or wallboard salvaged from nearby dumps were propped up on the edge of the clearings, as shields against the wind and rain. People slept in their lee. A few hundred yards away, automobiles drove by on the busy highways to and from New York City, but this teeming city was invisible to the motorists. As near as I could tell, it consisted of hundreds, perhaps thousands, of people, mostly but not exclusively men.

Every morning at dawn most of the residents of this "suburb" went out in search of work and food. Some of the food was purchased with money they got from odd jobs or begging. The rest came from the garbage cans of restaurants and food stores, or from friendly kitchen help and other workers. More solidarity. Every night some of the men returned with something, and what they brought was cooked in big cans and shared. Usually it was shared with those who had set up camp near the same firesite. But more than once I saw someone come over from another site, say that they hadn't scored much that day and be given a few cans of stew and coffee to take back to their little cluster.

The population was somewhat transient, but some people had settled in for a long stay. Every new arrival was welcomed and given his share the first night and morning, whether he arrived empty-handed or not. After that, he was expected to take his turn in the daytime search, provided he was well enough. Either that or take his chances at the end of the line. I continued to have good luck, because I made a new friend who let me go with him and knew just where to go. He had made a couple of connections in restaurants and diners. Every night or morning, they set something out for him in a garbage can or back entryway. If it wasn't there when we arrived, they told us to come back a little later. Every afternoon, we went back to the jungle loaded.

The stew and coffee tasted better than any I had ever had before. Perhaps they seemed so because I was influenced by the conversations and company, the inventiveness of the scavengers and cooks, the sharing of what little they had, the astonishing new level of freedom that I was experiencing and the joy of being accepted so readily in this strange new world. Undoubtedly everything was enhanced by my romanticizing the contrast between what I was experiencing there and the attitudes and relationships of so many of the people with whom I had spent most of my life. But whether the grub was as good as I remember it or not, I shall always cherish the people with whom I spent those days and nights. They helped strengthen my faith in human nature.

In my regular life prior to my journey to see how a relative handful of the "other half" live I had enjoyed some short-term "sensuous delights," as William Blake calls them, some fruits of the fullness of the earth, some products of nature and human labor that were not available to those I lived with on the road. I had been living in a world that seemed to exalt material things but robbed them of some of their magic by treating them as "private possessions" to be sought and consumed without sufficient regard to the fullness of our kinship with other living beings. Now, in hobo jungles, in boxcars and in sharing a cup of coffee or a warming fire on a street corner, I experienced material delights that surprised me by being more deeply and fully satisfying than most of the ones I had previously savored.

When I returned to Yale, I suffered for a week or two from the sores on my flesh left by lice and bedbugs. But my spirit had been cleansed. I knew that I had to work harder at fashioning a way of life that would not accept either the spiritual poverty of the rich or the material poverty of the poor, but would draw on the insights and true riches of both rich and poor.

10

I value highly many aspects of the education I received at Yale, distorted as some of it was by elitist influences and overvalued as a Yale education often is. But for years after I left, I would almost never mention that I had gone there. I did not want to be identified with an institution whose name would set up hierarchical barriers between me and other people. I wanted to avoid artificial separations from graduates of less prestigious colleges, from the poor noncollege people among whom I lived and worked, and from the prisoners whose lot I shared during my times in federal prisons.

To this day, I am more apt to mention the education I received in prison than the one I got at Yale. But that attempt at identification with some of society's rejected can also bestow a different kind of unwarranted prestige. Having spent nearly three years in prison for the sake of one's principles (and numerous shorter stays) is viewed in some circles as more impressive than it should be. So I point out that compared to most of the people I met in prison I was a short-timer. And for similar reasons, I have never kept count of how many times I have been arrested or in jail, a question I am frequently asked by the media and others. (One media writer wrote that I said "about fifty times," but he made that up.)

Since my children were in a better position than most to know the "real me," I had no reason not to talk with them about the Yale part of my life. Obviously I communicated some positive things about it because, twenty-seven years after I graduated, my second son, Ray (named after my father), went to Yale on a National Merit Scholarship. And I approved of his choice. He did well there academically and served as president of Dwight Hall. He was also elected to the Aurelian Honor Society and—if you'll pardon the ironic linkages—was chosen, like George Bush and me, to be a member of one of Yale's prestigious Senior Societies (*not* Skull and Bones, which George Bush and his father joined). That Ray was honored on his own, not as a "legacy" from his father, is indicated by the fact that he joined a different Society than I did. I think this choice to do so demonstrated a commendable desire to be "on his own," inside the Society and wherever else he was.

A few years later, he demonstrated this same desire to be himself in a more basic manner. At the height of the publicity concerning the Chicago conspiracy trial, he changed his name to Ray Sundance. When he did, he called me, told me how much he loved me and how proud he was of me, but that he had to be a person in his own right and the name Dellinger was interfering with it. Everywhere he went, when people heard his last name they wanted to know if I was his father and when he said yes, that changed the naturalness of the conversation and relationship. It was the same problem that my wife was having around the same time (see Chapter 64). And that I was too! So much so that I sometimes introduced myself to strangers as David Peterson, using my wife's last name. So I told Ray how much I loved him, how proud I was of him, and that I thoroughly agreed with his change of name.

Even before that, Ray had taken another step that was in accord with my views but was expressed in his own individual manner. Like me, he had reached a time when he decided that he did not want to trade on his Yale connections—or in any other way seek the kind of wordly success that Yale prepares its students for. But he made an earlier, more decisive break than I did. He withdrew a month before graduation. Here is how he explained his decision in "An Open Letter to the Yale Community" that was published in the *Yale Daily News*.

Dated May 9, 1969, it begins with a quotation from *The Loneliness* *of The Long Distance Runner* by Alan Sillitoe,* a popular book of the day:

> I won't budge, I won't go for that last hundred yards if I have to sit down cross-legged on the grass and have the governor and his chinless wonders pick me up and carry me there, which is against their rules so you can bet they'd never do it. No, I'll show him what honesty means if it's the last thing I do, though I'm sure he'll never understand because if he and all of them like him did it'd mean they'd be on my side, which is impossible. By God I'll stick this out like my dad stuck out his pain and kicked them doctors down the stairs: If he had the guts for that then I've got the guts for this and here I stay waiting for Gunthorpe or Aylesahm to bash that turf and go right slap-up against that bit of clothes-line stretched across the winning post. As for me, the only time I'll hit that clothes-line will be when I'm dead and a comfortable coffin has been got ready on the other side. Until then I'm a long-distance runner, crossing country all on my own no matter how bad it feels.

Dear Friends:
Yale University and the corporate capitalist system for which it whores has laid out the course of a lifetime long-distance race. The winners take their places among the powerful few. The losers are relegated to roles in the middle and lower classes and kept in the race through minimal material incentives and the elusive goal that they might someday become winners, if not for themselves then for their children. This is not my race; I do not choose to continue running.

This is no easy decision to which I have come. My love for this country is strong. My love for the people of the United States is deep and abiding. I am an American, born and raised. I cannot change this fact nor do I wish to. But the race which we are all conditioned to believe that we must run in order to

*New York: Knopf, 1960.

survive is not the race toward the future. It is a race toward decadence and death. The running of this race does not promote growth but rather sterility. It does not promote brotherhood among men but rather hatred and jealousy.

I have no simple answers to propose; no easy alternative to this rat-race of death. But certain things are clear. This system cannot be changed by a seizure of power but only by a dispersion of the power that the few hold over the many. And the means of changing toward a humane society must not only be consistent with that end but must be inherently a part of it; i.e. the means must be humane in the same way as are the ends toward which we strive. And any attempt to be a winner in the corporate capitalism's rat-race of death is not a humane act.

I will continue to be a member of this society. I will strive to grow more fully human, and to change the political, economic and social structures which block human growth. But I will not run society's race. I therefore resign from Yale College. I invite you to join me.

In peace, freedom and love,
Ray Dellinger, '69

From May 9, 1969, until October 18, 1988, Ray never abandoned this philosophy, though sometimes he became confused about how to live up to it or was distracted by other problems—both of which had also happened to his father and mother, his grandfathers and grandmothers. On October 18, 1988, Ray died from cancer, at age forty-two. Now, we hope, he lives comfortably "on the other side." And continues to grow.

I hope that something Kabir wrote—in a book that Ray and I used to read aloud together—is true:

If you make love with the divine now, in the next life
*you will have the face of satisfied desire.**

*From Robert Bly's translations of the fifteenth-century Indian poet, in *The Kabir Book* (Boston: Beacon Press, 1977).

II

Prison

11

After two years of working for Dwight Hall, I enrolled at Union Theological Seminary in New York City. I had not decided to become a professional minister, but I was seeking to deepen my understanding of the Hebrew Prophets, the Christian Gospels, "comparative religion" and some of the historical movements and groups (many considered "heretical") whose views and approach to life seemed more in line with my own than those of the conventional church. In particular, Union had a reputation for encouraging the application of the radical insights from such studies to contemporary life. But when I got there I found that it exerted both administrative and pedagogical pressures in the opposite direction.

My stay was cut short by the passage of the 1940 conscription law, so in the end I spent only one full academic year there. And because of the gap between what I had been looking for and what I found to be the reality, I lived the last five months of the school year in Harlem, along with four of my fellow students. The president of the Seminary said that we would be expelled if we broke the Christian fellowship by moving out of the school residency hall and leaving the seminary "community." I believed in a community of dedicated persons who wanted to gain insight and strength from one another, so I gave serious thought to what he said. But I concluded that I didn't believe in a community that had no meaningful associations with its poor, racially oppressed neighbors a few blocks away (or its poor white ones either) and lots of relationships with middle- and upper-class white people from near and far. After we moved out, I guess the president thought it over and decided it would cause a public scandal if he expelled us for moving into Harlem. Maybe it helped that I was president of my class and Howard Spragg was president of his. But early the next year he did expel four of us (and four others) when we refused to register for the draft and accept the privileged exemption that came with being a member of a "Christian community" of seminarians. By then, three of our Harlem five (Don Benedict, Meredith Dallas, and I) were attending seminary half time while living and doing community work in a poor, 60 percent Black neighborhood in Newark, New Jersey.*

When we first got the idea of moving out of the seminary and into Harlem, we asked the only Black student in my class, Clinton Hoggard, to join us. It's amazing how naive I still was, because I felt sure that he would want to move there with us. And when one of the others spoke to him and reported that he didn't, it crossed my mind that he might be trying to put his Black background behind him and make it in the white community as a white man with Black skin. I didn't want to jump to that conclusion, since he didn't seem to be that kind of a person, but I did think about it, if only briefly, because of an experience I had a year earlier when I was auditing a course that Richard Niebuhr taught at Yale Divinity School. I had tried to interest some of the seminarians there in a pressing social action project that I thought was in line with "Christian concerns." The response had been abysmal. When I mentioned this to Niebuhr, he said that I shouldn't have been surprised. "A high percentage of the students," he explained, "are from lower-middle-class families in the South who see entering the clergy as a method of improving their economic and social status. Graduating from Yale Divinity School with a good record is a first step in that direction."

The moment that Clinton and I began to talk about it, I knew for sure that his decision had nothing to do with any desire to improve his economic and social status by abandoning the Black community. The reason was that his needs were different than our needs and he didn't need, as we did, to find out what living in a Black community and being surrounded by Blacks would be like and might do to further his education. Later, when I spoke at a "radical" public meeting in Pittsburgh in the Fifties, Clinton came to hear me and renew our friendship. He had a

*Later, Don Benedict started the East Harlem Protestant Parish, which ministered primarily to Blacks and Puerto Ricans who lived in that area and included Blacks and Puerto Ricans in its leadership.

lively church in the Black community, and both he and it were noted for serving that community with their progressive Christian ideas and activities.

If a smaller percentage of the students at Union fitted Richard Niebuhr's trenchant observation about the students at Yale Divinity School, none of my professors excited me the way Richard Niebuhr, Robert Calhoun and Halford Luccock had at Yale. In particular, Richard's brother, Reinhold Niebuhr, was a grievous disappointment. His deeply religious, anti-imperialist, pacifist sermons at Yale had inspired me and had a lot to do with my desire to study at Union. But by the time I got there he had undergone what I saw as a terribly unproductive disillusionment. Overwhelmed by guilt over his own ego (which, as I observed it, remained tremendous in a perverse kind of way) he had turned against his earlier beliefs. Unlike Richard, whom I continued to love and for whom God was a loving companion, close at hand, helpful to us and deeply loved, Reinhold began to see God as "wholly other." Obsessed as he was with his own (and everyone else's) burden of the inescapable "original sin" that God had bequeathed us, he turned God into a distant, unapproachable, basically unknown and unexperienced monarch. According to him, God, for his own inscrutable, not-to-be-questioned reasons, had condemned us to a spiritual poverty that reminded me of the material poverty to which an earthly king condemns his serfs. And much as the serfs, according to the ruling society, were supposed to accept the sovereignty of their monarch and worship him, so "Reinhie" glowered and thundered that all true Christians should worship the Divine King. Inscrutable and unknowable as He was, and weighed down by sin as we were, in the end He granted us salvation through His Divine Grace.

No wonder that Reinhie condemned me and the other draft nonregistrants in 1940 for having the "arrogance" to assert our own egotistical wills by taking a "utopian" stand against the draft. He even preached a sermon in the Union chapel the day we were being carted off to jail, saying that his greatest failing as a teacher of Christian principles had been his inability to educate us on the realities of Christianity.

During the time I lived in Harlem, I had fun getting acquainted with some of our neighbors by playing stickball, shooting pool, having a beer and listening to the ball game at the corner bar, hanging out on the stoop on a hot night, and doing other things that neighbors naturally do together—even if it was a somewhat artificial situation. It took a while for us to break down the barriers, and we never did break them all down, but it helped that we were on the Black people's turf rather than they on ours. And we learned a lot more than we could have learned if the situation had been reversed.

After we had been there long enough to make some neighborhood friends and get our flat in shape (except for the bedbugs, which we never did get rid of), we held an open house for our neighbors and people from the Seminary. The next day, two of the three professors who had attended criticized us in their classes. And the day after that a faculty member who hadn't even been there continued the criticism in chapel. We had hoped that, unlike the Seminary president, they would be glad that we were trying to bridge the gap between the Seminary high on the hill and the Black people who lived in the slums below. But the main thing they noticed was that the women students had to walk past prostitutes in order to get to our flat. They said it was indecent and an insult to the women—the ones in the Seminary, that is. I don't know what the prostitutes thought, but the women students said that they were glad to have come face-to-face with a touch of reality. Several of them had stopped and talked with prostitutes and felt good about the contact. One student had arranged for herself and another woman from the Seminary to meet one of them later in the week for lunch. When I said this to one of the professors, he said, "Oh, she's not a real woman. Haven't you noticed how manly and aggressive she is? She even wants to be ordained." I think he was trying to dismiss her as a lesbian, but I didn't challenge him on that, as I should have. I was still too backward on anything having to do with sex and not sure yet that I approved of lesbianism, so I challenged him only on the legitimacy of women's ordination.

There was a special irony to the complaint about forcing the women students to see prostitutes. I learned it when I was discussing the criticisms with a Black employee who worked nights, guarding the Seminary entrance and running the late-night switchboard. The Seminary was on upper Broadway, near a stoplight and he told me that prostitutes gathered at the light during the summer months to solicit customers. But every fall, when the Seminary was about to open again, the president called the local police captain and asked to have the prostitutes moved a few blocks down the hill—which meant to Harlem or its outskirts. I guess he thought that it didn't look right to have them where the Seminary "community" and its distinguished visitors would see them. It wouldn't have looked like a Christian community. And who knows? Maybe he was worried that some of the male students would have been tempted by them. Or that some of the female students might invite one to have lunch with them in the Seminary dining hall.

We also came under attack for having served beer and wine at the open house, along with nonalcoholic drinks. We had thought a long time before deciding to do that, but knew that the guys we shot pool with at the corner bar or hung out with on the stoops wouldn't feel as much at ease if we limited the fare to tea and cookies in the fashion of the Seminary socials.

As things worked out, everyone else had a wonderful time, including four or five of the neighborhood people we had gotten to know best, those of our fellow students (both male and female) who had come and the third member of the faculty. The other two, we concluded, hadn't come with an open mind but as spies. No wonder I received more genuine religious stimulation in prison than in Seminary, just as I learned things there that I couldn't learn at Yale. And no wonder I decided not to return to Union Seminary after I had completed my first sentence in federal prison—and wouldn't have returned even if the president hadn't written us that we would be allowed to reenroll only if we signed a statement agreeing to obey all U.S. laws and all rulings and decrees laid down by the Seminary authorities.

Most of the prisons I have been in have a lot more Blacks in them than whites. It's even worse now than it was the first time I went to prison in 1940, fresh from Union Seminary and Harlem. In 1970, when I spent a month in Chicago's Cook County Jail during the Chicago conspiracy trial, close to 90 percent of the inmates were Black, Mexican, Puerto Rican, Native American or of Asian extraction. I could think of only two possible explanations: either Third World people in this country are criminal by nature, or the society, the economy and the court system are criminally racist.

Some people said I didn't belong in jail on either of those occasions. In a way they were right. But given the way things are, I knew that both times I was in the right place at the right time with the right people. Except that they didn't belong there either.

12

My last visit to the hobo cities in the Jersey marshes took place in the summer of 1940 after Meredith Dallas, Don Benedict and I had moved from Harlem to Newark. I had been asked to continue full-time in the job of assistant minister of an inner-city church for which I had worked part-time while studying at Union and living in Harlem. Now I was to head up an expanded program of activities for residents of the neighborhood and to take care of other churchly duties in the absence of the minister, who was taking two months off to pursue interests in Alaska. Dallas, Benedict and I figured that my salary was sufficient to support four people on the same scale as the other residents of the neighborhood, if not on the scale of the church members. Most of them had moved to the suburbs as the neighborhood "went downhill" with its influx of Blacks and other poor people. Sharing the money, and joined both by our girlfriends and student volunteers whom I knew through Yale's Dwight Hall or Student Christian Movement contacts in other colleges, eight or ten of us lived in a communal house and developed a full and exciting program of activities. Working closely with us were two relatively young Blacks (a man and a woman) from the neighborhood, whom I had persuaded the church to hire for the summer program.

We called our group the Newark Christian Colony but gradually it came to be known by many as the Newark Ashram, after Gandhi's centers of spiritual and political work in India. Like Dorothy Day and others at the New York Catholic Worker who had become our close friends, we offered hospitality to anyone who came to our door, sharing whatever food and clothing we had as well as shelter. Frequently there were more of us sleeping on the floor than in beds, and the food was always as elementary as in the marshes—and magically satisfying. Some of our guests came to us by way of the nearby jungles, and after I had mentioned the times I had stayed there, a couple of the men insisted on taking me there for a visit. I found that things hadn't changed much. The food, the hospitality and the discussions were as good as I had remembered them.

One of the men I went with was wearing a heavy white sweater with a blue Yale letter on it, from my track and cross-country days. I can't imagine how I still had it to give away, because there was such a rapid turnover of our worldly goods. Probably it had been sitting for years in a closet in my parents' home and I had retrieved it during a recent visit. Perhaps I had left it there originally because I didn't like to wear it but had been reluctant to surrender this last link with my past "accomplishments." In any case, I had no nervousness this time about being spotted in the jungle as a Yalie—and neither did the man with the gnarled hands and weather-beaten face who was wearing it.

My last ride on the freights also took place while I was living in the Newark commune. In 1942, after I had finished my first prison sentence, three of us hopped a freight to Scranton, Pennsylvania. We had been invited to speak at a church in the area about our life and work in Newark. By then, wartime production and jobs in the army had finally put an end to more than ten years of depression, so there were not many men on the road. But I found it convenient, appropriate to our finances and pleasant for old times' sake, to travel that way. Or so I thought until I found out how dangerous it had become, at least on that route. Everything was fine going to Scranton, but on the return trip we had a scary, narrow escape. We were attacked by club-wielding railroad police and forced to jump. Later, we found out that the head cop in that area was known as Killer Murdoch. (I'm not sure that I have the last name right, but there's no question about the Killer part.) According to some men who were hanging out nearby, he had killed a number of people, either by smashing them from behind with his club or by forcing them off fast-moving trains. We were saved by the moderate speed of the train when we had to jump. We hitchhiked the rest of the way home.

Before the Scranton trip, my last ride had taken place in early 1940, while I was still at Union. I had been invited by Mrs. Roosevelt to have tea at the White House, together with a small group of student leaders who had helped organize a demonstration that she supported. The demonstration was on behalf of the poor and racially oppressed and against

U.S. entry into the war, and the main speaker was John L. Lewis of the United Mine Workers. I traveled to Washington in a car with some friends, but before I entered the White House I had made arrangements with Don Benedict to meet him afterwards and travel back to New York by freight train. I had told him of my earlier trips and he persuaded me to go home with him that way.

I met Don outside the White House gate and we walked to the yards. All the boxcars were locked and we climbed into an empty coal car, close to the engine. Perhaps I shouldn't call it empty, because it was coated with coal dust that flew up into our faces when the train started moving. It was also a precarious place to ride because the inside walls of the car sloped down to two exit spouts that had been left open. We had a terrible ride, from the coal dust, the smoke and red-hot cinders, as well as the insecurity of our perch. When the train went through the long tunnel outside Baltimore, we almost passed out from the fumes. I think we were kept awake by the job of fending off the cinders—and by the ones we couldn't escape.

Don was as scared as I was, but he didn't lose the sense of humor that was one of his endearing characteristics. We had been warned in the Washington yards that the railroad cops were especially vigilant in Baltimore and I was worried about being arrested there. But he kept saying, somewhat unrealistically I thought, "I hope they nab us. Then you can tell them that you have just come from tea with Mrs. Roosevelt. If they don't believe you, you can put through a call to the White House and she will vouch for us." Neither of us knew at the time how often the authorities arbitrarily deny new prisoners their right to make a phone call—or delay it until after midnight. Fortunately, we didn't get caught and I didn't have to refuse to try the call. It was never my intention to make it.

A few months later Don and I went to jail, not for riding the freights but for our draft refusal. After we had been there a short time, Mrs. Roosevelt went to Swarthmore College to speak to the students. My brother, Fiske, was a student there and part of the welcoming committee that had lunch with her. When she heard his name, she asked if I was his brother and then pumped him for news of me. She also said, "When you write Dave, tell him that I admire him. Tell him that I think he is right in the stand he has taken."

All incoming and outgoing prison mail was censored. And when my brother wrote me with Mrs. Roosevelt's message, I was in solitary confinement and not allowed to receive any mail. But one of the officials, a Lieutenant Trainor, had showed me some sympathy from the beginning, visiting me in my cell and elsewhere and engaging in long, searching conversations. In prison, one always wonders whether a friendly officer ("hack" or "screw," as the guards are called) is trying to gather information for devious purposes. But I always hope for the best and try to be open, honest, and friendly without betraying any information about any of the other prisoners. Trainor seemed sincere and step by step we had become friends. Now he brought the letter to my cell and let me read it. But before he took it back to the office, he cautioned me not to tell anyone bcause he would get in trouble if other officials knew what he had done.

I never saw the letter again, not even after I got out of solitary and had my mail "privilege" restored. Like a lot of mail that the censor doesn't approve of, it was never delivered and it wasn't returned to my brother. So I didn't dare write out about the message, for fear of getting Lieutenant Trainor in trouble. Perhaps I should have told a visitor to ask Mrs. Roosevelt to visit me in the prison. It was the kind of thing she liked to do, though it kept getting her in trouble. Alternatively, Don Benedict, in whom I had confided after my release from solitary, suggested that I tell a visitor to ask my brother to tell the press what she had said. It would have been good publicity for our cause, but I thought it would be unfair to Mrs. Roosevelt. It was one thing for her to say in a moment of private enthusiasm and friendship that she agreed with my stand, but to have to defend the politics of supporting a nonregistrant publicly would have been something else. I was grateful for her support and admired her courage, but she was under frequent attack for her "Communistic" views, and I was worried that she would suffer additional attacks if the press learned what she had said. So except for a few trusted fellow war objectors I kept it to myself.

Twenty years later, in June of 1961, I saw Mrs. Roosevelt, about six weeks after the U.S. attack on Cuba at the Bay of Pigs and less than a year before her death. She came to a Quaker conference at which I was speaking and was asked on the spot to say a few words. In her remarks, she was critical of the Bay of Pigs invasion and lavish in her praise of

Adlai Stevenson, the U.S. ambassador to the United Nations. We met privately afterwards and I asked her, choosing my words carefully so as not to be crudely insulting, how she could speak so admiringly of Stevenson after he had told the United Nations that the CIA had nothing to do with the Bay of Pigs attack. Implied was my belief that he had deliberately lied as part of the cover-up.

"Oh," she said, "Adlai didn't know that the CIA was involved. The people in Washington kept him ignorant." I wondered if Stevenson had told her this and if, old, feeble and herself isolated from Washington inner circles, she had readily accepted it. Or perhaps he hadn't said it to her but she had stretched a point on his behalf because of friendship and general agreement with what she thought he stood for. After all, she may have stretched a point out of personal friendship with me when she told my brother to tell me that she agreed with the stand I had taken. And she certainly didn't know me the way she knew Stevenson, even though she had embarrassed me at the White House tea by seeming to single me out for special attention. Among other things, she had taken me by the hand and led me to a room where she thought John L. Lewis might be. She admired him greatly and said she wanted the two of us to meet. But he wasn't there, either because he had refused to enter the White House because of his conflicts with FDR or, for the same reason, had been refused admittance. I heard both explanations at the time.

My personal sympathy for Mrs. Roosevelt didn't lead me to accept her explanation for Stevenson's denial of CIA involvement. I thought of how a careful reading of information available for weeks *before the Bay of Pigs invasion* had made it clear to me, with far fewer sources of information than he had, that the CIA was organizing the attack. And I thought of a revealing incident that had happened to me on the first day of the invasion. I had been invited on short notice to discuss it on the Barry Gray show, an immensely popular radio talk show that was broadcast from New York. The battle was still going on and the outcome in doubt.

Besides myself, there were two other guests, a Cuban exile who belonged to a counterrevolutionary group that claimed "credit" for the invasion, and Sam Friedman, editor of the *Socialist Call*, an organ of the Socialist Party, U.S.A., who supported it. I remember thinking that Friedman must know of the CIA's involvement but was playing the same political game that had overtaken Norman Thomas and most of the Socialist Party's top leadership during World War II and from which it never fully recovered. I had resigned from the Party in 1943 when the *Call* refused to print an article I had written in Lewisburg Penitentiary. It had been smuggled out in a rubber glove inside a departing prisoner's anus.* Besides some comments on the prison system, I had expressed views about the war that the editors disagreed with. No matter that I was a member of the executive committee of both the Party and its youth section, the Young People's Socialist League, and was not alone in either section in holding such views.

Early in the Gray broadcast, I said that the CIA had organized the attack and had financed, trained and supervised the Cuban counterrevolutionary troops. Barry Gray acted shocked, interrupting me to say that I had made an outrageous statement. Then he turned to the other two panelists and said something like this: "Since Mr. Dellinger obviously has no respect for the truth and is just spouting propaganda, from now on I will address all the questions to you. Our listeners deserve an honest discussion."

He never looked at me from that moment on or asked me a question, but I managed to speak up some anyway. And I think the station's switchboard did connect me with a few hostile callers during the call-in part of the program. But I shall always remember what happened the moment the program went off the air. I had just taken off my headset when Gray turned to me and said, "Of course you are right about the CIA."

He said it in a matter-of-fact voice and without any explanation or apology. I told him that what he had done on the program was a good example of why the American government was able to get away with atrocious acts that a well-informed public would not tolerate. We argued for a few minutes, without my feeling that I was getting anywhere, and I left. I don't think that he even used the "national security" argument that is often used as a reason for lying to the American public or for withholding information that it has a need and right to know.

*The bearer of the article was Julian Jaynes, a war objector who later authored the voluminous and scholarly *The Origin of Consciousness in the Breakdown of the Bicameral Mind* (Boston: Houghton Mifflin, 1976).

When I got home, one of my new Jersey neighbors, a high school social-sciences teacher, who was a friend but didn't always agree with my politics, was waiting to see me. He told me that he had listened to the program, didn't know about the CIA's role in the Bay of Pigs, but had called in and tried to get on the air to defend my integrity. He wasn't put on, but he left a message that if Barry Gray didn't apologize on the air, he would come in the next day and punch him in the nose for having said such insulting things about me.

I don't know whether my friend would have carried out the threat if he hadn't come to see me first. But I thanked him for his support and told him that it would be more useful for him to organize a project in which he and his students would try to find out more about the CIA. I also told him what had happened in private the moment the program was finished and suggested he tell his students the difference between what Gray had said on and off the air.

For twenty-four years after that, I was never invited to the Barry Gray show again, not even during the height of public interest in the Chicago Eight trial. For a while I told the story occasionally, when it seemed relevant. But then it gradually disappeared from my active memory and repertoire, probably because there were too many more current examples to cite. But in 1985, I received a letter from "WMCA, Good Guy Radio." It came shortly after my name had been in the news in connection with my arrest and trial for a nonviolent action concerning the U.S. support for Nicaraguan Contras and Salvadorean death squads. This is what the letter said:

April 18, 1985

Dear Mr. Dellinger,
On April 10, 1985, at approximately 1:35 p.m., Barry Gray was talking about you and said:

"Well, that's David Dellinger, a man looking for a place to riot."

WMCA would like to offer you an opportunity to respond. Please let me know if you would like to do so.

Sincerely,
Nicole Sandler

This puzzled me because I doubted if Gray would have wanted me to tell on the air my story of what he had done on the Bay of Pigs program. So I thought it likely that he didn't even know about the invitation, but that it had been the idea of some program planner who didn't know of our history together. Even so, I should have accepted the invitation in order to see if I would have gotten on the show to tell the story. If not, it wouldn't have been the first time I had been canceled out by a higher official than the person who had invited me. At least I should have sent for the transcript to see the context of Barry Gray's comments about me and what else he said. But my life is pretty full, I usually have more to do than I can keep up with, and I never got around to answering.

13

When the draft law was passed in August 1940, I was exempt from military service as a divinity student. All I had to do was register. But I saw the draft both as a coercive militaristic intrusion into the lives of the country's young males and as a calculated preparation for U.S. entry into a war that I didn't believe in. And the exemption bothered me because it represented the same old business of my childhood all over again. It meant being treated once again as if I were somehow better than "ordinary people" and deserved privileges that were denied to them. The reasons were different this time, but a majority of males in my age group were liable either to be drafted or to go to prison for refusing. So I refused to register, seeing that as a method of expressing my opposition to both the draft and the privileged exemption.

My opposition to World War II was probably the most controversial stand that I have ever taken. And some of the reasons for taking it run contrary to the conventional myth that the United States ever had a principled position against Nazi racism and other oppressions. So let me tell you some of the personal experiences and mostly overlooked history of the period, the factors that played a major role in motivating me—along, of course, with my underlying commitment to nonviolent methods of resolving even the worst human conflicts. The history is from the way I observed and interpreted it at the time. And it still seems to me to provide a reasonably accurate picture of the major forces that were at work in U.S. ruling circles.

By the time I visited Nazi Germany in the summer of 1936 on my way to Oxford University, I had been for several years disgusted by U.S. governmental and corporate support for Hitler and the Nazis. A lot of Americans have forgotten this support by now, but from a range of sources I knew the reality behind something that Thomas Mann wrote in his diary in 1934. I had not come across the diary itself as yet, but during my undergraduate days at Yale, Mann was one of many credible sources of such formative information. Here is what he wrote in the diary:

> Russian socialism has a powerful opponent in the West, Hitler, and this is more important to Britain's ruling class than the moral . . . climate of the continent. . . . While horror of Hitler's methods is great, . . . the governor of the Bank of England was sent to the United States to obtain credits for raw materials for Germany, i.e. armaments credits. It can be said that German re-armament is taking place on Britain's orders and under British protection. [Need I add "and with U.S. money"?]
>
> Hitler is seen as the agent of capital, industry, the agrarian Junkers and the old state, the embodiment of fascism which maintains the status quo and has no intention to permit the dissolution of the existing state in the revolutionary party but the opposite.*

From my own struggles for the rights of the poor, the working class and the descendants of our country's slaves, I knew something of the reality behind these ruling-class sentiments. And I knew that in addition to the U.S. bank loans, General Motors, Ford, ITT and other U.S. corporations had jumped at the opportunity provided by Hitler's antilabor and other

*From *Leiden an Deutschland* [The Suffering in Germany] (Los Angeles, Privatdruck der Pazifischen presse, 1946).

reactionary policies to make profitable investments in factories inside Germany, including armament factories.*

So I did not go to Germany as a traditional "tourist," excited though I was at the chance to see German cities, cathedrals, museums, forests, rivers and mountains—and to attend German operas and concerts. I went as a cautious but determined protestor who wanted to find out as much as I could about the internal dynamics of this oppressive racist state that was supported by the antilabor, anti-Black and antidemocratic forces that I opposed in my own country. Accordingly, I usually went to the Jewish residential area of whatever city I was in and stayed in a bed-and-breakfast home of a Jewish family. And I visited bookstore after bookstore to ask for a copy of the poems of Heinrich Heine, the German poet whose works had been banned because he was Jewish. I went to the bookstores as an act of protest but also in the hope of establishing personal contact with booksellers (people whose calling I admired) and finding out how they felt about such acts of racist interference in their own profession. I found that such visits frequently led to searching conversations that included not only politics but also questions concerning the nature and meaning of life in this world of confusion, cynicism and conflict. I frequently met booksellers who were anti-Nazi and knew enough about the U.S. support for Hitler to complain about it. On at least two or three occasions, the owner or manager surprised me—after personal affinities had been established—by saying that he himself was Jewish. But, typical of the economic and other pressures that people are usually under, being Jewish did not stop them from continuing to run (or work in) a bookstore that was not allowed to sell the books of a beloved Jewish writer.

When I got to Oxford in September, I discovered that a German Rhodes Scholar was attending the same residential college as I, New College. To my surprise, he turned out to be anti-Nazi, more so than some of the upper-class British students and professors. This reinforced

*Soon afterwards, I knew that when the United States entered the war, it guaranteed these corporations "cost plus profits" for supplying matériel to be used in destroying the German factories (and people). Some years after the war, I learned that it paid them hundreds of millions of dollars as compensation for the plants they had invested in under Hitler.

the impression I had already gotten in Germany itself that totalitarianism is seldom (if ever) as complete or as devoid of active and potential internal opposition, as we are sometimes led to believe. His very selection by a German committee to be a Rhodes Scholar, and the failure of the Nazis to veto the selection, were signs of this, and as we became friends I learned more about the extent of the opposition. Later, I learned still more from some of his anti-Nazi friends in Germany to whom he gave me letters of introduction and trust. Having personal experiences of this kind strengthened my belief that there were better (essentially nonviolent) ways for the American (and British) people to work to eliminate Nazi totalitarianism than by the method of a devastating international war.

My final visit to Germany began in a nearly tourist fashion, because my parents came over in the summer of 1937 and we entered Germany in the big new car they had brought over from the United States. But when we crossed the border, the uniformed Nazi guards gave us the Heil Hitler salute and pasted a swastika on our windshield. I objected, both vocally and by tearing it off in full view of the guards. The guards took no action in response, but my parents were upset. They pointed out that "all the other Americans" accepted and displayed the swastika—and it was true. Once inside, I had contacts to make that would have upset my parents again, so I made a point of getting free from time to time, sometimes for a few hours and once by traveling alone for four or five days while they explored an area that especially interested them. During those interludes I carried a few messages from one anti-Nazi individual or group to another, at least partially protected by my apparent identity as an American tourist.

On all these visits to Germany, Nazi supporters and some of the middle-roaders used U.S. collaboration as an example of why I should support Nazism, while anti-Nazis decried it as an indication of what they were up against—and couldn't I and my friends do something about it back in the United States? But all the more serious anti-Nazis stressed that "the German people must be the ones to get rid of Hitler, not the rulers of Britain and the United States who first imposed the crippling Versailles Treaty on the German people and then helped bring Hitler to power." "War by the imperialist powers," they said "is the worst way to get rid of Hitlerism. We have to do it ourselves."

When I returned to the United States in the autumn of 1937, I joined efforts to get the United States to raise its immigration quota for Germans in order to let the Jews come here. But it never happened, even though famous individuals like Albert Einstein were admitted. In early June 1939, in what became known as the "Voyage of the Damned," the SS *St. Louis* was turned away by the United States and began heading back to Europe with more than 930 Jewish refugees, many of whom later died in Nazi concentration camps.

During the period when I was picketing and demonstrating against the quota, I was more upset politically than most of the U.S. politicians or press were by the August 1938 Munich Pact in which Great Britain and France agreed to the Nazi takeover of a significant part of Czechoslovakia. And my concern was *not only* because of the immorality and ultimate futility of an unprincipled "appeasement" that failed to deal with or solve any fundamental problems. (That failure, of course, has been cited since World War II whenever U.S. imperialists have wanted to invade a Third World country in which a dictator who formerly served U.S. corporate interests—even was installed by, or with the aid of, the CIA—had gotten too independent to satisfy his U.S. masters.) I was *also* upset because I saw the agreement as using Czechoslovakia as a pawn to be sacrificed in the geopolitical chess game through which the Western powers had been trying for years to get Hitler to move his Western-armed forces eastward toward, and they hoped into, the Soviet Union. On the other hand, by the time of Munich there were many staunch British and U.S. capitalists who had not changed their minds about the Nazi's domestic policies, but feared Germany's growing military power and commercial rivalry. They saw Munich as a delaying action while Britain continued frantically to bring its own armed forces to a level adequate for the dreaded alternative of an armed showdown with its German rival, similar to the one that had taken place in World War I.

Meanwhile, the Soviet Union was intent on having Hitler expand westward against the capitalist powers instead of eastward against them. When this effort culminated in the Nazi-Soviet Friendship Treaty of August 1939, most of the profacist U.S. capitalists turned decisively against Nazi Germany, with a division between those who thought U.S. commercial and power interests would be advanced by letting the Europeans fight it out amongst themselves and those who thought that joining the war would better advance the same selfish interests. At the same time, the U.S. Communist Party rejoined the antiwar movement in another of its famous "turns," which were based on its devotion to the Soviet Union as the exemplar and defender of the kind of society they envisioned for the United States.

This was the personal and historical background (historical at least as I understood it and still do) when I had to make some critical decisions about how vigorously to resist both the draft and the impending entry of the United States into World War II. Given what I had experienced and observed, I did not believe that the decision to pass the conscription law and lay the groundwork for entering the war represented a fundamental policy change to oppose racism and tyranny. Rather I saw it as a change of tactics that continued the United States' devotion to policies and practices that I continued to distrust and oppose.

Without necessarily sharing all the details of my outlook, a number of my fellow students from Union Theological Seminary opposed the war and were offended by the special religious exemption—bribe, we called it. So about a week before the time came for us to register, twenty of us made a public announcement that we would refuse to do so. Almost immediately, at least a dozen horrified peace leaders rushed to Union to get us to change our mind. Refusal to register, they said, would disgrace the antiwar movement and cause the government to crack down on it. The peace leaders who said this had lobbied Congress to secure special treatment for conscientious objectors who could prove that they were motivated by *special* "religious training and belief"—as were Quakers for instance, or as members of a pacifist church such as the Mennonites or Brethren. So they were the ones who would have felt disgraced, and the irony of this did not escape me.

For whatever reason, we never saw or heard from A. J. Muste of the pacifist Fellowship of Reconciliation during those agonizing days. But *after* the decision-making crisis had passed and eight of the original twenty had held out and refused to register, A.J. and Dr. Evan Thomas (a World War I objector and brother of Norman Thomas) issued a statement of support and mailed it to us, along with a personal note that included these words:

> You will be prepared to face any results that may flow from the decision which you took, including having to hear some in the pacifist movement express the conviction that your course is injurious to that movement itself. . . . [But] in a moral universe great good always results when men stand unflinchingly by their convictions and act upon them.

Julius Eichel and Ammon Hennacy (two other imprisoned World War I objectors) and Julius's wife, Esther, all agreed with our stance, but I did not know this, or them, at the time. Their support, along with that of Evan Thomas, became very important to me (and my wife) later. But as you will see, my relationship with Muste was more complicated and uneven.

Meanwhile, when I held out against the negative pressures, Clarence Pickett, the much-revered head of the American Service Committee (a dedicated man who was caught in a difficult situation that stemmed from his bureaucratic position and involvements) took me aside and told me that if I didn't believe in accepting the exemption as a budding clergyman, I should register for the draft, drop out of divinity school and apply for alternative service as a CO (conscientious objector). If I did that, he would see to it that I was made director of one of the CO camps that was being set up. There, he said, I could help create a model nonviolent community that would serve as an example for the country and world to see.

I thought it more appropriate for the kind of nonviolent action I believed in to stay as long as I could in the tumultuous neighborhood where I lived and worked rather than to withdraw in order to talk, meditate and pray with fellow pacifists in an isolated camp in the woods. In Newark we were acting nonviolently in tense racial and class conflicts, but inside the camps there was almost no opportunity for contact with the outside world. Moreover, I might be called the "camp director," but a National Service Board for Religious Objectors (a board of religionists who seemed more "passivist" in respect to a violent society than militantly pacifist) would be overseeing me. And by law the ultimate director of them, everyone in the camps and myself would be the military head of Selective Service, General Hershey.

Despite all this, and in support of my thesis that Pickett was a fine man caught, as A. J. Muste often was, in a difficult conflict between his bureaucratic role and his innate personal instincts, Pickett later wrote us a letter in which he said,

> I want to express my personal satisfaction that you have . . . maintained the right spirit in your dealings with the court. . . . Whatever happens, I shall not lose interest or confidence in you. . . . In our effort to rid the world of war, there will have to be many methods of attack used, and for certain people the instrument which you are using will probably be their fullest contribution.

Besides my other feelings on the subject, large numbers of people who were no more anxious than I to kill their fellow human beings were not eligible for exemption as conscientious objectors. Many of the Black men I knew in Harlem and Newark had no illusions about the U.S. government's supposedly humanitarian motives—in war or peace—even though many of them found it hard to turn down the chance to get regular food, clothing and spending money for the first time in their lives. And to be told for the first time that they were important in the scheme of things, serving their country by "fighting for democracy"—in a racially segregated army.

I don't mean to make the decision seem any easier than it was. One day I was wavering a little and chanced upon a "patriotic" parade in Newark. As I saw grade school and high school students marching behind the American Legion, Veterans of Foreign Wars and armed U.S. troops, I had a traumatic vision that these students—and thousands like them—would soon be in the trenches, killing and being killed. I was particularly moved because a lot of the young people marching came from the forlorn and desolate area of poverty and powerlessness in which I lived. And I thought about how that tragedy would be repeated for generation after generation unless we developed a nonviolent antiwar movement that denied itself special privileges and worked to achieve economic democracy.

So I refused to register and was sentenced to prison for a year and a day, as a felon.

14

When my seven Union Seminary colleagues and I arrived at the Danbury, Connecticut, federal prison, the captain took me aside and warned me that I would be living amongst "hardened criminals." "Keep to yourself," he said, "because a lot of them are naturally violent and you can never tell when they will turn on you."

But I had just come from a slum section of Newark where I worked with teenagers and adults who had been made "naturally violent" by the unnatural conditions of their existence. And before that I had lived on a block in Harlem that was thought to have the highest murder rate of any block in any city of the world. So I thought that was poor advice. In my experience, the best defense was to share a common interest and activity and gradually become friends. That was the reason (together with a natural love of life) that we organized a range of creative, fun activities in Newark, from clubs, sports teams, singing groups, drama groups, dances and free-for-all "bull sessions" to trips to the country. And why I did things in Harlem like playing pool in the corner bar. Moreover, the eight of us had just spent a week in New York City's West Street jail where a lot of prisoners were more hardened and violent than most of the ones in Danbury's "minimum security" institution were reputed to be. We had liked them and gotten along well with them, finding that they respected us as men of "courage" and principle, so long as we didn't get self-righteous about our views and way of life. A lot of them scratched their heads and tried to tell us how to become more worldly wise, but their goodwill toward us was obvious. "Holy Jeez," one of them had said to me, "I just had my lawyer give a judge five bills [five hundred dollars] so that I could get a shorter sentence and you won't even sign a piece of paper that would get you out of here. And if you signed it, you wouldn't have to go into the army or anything, just continue studying to be a priest."

Before I had time to assess the inmate population at Danbury and explore how they and I might relate to one another, I was put in solitary confinement for having sat in the Black section at my first Saturday-night movie. I was new and it wasn't part of an organized protest, just sitting next to someone I had been talking with when we walked in. But how could I obey when the guard ordered me into the white section and him into the Black section?

A few weeks after I got out of solitary, they put me in the Hole. Probably it was because I refused to go to the captain's office when the loudspeaker summoned me by my prison number. Earlier I had explained politely that I didn't object to the number if they used my name too, but that wasn't good enough for them. Or maybe it was the time I refused to remake my bed, with the guard standing over me after he had ripped it out and said it wasn't made the way they make them in the army. I was the one who slept in it and nobody saw it except me and the guards. Besides, I was there because I objected to the army, not just killing people and fighting for Big Business, but people becoming robots, doing whatever they are told.

I used to lie in my cell and recite a poem by e. e. cummings:

my specialty is living said
a man (who could not earn his bread
because he would not sell his head)
squads right impatiently replied
two billion pubic lice inside
one pair of trousers (which had died).

But I used to say public mice, because I didn't like calling people pubic lice, not even if they acted differently than I did on issues I considered important. Mice seemed a lot better: Are you a mouse or a man? You can become either at any time, it is up to you.

So now I was in the Hole for the first time, no light, no bed, shivering in the midst of summer in a cell that was damper and darker than the Swiss dungeon of Chillon that Byron had written about and that I had visited a couple of years earlier. "You won't come out," they had said, "until you agree to obey orders, *all* orders."

I was scared. Earlier, Tough Tony had been put in the Hole for sassing a guard. Tough Tony terrorized the prisoners and was supposed to be a hit man for the Mafia. In the middle of the night when everything was quiet, they had carried him out screaming, four guards carrying him screaming past my cell to the mental ward. The prisoner in the cell next to mine told me through the ventilator who Tony was, where he had been and where he was going. "Nobody can stand it," he said. "Don't ever do anything to give them an excuse to put you there." Perhaps he was a stool pigeon, saying what he had been told to say to an uppity troublemaker like me, but I couldn't tell. Three days earlier I didn't even know there was a Hole, let alone whether I could stand it.

Later I saw plenty of guys come out of there saying, "It was a vacation. I could have done it standing on my head, the motherfuckers." But others were broken by it. From then on they had a haunted, hunted look that I'll never forget. It wasn't just that they couldn't look the guard in the eye, they couldn't look anyone in the eye, not even themselves—like dogs that have been beaten until they are broken. That's what society calls "rehabilitating" them, making them good citizens who obey the laws and have proper respect for authority.

Some of the ones who came out claiming they loved it, it was easy time, never were the same afterwards either, but in a different way. They could look the guard right in the eye—with a cold, steely hatred. They were letting him know that one day they would kill him. Usually they don't; they kill someone else instead. It may be another prisoner or someone after they get out, someone who does some little thing that seems to interfere with their freedom and reminds them how impotent they have been made to feel—and this time they can do something about it. I know, because that was the history of some of the guys I did time with, then and later.

But prisoners had to be careful about looking at a guard that way or they got put back in the Hole for "silent insolence." In Danbury the authorities boasted that silent insolence had been deleted from their code book. But if anyone looked at the guards the wrong way they didn't have any trouble finding an excuse to put him in the Hole. Like the guard who had me put there after he tried to show me who was the boss by ripping my bed apart, and demanding that I redo it. So most of the prisoners looked at the floor when they passed a guard on the way to work or the mess hall.

I was plenty scared that first time, but I thought of the prisoner of Chillon, how a flower had grown through the stones and he had discovered that it was all the companionship and beauty he needed. I wished that I had a flower, or even a blade of grass, but there was no light and no cracks in the cement floor or walls. I laughed at myself for indulging in such romantic thoughts and wondered how long I could hold out until I cracked, as Tough Tony had cracked.

Then it began to happen. For no reason I can explain, I began to discover how little it mattered where you are or what anyone does to you. I was sure that what I had done to get there was right and somehow the longer I was there the better I felt. Maybe that wasn't it at all, but anyway I never felt better in my life, even if I was shivering and wished I had something to eat, or a cigarette. I was trying to sleep standing in a corner because it wasn't so cold that way and my hips ached from lying on the cement floor. But when I dozed off, I started to fall. If I wasn't careful, I'd hurt myself. If I cracked my head on the floor and knocked myself out, it might be hours before anyone found me.

I wondered how many hours it had been. Maybe it was only a few minutes, because I remembered a story by Edgar Allan Poe, about a man who had been locked accidentally in a sepulcher when he went back to look at his dead financée one last time. He thought he was there a week, but his friends missed him after a few hours and came back for him. His hair had turned white and he was shaking, as I was shaking then. He never got over it, he shook the rest of his life.

Then, unexpectedly, for no reason at all, I felt good again and I didn't care how long it had been or would be. I felt warm inside and filled all over with love for everyone, everyone I knew and everyone I didn't know, for plants, fish, animals, even bankers, generals, prison guards and lying politicians—everything and everyone. Why did I feel so good? Was it God? Or approaching death? Or just the way life is supposed to be if we weren't so busy trying to make it something else?

It didn't matter why. The only thing that mattered was that it was happening. It happened when I least expected it. I didn't try to make it happen, I didn't even know it could happen, not there, not anywhere that much. I never felt so good before, not even when I kissed Rena (which was a long time ago, but she was still the best). Or when I won the two-mile run in the Yale-Cornell meet (my first varsity victory) or fought Jimmy Dean in the fifth grade because he was punching out some little kid. He was older than me and beat the shit out of me, but I felt good anyway. The next day he had a black eye and everyone said how tough I was. I knew I wasn't, but it felt good to hear them say it.

I thought about how I had been in Spain during the civil war. The peasants and some of the soldiers from the People's University were the most inspiring people I had ever met, and I knew then that I would always be a revolutionary, it would never leave me—but a nonviolent revolutionary, because the other way is tempting but doesn't work.

I had almost picked up a gun on the third day in Madrid, in the People's Park, when Franco's troops were half a mile away and advancing. I thought that if my friends were going to die I was ready to die with them, and who knows, maybe we'll win. But by then I knew that the Communists were shooting the Trotskyists, both were shooting the anarchists, and the anarchists had shot at the car in which I had been riding in Barcelona when it made a wrong turn into their sector. Whoever won that way, it wouldn't be the people. I knew that I had to find a better way of fighting, a nonviolent way. I had at least a few ideas about that, from a few nonviolent actions I had taken part in, from Gandhi, and from a new book I had read earlier that summer, *Pour Vaincre sans violence* (To Conquer Without Violence) by R. Palme Dutt.*

That was the hardest decision I ever made in my life, not to pick up the gun in Spain. After that I knew I would never consciously injure anyone (but I have hurt people many times—it's not easy). After Spain, World War II was simple. I wasn't even tempted to pick up a gun to fight for General Motors, U.S. Steel and the Chase Manhattan Bank, even if Hitler was running the other side.

Now I was in the Hole and I felt the way I had in Spain, only more

*Years later I located a version of this book in English, under the disappointing title *The Conquest of Violence*, a title that shifts the emphasis slightly away from overcoming the kind of institutional violence that Dutt wanted to conquer without (using) violence to the more narrow concern of keeping oneself free from violence.

so. I had gone from freedom to jail, from regular jail to solitary confinement, from solitary confinement to a damp, black dungeon they called punitive isolation—and I had never been so free before. For the first time in my life, I had nothing, and for the first time in my life I had everything.

15

I heard a key in the door and they brought me something to eat. Hudson, who everyone called a stool pigeon and a fag, was standing there with a guard. He handed me a tray and whispered, "the light switch, the light switch." Then the door clanged shut and it was pitch black again.

I thought about how Hudson had gotten to me in solitary, when no one else could, and asked me to stand on the chair and stick my cock through the peephole in the door. I was afraid to, even though I felt horny and said to myself, "Why not? I wonder what it would be like." Now I was in the Hole and didn't know what he meant about the light switch because there wasn't any. I hoped the guard didn't hear him because I didn't want him to get in trouble, whatever he was.

I was pretty sure that there wasn't a light switch, but before I drank the cold coffee and ate the baloney sandwich, I felt the walls in the dark, up and down and all around, until I located a steel plate. The screws were loose and after I turned them with my fingernail the plate came off. Inside I found cigarettes and matches and I knew that the brotherhood of man was real.

Nowadays I call it the sisterhood, to even up a little for all those years of brotherhood. That's funny, because Hudson was a sister anyway. But maybe that isn't a nice way to think of it, something left over from my prejudices against homosexuals back when he helped me and I didn't realize that it might be a compliment to call a man a "sister," as I had felt complimented when angry white people called me a "nigger" for working to help Black people get a few of their rights.

Hudson was more human to me than most people are in their whole lifetime and I couldn't have cared less whether he was a sister, a brother or both. I just wished that everyone were more human, as he was. I was sure that he was a stool pigeon, but that only emphasized something I already knew, how mixed up and inconsistent everyone is, including me.

When I found the cigarettes, I felt a surge of love for Hudson. I loved him, and because of him I loved everyone. But I wouldn't have let him do to me what people like him do, even if he were locked in that dark cell with me. Not just because I was prejudiced but because I didn't need anything or anyone anymore. I didn't even need Sally, the girl I was engaged to, because I was already in heaven.

Ordinarily I don't use words like "heaven" (or "God," which in some cases can be even more confusing) because I'm afraid that people will misunderstand me, thinking that I am mouthing words that I don't really know anything about because they don't come out of my own experience or life. If so, they'll close up even more than usual, as I sometimes do when I hear some people use those words. I don't care about the words, only whether they are being used in an effort to describe something real. What's behind them is what counts. Even in divinity school I didn't get interested in most of the theology they taught. It seemed too much like using fancy words to describe things that can't be put into words, taking all the life out of them.

I am in the Hole, thinking about such things. Something is happening to me and I don't know what it is. Maybe I'm not in heaven. Maybe I'm drunk: "Jesus Christ, mother of fine apples, I feel drunk all the time" (Kenneth Patchen). I've never had more reason not to be drunk, but I am. I've never been more possessed of all my faculties and it's better than being drunk. If you fight clean and hard people can kill you but they can't hurt you. They can do terrible things to you—and probably will—but they can't hurt you unless you do it to yourself. From now on, no one will ever frighten or control me, no one will stop me from living to the full and loving to the full, loving everyone I know and everyone I don't know, fighting for justice without seeing anyone as an enemy.

After a while, I thought about going to sleep, not caring whether I was awake or asleep, alive or dead. Even dead I knew I would be alive, and if I weren't it wouldn't matter. Everything that happened was good. Life kept expanding inside and all around me, becoming more and more alive and making me part of it until I was floating in an ocean of live air. Really it was an endless ocean of music in color and there was no separation between me and the music. Where the color came from I don't know because that was years before color television. But I didn't know where any of it was coming from. It just came and swept me up in it, until everything was ocean and music and me.

It's hard for me to say that, even now when I'm trying not to hide. It's hard because of all those years that I heard people say that heaven was a place where angels played music all the time, on their harps. When people talked like that, it sounded sickly and pale, and I knew I'd rather play football, have a boxing match or climb a tree than listen to them—or than go to that kind of heaven. If someone started talking that way on the radio, I changed the station, hoping I could find Duke Ellington, Fats Waller or maybe Kate Smith singing "When the Moon Comes over the Mountain."

Was this what they had been talking about and I was too snotty to realize it? Or were they just mouthing words they had heard in church but knew nothing about, not having experienced anything similar to what I was experiencing? Had they known something that I didn't? Or was it the same as the way they sang in church about "the glorious cross" but wouldn't risk having to suffer a scornful word or raised eyebrow by speaking up for Sacco and Vanzetti who were crucified on my twelfth birthday.

I didn't know and I didn't have time to figure it out. I would have to think about it later, after I got out of the Hole and wasn't so busy. Right now I loved not only Hudson but the warden, Franklin Roosevelt, Winston Churchill and Adolph Hitler. But trying to explain that could lead to worse misunderstandings than saying "God" or talking about "heaven" and the heavenly music I was hearing and had become. So I *had* to think about it, trying to get my head to catch up with the rest of me. After a while I decided that I loved them as if they were kids who have to be pitcher or they won't let other kids play with their ball. Now they have grown up and are playing with prisons and factories, food supplies and banks, guns and armies, everyone's lives. Millions of people live grimly, suffer, get killed, so that they can be pitcher. I love them, but that doesn't stop me from being angry. I'm angry and sad because wars are going on, profits are up and people are down. I love them but I don't *like* them—or the things they are doing. I love everyone, but the ones I want to join forces with are the victims. Helping them will help everyone, even the ones who are doing terrible things to them.

Having figured that out, I went to sleep again. When I woke up, I was stiff and cold and did push-ups. But whatever it was that was happening just wouldn't stop. It was a long time before I realized that I was hungry and liked to eat occasionally, and wished that I could make love just once before I died. But the guards had told me that if I didn't straighten up I wouldn't get out of prison alive. If they were right, I would die without ever having made love, after all those years of coming close and stopping at the last moment for reasons I no longer believed in.

I asked Sally to make love the night before I went to prison, but she wouldn't, even though we were engaged and I might go off the next morning for five years—or forever. Thinking about it, I realized that it didn't really matter whether I made love before I died. But now I began to think that even if I got out of prison I might not marry Sally, because it did matter that she wouldn't make love on that last night together. She had to wait for permission from the government that was putting me in prison—and for some magic words by a clergyman. Most of the clergy were as ready to bless murder as marriage, so long as it was massive enough, approved and run by the government and in the name of democracy, peace and God. "Praise the Lord and pass the ammunition."

Maybe I was unfair to Sally, but I didn't know it or feel it. And I didn't know it or feel it when I got out of prison nine months later. I still loved her but decided that our love for each other had led her to go along with me in activities that expressed my deepest feelings but not hers. I felt that marriage would put her under pressure to accommodate to a more radical way of life than she was motivated to choose on her own. Conversely, I would be under pressure to lead a more cautious and conventional life than I felt was required in a world full of injustice, unhappiness and war. She wanted to marry a minister, but not the kind of minister I wanted to be—if I ever became one. I didn't want to give up my way of life and I didn't want to force it on her. Marriage would not be fair to either of us, and I was afraid that since I was more set in my ways, she would be the one who would be hurt the most.

I'll never know whether the real fault was my impatience and lack of faith rather than anything that would have persisted in Sally. But three months after I got out of prison Betty Peterson and I found each other, and around the same time Sally found a minister who was more conventional than I could ever have been.

16

When I got out of the Hole I was warmed by the number of prisoners who went out of their way to express their respect for me, even some who later objected to our campaign to end the prison's racial segregation. As near as I could tell, it was because they liked it when anyone refused for any reason to let the prison authorities push him around. But a couple of the inmates warned me that some of the guards were saying that I was a smart-ass college kid who thought he was too good to fight for his country. Someone ought to knock some sense into my head before I spoiled things for everyone.

The officials had told me that the other prisoners were untrustworthy, violent and inclined to harm me. But now the guards were trying to arouse the prisoners against me, saying that I was an unpatriotic troublemaker who might cause a crackdown that would make them lose their privileges. The maximum security cellblock into which I had been put was the only non-segregated unit in the prison; when one of the "biggest, baddest" prisoners in it, a huge Black man by the name of Al Harris, told me this, he said, "If anyone starts to fuck with you, just tell him to fuck off because if he so much as lays a finger on you, he'll look like a jelly fish when Al Harris gets through with him." Al was a long-timer who had recently arrived at Danbury's "minimal" prison to do a last, transitional year before release.

When Al got out of prison a few weeks after the eight seminarians did, he joined Don Benedict, Meredith Dallas and me in the communal house in Newark to which we had returned to continue our community work. He stayed with us for eighteen months, until the project ended when Benedict, Dallas and I were sent back to prison (separate prisons this time). By then our house and work had been flooded by other war objectors, all the other young men were arrested about the same time as we were and the women didn't feel able to continue on their own. While Al was with us, he took the lead in organizing the Essex County Equality League and led us and others in a series of nonviolent protests (some of them successful) against the city's racially segregated restaurants.

Early in our stay at Danbury, while our status with most of the other prisoners was still uncertain, the prison held a Ping-Pong tournament to select a team to compete against teams from the outside. The three best players turned out to be George Houser, Bill Lovell and Don Benedict of our seminary group.* For those who have never been in prison and observed the need felt by virtually every prisoner to find ways of improving his self-esteem and sense of worth, even if vicariously, it may be hard to imagine how much it endeared our group to the other inmates to see them outclass the visiting team. "Come on, George!" "Smash it again, Don!" "Attaway, Bill!" The cheers and applause came from a needful place, and the feelings of solidarity they expressed carried over into the dormitories and cellblocks and everywhere else.

But this was as nothing compared to what happened during softball season. Three or four of us, myself included, played on the prison team,

*In 1942 George Houser helped found CORE (Committee for Racial Equality), which was a prime organizer of the Freedom Rides and other nonviolent activities against racial segregation in the North as well as South. CORE changed after the controversial exclusion of whites during Black Power days, and it was eventually taken over by Roy Innis, a self-promoting opportunist. Meanwhile, George had become Secretary of the U.S. Committee on Africa. His autobiography, *No One Can Stop the Rain*, was published by Pilgrim Press (Boston) in 1988.

In February 1991, Bill Lovell wrote me, saying that an editorial I had written against the Gulf War in *Toward Freedom* (a newly renovated magazine of which I am chairman of the board) was "in line with our various organizations here in Chicago, including the North Suburban Peace Initiative in Evanston and beyond, whose board I have chaired for years."

along with a convict who was much admired for having played for the Brooklyn Dodgers. But the standout was Don Benedict again, one of the top softball pitchers in the country. All our games were "home games," and as the season approached its end we had won them all, largely because of Don's pitching. The final game was to be played against a team whose only loss had been in a close game with us early in the season. The prison was alive with anticipation of the showdown and expectations of victory were high. But then a crisis developed.

A few days before the game most of the war objectors were put in solitary confinement for having demanded ("threatened" to take) an hour off work in solidarity with a nationwide student strike against the draft and other military buildups.*

Without Don, the prisoners expected to lose. The tension and potential for a riot became so frightening to the authorities that the warden visited Don twice in his cell, asking him to agree to come out on the day of the game long enough to pitch. Don's response was that he wouldn't come out unless we all came out *and stayed out*. Finally, about two hours before the game, all of us were released from solitary in time for lunch in the prison cafeteria. When we entered the dining hall, we received the loudest, longest, most enthusiastic standing ovation that I have ever experienced.

The game was in no way an anticlimax. Don pitched a no-hitter, all of our group who played on the team either got a hit or made a spectacular fielding play and the prison team won the league championship. (Nowadays, whenever Don is telling someone about this incident in my presence, I always claim—for a while—that I saved the no-hitter for him by sliding on my chest and catching a sinking liner that would have scored the winning runs for the other team. Of course it's not true.)

*The group included Lowell Naeve and Stanley Rappaport. Stanley was New York chairman of the Young People's Socialist League. Lowell later wrote a book about his prison experiences entitled *Field of Broken Stones*. We printed and published it at the Libertarian Press, a Workers Cooperative, which was part of the intentional community in which I lived and worked most of the time from the fall of 1946 to the fall of 1968.

Despite the thrill of our tumultuous welcome in the dining hall and the subsequent joy of our (mostly Don's) having come through in the game, the most important thing that happened to me during that particular conflict with the administration was something different. It began when John V. Bennett, the director of the Federal Prison Bureau in Washington, visited the prison shortly before we were put in solitary. The morning he arrived, Lieutenant Trainor informed me that the reason for his visit was "to straighten [me] out." According to Trainor, the warden considered me the "ringleader" of the war objectors and the problems they were causing. Clearly he did not understand the democratic way that we worked or the independent strength of the other objectors, who would have been causing similar "troubles" for the prison whether or not I was there.

At that point, I could still laugh about it and got an extra laugh by comparing the warden to my mother. Like him, she was upset by the activities that I kept getting involved in and couldn't imagine that the group would be capable of engaging in them unless it had fallen under the domination of some sinister leader. Everyone else was following him. The only difference was that the warden thought that I was the leader, while my mother knew that it *couldn't* be me. Every time she visited, she wanted to know *who* it was who was leading me astray. Some "older person," she thought.

These conflicting views about me came to a head some time after we had been released from solitary so that Don could pitch. My parents received a phone call from the warden after they had gone to bed for the night. He had been speaking at nearby Andover Academy and called them after he finished his talk. He had to see them, *it was an emergency*. Shaken, they dressed and went to see him. As he had done earlier with Bennett, the warden told my parents that I was the ringleader of the troubles that worried them. The prison had been forced to put me in solitary confinement to stop me from stirring up the other prisoners. Now I was out but in terrible shape, showing signs of a nervous breakdown. If my parents could not talk some sense into me, the authorities would have to transfer me to the psychotic ward of the Springfield, Missouri, prison hospital, or perhaps to Alcatraz. He scared them half to death.

When they came as soon as they could to visit me, they soon ascertained that I was as calm, stable and inwardly peaceful as they had ever seen me—and they turned their wrath against the warden. The reason I was in such good shape was something that had happened during Director Bennett's visit and the ultimate, if delayed, effect it had on me.

True to Trainor's description of the reason for Bennett's visit, I was called in to meet with him. And the short-run results were traumatic. At first he sounded like the Freshman Dean at Yale, telling me the brilliant future that was within my grasp if I straightened out. Then he told me how mild Danbury was compared to other prisons, places like Atlanta, Lewisburg, Springfield and Alcatraz. Not only were the conditions of confinement more severe in those prisons, but my life would be in danger from the convicts. I told him that I had no trouble with the convicts at tough West Street (or at Danbury), just with authorities who refused to treat me and the others as human beings. I said that the country was finally speaking as if it opposed fascism, but every time I had gotten in trouble it was because of fascist acts on the part of the prison. I talked about having been put in solitary for sitting next to a Black man at the Saturday-night movie and made the connection with Nazi racism. I told about having been punished for refusing to answer when addressed as a number rather than as a person, etc. I shall never forget his response.

> Dellinger, the American prison system is the most authoritarian institution in the world, and if you don't straighten up and obey every order that it gives you, no matter what it is, the full weight of that system will come down on you.

It was one of the most chilling moments in my life. I had visions of being transferred to Springfield or Alcatraz and of terrible things happening to me there, death being the least of them.

Perhaps the impact of his words was greater because before I went to prison I had been told by a Quaker official who worked as a lobbyist in Washington that Bennett was an enlightened New Dealer who was trying to reform the system and would listen sympathetically to any complaints any of us forwarded to him. But mostly, I think, it was because I already knew as much as I did about the prison system, from my own observations and from the accounts of long-term convicts like Al Harris. And of course I remembered the warnings by officials that if I continued on my current path I would not get out alive.

I didn't "straighten up" and neither did my comrades, and soon we were all in solitary, under threat to stay there the rest of our sentence. The first day or two was routine, neither inspiring like my trip to the Hole nor particularly upsetting. But apparently Bennett's threat was reverberating in my subconscious, because one night I found myself going through a period of anguish such as I had never experienced before. I felt absolutely certain that there was no way I could continue on my present path, not just inside prison but on the outside—if I got out—and manage to stay alive. But, in a way, death was the least of it. Before it came, I visualized anything from months of agonizing misunderstandings with people whom I loved—or at least wanted to interact positively with—to periods of unbearable physical torture. All night, I experienced this future in all its frightening intensity.

Then something happened similar in its own way to what had happened in the Hole. There is no way to describe it except to say that I died. I faced my own death and embraced it. I know that it must sound fanciful but I emerged from the experience convinced that I had died and that nothing that any human being could do to me could ever harm me. I had faced the worst, had decided to continue in the direction that life was taking me and suddenly, unaccountably, I was free. I had died and, if you will forgive the phrase, had gone to heaven—much as I had done earlier in the Hole.

Death, be not proud, though some have called thee
Mighty and dreadful, for thou art not so.
. . .
Death, thou shall't die!
—from a sonnet by John Donne

During those hours of anguish I had lost contact with my experience in the Hole but in the end it returned, coming just as unexpectedly as it had the first time. I became filled with the peace and love that surpasses understanding, and I "knew" that I could never again be separated from feelings of human solidarity and love—and the ultimate love that undergirds everything. But this time, I had more feelings about death and rebirth. Perhaps because in the Hole I had not died, though I had been willing to. I had been scared at first but mostly I had gone directly to heaven without having had to go through any extreme agony.

From then on I felt for years that, having died, I was having the incredible fun of living some bonus time, however long or short it would turn out to be. It was an unearned gift that could be taken away at any time without making any difference to me. That's how I felt in Lewisburg Penitentiary in 1943 and 1944, on a number of occasions when I prepared to die. And when I stood nonviolent guard at the Koinonia interracial community in Georgia in 1956 after it had been firebombed and shot into, I felt no fear at all—not because I was brave but because I was already dead and nothing could harm me. And the same held true in 1963, when I was shot at during an interracial march in the South. And when, a month or so later I was separated from my companions in Albany, Georgia, and had a sinister white man follow me for an hour or more, muttering imprecations about "nigger lovers." I tried to talk with him but he wouldn't listen and kept following me, ostentatiously displaying a long-bladed knife that I expected him to plunge into me at any moment. That time I felt a little nervous, but no real fear. And so it was the time I was put into the white section of the jail in Americus, Georgia, with no companions except prisoners who hated civil rights troublemakers and were told that I was a "nigger-lovin' agitator from New York."

The first time anything seriously different happened was in 1967 and '68, when, after a number of death threats, a series of bombs were sent to me in my home in Glen Gardner, New Jersey. That time it was different because a terrifying new element was added. It was only sheer luck that my wife, children and our first grandchild were not killed. *That* stuck a dagger into my heart and I *felt* it. It was one thing for me who was already dead to be killed again. And though I felt awful about the danger to my wife, at least I knew that she had chosen our way of life and danger. *But the children!*

It's hard for me to remember when I lost that sense of being dead and having been granted some unbelievably enjoyable bonus time. But somewhere along the line it gradually slipped away until a time came when I realized that it was no longer a part of my everyday consciousness. The best I can guess is that I lost it after I got old enough for there to be a more conventional reason to think about a second death. By then my bonus years had taken me beyond the time in life when most people die, and I had been frequently reminded of this by the death of friends and relatives who were my age or younger.

All I know for sure is that all through my first bonus years, it was natural to say (and feel), "What the hell, live it up, there's no way anyone can harm you and you have nothing to lose." And that living another kind of bonus years now, I still say and feel, "What the hell, live it up. Live to the full. Enjoy life. Enjoy every magnificent minute of it!"

17

A Snapshot

When I was in Danbury in the fall of 1940, the Communist Party opposed U.S. entry into the war that was soon to become World War II. It was the period of the Nazi-Soviet Friendship Treaty, which meant that Roosevelt no longer valued Hitler as an ally in the fight against Communism and was maneuvering to get public support for going to war. By contrast, the Communist Party was muting its anti-Hitler rhetoric, so much so that sometimes it seemed almost to be embracing Hitler. I wasn't embracing either Hitler or the Soviet Union, but because of my antiwar stand I was hailed as a hero, practically a saint, by a dozen or so Communists who were doing time there for some reasons not connected with the war.

A group of them were members of the furriers union in New York and worked in the prison's tailor shop. My job was to collect the trash six days a week from all the various units of the prison, so I saw them there every day except Sunday. Besides praising my stand, they plied me with prison niceties that they managed to have access to—hot coffee and rolls, an occasional cigar, nicely tailored, carefully ironed shirts and pants, etc.

One day, I walked in as usual and they called me a "fascist" and a "coward." When I tried to talk with them, two of them literally spat at me and I left, totally confused. At my next stop, I told someone what had happened. "Didn't you know?" he said, "Germany invaded the Soviet Union." I hadn't known, but it was June 22, 1941, and true.

They didn't even ask me if, given the new circumstances, I would decide to change my position. Or try to convince me that I should change. They were right in assuming that I wouldn't, but suddenly I had become not just a political opponent but subhuman. It reminded me of the attitudes toward Socialist Party members and Trotskyists I had observed a few years earlier at the Connecticut State Communist Convention.

III

Meeting Betty

18

Nothing else ever happened to me as important as meeting Betty (now Elizabeth) Peterson. I met her at a National Conference of the Student Christian Movement (SCM) in Miami, Ohio, during the Christmas holidays of 1941–42. Here is the complicated emotional background that I took to our meeting.

Shortly after I had finished my prison sentence at Danbury I was asked to make a major address at the conference. The invitation made clear that I was to speak as an antiwar activist who was committed to nonviolent methods of overcoming domestic and international injustice. But then Pearl Harbor was attacked, the United States declared war on Japan, Germany followed with a declaration of war against the United States and I wondered if my antiwar and anti-imperialist criticisms of the United States would be as welcome as when I had been invited.

Even before Pearl Harbor, the circumstances of my release from prison had suggested that I would be rearrested as soon as I made a speech at a major forum in favor of nonviolent resistance to U.S. militarism. On the day of my scheduled release, I had been issued civilian clothes, taken to the warden's office, handed a draft-registration form and told to sign it. When I refused, the warden said that he could not release me unless I did. When I still refused, he said that my seven Seminary colleagues had all signed and that he hated to see me be the only one not to get out. Then I was left alone in a small room to "think it over." Perhaps an hour later, I was ushered into his office again and again I refused. "Well," he said, "I'm going to release you but I will have to notify Selective Service and the FBI that you have refused to register. Since you won't be carrying a draft card, the government may pick you up at any time. Perhaps they will do it at the Danbury railroad station or perhaps when your train arrives in New York. If they don't and you want to stay free, don't speak out against the draft and don't organize or take part in any antiwar demonstrations." Free?

When I got to the van that was waiting to take me to the station, I found my seven colleagues in it. None of them had registered.

Given this background and the hysteria that followed the Japanese attack on Pearl Harbor, I wondered what would happen when I spoke at the conference. At first, I thought that I might be arrested and dragged away in the middle of my talk. But then I reasoned that the government must know that this would raise too many questions in the audience, so it would be more apt to arrest me discreetly after I had finished. In any case, I felt that I should speak as forthrightly and forcefully as I could, since it might be my last chance to present a large body of students with a view that was being rapidly overwhelmed by war propaganda.

By now, I have forgotten what I said, but it did not lead to my arrest. And I received a more enthusiastic response from the students than I had anticipated. When I finished, I was handed a number of slips from students requesting private interviews, a procedure that had been set up to facilitate meetings between students and outside speakers. One of the slips was signed "Betty Peterson, Pacific College, Newburgh, Oregon."

Reminiscing with Elizabeth and some friends about this incident a few years ago, I teasingly suggested that my speech must have been even better than I thought because it led her to ask for the interview. "I thought that if I gave the best speech of my life," I said, "it would probably cause me to be arrested, but instead it brought Elizabeth into my life." Her honest response was that she had filled out the request *before* I spoke and that she doesn't remember much about the talk. She asked for the interview because the conference program had mentioned that I was a draft objector who had been in prison for his beliefs, lived in a commune and was working in an interracial project in a city slum. She opposed the draft, wanted to live in a commune and had been working the previous summer with Mexican migrant workers in Yakima, Washington.

The story of our meeting would be incomplete if I did not say that I was twenty-six at the time and lonely for a female partner. Shortly after I had broken my engagement to Sally, another young woman, one of fine qualities and a fellow member of our commune, proposed to me. I knew that she was not the answer to my search, but I was sorely tempted to accept her follow-up offer. It was that we should live together as lovers and "find out where that takes us." In the end I declined. By now I have no way of knowing how much it was because I was still saddled with the sexual morality of my upbringing and how much because I was afraid that it would get us into a dishonest relationship that would not be good for either of us.

To add to the complications, another young woman asked if she could hitchhike with me part of the way to the conference. She said she wanted to visit an aunt who lived near Pittsburgh, which was on the way. She was a married friend who was a part-time volunteer in our community project, teaching art to both children and adults. We spent a night in a hotel in Pittsburgh and although I arranged with the clerk for separate rooms, she invited me to her room and then to her bed. This time I half-reluctantly, half-eagerly accepted the invitation. But at the last minute I decided that for us to commit adultery would be unfair to her husband and unworthy of both of us. When she told me that she wanted to leave him and marry me, this might possibly have made the act acceptable if I had been clear about being ready to marry her. But I was not. I loved her deeply but felt that somehow the chemistry was not quite right for a marriage. When she and I had dated before her marriage, I had felt less spontaneous sexual excitement from her than from a number of other young women.

I did love my bedmate in Pittsburgh enough to think seriously of marrying her after she divorced her husband. After all, what did I really know about sexual matters, inexperienced as I was? And I felt more secure in her lifetime commitment to the kind of life that I wanted to lead than I had with Sally. In the end I said, "Let's both think it over and when we get back to Newark, we'll decide."

So on to Ohio it was, still uncommitted but leaning toward saying yes.

My first meeting with Betty lasted only a few minutes, just long enough to arrange the time and place for the interview. But a few minutes after I looked at her, heard her voice and watched her walk down the aisle of the lecture hall to her seat, I called my married friend and told her that I had decided that I would not be able to marry her. "You've met someone else," she said, and I said she was right. To give you an idea of how much my friend, Betty and I had in common, the three of us were the closest of friends for the rest of her life. About thirty-five years after our trip to Pittsburgh, my friend died from a stroke. She never did divorce her husband, and, as far as I could see, they were happy together.

I don't believe that there is only one person who is destined to be another person's true mate, but that is my story of what happened to me. Something about Betty in that first brief meeting made my whole being want to get to know her whole being. I never doubted for a second that I wanted to spend the rest of my life with her. After fifteen years of troubled, postpuberty virginity, five of them after I had graduated from college, I finally had found someone with whom it felt overwhelmingly right to share the miracle of sex and the added miracle of bringing children into the world and becoming a family. I longed to spend a lifetime of all-encompassing adventure with her, each of us helping the other to live the revolution now.

It didn't take long for Betty to let me know that she felt much the same. The conference lasted five more days and we spent almost every waking moment together. As soon as I got back to Newark and she to Oregon, I called her on the phone, we jointly decided that I should come out as soon as possible, and a few days later I hitchhiked to her. The day after I arrived, Betty withdrew from college and we traveled to Seattle, where her parents lived. On February 4, a month and a few days after we had met, we married. I had originally suggested that if she had any hesitations, she should join the community, we would live together and "see where that takes us." But she wasn't very radical in that area, even though once I met her I had finally become so.

Her father was a Presbyterian minister and he performed the ceremony, but Betty and I wrote most of the words. We wanted them to express our joint commitment to the kind of life we planned to live together, dedicating ourselves not only to one another but to a life of working together for justice and peace. We pledged to become a small community of love that, to the best of our abilities, would reach out to include the entire human family.

When we made this commitment we both knew the uncertainty of our situation. It was less a question of whether I would be sent back to jail than when. I told her of a close call I had hitching out to meet her. After I had ridden for two days with a young couple, a snowstorm halted all traffic at the top of the Donner Pass in the Sierra Nevada Mountains. While we were sitting in a restaurant waiting for the roads to be cleared, the police arrested the three of us for possession of a stolen car.

Because they could not drive us to jail on the snow-blocked roads, they walked us to a nearby small hotel and locked us in a room on the top story. I thought I could explain my relationship to the car, but knew that I would be in trouble the next morning for not having a draft card. I discussed the matter with my friends and they agreed that I should try to escape. The police had made a point of having us put in a room that did not have a fire escape, but I felt that by taking a slight risk I could probably get to the one outside the room next to ours.

The couple assured me that they had bought the car before they started on the trip and felt they would be all right. So I gave them most of what little money I had, to help them hire a lawyer. Then I sat at the window of our room with my eyes glued to the road below. Finally, as the first faint light began to appear, I saw the cars begin to move. With a leap, I got a grip on the nearby fire escape, pulled myself on, climbed down as far as it went, dropped to the ground, and managed to find a ride without being caught. At the first large city I holed up in a fleabag hotel for the rest of the day and till the next morning, hoping that the hunt for me wouldn't last longer than that. Then I managed to make it to Newburgh, Oregon, without being apprehended.

After our wedding, Betty and I drove in her parents' car to a honeymoon cottage she had arranged for us on Puget Sound. After a wonderful four or five days and nights there, we returned to Seattle, said our goodbyes and took a bus to Salt Lake City. From there we hitchhiked to Newark. We didn't want her parents to be upset by our hitchhiking out of Seattle, but we didn't have enough money to take the bus all the way to New Jersey. For the first time, I wondered if I had been right to give most of my money to the couple interned at Donner Pass, but Betty said that she was glad I had.

In Iowa we were given a ride by a man who turned out to be a sheriff. He spent a lot of time talking about the war and his distaste for people who refused to fight for their country, and we were sure that he was preparing to ask to see my draft card. He didn't, but tried to get me to promise that I would put Betty on a bus and hitchhike the rest of the way alone. I said it was a good idea. Once we were safely on the sidewalk I told Betty that I thought we had just enough money to do that, but she would have none of it.

After an adventurous week, we made it safely to Newark, hitching the last couple of days and nights without stopping, except from time to time to get a new ride. We walked the last few miles, bags and all, from where the last ride had left us off. By then we were physically exhausted. But dawn was breaking on the new day and on our new lives so I can still remember how joyous we felt in our togetherness.

19

Between our arrival in Newark and my arrest about sixteen months later, Betty and I found out that neither of us was perfect but that our love was not seriously challenged by that reality. Besides having to learn how to deal with each other's foibles and quirks—neuroses even—our greatest problem was finding time to be alone together.

The communal house in which we lived was crowded with the eight or ten of us who were regular residents, but on top of this we were deluged with visitors. Some were adults (mostly men) who came in search of the hospitality we offered to anyone in need—food, clothing, shelter and friendship. Others were young men who were resisting the draft, or planning to, and usually had parents who disapproved. They needed at least a temporary home where they could get moral and political support. Besides endless discussions on the nonviolent way of life, they could participate in community work that served as a laboratory in which to test the practicality of their ideas about moral alternatives to society's ceaseless wars between races, classes and nation-states. If they didn't come to us with community work high in their priorities, almost all of them grew to believe in it and like it. After spending a few months with us, a group of seven or eight of these young people (men and women) set up a separate commune in another depressed area of Newark.

Additionally there was a host of visitors who came for anything from a few hours to a few days or weeks to share religious or political ideas and experiences with us—personally, in group meetings and in the project's other activities. They included people we met when we spoke at churches or secular political events, mostly in the suburban areas surrounding Newark but sometimes in New York or further afield. Others came because they heard of our antiwar stand or community work, whether by word of mouth or through the publicity that both generated. We gained a lot of intellectual, spiritual and material sustenance from these people and made a lot of good friends.

In this setting, Betty and I poured ourselves into relating to our varied guests and trying to keep up with the project's other work. She helped get a hot lunch program started at the local grammar school, helped carry it out and worked with a food cooperative that the commune had organized among neighborhood adults. She also found time and energy to interact—with a creativity that amazed me—with the many small children of the neighborhood.

I continued my clubs of teenage boys and coached a couple of athletic teams—in baseball, football and basketball, depending on the season. And five nights a week I worked the graveyard shift in a huge commercial bakery. Because a war tax had been levied on everyone's weekly paycheck, I worked out an arrangement with the management whereby they could count on my showing up regularly but would not put me on the regular payroll. After each night's work, I would get paid and confirm that I would be in the next night. I have been a war-tax resister ever since.

I shall never forget the first large-scale, daytime trip to the country that Betty and I led together for the youth of the neighborhood. Suddenly the bus nearly tipped over because a girl by the name of Maggie Demer had just seen her first cow. "*Ooh, a cow!*" she screamed, and every other kid on the bus rushed to that side of the bus to see their first cow. And when I took one of my boys' clubs to New York for an outing, I was shocked to discover that not one of them, teenagers all, had ever been across the river to New York. After a while, we rented a small farm about fifty miles away (outside Chester, New Jersey), installed a resident organic farmer (Robin Rae, a draft resister whom Dallas, Benedict and I had met at Danbury) and made it available for family vacations and weekend outings for our Newark neighbors. Sometimes volunteers from the *Catholic Worker* or the Friends Service Committee came to engage in work camps there with neighborhood volunteers.

All of these activities were complicated by the racial tensions of the neighborhood and by the presence of volatile youth gangs. Some of the successes we had in dealing with both problems strengthened my belief in the theory I had held for years (with less concrete experience to back it up) that such conflicts are endemic to our kind of society but not beyond solution through patient and creative friendship and other forms of nonviolent work. I think, for instance, of the time my efforts to work with two rival gangs culminated in my having to intervene in a confrontation between the two rival leaders, each with an open knife in his hand and his similarly armed lieutenants standing a step or two behind their leader. One of the members of one of the gangs had come to the house to get me when he knew that the other gang had challenged his gang to meet them and "have it out." I managed to avert the fight and to get the two groups to agree to sit down with me the next day to talk things out.

On the personal side, Betty and I used to escape upstairs to our bedroom whenever we could, for an hour together before I left for work and she went to sleep in order to rise early to join in preparing and serving breakfast. Usually we spent a good deal of that time reading aloud to each other. Besides the inevitable poetry, our first major text was Marcel Proust's *Remembrance of Things Past*, but after a hundred pages or so we had both had enough and moved on to something else. Kafka, I think, and Kahlil Shridharani's *War Without Violence*.

Betty kept her maiden name after we were married and when she wrote her first letter to my mother after a weekend visit to Wakefield, she wrote it on her personal stationery, with the name Betty Peterson at the top. The day my mother received the letter, she called me on the phone. "What's the matter with the name Dellinger?" she asked. "Isn't it good enough for her?"

Both Betty and I were well aware that I might be arrested at any time and go to prison for anything from one to five years, but we jointly decided that we wanted to have a child anyway. I knew that it would be hard on her if I went for long—or forever—but, if anything, the fact that I might be sent away increased her desire to become pregnant. She said that she would carry part of me inside her for a time and then have a reminder of me close at hand.

She became pregnant soon enough, but after several months had a delayed miscarriage. I feel sure that one of the causes was the rigors of her daily life, but we also found out that she had a tipped womb that would have made the pregnancy difficult under any circumstances. After the physical and spiritual trauma of having carried a dead fetus inside her for a month or more, it took a long time for her to get back into sufficiently good health for us to decide on another pregnancy. By then, the likelihood of my being sent to prison was increasing, so we felt a special urgency to accomplish the pregnancy before that happened—and we did.

The reason we knew that arrest and sentencing might be in the offing was the decision we had made (along with others of course) to launch a Peoples Peace Now Campaign. We felt that the war had reached a stage of genocidal bombings of civilian areas in Germany and demands for "unconditional surrender" that made it necessary to do this, but we also knew that doing so was apt to provoke the authorities to crack down on me. Again, the decision to launch the campaign was Betty's as well as mine, and she risked arrest in the Committee's public actions, both outside the Capitol in Washington, D.C., and in Newark.

These are examples of how in testing times and despite the discovery that neither of us was flawless, our basic unity of purpose and belief prevailed. The mysterious magic that had thrilled us at our first meeting never left us for long, transcending and seeing us through whatever personal strains and temporary misunderstandings we experienced. So my life was filled with love, joy and gratitude.

IV

Prison Again

20

The first public action of the Peoples Peace Now Committee took place outside the Capitol building in Washington, D.C., on April 6, 1943,* with about a dozen participants. We didn't issue a general call for others to join us, or make any public announcement, because we wanted to be able to get to the Capitol and demonstrate long enough to get our message out to the public through reports in the media. If we were arrested (as we expected to be) others who felt as we did would be out of jail and able to conduct local or regional follow-up actions.

Here are a few excerpts from the leaflet we took to distribute:

> Truth and Brotherhood will not be helped by Unconditional Surrender. In Germany, Hitler is insecure. The German people will overthrow him. They long for a just peace. They could be our allies in the fight against fascism, but we separate them from us by demanding "unconditional surrender," a demand which any people would fear.
>
> CALL FOR A PEACE IN WHICH:
>
> 1. *There will be no military victory for Axis fascism, for British-American imperialism, or for Russian Communism.*
> 2. *Every country will be free and equal in solving their mutual problems.*
> 3. *There will be no blockade to prevent the feeding of Europe.*
> 4. *The mills, mines, factories and natural resources will be democratically owned* ***by the people.***

*The twenty-sixth anniversary of the U.S. entry into World War I.

5. *The products of industry and agriculture will be distributed fairly among all races, communities and individuals according to need.*
6. *All anti-Semitism and Jim Crowism will be outlawed, together with all exploitation of India, Asia and Africa.*
7. *The crushing burden of armaments will be lifted off the backs of men.*

We got to the Capitol all right but were immediately set upon by obviously prepared police. They confiscated our signs and leaflets but did not arrest us. Not a word of the attempted action appeared in the media. But by coincidence (synchronicity?) the *Washington Post* carried an editorial on April 7 in which it said that "the Government should go the limit in relying upon the press to be self-disciplined. For voluntary censorship is the ideal arrangement in a democracy engaged in what we are pleased to call a peoples' war."

When I got home and went to work the next night at the bakery, I took a few copies of our leaflet and showed one to two of my coworkers whom I knew to be sympathetic. They got excited, called over others and most of them responded favorably. They were all white, but, together with an experience I had a short while earlier in the Black ghetto, I concluded that a lot of ordinary people were more ready for a Peoples Peace than the media was. A Black friend had taken Dallas, Benedict and me to a popular nightclub to hear a jazz band that he particularly liked. We were the only white persons there. During a break, our friend introduced us to the band leader, with a word about our having been in prison for our stand against the war. The band leader got excited, talked with us for a while and then introduced us to the audience. When he told our story, we were greeted with thunderous cheers and applause. For the rest of the night, we were surrounded by people who came up to congratulate us and say that they felt the same way we did. A few of them were even in uniform.

The first day of the Peoples Peace Now follow-up demonstrations Betty and I marched and leafleted in downtown Newark with about thirty people. No one interfered with us, and we got a number of enthusiastic responses from people who took our leaflets and talked with us, so we were exultant. But when we repeated the action the next day, the police stopped us and, like the Capitol police, confiscated our materials without arresting us. And when we got home, federal authorities were waiting and I was arrested on charges of draft refusal.

Ever since I had gotten out of Danbury, the FBI had intermittently threatened to arrest me, but members of the clergy or other people of influence had intervened in my behalf, citing the importance of the community work I was doing and saying that a second arrest would amount to "double jeopardy" for the same offense (illegal under federal law). Most notably, about a hundred members of the Congregational Church's clergy had signed such a statement when Bill Clark, a young Congregational minister who had been with me in Danbury as a nonregistrant, circulated it at one of their annual conferences. To get around the double jeopardy, the authorities had ordered me to take a physical for induction into the army, as if I were registered, but until then they hadn't followed up on my refusal to take it. But now they apparently decided the time had come to get me (and others of the Committee's organizers) off the streets and into prison.

After I was arrested I spent three weeks in the Hudson County jail because I refused to pay bail while awaiting trial. I don't make bail refusal an absolute, but I usually refuse because I believe the amount of money that a person can command should not determine whether or not he or she stays in jail. Every jail I have ever been in has been crowded with people who have been there for weeks or months (sometimes a year or more) without having been tried, convicted or sentenced. It makes a mockery of the idea that everyone is innocent until proven guilty. Such people are hostages who have been captured by a system that puts a money value on everything, including freedom and justice. It is holding them for a ransom that neither they nor their families or friends are able to pay. Who knows what the long-term effect of my refusal to pay bail may be on the judge who set it or on other people, but I have thought it worthwhile to raise the issue. Whatever effect it may have on the judge or the court system, it is an important act of solidarity with people who are being held for lack of bail money. And it often leads to wonderful discussions and friendships.

Betty, my newly pregnant wife, supported the refusal, but after I had spent three weeks in jail, she decided to get in touch with the judge and explain my reason. After talking with her, he decided to release me on my own recognizance.

Earlier, when I had arrived at the jail and was being taken upstairs in the prison elevator, a guard started handling a prisoner roughly. When the prisoner protested, the guard began punching him. I got between them, and the combination of my body and whatever I said stopped the blows. Afterwards, I was put into a small, overcrowded cell that had no one in it except seven or eight murderers and me. The murderers greeted me not with violence, as the officials may have earlier suggested they do, but as a hero who had just intervened on behalf of a fellow prisoner. They told me that he was a leading member of the Mafia and when they mentioned his name I immediately recognized it from the newspapers. He sent me a message thanking me for what I had done, saying that he had heard that I was there for lack of bail money and would pay it for me. I sent word back thanking him and explaining why I would not accept his offer.

In the Cook County jail nearly thirty years later I was again offered bail money by a fellow prisoner who was in the Mafia. This time I was one of five prisoners from the Chicago Seven trial who had originally been denied bail by our judge. When this was overturned eight days later by an Appeals Court, the prisoner heard it on prison TV and expected me to leave. But two days passed, I was still there, and he thought it was for lack of money. He did not know that the delay was because the five of us had refused to accept bail from our supporters until they raised an equal amount for other prisoners who had been there a long time but couldn't raise it. So when I passed his cell on my way to see our lawyers, he handed me a slip of paper and said, "I guess you're having trouble raising bail, Dellinger, so give this to your lawyer. If he goes to this address with this note, he will be given whatever he needs to bail you out of here." I am sure that he did it out of the goodness of his heart and because he had followed accounts of the trial on television and liked the way we were standing up for our beliefs. But I thought about other instances in which the Mafia undoubtedly supplied bail money to someone who would be tempted afterwards to work with and for them.

During my 1943 stay in the Hudson County jail, after midnight one night a prisoner named Henry M. was thrown in with us. We soon learned that he was charged with having committed a particularly gruesome murder that was headlined in the next day's papers. He had done it all right and was even more horror-stricken than anyone else. As I got to know him, he told me the story. A seaman, he had returned home one night to his apartment in a row of buildings that had identical appearances and entrances. Drunk on his first night in port, he had burst by mistake into the building next to his and had been immediately attacked by its occupant. Enraged, and thinking the other person was the intruder, he had responded by brutally beating his assailant, killing him. I have never known anyone more conscience-stricken than Henry was. He couldn't believe that he had done it but knew that he must have. I gave him what comfort I could during the rest of my stay and managed, with Betty's help, to get him a socialist lawyer I knew, who took his case for free. The lawyer was as impressed with Henry as I was and eventually succeeded in getting him a sentence that wasn't quite as long as it might have been—or perhaps in saving him from the electric chair.

Getting to know Henry was one of many instances in which I found that prisoners who had committed horrible crimes—though usually not by accident—were not that different than myself or most of the people I knew on the outside. To cite the most extreme case I had experience of, I got to know someone at Lewisburg who had intentionally committed a far more gruesome crime than Henry had. He kidnapped a man and tortured him while trying to collect ransom. Each day he scalped his victim a little more, pulling back the skin an inch a day and sending a picture of the day's results to the man's family. Hearing of his crime, I was horrified and felt sure that he would prove to be an exception to my previous experiences and general view. But when I got to know him, he wasn't. I never did find out what had caused the anger that had driven him to such an excess of calculated cruelty, but after a few months of our friendship I would have felt comfortable taking him into my own family for a period of adjustment to the outside world—if there had been any chance of his getting out. My willingness to do so stemmed from experiences through which I had learned that when I had enough personal contact with such a person and treated him with enough love and creativity, it might not cure all his psychic illnesses or get rid of all his frustrations and cruelty, but invariably it led to his responding in kind to me (and, to a surprising extent, to others as well). If the person joining me and my family were Henry, I would probably have made sure that he got treatment for alcoholism, and similarly I would have gotten this friend in touch with some kind of treatment to prevent him from taking out any remaining aggressions on people other than me and my family, though I didn't think there was serious danger of that happening.

Sometimes, people who understand the core similarity between the criminal and themselves express it by saying, "There but for the grace of God go I." Perhaps that shows a glimmer of understanding of how similar we all are to the people who do terrible things—or do things that are more obviously terrible than some of the things we do un-self-consciously. But I would have no respect for a God whose grace made such an invidious distinction between those whose privileges (of color, class, family—and sometimes personal health) made it less likely that they would commit such crimes than those whose circumstances made it more likely that they would. It wasn't this kind of God that saved me from being sent to reform school when I was ten to fifteen years old and did many of the things that caused my jailhouse companions to be arrested and started them on their way to more serious crimes. It was my parents' status and connections.

After the judge with whom Betty had talked issued the order to release me from the Hudson County jail on my own recognizance, she came to get me. She came in a flamboyant new sports car that was owned and driven by a lieutenant in the navy by the name of Louis McMillan. Louis and his wife, Peggy, were New York friends who liked our work in Newark and admired me for going to jail for my beliefs, even though Louis did not fully share them. It was fun seeing him at the prison door in his naval uniform, driving to their house in his fancy sports car, having a relaxing drink, home-cooked, gourmet meal and stimulating conversation. In those days, Betty was a teetotaler, but when I took the just opened bottle of liquor and jokingly passed it under her nose with a warning not to let it get her drunk, she became pleasantly giddy. I couldn't tell whether it was from the aroma or because we were back together again.

David Dellinger, *right*, and his brother, Fiske, *left*, 1939.

Patch, Elizabeth, Dave, and Ray in Newark in 1946.

With his wife and children in 1947. *Front row, left to right:* Patch, Ray, and Elizabeth.

With Bill Lovett, *left*, at the Libertarian Press in 1948.

Left to right: Bill Sutherland, Art Emery, Dellinger, and Ralph DiGia on the S.S. Anna Salen in 1951.

In France at the Rhine in 1951. David Dellinger, *standing left*, and Ralph DiGia, *standing right*. Sitting are Art Emery, *left*, and Bill Sutherland, *right*.

Elizabeth Dellinger with two-year-old Michele in 1958.

The Dellinger family in 1962, *clockwise from far left:* Dan, Ray, Patch, Tasha, Dave, Michele, and Elizabeth.

Barbara Demming greets Dellinger as he is released from jail after a hunger strike in Albany, Georgia, in 1963.

Dellinger, *far left*, addressing microphone with paint-spattered fellow demonstrators in 1965.

Conferring with Tom Hayden at the House Subcommittee on Un-American Activities hearings in December 1968 about the "police riot" in Chicago during the Democratic National Convention. (AP/Worldwide Photos)

Prison Again

21

The sentence I received in the aftermath of the Peoples Peace Now activities was to serve two years at the Lewisburg maximum-security penitentiary, as the prosecution had recommended. But the judge changed the emphasis by recommending that I do my time at the prison farm outside the walls of the main prison. And contrary to precedent and custom, he suggested that I go home overnight and come back on my own the next day to be taken there. My feeling was that he had done this partly because of exchanges we had in which I was firm but had reached out to him as a fellow human being, and partly because of my bail refusal and Betty's intervention. The irony was that when my friend Bill Sutherland had reached out in similar fashion to the judge in his trial a few months earlier, saying, "I just want to discuss this with you as one human being to another," the judge had sentenced him to four years at Lewisburg. I think the difference was that Bill was Black and the judge he was trying to approach "as one human being to another" was a racially prejudiced judge from the South who was temporarily sitting in for the judge who later sentenced me.

When I got to Lewisburg and was being processed inside the main prison, I discovered that about a dozen war objectors (out of twenty or thirty) were on strike. So I asked the officials to let me talk with them so that I could decide intelligently whether to work or to join the strike. I wasn't surprised when they refused and took me to the farm. Once there, I learned that before the war it had been used, as Danbury had been for Al Harris and others, as a more relaxed, transitional place for long-termers to finish their sentences. A few of them who were there told me of resentments among regular prisoners that a few "conchies" and a large number of Jehovah's Witnesses, all of whose sentences were "short" to begin with, were given the privilege of doing their time at the farm, robbing long-timers of their right to spend the last few months there.

Like me, the Jehovah's Witnesses were draft refusers, but they were not pacifists. Their position was that they would fight only in the forthcoming "holy war," Armageddon, between the saved like themselves and the forces of Satan—most everyone else. Unlike them, I did not want to be taking a place that could be filled by a needy long-timer, so I told the officials that I would not work there. Then I got to meet the strikers since I was taken inside the main prison and put in the isolated cellblock where they were.

Once there, I discovered that the strike had begun over racial segregation, starting when Bill Sutherland had been forbidden one day to sit at a table in the dining room with some of the white objectors. But it had gradually broadened to include what I saw as an unrealistic "shopping list" of demands. To me, that meant that in essence it had become an "absolutist" strike of the kind that I had decided at Danbury I would not engage in. I preferred to work as often as I could at a prison job, both because of the associations with other prisoners and to be in a position to take action with maximum effect when I was confronted by a specially obnoxious act or saw a concrete objective that I thought was potentially winnable.

As we discussed the situation, it became clear that the other strikers tended to think along similar lines and felt that they had unintentionally backed themselves into the absolutist position and were getting nowhere. In the end, everyone gave up that all-purpose strike and five of us went on a hunger strike for two specific objectives. One was to end the policy of putting people in the Hole, with its hole in the floor replacing a regular toilet (maybe that was why it was called the Hole) and with its lack of bed, reading or writings materials and everything else, even a toothbrush. We used to ask the officials what kind of "crime" justified taking away one's toothbrush so that one's teeth would decay. The other demand was for an end to the repressive prison censorship of incoming and outgoing letters and incoming reading material. We said that we had no objection to the prison's opening letters and packages to inspect them for drugs and weapons, but we demanded delivery of all incoming mail, including newspapers, magazines and books. We presented a symbolic list of publications that would have to be admitted to show that the policy had been changed. Besides some of the material that we wanted to read, we included both *The Witness*, a publication of the Jehovah's Witnesses, and the Communist Party's *Daily Worker*. And we made clear that the contents of the publications should not be censored in the manner they had been at Danbury. There the censor cut out of the *New York Times* all stories and articles about crime, and when someone sent me a book entitled *The World's Great Letters*, the censor tore out the letter by Benjamin Franklin in which Franklin advised the reader to "choose an old mistress rather than a young one."

Each of the hunger strikers was put in a separate cell, with an empty cell on each side of it to prevent communication. The warden stressed that neither he nor any other official would meet with us or discuss the issues until we started to eat. And a guard who brought us the daily offering of food that we rejected told me that the orders were that not even the guards should speak to us. We were to be completely isolated from all human contact until we had either given up or had collapsed and been carried to the prison hospital.

The first to fall was Paton Price, a skilled actor and former roommate of Kirk Douglas. Paton was skin and bones even before the hunger strike, so I was not surprised when he collapsed after a very short time—eighteen days, I think. The warden let us all out of our cells to see him as he was being carried past us on a stretcher, eyes closed, looking like a ghost and at the very least unconscious. "See what you have done," the warden screamed at us, "you've killed him." And Paton surely looked dead. But when the warden moved away, preparing to lead the guards and the corpse they were carrying to the hospital, Paton opened one eye, winked at us and whispered, "I'm fine. Don't give up!"

A few days later I saw the warden again. He came to my cell and told me that my wife was dying from complications connected with her pregnancy. After the earlier experience in which she had carried a dead fetus inside her long enough for it to have poisoned her severely, my first thought was that it was true.

"She's dying," the warden said much more solemnly than he had announced Paton's death. "She has sent a message telling you to go off the strike so that she can die in peace."

Not having signed a slip authorizing the prison to censor my mail—and denied any mail anyway while on strike—I had heard nothing from her since my arrival. For a terrible moment, I believed him. I don't know what I would have done if I hadn't already served one sentence and learned how shamelessly the officials lie to the prisoners in order to bend them to their will. Also, I knew Betty well enough to question whether she would have sent such a message. On the other hand, why not if she was dying? There was only one thing to do and, shaking with fright, I did it. "Take me to her," I said.

The warden refused and I felt a glimmer of hope. "If she's dying, you *have* to arrange for me to get to her," I said. "You have no right not to!" He said he wasn't allowed to and left. Alone again, I was in agony, but the more I thought about it the more I thought that he had lied to me. The best I dared hope was that she was ill but not dying. In either case, going off the hunger strike would not help.

Weeks later, the hunger strike ended when we won on the question of censorship and felt that we had focused a certain amount of attention on the scandal of the Hole—both within the prison and outside, through prison visitors and movement publications. A pile of letters was given to me and in every one from Betty she made clear that she was having no special problems with the pregnancy and supported the strike, encouraging me to keep it up as long as I could.

On January 2, 1944, our first child, Evan Patchen Dellinger, was born. He was fourteen months old when I got out. One time while I was still in prison, I held him momentarily in my arms. In the visiting room, the prisoner and his visitor faced each other across a wide table, with a low barrier in the center that was supposed to prevent the passing of contraband, even though visitors had to pass through a metal detector and be searched before being allowed in. Elizabeth brought Patchen and we planned our move at the beginning of the visit. When it was time for her to leave, we would both stand and lean forward and she would hand him to me. We did, she did and *I held him!*

Before the guard got to me, I handed Patch back to her, to prevent any mishaps. If the room had not been filled with visitors, I don't know what the guard might have done on the spot. As it was, he jerked me out the door without any resistance on my part, shut the door, screamed something at me and drew back his clenched fist as if to strike me. Whether because of the joy that I felt from holding our child or because I knew that in a sense I had "betrayed" the guard by doing something for which he might be reprimanded, all I felt for him was sympathy. So I held out my open palms and said, not tauntingly but approvingly, "It's okay, hit me. I didn't mean to get you in any trouble but if you want to, go ahead and hit me. Go ahead." He gave me a funny look, unclenched his fists and turned me over to another guard who took me to my cell.

Earlier, getting to the point where we felt we had won enough to end the hunger strike was not easy. The last of the other four strikers went to the hospital the twenty-fourth or twenty-fifth day, but I stayed in my cell eight or nine days longer. By then the effects on me were fascinating. Some of them were caused (as I was told later) by changes in bodily chemistry produced by over a month of not eating. Others, which had harmful, long-lasting consequences, resulted from the setting in which the fast took place. Before it began, I was severely constipated from the prison food and spending several weeks in a small cell without outside exercise. Under the best of conditions, doctors recommend an enema (or a couple of them) in the early days of a fast. This would have been impossible under such circumstances, even if I had known about it. Eventually the prolonged presence of unexpelled fecal matter in my colon led to acute colitis, the aftereffects of which I experienced for nearly thirty years. I don't know how to explain it but I lost most of the aftereffects in 1972 when I had a ruptured appendix. The appendix ruptured only because I had thought the acute pains I had felt for a week were the usual pains from colitis, so I didn't go to a doctor to be examined.

On the chemical side, I reached a period during the hunger strike when I had almost constant "out-of-body" experiences, as they are called. While my body was on the bed, I would find myself floating on the ceiling or around the room in the air. Once I even floated outside and experienced the trees and the sky. It was fun. And there were strange visions and happenings, including feelings of exaltation similar to those I have described from my first visit to the Hole. In the Sixties, when a lot of people were taking LSD because of the visions they apparently got from it, there were a lot of reasons I had no interest in taking it. But one time when some people were pressing me to try it, Abbie Hoffman was there. He said to them with convincing firmness, "Leave him alone. Dave already has enough visions and expanded consciousness. He doesn't need to take LSD. He experienced in prison during his hunger strikes anything that LSD or any other drug could do for him."

So far as I knew I had never discussed these particular effects of the fasts with him. I think that he said this because, for all his lovable spontaneity, Abbie studied any drug that he himself took and undoubtedly knew the similarity between the chemical effects of LSD and a long fast. And of course there was another reason he spoke as he did. Instinctively, he offered support to anyone who was being pressured to do something that didn't come out of that person's inner sense of who he or she was and what he or she wanted to do. Chemically, Abbie was manic-depressive, beginning long before he used any drugs, and sometimes when he was in one of his manic phases he didn't fully live up to this. But mostly he did, even in these phases.

During the strike, I never did tell anyone that I needed to go to the hospital. I was doing fine. But on the thirty-third day, the guards came and got me. They came with a stretcher to carry me, but to my surprise I managed to convince them that I didn't need it. So I walked—floated!—to the hospital.

Before I report on what happened there, there was one other time during those first thirty-three days when I was startled to hear my cell door clang open and see the warden standing there. This time a high official from the State Department was with him. He had come from Washington to offer me a job in the department, "where I could do a lot of good," he said. All I had to do was to stop the hunger strike and go through the "mere formality" of filling out a registration card for the draft.

Mostly he stressed that staying in prison and continuing my present course would cause permanent harm to me in whatever future career I might want to pursue, whereas taking the job in the State Department would lead to a brilliant and useful future. Beyond the flattery, I got the feeling that this particular envoy felt genuine respect for people like me. On the other hand, I doubted if he could have undertaken this initiative purely on his own, and my doubts were increased when he said that my determined resistance was an embarrassment to a government that stood for democracy and political freedom. I immediately connected this with the growing dismay in some circles over the tactics of unconditional surrender and obliteration bombing, a dismay that we had been trying to bring to a head with the Peoples Peace Now campaign. And I thought of signs we had seen that the traditionally cautious peace bureaucrats were also beginning to come a little more alive politically, moving cautiously out of their preoccupation with what a recent biographer of A. J. Muste, one of the best of them, has written: "However acute his observations of its causes and consequences, Muste's deepest personal involvement in World War II was in the internal affairs of the pacifist movement . . . [not in trying] to exercise influence in a wider sphere."* He and other pacifist leaders had to know of our hunger strike and had also to be challenged by it to broaden their involvements. So maybe our hunger strike was frustrating the government's objective of silencing us by putting us in prison, and the time had come for it to try a new tactic. Why not offer me (and others) a bribe that would silence us more effectively?

I didn't accept the offer, but about a year later a fellow prisoner, Al Hassler, who was an official of the pacifist Fellowship of Reconciliation or F.O.R. (headed by A. J. Muste) and editor of its monthly magazine, was offered—and accepted—parole on terms that forbade him to write or speak against the war. Ironically, about a dozen of us were on another, shorter hunger strike at the time (probably two or three weeks) and first learned of that deal when A.J. came to visit us after having sent a message to us through the warden, telling us that he was coming to negotiate the issues for which we were striking. To our dismay, he met with the warden first, then reported to us the "good news" about Hassler's release and tried to persuade us to abandon the hunger strike, citing the prison administration's now more enlightened attitude toward war objectors. We all felt betrayed. Although I later came to love and admire A.J. in his changed post-F.O.R. phase, many of the objectors at Lewisburg never forgave him for this and other actions he took during that period.

Nothing was mentioned about such a restriction in the earlier offer to me, but my guess is that it would have been brought up when I was about to be released, or as soon as I got to the State Department and met with superiors who were anxious to help me "have a successful career in the service of our country."

If unwillingness to mute my stand against the war had not been reason enough, I would have declined anyway. The routine brutalities imposed on the inmates of U.S. prisons had become so offensive to me

*Joann Ooiman Robinson, in *Abraham Went Out: A Biography of A. J. Muste* (Philadelphia: Temple University Press, 1981), p. 93.

that I would not have abandoned the strike and the prisoners by accepting the deal. Not for the dubious benefits of making a false peace with an Establishment that considered criminals as less than human and treated them accordingly.

22

The psychological warfare did not end when I got to the hospital. For my part of it, I refused to open my mouth to allow Dr. Rink, the head doctor who was conducting the first feeding, to insert a feeding tube. But I told him that other than that I would not resist because I had no interest in a strictly physical battle.

Who knows the significance, if any, of making him insert the rubber tube through my nose instead of through my mouth but I wanted to emphasize my continued determination. The negative aspects were minor: it was painful at first, though it got less so after repeated insertions had either widened the channel or toughened the membranes. And it may have been the reason that I experienced sinusitis for years.

As for Dr. Rink, he seemed to take my refusal in stride and proceeded to force the tube through my nose and down into my throat while an attendant held my head. But then he shook the glass container that held the liquid that he was about to pour into me. "Aha," he said, "what was that?" And he shook the container again, next to my ear so that I could hear what he had heard. "Oh my God," he said. "Someone is trying to kill you. There's ground glass in it." He shook it a third time, and clearly there was.

I have no way of knowing how the glass got there, but my suspicions were that it had been put there by someone in charge, with Dr. Rink's knowledge. But the doctors and other officials kept telling me that it had been done by a hostile inmate. They had saved me this time, but clearly my life wouldn't be safe if I insisted on continuing the strike.

It took another thirty-two days before we finally won enough of our demands to end it. But before that happened there was another dramatic incident. The doctors had been telling me for some time that I had gone too long without eating and that the tube feeding, limited as it had to be, was not having the desired effect of restoring the functions of my body. "You're in bad shape," they kept saying, shaking their heads gloomily. One day I got up to see if I could move my bowels, made my way to the nearby bathroom and sat on the toilet. Suddenly a strange vibration passed over and through my entire body. To my surprise, I felt that I was dying. And when it happened a second time and a third, I was sure of it.

I decided to die in my bed, if I could get there, and somehow I managed to. Almost immediately, still feeling periodic tremors and lying there gasping for breath—but not having said anything to anyone except a silent good-bye to Betty—someone spoke to me. I opened my eyes and saw that I was surrounded by doctors. "We just studied the cardiogram we took this morning," one of them said, "and your heart is giving out. It can't take the strain any longer. If you don't eat right away you will die."

I was too weak to say anything, but I shook my head feebly to show that I wasn't going to eat—and I didn't. But after a while the sensations stopped coming and I decided that I probably wasn't going to die.

I can't prove anything, but the circumstances were such that the more I thought about it the more I believed that the sensations I experienced had been caused by something the doctors had inserted in the liquid they had poured into me that morning. Not only didn't I die, even though I didn't eat, but from a few days after I got out of prison until the present, no cardiogram has ever shown anything irregular in my heart or the slightest damage of any kind.

All during the sixty-five days of the hunger strike, we had been treated to a combination of threats and tempting inducements to eat. The inducements ranged from bringing us succulent steak dinners in the early days (and other items not included in the regular menu) to offers of tea and toast in the hospital. When the strike finally ended, we were given the milk, tea and toast that we asked for to break the fast, but an hour or two later the regular supper of the day was served to us in our hospital beds—hot chile con carne. Since I foolishly—and against my better judgment—ate some of it, this probably contributed to my physical problems during a time of crisis the following day. But mostly I think the problems were almost inevitable effects of the long fast under prison conditions.

The next day we were served the regular prison meals again and transferred to regular cellblocks or dormitories after supper, each of us to a different one. While I was still weak, nauseous, dizzy and bothered by a ringing in my ears that impaired my hearing, two guards led me to a dormitory that was known as the "fuck-up dorm." Most of its inmates were military prisoners from the South, white of course, who had committed violent crimes.

One of the guards addressed the curious prisoners: "This guy is one of those phonies who says he's too good to be in regular prison with the rest of you." This was a total lie. Unlike a few war objectors, I had always opposed special classification and treatment as a political prisoner. "He's a nigger-lover who says that you guys should eat and sleep with niggers and use the same toilets and showers as niggers do." True. "And he's a Nazi who spits on the American flag and refuses to fight for our country." And after a pause, as if to let his words sink in:

"We're leaving, so that you guys can take care of him."

By then, I had thought that I had heard the worst, and basically I had. But just before they closed the door, the other guard spoke for the first time: "When we come back, we hope you give him back to us with his head in his hands."

The door clanged shut and despite what I have written earlier, about having died in Danbury and therefore not fearing any more for my life, somehow I didn't feel as calm and unperturbed as if I were about to have tea with some friends. But instinctively I knew what I had to do. I could hardly stand from dizziness, but I had to take the offensive.

Instead of waiting for them to come for me, I staggered over to the largest group. Some of them had been playing cards while others watched. When they saw me coming, someone picked up the cards and everyone walked away. No one said a word. I tried another little cluster and the same thing happened. So I walked over to where two guys were sitting on a bed, and they got up and walked away, also without a word.

I decided that they were waiting for the lights to go out before attacking me. So I leaned against a wall for strength and addressed them in the loudest, firmest voice I could muster. Here I will have to paraphrase what I said because I don't remember it word for word the way I remember what the guards said. All I remember is the line of attack—and the prison language I used. It went something like this and it drew on things I had learned from my earlier prison experiences:

> You guys know enough not to believe those motherfuckin' hacks. That's a lot of bullshit they're trying to shove down your throats and you know it. Any prison-wise convict like you guys know better than to believe a word the hacks say. They're lying through their motherfuckin' teeth. It's the hacks who act like Nazis, not me. You know how they treat you. I've been up there in solitary fighting for you guys. Five of us have been up there fightin' to get rid of the goddam fuckin' Hole. We're fighting for the cons, and the hacks don't like it. We've been fighting for the con's right not to be put in the Hole every time they look at a motherfuckin' hack cross-eyed. Fighting for everyone's rights to be treated like human beings for a change. I know a lot of you guys have been in the Hole, so I don't have to tell *you* what it's like. I don't have to tell *you* why we've been on hunger strike demanding that they stop acting like Nazis and do away with the Hole once and for all. You want to know why they're tellin' all those lies about me? To get you and me fighting amongst ourselves instead of stickin' together against *them*. Anyone who has been doing time like you guys have won't fall for that shit. You know the score. And so do I. So let's cut out the crap and not let the motherfuckin' hacks fuck us over.

I feel that the words were a lot better then, but that was the approach I took. And I remember pausing a couple of times in hopes of a response, not getting it, not being sure what to do and starting up again, saying more or less the same thing in slightly different words.

Nobody said a word to me from the time I finished until the lights went out. No one came near me and I didn't approach anyone or try to talk to anyone. I went to bed expecting the worst. In a few minutes, the lights went out and I heard the noise of some guys murmuring excitedly to each other, getting more and more agitated. Then I heard the sound of a lot of feet coming down the aisle toward me. It sounded like a stampede. "Here it comes," I thought.

This time I didn't take the offensive. Maybe because I was completely exhausted and had begun to fade out the minute I lay down. Perhaps because of what I have said about the effects of my death in Danbury. Anyway, I lay there barely conscious and ready to die peacefully, not even worried about the details of how it would happen.

The stampede went right past me and the next thing I knew it was morning. I soon found out what had happened to the guys whose onrushing feet I had heard coming down the aisle. They had gone to the bed of another guy at the far end of the dorm, dragged him into the john and gang-raped him.

He was a little guy called "Red" and he got out of the hospital the next afternoon. The "fuck-ups" were assigned to the kitchen and I was there trying my best to work, in bad shape but encouraged by the fact that a couple of guys had spoken to me. They didn't make any references to what the guards had said or what I had said, and I didn't bring up the subject. The best tactic now was to be patient and let the ice melt gradually. If I had gotten through the first night, I might get through the second one if I didn't make any false moves by trying to rush the process.

Then the hacks brought Red in and he began to work. As soon as I could, I went over to him and said something like this: "Geez, Red, I had no idea what was happening. I thought they were coming for me, and when they went right on past me I didn't know where they went or what happened. If I had known, I would have tried to help you. If they try it again, I'll do my best to help you." Glaring at me, he picked up a long kitchen knife that was used to carve the meat, held the point about an inch from my chest and said: "Get away from me, you motherfuckin' Nazi. If you ever speak to me again, I'll jam this so far into you that it'll come out the other side."

Gradually, I made a few friends but a lot of the guys continued to give me the silent treatment. I did manage to speak to Red a couple of times—in the dorm where there were no kitchen knives (though a lot of the guys had the usual shivs—short knives made by the cons in the machine shop). He began to loosen up a little and so did several others, but not enough for me to feel safe. Then something happened that changed everything.

A prisonwide Ping-Pong tournament was announced and I knew, based on what I had learned at Danbury, that if I could compete and do well it would help. I'm not sure how long I had been in the dorm by then but when I entered the contest I was still weak, groggy and hard of hearing. Mostly by sheer nerve and willpower I beat a few opponents and made it to the semifinals. When I came back to the dorm, accompanied by another guy who had competed and lost, he announced to everyone who would listen: "Guess who's in the semifinals? Dill here. Ya shoulda seen 'im. He's terrific. *We're gonna be the champs.*"

I'm sure that I wasn't nearly as good as the two guys I played the next week, but I won the championship. From then on, I had it made. I was a hero because the most looked down on dormitory in the joint, filled with insecure fuck-ups, had produced a winner and it was me.

Even so, it was another month before I put in a request to be transferred to a cellblock, as I desperately needed. I was still weak and intermittently dizzy and needed the relative quiet of a cell compared to the tumults and carryings-on of that noisy fuck-up dormitory. But the one thing you can't do in prison—or most anywhere else—is to run away from threats, particularly if you are pursuing a nonviolent course. I didn't want to take any chance of seeming to do that because I knew that if I did, the wrong reputation would follow me wherever I went.

Meanwhile, another crisis had developed, one that involved the warden rather than the prisoners. When we ended the hunger strike, we were given a large pile of letters and a few magazines, but from then on we had never received a magazine of any kind, and no *New York Times* had come in. We decided that the authorities were not living up to the agreement. So three of us decided that we had to confront the warden and, if necessary, go on hunger strike again. The other two encouraged us but said that they did not feel up to it. We got an appointment, but the warden explained that he was seeing to it that we got everything that came in. If we hadn't gotten any magazines or the *New York Times* it was because none had arrived. After a little back-and-forth, we told him that as of that moment we were on hunger strike again and stood up to leave. Without any apparent embarrassment, he said, "Let me just check in case anything came in today." He rang a buzzer, walked over to say something that we couldn't hear to a guard who had come to the door, and sat down at his desk again. In a few minutes, the guard came back and gave us a huge pile of letters, magazines and copies of the *Times*.

23

Shortly after my transfer from the "fuck-up dorm" to a cellblock I learned that the "absolute knowledge" I thought I had acquired from my fistfight at Yale—that I would never again be able to hit another human being—was not quite absolute. The spirit of what I had felt remained, but it had to be worked out experimentally in ways I could not have predicted back at Yale or at any other time. "Our truths are not absolute. They are biographical."

I learned this when one of the members of our recent hunger strike, a twenty-year-old Quaker by the name of Bill Lovett, came to me for help. He came because three prisoners in my new cellblock had selected him as the object of their sexual desires. He was to be their "boy." They had come to his cell the night before and announced that they were going to fuck him. Somehow he managed to hold them off, but when they left they said that they would be back the next night and would not take no for an answer. Saying this, they had displayed a shiv and the "key" with which they had entered his cell and could enter it again. (Like shivs, "keys,"devices used to open the cell doors, were made surreptitiously in the machine shop.) "Tomorrow night," they had said, "it's fuck or fight." That was the legendary ultimatum of Lewisburg's sexual bullies.

Because I was new in the cellblock I hadn't worked out a relationship with any of the aggressors, but I knew two of them slightly. Both were in for crimes of violence, as were most of the prisoners in that block. Frequently those of us who were war objectors (particularly rebellious ones) were put in with the most violent inmates. For the more thoughtful officials, it was a way to "show you people what the real world is like," as one of them had explained to me. That would cleanse us of our "romantic notions" about nonviolence. For other officials, the assumption was that anyone who wouldn't go to war was "yellow," so they were only too glad to have us get what we deserved at the hands of violent inmates. Alternatively, we would be so intimidated by them that we would come crawling to the officials, our spirits broken, and ask to be moved to a safer cellblock or dormitory. Then they would have the upper hand. Perhaps we might even decide to comply with the draft law so that we could be set free.

When Bill told me the trouble he was in, I was as upset as he was and uncertain what I could do to help him. But I knew I had to try. In the end, I decided that the only thing I could do was to get out of my cell at the appropriate time and stand guard in front of his cell. I would try to talk the would-be rapists out of their goal, but I had to be ready to fight. If it came to that, my somewhat unrealistic hope was that I could fight the biggest of them without the others ganging up on me, win a victory, establish my dominance (a word and concept I usually hate) and save Bill.

There was one trouble with fighting that had nothing to do with my previous decision never to get into a fistfight again, no matter what the circumstances. A year after the fistfight I had broken one of my wrists playing football in an intermural league and the wrist had never mended. I had undergone a bone graft, but it didn't take; and hardly was the wrist out of its cast when I broke it again, and again it failed to mend. From that time on, if anything put any pressure on the underpart of that hand it caused intense pain. (It still does.) I was afraid that if I got into a fight with the guys who were after Bill, I would collapse from the pain the first time I so much as parried a blow, let alone hit anyone. Fortunately, Bill worked in the hospital, I got him to steal some tape and I taped that wrist as firmly as I could. I didn't know if that would solve the problem, but what else could I do?

As soon as the lights were out and the guard had disappeared, a bankrobber friend with a key sprung me from my cell and I went down to Bill's cell. I wasn't worried about the guards because it seemed to be their practice to leave the prisoners alone long enough for them to take care of their sexual needs or otherwise get rid of their pent-up emotions. Better that they work out their frustrations on other prisoners than take them out against the guards or in prison riots.

I had hardly gotten to Bill's cell when four, not three, prisoners arrived. The fourth one was a guy called Sarge, an ex-sergeant in the army who had killed two people in separate fights. As the phrase went, he was a mean sonofabitch. I gulped and said, "Hi."

I began by engaging them in conversation. They seemed puzzled by my presence but talked. Acting as casually as I could with my back to Bill's door, I said nothing about him but talked about the prison, asking them questions about their "raps" (charges and sentences), work crews, times spent in the Hole, knowledge of other prisons, etc. At last, I mentioned the long hunger strike that Bill and I had been on and how we had been force-fed through a tube that was shoved through our noses and down into our throats.

I told them that in my case I had been force-fed after thirty-three days of refusing all food, but that since Bill was younger and less experienced he had collapsed after three weeks and been tube-fed earlier. Not knowing whether it would help or hurt, I mentioned—for a reason—that Bill was the only one of the five hunger strikers who had opened his mouth and allowed the guards to insert the tube rather than making them do it through his nose. "He's brave,' I said, "but he's still a kid. He's hardly been around at all. He's never even been in prison before. But he laid it on the line when he went on a hunger strike for prisoners' rights, and I'd hate to see him get messed up now." This was my first crude attempt to gain a little sympathy for him, but not surprisingly it backfired. "Oh, that's it," Sarge said, "he's your boy. *That's* why you're here."

"Hell, no!" I said, "I don't go in for that stuff and neither does he. But he and I were on that hunger strike together and I don't want to see him in any trouble, not after what he's been through fighting the hacks."

They changed the subject but made no move to leave. Clearly it was too early for me to bring things to a head, so I asked them about their families and told them about mine. They told nostalgic stories and so did I. One of mine was about having a son born while I was at Lewisburg, how my wife had sent me a picture of him nursing at her breast and how the warden had showed it to me in his office but wouldn't let me have it. "One of the other prisoners would steal it," he had said, "and a bunch of them would jack off together looking at it. I know you wouldn't want *that* to happen." I said that I had told the warden that having the photo meant so much to me that I'd take my chances, but he wouldn't let me have it, "the lousy motherfucker."

Soon it was clear that, hit-and-miss, I had reached something inside my companions that was establishing a bond of common experience and shared feelings. I can't make our exchanges come as alive as I think they did then, but I could tell that I was on the right track. The best I can say is that it was a case of my harking back to the days in high school when I had learned that my refusal to fight wouldn't work unless I had the goodwill and patience to reach my opponents at a level of common outlook and friendship that bypassed and transcended the conflict. Now I was doing the same with more hardened antagonists and more awesome stakes, trying to convince them of my genuine respect for them and desire to be friends. Gradually, I became so involved in this—and went so deeply into myself and them—that I almost forgot why I was there talking with them.

But I don't want to overstate matters. The reality of why I was there never left me for long and when it did I was brought back to it by the way in which one or more of the less talkative men grumbled impatiently around the edges of our little group. Obviously, they wanted to get beyond all this talk and get their rocks off by fucking Bill in the ass.

Luckily I seemed to have made the best contact with the one who worried me the most—he had a terrible reputation and seemed to be their leader. I had decided earlier that he, not Sarge, was the one I would try to fight, if it came to that. It will do no harm by now to say that his name was Steele and that, true to his name, he had the coldest, most steely eyes and voice that I had ever seen or heard. Or so I felt at the time. But gradually I could see that he was affected emotionally by the discussion. This helped for a while, but a time came when I felt that I was losing the battle. I had seemed to reach them in somewhat the manner I had hoped, but apparently it wasn't enough. They wouldn't leave and we were running out of conversation.

I thought that I had made enough good contact that they probably wouldn't jump me, but felt that any minute they would tell me to get the hell out of the way so that they could get down to business. That would be the time when, according to my original plan, I would have to fight the leader. But by then I had convinced myself that fighting wasn't the answer. It wouldn't solve the problem for long and would violate the progress I had made. So I proceeded with an alternate plan that had been in the back of my mind all along as a last desperate measure. Fortunately, I was able to adapt it to the goodwill that had developed between us. First, I said openly for the first time that I knew why they had come. Then I said how upset Bill was—*and I was*—at the prospect of his being fucked against his will. "So," I said, "I decided to come down here and do my best to prevent it. And if necessary, I was going to tell whoever it was that they would have to stick a shiv into me before they could stick it into Bill. You can imagine how relieved I was to find out that it's you guys and not someone who would do that."

I suppose that it didn't have to turn out as happily as it did. But shortly after I had laid things on the line that way three of them faded away wordlessly, first two of them and then Sarge. That left only Steele and me. "Motherfucker," he finally said, "what a pisser. For a while I thought he really *was* your sweet-ass, cock-sucking boy and that you were trying to save him for yourself. But now I can see that's not it at all. I've got to hand it to you. I can't believe what you just said. You'd let someone stick a shiv into *you* to save *him*. Holy motherfuckin' Christ!"

That was about the most welcome, genuine praise I have ever heard in my life. Soon after that we left together. And from then on, we were all friends, and none of them ever bothered Bill.

When I had been in my cell waiting for the confrontation to take place I had felt real fear for the first time since I had died in Danbury. Perhaps the post-Danbury feelings had been tested too often in recent months and I was emotionally drained, unable at first to find them for this new crisis that came so soon after I thought I had been transferred to the "peace and security" of a cellblock. But I had worked on myself and had recaptured those feelings by the time of the encounter. So I had felt relatively fearless again and ready for whatever happened. When I walked away with Steele, leaving him by his cell and continuing to mine, I was exultant. But once inside, with the door closed, I began shaking all over, sobbing uncontrollably.

It's a story that I never told for years, not to Betty and never in intimate discussions with friends. Certainly not in public talks, even when the subject has been prison or the power of active nonviolence. But after more than four decades of silence, twice in recent years I tried to tell it. Both times, a deeply probing discussion period had followed a talk in which I had drawn on other prison experiences and finally I thought I was ready. But both times I choked up and couldn't continue. I am crying now.

24

Despite everything that happened in Lewisburg, I received my "conditional release," commonly known as a "good time" release, about four months before the completion of my two years. Perhaps they were anxious to get rid of me, as the offer from the State Department had suggested. The conditions required that I have an approved job on the outside, and Betty had arranged one for me. I was to work for a Quaker apple farmer in Westchester County, Pennsylvania. Betty, Patch and I would live in his tenant house, and I would work forty hours a week, picking, sorting and packaging apples and doing whatever odd jobs the farm required. The forty hours a week was a condition I had insisted on, not with the prison but with the Quaker farmer, through Betty. I had made clear that I needed the rest of the time free, mostly for writing.

The writing was particularly important to me because it had been impossible for me to do any substantial writing in Lewisburg and know that I would be able to take it out with me. There was some confusion about the rule, if there was a rule, but everything we took had to be inspected. What happened seemed to be mostly a matter of last-minute whim on the part of the authorities, together with a desire to crack down on rebels like myself. The things I had been writing kept disappearing from my cell during the periodic searches for contraband; when I complained to the warden he said that he didn't know anything about that but it didn't matter since I wouldn't be able to take most of my writings out with me anyway. Nothing written about the prison or in support of the offense that had gotten me there would be allowed. So after a while I stopped most of my serious writing, though I did make and get out some scattered notes.

When I arrived at the farm, it was haying season and I worked sixty hours or more the first week or two without complaining. But by then, we were behind on apple picking and the next week was the same. Then it was sorting and packaging that we were behind on, and I finally reminded the farmer of the forty-hour-a-week verbal contract. "I know that we said something about that," he replied, "but it doesn't seem right for the owner to be working overtime and the tenant sitting around in the tenant house taking it easy." So I began to explore arrangements to leave.

I telephoned my friend Kenneth Patchen, who had been on my correspondence list at Lewisburg, and told him of the crisis. He responded by saying that he and his wife, Miriam, were about to move into a cottage in the Catskills on the property of his friend Annie Rush, that there was a vacant second cottage, and he was sure he could arrange with Annie for me, Betty and Patch (his namesake) to move into it. The place was in Mount Pleasant, New York, and it didn't take us long to get there. Typically I guess, I didn't ask permission from my parole officer but stopped in his office in New York on my way and informed him where I was going and why. Luckily, he said "Fine," typical of the understanding from individual officials that one sometimes finds within the system.

I got a job working for a dairy farm about four miles away, walking to and from work. I spent the first few hours shoveling manure and cleaning the pasteurizer. Then I delivered milk in a truck. On the first or second weekend, Betty and I walked about ten miles to visit Holley Cantine, an anarchist who, doing his own printing, published a small magazine that I liked, *Retort*. It was in *Retort* that I had first read one of Kenneth Patchen's poems, after my first release from prison and just before he showed up at a meeting at which Paul Goodman and I were speaking. I was thrilled to meet Kenneth, and he seemed just as thrilled to meet me; we became close friends.

It turned out that Holley knew of a hand-feed, foot-pedal press for sale by another writer, Jimmie Cooney, along with some hand-set type. We bought it (on credit) and before long Ralph DiGia, Bill Kuenning and I were on the way to launching a magazine called *Direct Action*. Bill had been one of the five hunger strikers against censorship and the Hole at Lewisburg and both he and Ralph got out of Lewisburg shortly after our move to Mount Pleasant and joined us there. Betty and I were in a commune again.

The first issue of *Direct Action* was forty-eight pages and it took us forever to handset the type, make up the pages and print a few hundred copies, two pages at a time. One night when we were working late at it, after a few weeks of endeavor, Bill suddenly said, "And to think that they get out the *New York Times* every night!"

In the first issue, I wrote a book review of *The Trial* by Franz Kafka and an editorial that drew on the recent atom bombing of Hiroshima and Nagasaki. The editorial expresses the basic philosophy that I have tried to live by ever since, whatever my temporary deviations and less than ideal imagination and creativity. The only disclaimer I would make concerns the somewhat casual way in which I referred to sabotage as one of the methods we might employ in our loving, nonviolent warfare. For those who want to pursue that subject further, I have included in the Appendix a few words concerning my views on it as they have evolved through the years.

Here is the editorial, with the original emphases preserved.

Declaration of War

The atom bombing of Hiroshima and Nagasaki destroyed whatever claims the United States may have had to being either a "democratic" or a "peace-loving" nation. Without any semblance of a democratic decision—without even advance notice of what was taking place—the American people waked up one morning to discover that the United States government had committed one of the worst atrocities in history.

Hiroshima and Nagasaki were atomized at a time when the Japanese were suing desperately for peace. The American leaders were acting with almost inconceivable treachery by denying that they had received requests for peace, rumors of which had been trickling through censorship for months.

The atom bombs were exploded on congested cities filled with civilians. There was not even the slightest *military* justification, because the military outcome of the war had been decided months earlier. The only reason that the fighting was still going on was the refusal of American authorities to discontinue a war which postponed the inevitable economic collapse at home,* and was profitable to their pocketbooks, their military and political prestige, their race hatred, and their desires for imperialist expansion.

The "way of life" that destroyed Hiroshima and Nagasaki (and is reported to have roasted alive up to a million people in Tokyo in a single night) is international and dominates every nation of the world. But we live in the United States, so our struggle is here. With this "way of life" ("death" would be more appropriate) there can be no truce nor quarter. The prejudices of patriotism, the pressures of our friends, and the fear of unpopularity, imprisonment or death should not hold us back any longer. It must be *total war* against the infamous economic, political and social system which is dominant in this country. The American system has been destroying human life in peace and in war, at home and abroad, for decades. Now it has produced the crowning infamy of atom bombing. Besides these brutal facts, the tidbits of democracy mean nothing. *Henceforth no decent citizen owes one scrap of allegiance (if he ever did) to American law, American custom or American institutions.*

There is a tendency to think that the bombing of Hiroshima and Nagasaki was an excess that can be attributed to a few militarists and politicians at the top. That is the easy way out. It enables us to express our horror at the more obvious atrocities of our civilization while remaining "respectable" supporters of the institutions which make them inevitable. But obliteration bombing by blockbusters, incendiaries and atom bombs was a logical part of the brutal warfare that had been carried on for nearly four years with the patriotic support of American political, religious, scientific, business and labor institutions. The sudden murder of 300,000 Japanese is consistent with the ethics of a society which

*I was wrong on this one. The collapse didn't come until much later than I had anticipated.

300,000 Japanese is consistent with the ethics of a society which is bringing up millions of its own children in city slums. The lives of 300,000 "enemies" are distant and theoretical to business and labor leaders who find excuses for enjoying $15,000 incomes (and $150,000 incomes) while hiring workers for less than $1,500. Workers who passively accept starvation wages, periodic unemployment and relief checks, at the order of private owners and civic authorities, will also accept orders to put on a uniform and mutilate their fellow men.

No, the evil of our civilization cannot be combatted by campaigns which oppose militarism and conscription but leave the American economic and social system intact. The fight against military conscription cannot be separated from the fight against the economic conscription involved in private ownership of the country's factories, railroads and natural resources. The fight against the swift destruction of human life which takes place in modern warfare cannot be separated from the slow debilitation of the human personality which takes place in the families of the rich, the unemployed and the poor. *The enemy is every institution which denies full social and economic equality to anyone. The enemy is personal indifference to the consequences of acts performed by the institutions of which we are a part.*

There is no solution short of all-out war. But there must be one major difference between our war and the war that has just ended. The war against the Axis was fought as a military campaign against people, with all the destructive fury, violent hatred, regimentation and dishonesty of military warfare. The combatants were conscripts rather than free men. Every day that the war went on they were compelled to act in contradiction to the ideals which motivated many of them. Therefore, "victory" was predestined to be a hollow farce, putting an end to killing that never should have been begun, but entrenching white imperialism as the tyrant of the Pacific, and contributing unemployment, slums, and class hatred to the United States. The American people won half the world and lost their souls.

The war for total brotherhood must be a nonviolent war carried on by methods worthy of the ideals we seek to serve. The acts we perform must be the responsible acts of free men, not the irresponsible acts of conscripts under orders. We must fight against institutions but not against people.

There must be strikes, sabotage and seizure of public property now being held by private owners. There must be civil disobedience of laws which are contrary to human welfare. But there must be also an uncompromising practice of treating everyone, including the worst of our opponents, with all the respect and decency that he merits as a fellow human being. We can expect to face tear gas, clubs and bullets. But we must refuse to hate, punish or kill in return. We must respect the owners, policemen, conservatives and strike-breakers for what they are—potentially decent people who have been conditioned by a sick society into playing anti-social roles, the basic inhumanity of which they do not understand.

This is a diseased world in which it is impossible for anyone to be fully human. One way or another, everyone who lives in the modern world is sick or maladjusted. Slick businessmen and bosses, parasitical coupon clippers, socially blind lawyers, scientists and clergymen are as much victims of "a world they never made" as are the rough and irresponsible elements of America's great slums. The only way we can begin to break the vicious cycle of blindness, hatred and inequality is to combine an uncompromising war upon evil institutions with an unending kindness and love of every individual—including the individuals who defend existing institutions.

This is total war. But it is a war in which our allegiance transcends nationalities and classes. Every act we perform today must reflect the kind of human relationships we are fighting to establish tomorrow.

25

In October 1945 we were working on the second issue of *Direct Action* when a fire broke out in the Rush's icehouse, where we did our printing. It damaged the press, though not beyond repair. With that and the imminence of winter, Betty and I moved with Patch to Newark and I got a job in the Collier Printing Company.

I had known for a long time that I wanted to earn my living by doing work that directly served my spiritual and political goals and involved the use of both "hand and brain." Besides being natural to my body, mind and spirit, combining hand work (and other physical labor) with brain work challenges the artificial class divisions of society into brain-workers and laborers. Now, after getting out an issue of *Direct Action* and getting some enthusiastic responses, the much-quoted but seldom-followed axiom that the pen is mightier than the sword had come newly alive for me. It motivated me toward developing a printing and publishing business that could make my pen and those of other rebels reach people more surely and clearly than if we depended on the capitalist press—or, for that matter, on the press controlled by the bureaucratic leadership of the established peace and socialist organizations. The editor of the Socialist *Call* had turned down my article that had been smuggled out of Lewisburg in a prisoner's anus. And when sixteen of us imprisoned there (including several members of the Fellowship of Reconciliation) had written a letter critical of it for publication in the FOR's magazine, *Fellowship*, A. J. Muste had written back saying that it had not been printed because it did not represent our best selves. If people like me wanted to be sure of being published, we needed presses of our own. For me, the first step was to become skilled as a printer.

I stayed with the Collier Company for six months but there were two serious problems. I had purposely selected a union shop because I believed in unions, but it turned out that Blacks were not allowed to join either the Typographers Union or the Printing Pressmen. The only Blacks allowed to work there did the dirty work of cleaning the presses and sweeping and mopping the floors. Denied the joys that come from being a craftsman, they were also deprived of union wages and benefits. Second, an apprentice was permitted to apprentice to only one of the unions and to learn only its part of the craft. I worked in the typography department and felt that it was a one-sided apprenticeship that reflected the overly specialized job assignments that dominate modern industry and minimize the human development of the worker as a person of many talents. I wanted to become a master printer in the tradition of my great uncle Benjamin Franklin,* able to see and feel the job as a whole and occasionally to carry it through from beginning to end.

At the end of six months, I was ready to leave. I got the small press repaired and installed an electrical hookup to eliminate the foot-pedaling. So Betty and I opened a one-man, one-woman printing business—or as much one-woman as Betty was able to make it, given that she was first carrying, then delivering and nursing our second child, Raymond, as well as spending more time taking care of Patch than I was. But we installed a crib and a chair swing in the shop to make it possible for us all to be together as much as possible, and for me to take care of the two boys while she got a little time off.

Pressman friends from the Collier Printing Company stopped in regularly after work and gave me much-needed help in solving whatever problems had stumped me. The business grew, with a lot of political work, including the second and third (final) issues of *Direct Action*. But we were not a union shop and, lacking the union label, could not print for some of the organizations we wanted to, not even the War Resisters League (WRL), in which Betty and I were active. The only exception was when we donated the labor: the product could carry the words "Printed by volunteer labor." After a while, we joined the Industrial Workers of the

*Franklin was one of my great uncles, by way of one of his grand nephews and a full-blooded Cherokee Indian. Growing up, I heard a lot about Franklin, but didn't learn of my Cherokee great-grandmother until I was in my sixties.

World (IWW), the still-extant union of the almost-extinct Wobblies. This opened up some additional work of the kind we wanted, but not with the WRL. That came only after Igal Roodenko joined the shop and we became "A Workers Cooperative." The WRL decided that a workers cooperative was at least as good as a privately owned shop with a union contract and a policy of racial exclusion. About that time, my father gave me enough money to add a slightly bigger, machine-fed press* and we flourished—work-wise and satisfaction-wise, but with our little family barely surviving economically.

Meanwhile, Betty and I worked out plans with three other couples, Bill and Charlotte Kuenning, Adele and Ralph DiGia, Taddy and Bent Andressen (Bent was also an ex-con war objector) to start what we called "an intentional community." In 1947, we bought twenty acres of land in western New Jersey, in rural Hunterdon County near the village of Glen Gardner. We formed a "cooperative," with each family having separate living quarters and finances but all of us holding the land and buildings in common. One or two days a week, depending on the pull of outside political activities, we worked together on community projects and ate the main meal together. Doing all the work ourselves, we converted an old chicken house into living quarters, divided the one regular house into two apartments, and added electricity, a bathtub and kitchen to a two-room summer cottage. Betty, Patch, Raymond and I lived in the cottage—along with a new family member, Howie Douglas. Howie was a thirteen-year-old refugee (from an oppressive Newark orphanage) whom Betty and I adopted, though not by signing legal papers. He joined us as soon as we moved in.

We first met Howie (and his older sister, Dottie) a few years earlier through one of my coworkers at the Fischer Baking Company, their half-brother, Fred Boumal. After our first visit with Fred to the orphanage, we took the two of them out from time to time for a treat and a visit at the Newark Christian Colony. One time Howie ran away from the orphanage, came to the communal house and, after a short visit, was taken back by whoever was there at the time. A couple years later, after Betty and I had moved back to Newark and opened the print shop, we reestab-

*A Miehle Vertical.

lished contact with Howie. Soon he ran away again and came to the shop. When he begged me not to take him back, he seemed so scared that I asked him what had happened when he ran away earlier. "The nuns beat me," he said, "and made me go without supper for a week." So after conferring with Betty, I whisked him across the river to New York City, to the Kuennings, and arranged with friends in Ohio, Jean and Harold Smith, to take him until we were set up in our intentional community, which was then in the early planning stage.

When Howie came to live with us, we notified the State Board of Guardians and they immediately announced that they would have to pick him up and return him to the orphanage. But when we said that Howie, Dottie and Fred would testify in court about the abuses Howie and Dottie had suffered there, they changed their mind and said that we could keep him. After a while, they even listed us as the official foster home to which he was assigned and helped us with a clothes allowance and free medical care. Howie stayed with us until he married. Whatever minor problems we had with him and he with us—and after some intervening years during which we had only rare contact—he and his current wife, Betty, are much-loved members of our family. So is Howie's son, Brian, who recently phoned to invite me to speak at an antiwar teach-in he was involved in. When we phoned Howie and Betty on Christmas Day 1991 to wish them a Merry Christmas, they were fasting for the day "to increase our sensitivity to the homeless and other people who have to do without." They said that it meant that they could "give a little extra this week" to the places they regularly take it to. They had shared a family Christmas celebration three days earlier, on Sunday.

A few months after the Glen Gardner intentional community got underway, Bill Lovett, my Quaker friend from Lewisburg, joined it, along with his wife, Janet. He took on the full-time job of constructing a building on the community's land into which we could move the print shop. When that was accomplished, Bill joined Igal and me in the printing cooperative. We called it the Libertarian Press, a Workers Cooperative. Igal, a born-and-bred city man, didn't join the community but lived with us during the week and worked at the shop. He did this for about a year before the traveling and long absences from the city got to be too much for him.

After five years the original community lost some members, added some, and was reorganized on a more communal basis. We kept the separate family living quarters but not the private finances, and the printing and publishing became the main economic activity for all of us. Everyone who worked at the shop took his or her share of both intellectual and physical work, whether operating and cleaning the presses, unloading heavy skids of paper, editing manuscripts, working with authors, doing typographical work, collating and stapling magazines or whatever. There were no artificial divisions between owners, managers, skilled craftsmen and laborers.

Step by step, between 1947 and 1956, *Direct Action* (which had the shortest life of all) was succeeded in turn by *Alternative, Individual Action* and *Liberation* (which lasted more than twenty years). After three or four years of publication, an issue of *Alternative* was confiscated at the post office and destroyed, apparently because an article by Paul Goodman had the word "fuck" in it, or perhaps because I had written urging young men not to register for the draft. Or maybe it was the combination of the two, because we never did get a satisfactory explanation from the post office. But clearly we were a danger to public morality on both counts. We got out only a few more issues. Besides the uncertainties, one of the editors left the country to find freedom in Africa, and Ralph DiGia, Bill Sutherland and I went to Europe for five months on a world-citizenship peace project.

Besides the writing that I did, Betty wrote an article for the March-April 1949 issue of *Alternative* entitled "What Can We Do Now?" She discussed the importance of "creating something with our hands (or physical effort) along with our brains." Referring to the "sterility" that sometimes appears "in national offices," she suggested "a maximum term of office for executives and leaders [so that] "individuals who find themselves in these positions might . . . change periodically into other activities of direct creativity, to recreate themselves." "Teaching should be by example as well as by theory," she said, and "although street meetings, pamphlet and leaflet distribution should be utilized to present the radical pacifist way of life, I think the most helpful is child education." She thought that "a living community offers the best opportunity" for that. "For those who want to make a change late in life . . . [and] do not feel that they can participate in a total civil disobedience campaign, they might seriously consider refusing to pay their income tax, on the basis that its largest use is to support the military and war system." Finally, in the spirit we tried to live by, she asked for suggestions from the readers about "other alternatives to the destructive course of our civilization . . . as they discover them."

Individual Action was started in early 1952 by a former reader of *Alternative*, John Goldstein,* an anarchist who came to me with the idea for the magazine. I hadn't known him but encouraged him and soon was writing regularly for it. Two of my articles took strong stands against the public hysteria whipped up by the government and media against Julius and Ethel Rosenberg, criticized the flagrant abuses in their trial and argued against their execution. In line with the articles, I first attended and then spoke at public rallies in their defense at New York's Union Square.

In doing this, I took a principled stand against virtually all of the anarchists, socialists and pacifists with whom I worked, with the notable exception of John Goldstein. The others stayed aloof from the case (or spent more time attacking the Rosenberg's pro-Sovietism than criticizing the government) because their anti-Communism affected them differently than my disagreements with the Communists affected me. I was much criticized for it, but it is one of the decisions of my middle years that I am most proud of. Two years later, when A. J. Muste suggested to me that he and I launch a new magazine together (*Liberation*), one of several hesitations I had about working with him in such a venture was caused by his failure to speak out forthrightly in the Rosenberg case.†

*After a few issues, Felix Ortiz, a young Puerto Rican joined him as coeditor. I benefited a great deal from the long discussions the three of us had at the shop while we worked on each issue.

†Muste's mostly admiring biographer has written, "When, in 1953, Julius and Ethel Rosenberg were tried, convicted, and sentenced to death . . . the International Committee to Secure Justice in the Rosenberg Case was formed in an effort to save their lives. The F.O.R., with Muste at its head, remained aloof from the Committee because of its Communist overtones. This position, while politically prudent, cut pacifists off from first-hand familiarity with the case and from a full sense of the patent injustices which had occurred in the Rosenberg trials. Consequently the F.O.R. response was framed in terms that history would show to be unduly respectful of the judicial system and the authorities that sent the couple to their deaths." (Joann Ooiman Robinson, *Abraham Went Out*, p. 105).

After consultations, A.J. and I did launch *Liberation* in early 1956, with Bayard Rustin, Charles Walker and Roy Finch as comembers of the editorial board and Ralph DiGia as business manager, all unpaid of course. It was the beginning of my permanent reconciliation with A.J., who had changed significantly after the FOR had relieved him of his duties as its executive secretary, praising him lavishly and giving him a pension but basically firing him on the pretext of old age. I had a hard time, though, persuading Roy Finch that A.J. had really changed, not just taken another of his temporary turns in search of broader support. Ironically, when Roy finally became disillusioned with *Liberation* and resigned, it was over articles I had written in support of the Cuban Revolution after my visit to Cuba in 1960. A.J. supported what I had written, but I was the main villain.

Liberation soon grew to include an impressive list of well-known writers (and unknown writers, some of whom later became well known). During the Sixties, the board of editors included Sidney Lens, Barbara Deming, Paul Goodman and Staughton Lynd, with Kay Boyle and Tom Hayden as associate editors and David McReynolds and Richard Gilpin, in that order, as members of our one-person staff.*

*Besides the editors, associate editors, and staff member David McReynolds, here are a few of the better-known people who wrote for it: Edmund Wilson, Todd Gitlin, Jeannette Rankin, Dorothy Day, Daniel Berrigan, Waldo Frank, Michael Harrington, E. F. Schumacher, Richard Gregg, Paul Jacobs, Norman Mailer, Milton Mayer, Lewis Mumford, Robin Morgan, Kenneth Patchen, Michael Lerner, Adam Hochschild, Barbara Ehrenreich, Richard Barnet, Lawrence Lipton, Walter and Miriam Schneier, Mulford Sibley, Kenneth Rexroth, Pitirim Sorokin, Vera Britain, George Woodcock, Martin Luther King, Jr., Thomas Merton, Jules Feiffer, James Baldwin, Kenneth Boulding, Mitchell Snyder, Howard Zinn, Adrienne Rich, Gary Snyder, Jack Newfield, Michael Klare, Eric Bentley, Lawrence Ferlinghetti, William Davidon, Erich Fromm, Nat Hentoff, Margaret Halsey, Linus Pauling, James Peck, Gerard Piel, W. H. Ferry, Vincent Salandria, Arthur Waskow, Nirmal Kumar Bose, Alex Comfort, Vinoba Bhave, E. D. Nixon, Homer Jack, Helen Mears, Muriel Ruykeyser, Arthur Kinoy, Julius Lester, Norman Thomas, Joan Baez, Rajandra Prasad, Judith Malina, Charles Cobb, Jayprakash Narayan, Michael Ferber, Julian Beck, Murray Bookchin, Krishnalal Shridharani, Diane Di Prima, Harry Elmer Barnes, Lorraine Hansberry, Robert F. Williams, Andre Gorz, Stanley Aronowitz, Noam Chomsky, Allen Ginsberg, E. P. Thompson . . . But I am going to stop there, after looking

All the magazines I have mentioned were printed at the Libertarian Press, along with *Cooperative Living*, the magazine of the Fellowship of Intentional Communities, for which I wrote and served as editor for a time. Besides magazines, we printed some books and did a lot of local printing, some of it run-of-the-mill stuff and some that was more exciting, such as for the local art gallery. Exciting in a different way was the question of whether or not we would agree to print some routine work for the local chapter of the Veterans of Foreign Wars. After considerable debate, we decided to, with myself arguing in favor, perhaps partly because I played with some of its members on the local baseball team and treasured the relationships (see Chapter 29). The books included *Field of Broken Stones*, a prison memoir by two friends of mine (fellow ex-imprisoned war objectors), Lowell Naeve and David Wieck; *The Revolution of Our Time* by Scott Nearing, with whom I had been a cospeaker at a number of conferences; and the *Autobiography of a Catholic Anarchist* by Ammon Hennacy, who lived in our community for several months while it was being printed. We also did some books for the newly created Grove Press.

During the period from 1946 until the Sixties, Betty and I managed to be quite active politically, despite the demands of a growing family. And so did most of the other community members. In the Sixties one family who had been there a few years, the Landrys, left because they thought that the community should confine itself to being a "pilot project" that served as a model and example for the larger society. They considered work outside the community in civil rights and antiwar work to be a distraction from that function. The outside work did require periodic absences, including jail time, and deciding when to be absent required community discussion and sensitivity. I won't try to estimate how sensitive I was, but the idea held by most of us was that we should take turns in such activities and the remaining community members would fill in for

---

through the contents pages of less than half the issues. That's more than enough to give a sense of the quality and diversity of the writers. And I apologize to anyone whose name was left out because the list became unwieldy. I will also add that wherever I go I meet people (many of whom I have not known before) who tell me what an important influence *Liberation* was on their lives.

those who were temporarily absent. Probably we had not made this clear enough to the Landrys, whose membership we had welcomed for other reasons. Not everyone who believes in community belongs in the same community. But Gerry and Denise Landry made a lot of valuable contributions to our community before they left. They suggested naming our community Saint Francis Acres and changing the deed to declare that the land belonged to God with us merely as the trustees, two changes that we gladly made.

All through the late Forties and the Fifties, I journeyed to Washington and New York for antinuclear demonstrations and civil disobedience actions. There is no way I could list even half of them and there is no reason to. But I will mention a forty-four person, two-week fast in Washington in April 1950 against the making of the hydrogen bomb, and two sit-ins at the Atomic Energy Commission, one inside the AEC building in Maryland and one at the entrance to its New York office. Among the anti–hydrogen bomb fasters in Washington were seventeen-year-old Howie Douglas, my old colleague Bill Sutherland (from the Newark Christian Colony/Ashram and Lewisburg) and two Hopi Indians. I had met one of the Hopis in Danbury prison ten years earlier, and when I wrote him of our plans he decided to join us and came with his chief, Tom Banycya. During that fast, we held public meetings (including street meetings), picketed and distributed literature every day. In the AEC sit-ins, in New York I sat between Judith Malina and Julian Beck of the Living Theater, two beloved friends. In Maryland, one of the protestors was Jim Peck. During that sit-in we fasted, but every day Jim and I would go off in a distant corner, where we thought that our smoke wouldn't bother the others, and have a cigar from the box he had brought with him. Some of the Quaker women on the fast were surprised, but when we consulted with them they told us to go ahead if we enjoyed it.

In May 1963 Jim was beaten nearly to death in Birmingham when the FBI and city police purposefully withdrew from the scene in order to allow the KKK to attack the arriving Freedom Riders. On the bus's way to Birmingham, Jim had stopped and joined me for an hour in front of the CIA headquarters, which were in Washington at the time. A group of us, including Bob Steed and others from the *Catholic Worker*, were picketing and fasting against the Bay of Pigs invasion of Cuba. I seriously considered joining Jim on the Freedom Ride but the Cuban invasion was still going on and because of my recent visits to Cuba and the depth of my opposition to the invasion, I did not feel right about leaving that protest. In the end we were arrested, fined and jailed for two weeks when we refused to pay the fine.

During the Fifties, I also worked with others to form a series of nonviolent committees and organizations, each of which, like the magazines, generally grew out of an earlier one, usually with an expanded membership, both numerically and geographically. These included the Committee for Nonviolent Revolution, Peacemakers, the Committee for Nonviolent Action and the somewhat different Fellowship of Intentional Communities. I also served on the executive committee of the WRL and later as vice-chairman.

It would be hopeless, though, for me even to try to list the committees and projects I worked on. Perhaps the most important point is that during the Fifties I was involved in as many activities as at any time during the Sixties, and so were at least a few hundred people whom I knew personally and thousands whom I didn't know. The main difference for me personally was that at that time I did them from my base in the intentional community and the Libertarian Press, whereas by 1968 both the community and the press had been driven out of existence because of our activities (see Chapter 29). From a larger point of view, the difference was that the Fifties was a time for sowing seeds, whereas the Sixties, to some extent, was harvest time. (Of course, some new seeds were sowed in the Sixties that haven't come to full fruition yet.) During the Korean War we were pleased when we held a mass demonstration that included a few hundred people. During the Vietnam War, we held planning meetings that gradually grew to involve several hundred people for demonstrations that gradually grew to include several hundred thousand—and eventually close to a million. But I consider the work that I did in the Fifties to have been at least as important as the work I did in the Sixties, probably more so.

26

When the Korean War broke out, Bill Lovett and I journeyed to New York to meet with antiwar leaders and activists, hoping to unite with them on a speedy, large-scale response to what we saw as a hypocritical and extremely dangerous war. But it was not to be. We had somewhat naively failed to anticipate the extent to which the leaders of the established antiwar organizations would be seduced by the support of the U.N. for a "police action" that in our eyes was mostly a U.S. war against North Korea for the purpose of ensuring U.S. domination of the area on or near the Pacific Rim.

Abe Kaufman, Executive Secretary of the WRL, produced a written analysis that I characterized ("unfairly" he said) as an endorsement of the war against Communist aggression and an apologetic reminder that pacifists would not be able to fight in it because of our personal inability to engage in violence. A. J. Muste was the organizational leader whom I had particularly counted on to be ready for militant action, since he had participated two months earlier in the Washington fasting, leafleting and street meetings against manufacture of the H-bomb. And indeed his political analysis was much better than that of the others. But the confusion created in liberal circles by the U.N. fig leaf under which the war was being fought made him hesitant to get too far out front in relation to his colleagues and some of the more weighty members of his own organization. So he wasn't ready to join in a call for militant protest and resistance. His attitude reminded me of the role he had played during World War II, when he took the principled and risky step of refusing to register (when the draft law was extended to his age group) but represented the FOR on the National Service Board for Religious Objectors, the board that was clearly taking orders from General Hershey and imposing repressive restrictions on the conscientious objectors who were subject to its (and Hershey's) supervision. Now, when A.J. said that he favored protests against the Korean war *but not yet*, not until we could build more substantial organizational support, it reminded me of how during that earlier period he had told me for over a year that he agreed that the FOR should resign from the National Service Board, *but not yet, not until more converts had been won to this position.* In that case, I had attended a meeting of the FOR governing board (on which I sat) when an apparent majority of members finally indicated their readiness for the organization to resign, but A.J., contrary to what he had said to me privately on the subject, responded by arguing against "precipitate action" and stalling the resignation for another year. So I wasn't in any mood to defer action against the Korean War until A.J. felt the time was ripe.

The New York secretary of the American Friends Service Committee, Robert Gilmore, took a cautious position somewhere between those of Kaufman and Muste and wasn't about to help organize or to participate in the kind of action we felt was needed. Every suggestion for strong immediate action was opposed by all three, although they called for additional planning meetings to discuss the situation. Meanwhile the war was getting into high gear, largely unchallenged except for verbal attacks by the Communists. But eleven Communist leaders had been convicted in 1949, under the Smith Act, of working for the "forceful overthrow" of the government, and most of the Party's energies were going to fighting that. With some of its leaders going to jail and others going underground, the Communist Party was in no position to do any significant public organizing against the war.

After we had gone to two other meetings that went nowhere, our little community at Glen Gardner decided it was better to act locally than to stay endlessly involved in "high-level" talkfests with leaders who were influenced by factors we did not value. So five of the six people living full time at the community (Bill Kuenning, Janet and Bill Lovett, Betty and I) announced a two-week fast. The sixth, Charlotte Kuenning, supported the fast but was nursing a child.

On the whole, the fast seemed fairly successful, getting some attention in the media (including a story on page three of the *New York Times*) and stimulating supportive letters from all over the country. While fasting

I continued to work full-time in the print shop, in our organic garden and helping Betty prepare and serve three meals a day for the kids. What a difference from the hunger strike in prison during which the warden had come to tell me that Betty was dying and had sent a message for me to stop.

After the end of the fast, I started traveling to New York once a week for antiwar street meetings, mostly organized jointly with Bayard Rustin, youth secretary of the FOR, and Jim Peck, Ralph DiGia and Igal Roodenko of the WRL. We would set up a stepladder at a busy corner and take turns speaking from the top of it while our associates supported it (and us) from below. We had some exciting times, but nowadays I sometimes wince when I hear born-again Christians and similar groups self-righteously declaiming on street corners simplistic solutions to all of life's problems. I hope we were neither self-righteous nor simplistic, but I don't dare say that we avoided all tendencies in those directions.

A climax came when Bayard brought in a collection of young people from suburban areas to join us in a march, with an opening and closing street meeting. Starting in Harlem, where we got an excellent response, we carried signs, distributed leaflets and conversed with everyone we could as we walked to Times Square. There we set up our stepladder and started addressing a small but growing crowd. The response was the usual mixture of catcalls and shouts of approval until a man arrived who was unusually agitated and violent. I was speaking at the time and saw him hit a couple of our people when they tried to reason with him. Soon two big guys from the *Catholic Worker*, Roger O'Neill and Charlie McCormick, were holding him, and he was shouting in such a rage that I wondered if anyone could hear what I was saying. I barely knew Roger and Charlie at the time and wondered, somewhat uneasily, if they were pacifists familiar with how to handle him sensitively enough. (Later I found out that I needn't have worried. Roger and his wife, Mary O'Neill, joined our New Jersey community and Charlie and his wife, Agnes Bird, became good friends and frequent visitors.)

Soon, I decided on a way to try to solve the problem. I tried it for the man's sake, as well as for the two men from the *Catholic Worker*, the young visitors from the suburbs and the rest of the listeners and spectators. And it seemed to be in line with the approach I usually took, as when I had confronted the would-be rapists at Lewisburg. "Let him go," I said to the fellows who were holding him. "I'll come down and if he wants to hit someone he can hit me." And I came down from the ladder.

He rushed at me so angrily that I sidestepped a couple of times as he swung wildly and missed me. Then I realized that he wasn't listening to anything I was trying to say to him, and that I wasn't living up to my promise. So I said, "Okay then, go ahead and hit me if it will make you feel better," and I stood motionless, arms at my side. He did and the next thing I knew I was coming back to consciousness on the sidewalk, with Agnes Bird leaning over me. Later, I found out that after knocking me unconscious, the man had started kicking me in the head. Agnes had thrown herself on top of me and said, "If you have to kick someone, kick me," and this time her nonviolent approach had an effect on him and he stopped.

I also found out that the man had just learned that his son had been killed in Korea. Some of our people had finally been able to talk with him and he had told them. After they had talked, he came up and apologized to me, but I was too groggy to do much except to shake his hand and thank him. I wish I could say that I or someone else had gotten his name, address or phone number and that we had some later contact with him, but I didn't, no one else did and I never saw him again.

I can't really justify the way I acted. It would have been better to have done what I did on a similar occasion a couple of years later. That time I had announced from a speakers' platform on New York's forty-first street that we would give the hecklers (anti-Communists from Eastern Europe) a chance to alternate with us on the platform. It worked, had a good influence on people on both sides of the dispute and led to a favorable article in the *New York Times*. I must have thought this time that the man was too upset for such an approach, but I should have tried it anyway. Or I should have found some other way to establish better contact with him before dismounting. I did try it for a while *after* I had dismounted, but by then it was too late and, given what I had promised, I saw no alternative but to stand motionless and let him hit me. Foolishly, I issued the original invitation without having established an initial bond with him, as I had done in the confrontation at Lewisburg. In the end he did apologize, though I have no idea what the final effects of our actions were on him. What I do know is that the physical effects on me were serious and lasting.

When I got to a doctor he determined that I had a broken jaw and a badly damaged right eye. The jaw wasn't serious, but the eye was. After its initial recovery, which took a month or more, I had recurrent bouts of crippling "iritis" for more than twenty years. They required me to patch my eye, and the pain sent me to bed two, three or more times a year. On a number of key occasions they interfered with actions I was taking part in or wanted to take part in. I was suffering from such an attack on April 24, 1971, when we held the largest anti–Vietnam War demonstration of the war, in Washington, D.C. In a subsequent letter, in which Betty was reminding me of how stubbornly foolish I could be on such occasions, she wrote, "In April 1971 you insisted on going to Washington, D.C., when you knew you were too ill to stand up." And she was right, because when my time came to speak, I could hardly stand to mumble some words to the crowd before being taken to a hospital. I was there all through the exciting two weeks that followed, including the tumultuous May Day revolts of May 3. Ironically, I had been one of the few older sponsors of the April 24 demonstration who had also sponsored and organized the May Day plans to "close down Washington." That was why I felt it urgent for me to be there on April 24 to promote that cause from the platform. I finally got out of the hospital just in time to give the baccalaureate address at Columbia University, having been chosen for that task by a vote of the graduating seniors. I spoke, but with the patch over my eye and not feeling well enough to do as good a job as I wanted or to interact adequately with the seniors who flocked around me afterward.

Fortunately, the iritis attacks became less frequent and less serious after that, and sometime in the mid-or late Seventies they stopped altogether. Meanwhile I had become legally blind in my right eye.

27

The Times Square incident took place in 1951, a few days before I was due to leave for Europe on a World Citizens peace project that had been conceived in the context of the hot war in Korea and the intensification of the Cold War. Besides myself, the participants were Ralph DiGia from the Glen Gardner community, my old friend and colleague Bill Sutherland and a young dairy farmer from Iowa, a Quaker by the name of Art Emery. Ralph and I had decided to be part of the project even though the community was beginning to fall apart. Ralph was leaving the community and he and his wife were separating. But I wasn't leaving either the community or my wife, and Betty had urged me to go. Art's wife, Caroline, would stay with Betty and help with the children.

Our plan was to bicycle from Paris to Moscow, talking with people on both sides of the Cold War and distributing leaflets that were printed in English on one side and in the language of the country we were going through (French, German, Russian) on the other. They analyzed the artificial nature of the hot and cold wars and the futility of armaments. And they urged people on both sides of the Iron Curtain (or "Dollar Curtain," as we sometimes called it) to lay down their arms and make a people-to-people peace. (The English text is reproduced in the Appendix.)

The four of us had secured free passage on a ship full of college students in return for conducting classes for the students. But I couldn't help much, being unable to talk more than a few mumbled words because of the broken jaw and having trouble seeing because of the bandaged and painful eye. After a week we got to Le Havre okay, but then we experienced our first crisis.

As soon as we arrived, Bill and Ralph ordered a beer and I some

French wine. Art Emery exploded: As a teetotaler, he disapproved. As we were discussing it, he came up with an argument that we couldn't answer. Enough funds had been raised to carry us through the first weeks of our journey but more fund raising was going on, with additional money to be sent to us in Paris. Art said that the people he knew who were scrimping and saving to contribute would not want us to be spending their money on beer and wine. Since Bill, Ralph and I were old friends, but none of us had known Art, we quickly decided that to preserve the unity of the group we would agree not to buy any more beer or wine. A few minutes later, Art bought a double-decker ice cream cone, and we pointed out that in France this cost more than either the beer or the wine. But we didn't get anywhere with Art and from then on he kept getting his ice cream and we abstained from the wine and beer, both in and out of his presence.

I kept a journal during much of the ensuing trip and used it to start a book (which I never completed) after my return to the United States. Here are some excerpts:

> You save money by living there, but it won't be safe to walk in the streets at night. Outside of the tourist sections, the anti-American feeling is so strong that you must not be heard speaking English, even in the cafés and restaurants."
>
> This advice was given to me by a French journalist . . . when we moved into a tiny hotel in a working-class district of Paris. Two months later, after the tourist season and outside the tourist routes, the four of us were bicycling through a tiny French town on our way to the German border. Someone recognized us as Americans and set up a shout. Immediately a small crowd gathered, but instead of being hostile they were friendly. People called to their neighbors that "the four Americans" had come. The mayor of the town entertained us in his home. A group of French workmen fêted us in a café.
>
> While we were at the mayor's, he took time out from the festivities to warn us against the local Communists. In the café some of the workmen confided that they were Communists and warned us bitterly against the anti-Communist mayor. In other towns our experience was similar. We were befriended by generals

and pacifists, university professors and illiterate laborers, Jews whose families had been killed by the Nazis and Alsacians who had fought in the armies of Hitler.

When we arrived in Paris, we were just four more Americans who could be identified in people's minds with the might, power and foreign policy of the United States. Two months later we were "The Four Americans." We had publicly criticized the militarism of *both* the United States *and* the Soviet Union. We had announced our desire to bicycle from Paris to Moscow, appealing to the people of both blocs to refuse to take part in the preparations for another war. People knew from the newspapers and radio accounts that this was not just a publicity stunt—that the four of us had served prison sentences totaling ten and a half years in the United States as conscientious objectors to war.

We never got to Moscow—and for that matter we didn't even get into Germany. The Soviet authorities took care of the former and the United States government refused to let us have visas for Western Germany. In the end we took another route and made an underground sortie behind the Iron Curtain. When we did, we succeeded in conversing in broken Russian with over sixty Soviet soldiers and civilians, mostly in groups of twos and threes. (We had prepared for this by studying the language in Paris for two months, with a Russian refugee woman.) Besides giving each of them Russian-language leaflets (with extras for their friends), we also distributed several hundred of the leaflets at the Austrian headquarters of the Soviet Army.

At first we were bowled over by the enthusiasm of the French for our project. We were not used to being greeted as heroes for asking people in our own country to lay down their arms. But as our heads cleared, we realized that in most cases the mothers who tearfully embraced us, the wounded veterans who gripped our hands and the youths who distributed our leaflets were not pacifists themselves. Most of them were not prepared to take actions similar to ours. What they desperately hoped was that somebody, anybody—maybe we four Americans with our appeal to both sides to lay down their arms—would succeed in performing a miracle and alter the expected course of events.

It was not entirely an accident that their enthusiasm was

linked to a project that called for immediate total brotherhood and immediate nonviolence on both an individual and international level. There were many indications that they felt that in the end this is the path mankind must take if it is to survive—and if human beings are to preserve enough decency to make survival of any value.

The longing for something new, similar in its broad philosophy to what we were talking about, together with the reluctance to make what might turn out to be a useless personal sacrifice, could be seen clearly in Alain, a brilliant young graduate student at the University of Strasbourg. A half hour after we met him, he offered to help us with our project. At the time we had just received our second and final denial of visas for Western Germany. We did not want to become too embroiled in a conflict with our own government, since the central purpose of the trip was to reach out in love and friendship to the people of so-called enemy countries. But we felt that before moving toward Russia by another route we should do something to call attention to this "U.S. Iron Curtain." So we decided to camp at the border on the Rhine, fasting for a week and giving our message, both verbally and through our printed leaflet, to all who showed interest.

Alain was one of a large group who showed immediate interest. He rounded up a tent, blankets and pillows. With other French youth, he put up the tent for us, mimeographed announcements of what we were doing, ran errands and spent ten or twelve hours a day helping us. Like us, he was shadowed constantly by the police and subjected to other indignities. His house was ransacked, his concierge interrogated, etc. But from the first, he made only one reservation: he would not distribute our leaflet. This, he explained, was because of the expert legal opinion we had received that the section which appealed to individuals to refuse to make or bear arms was in contravention of French civilian and military law and carried a potential penalty of sixty-six years under the civilian law and court-martial by a special military tribunal. Naturally, this reservation made us feel better about the risks he was already taking. We did not wish to implicate others, particularly those whom we hardly knew and who might be approaching the project out of temporary enthusiasm, without the long preparedness we had undergone.

Something happened, however, that changed Alain's plans. The first night that we tented at the Rhine about fifteen policemen descended on us while we slept, pulled the tent down, and tried to deport us to Paris. After being taken to police headquarters and threatened with the sixty-six years of prison if we did not cooperate, we explained to the police that we would employ the Gandhian technique of nonviolent resistance. We would be friendly with all the individual policemen, understanding the pressures they were under from their superiors. (It was not until later that we received evidence that the whole raid was undertaken at the instigation of the U.S. consulate.) At the same time, we would do nothing to make their task easier. We would not walk onto the train to Paris or do anything except sit relaxedly on the ground while they were attempting to deport us. Perhaps these attitudes contributed to the decision of the authorities to take us to the outskirts of town, in the direction of Paris, leaving us and our bicycles by the roadside.

We slept in a field that night, rode our bicycles the next morning back through the center of town, accompanied by French supporters on their bicycles and cheered by spectators along the route. We pitched camp again and the police did not disturb our encampment but seized the leaflets we were distributing. Once again, we were threatened with the penalties we were exposing ourselves to.

Naturally, we had only a small portion of the leaflets at our camp where they could be seized, but it took us the rest of the day to decide that we should continue with the distribution whatever the consequences. After all, we had decided early that if by some chance the Russians decided to capitalize on the publicity by granting us visas and taking us on a conducted tour, we would not go to the Soviet Union unless we were able to take our leaflets. Once there, we would insist on distributing them whatever the consequences. If it were so important for us to insist on presenting our full message to the people of the Soviet Union, how could we back down when a similar freedom was challenged in the West?

The next morning we went, however apprehensively, to the bridge to resume distribution. Alain was one of our supporters who went with us. We thought he had come to lend moral support and to observe what happened. But as we approached the bridge, and after one of the many policemen had informed us that we would be breaking the law if we handed out the leaflets, Alain and several others pulled leaflets out from under their shirts and insisted on giving them to all who passed. The police did not interfere and no one was arrested. Perhaps this added evidence of our widespread popular support in France was a factor in the decision of the French authorities—and the American consulate!—not to carry out the threats against us.

During the next ten days, we seldom had any time to ourselves. Persons who had learned of the project came from the entire surrounding area to assure us of their support. We spent sixteen to eighteen hours a day in conversation with them.

One of our daily visitors was a policeman who had participated in our arrest and expulsion. It hadn't been easy that first night for us to be friendly with each of the police, after the tent had been pulled down on our heads and we had been tossed, pell-mell, half-asleep and fasting, on top of our disordered belongings into the back of a pitch-black police wagon. But when we had been handled roughly and cursed at, we had not replied in kind and when we got to the police station we were soon conversing in friendly fashion with our captors. The next day we had been left in a courtyard of the prison (in preparation for deportation) while the distracted chief had consulted with his superiors on how to deal with the four young American who were unmoved by his threats and were practicing nonviolent noncooperation. Noticing our leaflets scattered in a heap of our belongings, I had started to pass them around to the curious policemen, saying "Here, this tells better what it is we are trying to do." Because it was the time for the shifts to change, soon twenty or thirty policemen were reading the leaflets, apologizing for the "brutality" we had suffered and in many cases assuring us how much they agreed with us.

"It's the only hope," said one of them. "Something has to

be done to break down the barriers which make enemies of people who have never even seen each other." All during the hour, I had waited for the "meeting" to be broken up, but instead the crowd of sympathetic listeners kept growing and after a while it had included lieutenants and captains.

Even so, we were surprised the next afternoon when two motorcycles came chugging up to our tent, one bearing the policeman who became our daily visitor and the other carrying another of the several off-duty cops who came to see us from time to time. They had to pass the radio car and police lines that were constantly present in order to get to our tent and knew that their visits were noted in the records. "Oh well," one of them said, "I lost all chance of promotion already when I came to visit Garry Davis when he was here a couple of years ago." Davis was the U.S. pilot in World War II who had announced that he had become a World Citizen and advocate of World Government. Our intentional community in New Jersey, with its emphasis on grass-roots participatory democracy, had serious reservations about the dangers of World Government, but responded to part of Davis's message by formally declaring itself a World Citizen Community.

While all this was happening, accounts of our fast appeared in various American papers. But instead of giving the true reason for it, they said that we were protesting the refusal of the Soviet Union to grant us visas to Moscow. At the time we had not received any word of the Soviet Union's response to our still recent applications for visas, but a West German official in Bonn had informed us that it was the U.S. Military Command who had insisted on the refusal to admit us to Western Germany. Meanwhile, the Paris daily, *Liberacion*, which was accused of being an undercover Communist paper, printed front-page stories and photographs of our activities, with exactly the same degree of accuracy as the parallel (but much smaller) stories in the back pages of the *New York Times*. The difference was that they had a reverse conception of "all the news that is fit to print." They left out the anti-Soviet quotations and printed only those that could be interpreted as anti-American.

While we were at the Rhine bridge in Strasbourg, I was asked by a broadcaster who ran his own program to speak on the government-controlled radio station, but when I got there the manager canceled my appearance. This didn't surprise me because a few days earlier the acting prefect of Alsace (comparable to governor of a U.S. state) had told me that France was a "very restless country," and that our project was having "serious internal and international repercussions." But I was surprised when three representatives of the radio station came to our tent shortly afterwards, apologized and said they had arranged for me to speak on another station. Ralph and Bill went with me, and Art stayed to guard the tent and talk with visitors. This time, we got an unpleasant surprise of a different kind when we arrived at our destination. Here is a condensed version from my journal of what happened:

> Only then did the radio representatives explain that we were to make a personal appearance in a night club. The scene was such a contrast with our damp, foodless tent that we drew back instinctively. Not that we wouldn't have enjoyed an evening at a night club—if we had been able to eat and drink, but that we were afraid that the setting would be a poor background for what we had to say. The thought flashed through my mind that the M.C. might say: "Well look at who is here. The Four Americans just dropped in at the Naked Girl to enjoy themselves. (I don't remember the name but that one would have been appropriate.) Please come to the microphone and say a few words. Tell us how you like France. How do you like French women?" I wondered what the effect would be on the Alsacian mothers who had gripped their babies closer to them as they told us of the horror of American bombings of their homes during World War II and thanked God that there were Americans who want peace. I thought of the grimy laborers who had brought us beer a few hours earlier and to whom we had explained that we were eating nothing and drinking only water.
>
> Before we would go in, we held a hurried conference with the radio men. "Oh no," they said, "we brought you here because you must be allowed to tell your story to the French people. This is the only way we could arrange it." Even so, we did not go in

until the Master of Ceremonies came out and impressed us with the seriousness of his intentions. Still apprehensive, we followed him into the room. "The Americans," someone shouted, "The Americans!" And suddenly the place was a bedlam of cheering and clapping. Some of my fears returned when the program began with a platinum blonde doing a French can-can while singing a sexy ballad. Her breasts were covered only by a thin veil and as they bounced around inches from my face, I wondered what would happen if a newspaper photographer chose that moment to snap a candid shot. I also wondered how much of this I could take and still concentrate on the need for peace as single-mindedly as I had asked the M.C. to do.

When our turn came, the M.C. did not let us down. He immediately expressed his great admiration for what we were doing and asked a series of serious, intelligent questions. Frequently during my replies we were interrupted by applause and shouts of approval from the audience. But it was not until the next day that we learned that his particular variety program was the only program originating in Strasbourg that had a nationwide hookup. It was one of the most popular programs all through France. After the official refusal to let me speak on the earlier program, some of the people who were anxious to have us broadcast had cooked up a plot to smuggle us onto the nightclub program, knowing that the Master of Ceremonies held too commanding a position either to have the program tampered with during the broadcast or to suffer any consequences afterwards.

From Strasbourg, we set out for Vienna, where we hoped to speak personally to Soviet authorities about our application for a visa that would enable us to get to the Soviet border and bicycle to Moscow. Vienna, like Austria itself, was divided into four sectors at the time, one occupied and controlled by the Soviets and the others by U.S., French and British forces.

Those were the days when there were many stories about citizens from other countries who wandered into the Soviet sector and disappeared, never to be heard from again. When we visited the Quaker center in the American sector, the staff stressed these disappearances, said they never entered the Soviet sector and warned us not to. But we did, met with some Soviet officials and came out. The Quakers were astonished. Later, after we had returned to the United States, Spencer Coxe, one of the Quakers who had warned us, wrote us a letter in which he said that he and the others had been much too cautious and that our bravery had stimulated them to follow our example, with beneficial effects for their work.

After that, we made frequent visits to the Soviet area while waiting for the authorities to hear back from Moscow about our planned visit. Eventually, they said that we could go to Moscow, where we would be welcomed. But when we pressed them for details, they said that there was no point in our bicycling through the countryside and we could not bring in bundles of leaflets, only a few samples. If the Soviet Peace Committee decided in Moscow that we could distribute any literature, it would have to be printed there. We didn't want that kind of a visit, so again we developed an alternative plan. This time, it was to go to a Soviet army camp deep in the Soviet-controlled section of Austria, contact the soldiers, converse with them as best we could, and distribute the leaflets.

Here I return to my journal:

> "You can do what you want with your own lives, but you have no right to cause the death of innocent people." The speaker had been wildly emotional earlier, shrieking in an hysterical voice that threatened the secrecy of our meeting. But now she spoke with a controlled quiet that sent an involuntary shiver through my body. I looked around uncertainly at the closely drawn circle of eight or nine persons to whom we had decided to disclose our plans for penetrating the Iron Curtain. They were the persons in Vienna from whom we had expected the most support, including some of the Quakers who had come to think better of our penetration of the Soviet sector of Vienna. They were also the ones who would have to report our "disappearance," if that was the outcome.
>
> "She's right," all but one agreed. [My journal doesn't say who that one was, but probably it was Spencer Coxe.] "In the first place, you'll never get to Baden. But if you did, the Soviet soldiers would not accept your literature. They know that to be seen taking a leaflet or to be caught with it would lead to their death. You might be able to get it into the hands of one or two

> before you are seized, but in doing so you would be jeopardizing their lives. It's bad enough that the four of you will disappear without having accomplished anything, but you have no right to jeopardize the lives of innocent people."
>
> We never convinced any of them (except the one early dissenter), but decided to go anyway.
>
> We worked out a plan for getting there by buying a train ticket for Murzzuschlag, a British-occupied town on the other side of the Soviet zone. In twenty-eight minutes, the train would make its first stop, at Baden, the Russian Army headquarters. No one except Soviet-approved travelers were allowed to get off at Baden, but our plan was to wait until the train was pulling out of the station and jump off as inconspicuously as we could manage.

The night before we were to carry this out, we separated during the afternoon and arranged to meet for supper at a restaurant. Ralph and I got there first and then Bill arrived. It was Bill's turn to explode. "No one knows what is going to happen tomorrow," he said. "By this time of night we may be dead. Or on our way to a Soviet concentration camp in Siberia. *I don't give a damn what Art says. I'm having a beer.*" Ralph and I said, "*Great. We'll have a drink, too.*" A few minutes later Art arrived, saw us drinking but didn't say a word about it. So we explained our rationale as best we could and he said, "Fine, I don't blame you." I think that the difference between then and our set-to in Le Havre was not just the dangers we were facing, but that we had become bonded as four friends and were no longer the three close friends and one outsider that we had been earlier.

The next day our plan worked. We jumped off the train after it started moving slowly out of the station, and to our great relief the train kept going and no one paid any attention to us. After our first few successful encounters with Russian soldiers, we separated in order to cover the town better, while being less conspicuous. We spent a couple of hours passing out leaflets to everyone, but concentrated on the areas where soldiers were plentiful. Sometimes it was on street corners or on the stoops of houses in which they were billeted. Sometimes we handed leaflets through open windows, and I went inside a few houses. Our policy was to avoid officers, and we passed up soldiers when our encounter would have been seen by officers. Never did we expect the interest, the surprised but natural friendliness that we found. We experienced none of the hostility we had been led to expect. Three Russian civilians took leaflets, exchanged a few words with us (we in our halting Russian) and insisted on taking more copies for their friends. As they left, they gave us six shillings toward the printing costs.

No one challenged me, and when I got back to our prearranged meeting place Art and Ralph were already there. We expected Bill any minute. We had known when the next train was to stop on its way through and had arranged to meet nearby, out of sight from the station, five or ten minutes ahead of time. Soon we heard the approach of the train but there was no sight of Bill. Our hearts sank and we thought we knew what had happened. Since Bill was Black, he was much more likely to be spotted as an American. "So that's it," we said, "They grabbed Bill and that's the last we will ever see of him."

We quickly decided not to leave without him. But just as the train was pulling in, Bill came puffing around the corner and said, "Let's get out of here. I've never been so scared in my life." We jumped on and that ended that phase of the project.

We made a number of stops on the way back to Paris, reporting each time (and in Paris itself) on the trip and planning future contacts. In Paris, Bill Sutherland reaffirmed what he had said during our first weeks there: "This is the first time I have ever been anywhere where I was treated as a full member of the human race. I shall never live in the United States again." Now he said, "I'm going home to get my affairs in order, say good-bye to friends and family and move back." Since then his residence has always been abroad, though he visits the United States regularly.

A few months after our project, Bill worked closely with Kwami Nkrumah in the nonviolent campaigns that transformed the British Gold Coast colony into Ghana. Years later, after corruption and dictatorship had set in, he moved to Tanzania, where he worked closely for years with Julius Nyerere. His home is still there. During most of the years Bill has served as a representative of the American Friends Service Committee, and most of his trips to the United States have been for consultations with them and to go on tours they have sponsored. But in 1987 he was a Fellow of the John F. Kennedy School of Government at Harvard. He invited me to give the opening lecture in the course he conducted—and I did. By then both of our lives had been so full and we had so many current concerns that I can't remember if we even mentioned the trip we had taken together in 1951.

28

For all the joys that Betty and I shared, we experienced periods of difficulty in our relationship. One was caused by the 1951 European project. Shortly before the time for me to leave we learned that she was pregnant and seriously discussed the possibility that I shouldn't go. Then I was hurt at the street meeting and, as Betty remembers it, the concussion made it hard for me to think straight and for her, given what I had just been through, to deny me participation in a project that meant so much to me. I think she is right about herself but overly generous to me, given the difficulty I always had in knowing when or when not to participate in a risky project that threw an extra burden on her. In any event, the strains that she had felt but not expressed came to a head when the project lasted longer than expected (five months) and when she learned that we had risked our lives by going to the Soviet army camp. (I telephoned her after we got out of the Soviet sector.) But after my return, the natural magic in our relationship gradually reasserted itself, in part because—for once—I took several steps that helped.

One was to accept her proposal that I not reopen the print shop, as I dearly wanted to. It had closed "temporarily," either when I left or shortly afterward, when Bill Lovett developed TB and had to go to a sanatorium. Contrary to what I would have done on my own, I took a job with the War Resisters League for about a year, commuting to New York every day on the train. Then Bill got out of the sanatorium and, with Betty's approval, we reopened the shop. Marty and Rita Corbin from the Catholic Worker joined the community and Marty worked full-time in the shop; Rita helped us out from time to time and continued as art editor of the *Catholic Worker*.

I also tried to cut down on my outside activities, though it would be an exaggeration to say that I ever solved the problem of how much time to spend at home with the family and how much to spend away in activities that served our other goals. But I learned to stay home more, and when the lure of an outside activity was especially strong we made an extra effort to participate as a family, traveling together to conferences and demonstrations. In 1957 our whole family went to the Koinonia Community in Americus, Georgia, when it was under attack, and Betty and I took regular turns of standing nonviolent guard together. That kind of shared experience helped immensely.

But there were occasions when joint trips were not practical and when I resisted tempting activities because of the needs of our growing family. One was going into the Pacific in 1958 as a crew member of the *Golden Rule*, a small boat that traveled into the nuclear-testing area to interfere with, and witness against, the tests (the first of many such expeditions). I did manage to go to California to organize support and to visit the dock in Sausalito from which the boat set out.

I also turned down an invitation from Martin Luther King, Jr., to go with him to Bimini in the Bahamas to write a book for him. My decision was simplified by my having previously written an article for him and having reservations afterward about having done so, particularly after people kept praising the article in my presence without knowing that I had written it. I doubt if proxy authorship is ever a good idea, particularly of a whole book, but when I discussed my reservations with Bayard Rustin he said, "Well, Martin is going to be busy with a lot of other matters, mostly having a good time—*you know Martin.*" And indeed I did—in matters that my friend Ralph Abernathy was to get in trouble for writing honestly about more than thirty years later. According to Bayard, the idea was for me to talk with Martin from time to time, draw on the conversations, add ideas and phrases from his speeches, and check with him occasionally to get his response to what I had written. This made the invitation more attractive, but between my general reservations and the needs of my family, I declined.

The period of my lessened activities outside the family continued until the fall of 1963, when I began to expand my activities away from home. By then Michele, our youngest, was seven, and the other children eleven, fourteen, seventeen and nineteen. Also, the Sixties were heating up and I thought that our community was helping Betty more when I was absent. Checking with her now, I find that she says, "No, they weren't." So maybe the strength of my desire to go led me to fool myself. Anyway, I made the first of several new trips to the South.

As late as 1965 I decided that it would not be right for me to accept an invitation to travel to North Vietnam. Herbert Aptheker, a leading intellectual in the Communist Party, had met some Vietnamese at a World Peace Conference and had been invited to come and bring two American friends. He asked Staughton Lynd, and Staughton suggested me. Aptheker agreed, but I didn't think it was right to leave the family just then, so Tom Hayden went in my place. But slightly less than a year later, I went and was gone much longer than I would have been on the first trip. The first one came at a time when Betty didn't want me to go, the second when she felt better about it.

So I did a little better for a few years, but the truth is that from my release from Lewisburg on I was never sure exactly when to stay home because of family responsibilities and when to go on a project that responded to my (and her!) wider concerns. Perhaps it should have been easier to know because of the nature of our marriage and supposed nature of our community. Within the marriage, Betty was never one to let me be the sole head of the household, and I did not want to be. And the community had been established as a self-styled feminist community, at least partly in response to the brief, partial resurgence of the women's movement that occurred toward the end of World War II. All the women considered themselves feminists, and the men assured them (and ourselves) that we were committed to live in accord with that principle. The problem was that all of us (men and women) had internalized the dominant sexual stereotypes of the society more than we realized.

To add to our difficulties, the residual sexism in us and in the organizations with which we worked was aggravated by a second problem. For all the hostility and calumny that my jail sentences and hunger strikes brought me from certain quarters, in others I was automatically viewed as the more glamorous and heroic member of the family. This overlooked the reality that Betty's unpublicized role during my time in prison had required at least as much determination, staying power and creativity—along with a different kind of "heroism" (I hate to use the word, given the artificial and divisive ways in which it is usually used) than my imprisonment had. But I was the one who was invited to most of the outside activities and to speak at events such as the War Resisters League Conference in the summer of 1946. When the next summer came and the WRL asked me again, I suggested that Betty be the speaker from our family, but for a lot of the people whom the organizers wanted to attract to the conference she had no history, especially under the name of Peterson, and they said no.

She and I discussed it and at her urging I spoke again. By the third year she did speak, not instead of me but in addition to me. For a variety of reasons, though—including her lack of prison glamour and perhaps her socially created inexperience as a public speaker—people appeared to be less interested in what she said than in what I said. The more personal things she spoke about were at least as important to such a movement as the subjects I covered (probably more so because of their customary neglect), but they weren't considered as vital to the primary work the organization was engaged in. And I was not advanced enough to have suggested that I talk about the family things and she talk about the "political" things. It took the reenergized women's movement of the late Sixties and the Seventies to *begin* to establish a sounder perspective in such matters—in me, in Betty and in the Movement.

Within the family itself, I succumbed from time to time to the male failing of wondering why Betty was not more content to put in extra time with the kids while I was away on an important mission—even during periods when living in a community was not relieving her of the extra burdens as much as we had hoped it would. On her side Betty succumbed at least occasionally to wondering why I, the male "breadwinner," was not doing a better job of seeing that the community—and therefore our family—got out from under its crushing debts. After a while, she solved that problem creatively. First she started working to get her B.A. degree by completing the college work that she had given up when we met. Then she took a job as a grade school teacher, beginning during a 1960 trip I took to Cuba. When we moved to New York in September 1968, she resumed studying and got her M.A. while doing full-time day-care work.

Eventually she became the Education Director of Talbot Perkins, a child development agency that specialized in foster care and adoptions.

In the interim, high points of sharing for both of us were the birth of our last three children at home, "delivered" by me. Of course it is the mother who does the work and delivers the child, but I loved being there and helping out. Typically, Betty took the initiative in setting up the location and plan, in accord with her naturally pioneering spirit and because of the frustrating experiences she had undergone in the hospitals where she had given birth to the first two. In both cases, the hospital gave her anesthesia against her will and gave her a hard time when she insisted on breast-feeding the babies instead of accepting an injection to dry up her milk.

For the third child, we thought we had found a nearby "country doctor" who believed not just in home deliveries but also in "childbirth without fear," but he disappointed us. When we called him after Betty's water had broken and she felt that birth was imminent, he came to our house, examined her and said she was not ready. I spoke to him privately, saying that if she thought she was ready, I felt he should take her more seriously, given her experience of two previous births and the studying she had done on the subject. He would have none of it. "Let her scream a while first," he said, "then she'll be ready and you can call me."

I immediately decided that I would not call him again, and that I would help her deliver the child. Luckily, I had boned up on a government pamphlet for midwives (in case the doctor didn't get there in time) and was somewhat prepared. Sharing the experience, with me helping the baby out, cutting the cord and laying her on Betty to be breast fed, was so fulfilling for both of us that we decided I would help in the same way with any future births.

After that first home birth, on July 26, 1949, we notified the doctor and he came back to check everything. We had not decided on a name, wanting to watch the child first and select from the names we liked one that seemed to fit her personality. He came back three days in a row, asked for the baby's name and left. On the fourth day, we had finally decided that her name would be Natasha, a name that we liked from Dostoyevsky's novel *Crime and Punishment*. "Oh," he said, "Chinese!"

and left. Later, we found that he had neglected to register her birth, even though we thought it was for that purpose that he had come back every day to ask the name.

The second "home" birth, Danny's, took place at the Catholic Worker Farm on Staten Island, on January 21, 1952. It happened there because this was the period when the community was at its weakest point and I could commute between Staten Island and my War Resisters job in New York City. Dorothy Day had invited us to take advantage of a "birthing room" at their farm. She had visited us during the later stages of Betty's pregnancy, told us that her daughter Tamar had recently had a baby there, and said the room was still set up and ready for another birth.

After the joys of the delivery, I opened the door of the room to let our friends know that everything had worked out beautifully and that the baby was a boy. "Yes, we know," they said. That surprised me but later, when I finally had time to ask someone how they had known, she replied, "Father T. told us." Father T.'s room was directly above the birthing room and there was a heat register between our ceiling and his floor. Apparently he had watched the birth through the register.

Each time that we planned for me to help deliver the baby at home, Betty was examined in advance by a doctor, to be sure that there were no special complications. Each time everything was in order, but the doctor advised strongly against our plan; everything worked out wonderfully anyway. In Danny's case, I had to reach in and turn him to get him to be in the right position to come out. When I saw that the cord was around his neck, I gently worked my hand between the cord and his neck and disentangled it. After the third home delivery, Michele's, I had trouble with the afterbirth. It wouldn't come out and I was scared. A friend of ours had died a few months earlier from hemorrhaging while giving birth *in a hospital,* and I had visions of Betty's hemorrhaging. I telephoned a sympathetic doctor in New York who had examined Betty after we had become upset by the hostile attitude of our local doctor. He told me to "pull a little harder" while Betty pushed a little harder. I did, she did, and out it came. Thinking of what had happened to our friend, we had both been overly cautious.

Michele's birth took place in October 1956 at our house in the St.

Francis Acres community. By then we had lived there for nine years. We lived there for another twelve years, until a series of hostile attacks forced us to leave.

29

For twenty-one years we had gotten along well with most of the people in the neighboring towns and outlying rural areas, despite our unorthodox way of life and radical political activism. Having children in the local schools had helped us get to know a number of families in a natural way, and my playing on the town baseball team had helped. Dropping in occasionally at one of the two local bars to have a beer and watch sporting events with the other men broke down a few tensions. I had met some initial hostility on my first visit to a bar a week or two after our arrival, but having had to face it led me to come back from time to time. Inside our own little community, I used to refer to my visits there as "group therapy," making it clear that I benefited from it as much as my bar mates did.

Finally, in 1967, a series of events began that made it difficult for us to continue living in the area. I had made my first trip to Vietnam in the autumn of 1966 and stories about it and my other anti–Vietnam War activities were appearing more and more in the press and on television. The first crisis came early in the year when the print shop, the center of our communal work and economy, was vandalized at night when none of us was there. The presses, Linotype and binding machine were smashed, and drawers of hand-set type scattered on the floor, along with card files and other office materials. A message that seemed to be a death threat was printed in large letters in a prominent place. NEXT TIME IT WILL BE YOU, it said, in red ink with what looked like blood dripping from the letters.

As soon as the news got out, the president of the local chapter of the Veterans of Foreign Wars came to the house with two other members. They expressed their indignation and told me that "Nobody local would *ever* do such a thing. It has to have been someone from outside the area." They said that at the last two national conventions of the VFW, they had been approached by men whom they had never seen before and criticized for letting a Communist like me live in their town and keep getting in the papers with anti-American statements and carryings-on. "It's a disgrace to you and the town," the men had said. "Why don't you beat the shit out of him and get rid of him?"

"We told them," they said, "that we like you, even if we don't always agree with your ideas and activities." For a lot of reasons I believed them, including the good personal relations we had established on the baseball team and at the bar. My own inclination was to believe that some branch of the government was behind the attack, perhaps acting through one of the anti-Communist refugee groups that they worked with, early domestic versions of the Nicaraguan Contras. The fact that my friends had never before seen the men who tried to instigate them to take action against me added to this impression.

In May of 1967, Betty's contract for teaching in a grammar school about twenty miles away was not renewed, after she had taught there for six years without any complaints and a lot of compliments. There was no adequate explanation offered, but some embarrassed apologies. I had been told years earlier by the local postmistress and local store owner that the FBI had visited them and warned them against me, so I wondered if now they had put pressure on Betty's employers.

While we were still reeling from these events and trying to figure out how to survive economically, I received a bomb in the mail. It came in the form of a Christmas present, on December 31, 1967,* ostensibly a bottle of Johnnie Walker Red Label Scotch, which was the brand I drank on the few occasions when I had enough money to buy it.

*Sixteen years ago, in my book *More Power Than We Know*, I inadvertently gave the date as Christmas Eve of 1968, but we had already moved to New York by then. Also, Elizabeth has convinced me that the incident happened not on Christmas Eve but on New Year's Eve.

Our family had spent the day in New York, seeing friends, doing some holiday shopping and stopping in at the office of the Vietnam Peace Parade Committee, of which Norma Becker and I were the coordinators. On the way home, we had picked up some letters and packages at our rural-delivery mailbox at the bottom of the dirt road that led to our house. Now we were sitting around in our living room, a Yule log burning in the fireplace and opening the packages. All our five children were there, plus Tasha's daughter of a few months, Michele Burd, and Patch's wife, Lissa.

When we came to a package that had as a return address the words VC and the New York address of the Peace Parade Committee, I became suspicious. VC stood for Vietcong, and somehow I didn't think that anyone at the Parade Committee (where I had already received a present that day) would play such a cynical joke on me. I took off the outer wrapping and found the carton in which that brand of scotch was sold. Pondering my suspicions, I held it in my hand for some time without opening it.

"Look at the old man, savoring his Scotch before he opens it," my oldest son Patchen suddenly remarked. "Come on, Dad, open it and you and I'll try some."

I didn't want to alarm my family and I was nervous about opening the carton, but I had to do something. Finally, I gingerly separated the carton a little at the bottom to peek inside. Inside I saw wires and black powder. I stood up, said to Patch, "Come with me, Patch," and walked outside. "It's a bomb," I said, and told him what I had seen. Then I deposited it in the snow, well away from the house, and we decided that we should tell Betty but not the kids. We went inside and I called the state police. I told them where I had put the package, and since it was New Year's Eve they decided to wait till the next morning to send someone from the bomb squad.

On New Year's morning, they came, somehow defused it (outside my presence) and opened it. Inside was a live hand grenade, a small bottle of gasoline, which they said was to start a fire that would destroy the evidence, a battery and a pile of explosive black powder, apparently as insurance that the package would do its deadly work. They showed me how opening the carton in a normal manner would have brought two sets of wires into contact and set off the bomb.

Present with the bomb squad was an inspector from the Postal Service. "We're going to track these people down," he said. "We're going to get them. This is the same type of bomb that exploded twice in the Jersey City post office. They maimed two of our employees for life. It's an unusual construction and there's no doubt that it's the same outfit. This is no homemade bomb but something made by professionals in a well-equipped shop." He told me that one of the bombs had exploded on a conveyor belt and the other when an employee had tossed a package into a canvas receptacle.

I had read in the papers about the explosion of the two other bombs, a week or two apart and a week or two before mine arrived, but it had never occurred to me that they might have been sent to me. It occurred to the inspector, though. "The post office that the other bombs went off in," he said, "is the regional office in which all mail addressed to you is sorted. Clearly this is not the first bomb they have sent you."

Despite the inspector's vow that he was "going to get them," I never heard from him or anyone else from the postal service again. Nor from the state police either. And I didn't contact them. It increased my suspicions that the government was behind sending the bombs and made me think that it was making sure that the investigations didn't go too far.

What really got to me was that Betty, our own five children, Tasha's little Michele, and Patch's wife could all have been killed, some of them quite possibly burning to death while lying wounded and helpless. Irrational as it may seem, the inclusion of the gasoline and the presence of the roaring fire in the fireplace around which we had shared so many good times made everything seem even more horrifying.

Another even more terrifying thought haunted me for years. If it had not been Christmas vacation, Michele and Danny would have picked up the package from the mailbox on their way home from school, carrying it for over a mile along the winding, uphill dirt road. I thought of what had set off the earlier bombs in the sorting station and visualized them bouncing up the hill with this one, possibly tossing it back and forth on the way, or dropping it. . . .

The children weren't killed, but the bomb made a lasting impression on them. Eight years later I walked into the office of *Seven Days* magazine, where I worked, and found a package on my desk. On top of it was a note from Danny telling me not to open it until I called him on the phone. When I did call, he said that he had stopped by earlier to see me, had seen the package and was frightened that it might be another bomb. I opened it gingerly, and it wasn't. To this day, one or another of my kids sometimes warns me to be careful when they are around and a package arrives from UPS, Federal Express or in the mail.

"Do you know the person whose name is on the outside, Dad?"

"Do you think you should open it?"

"Be careful, Dad. Remember!"

30

Three Snapshots

Why Did the Lights Go Out?

It is February 1990 and I am in a two-room second-story apartment of a small cottage in an isolated spot on the coast of Maine. The cottage is part of a larger complex that hums with vacationers in the summer months but is completely abandoned at this time of year. That's probably why there are three floodlights outside my window, one on a corner of our building, one on the roof of the garage and one about fifty yards away on an adjacent building. They go on automatically every night, at dark. Usually, the couple who owns the building is downstairs, but they have gone South for two weeks.

I have come here to work on my book, and at the moment I am writing about how I "died" in solitary confinement in Danbury in 1940. That made me think about the bombs that were sent to me in the mail in 1967. Suddenly all the lights go out, inside and outside. A few seconds later my own lights go on but the outside lights do not. The windows have no shades—and I feel like a target. Am I being set up? What shall

I do? I have just written that ever since I died in solitary, I have not been worried about dying, violently or not. Having felt a definite twinge of nervousness, I realize the irony of the situation and smile. I go back to work.

A few hours later I finish, get up and prepare for bed—and realize that the three outside lights are on. They are so bright that usually they bother me, but I have been too preoccupied with what I was writing to notice. I have no idea when they came back on. After that first brief twinge, I haven't been concerned enough to pay attention to anything except trying to make my thoughts and memories clear enough to record them on the computer.

Marching Through Georgia

It is autumn 1963, and I am marching through Georgia. There are about twenty of us, members of the Quebec to Guantánamo March. Leading the march are Ray Robinson (Black) and Michele Gloor (white). Directly behind them are Barbara Deming (white) and Carl Arnold (Black). The signs we carry say things like ABOLISH ALL RACIAL DISCRIMINATION, FREEDOM NOW, PEACE THROUGH DISARMAMENT, FREE TRADE WITH CUBA. Dennis Weeks, who is limping through the South on a bad foot, is carrying a sign that says REFUSE TO SERVE IN THE ARMED FORCES, though some of the walkers advised against it. It is like walking through territory that has been mined: so much is pleasant, easy and inspiring, but we never know at what point our next step will set off an explosion. So far we have survived despite being shot at, jailed, shocked with electric cattle prods (some of the walkers but not me) and forced to play chicken with cars that sometimes have forced us into a roadside ditch.

We are walking through the small town of Marshallville with police watching our every move. We turn onto a magnificent avenue lined with stately Southern mansions, huge trees and well-kept lawns. We come to a church, with two white men standing outside. Barbara Deming walks toward them, is ordered by the police to move on, but advances toward the men anyway, smiling and holding out a leaflet. They beat a hasty retreat into the church. Apparently they feel they will find greater peace of mind there.

At the end of the luxurious avenue, perched precariously on top of a mud bank, is a wretched shack, the outpost of an impoverished Black settlement and the only Black house to adjoin the paved road. Standing on the ramshackle steps, erect, motionless and in rags, are seven or eight Blacks, apparently a mother and her children, some of them teenagers. The police car has driven ahead of us and stops directly in front of the house. As we arrive and Michele Gloor starts to mount the bank with some leaflets, one of the policemen jumps out to restrain her, apparently thinks better of it, and says, "Don't go up there."

The line of march stops. The Blacks remain motionless, like an inspired grouping of statues. "This is those people's house," Michele replies gently, "and if they want a leaflet I want to give them one." "If they wanted a leaflet, they would have come down to get it," the policeman replies.

For a long time, no one moves or speaks, not the Blacks (who have not moved perceptibly since we first saw them), not Michele, the policemen or the silent walkers. Then there is a slight movement, and with infinite grace a girl of perhaps fourteen slowly detaches herself from the group in front of the shack, walks down the bank and takes a leaflet. A moment later, a slightly older girl does the same. Satisfied, we move on.

After we have walked a short distance, someone notices that the police car has not left the house and that a sheriff's car has joined it. We stop walking and turn back to face the house. After a few minutes the police car drives toward us and we resume walking. It turns around and goes back to the house. We stop again and face the house again, but we are too far away to observe clearly. A third car and then a fourth pulls up in front of the house. What shall we do? To go back might inflame the situation, but we can't abandon them either. So we move a little closer, to see better and decide what to do.

After a seemingly interminable five or ten minutes, two cars come out of the Black section and come to us. They are followed by a police car that parks behind them. In each car is a Black couple. Unseen by us, they have observed the whole scene, have come to get leaflets. They tell us that no one has been arrested or attacked, they think it's better for us to continue our march. We give them the phone number of the Black church where we will be staying that night and urge them to call us if there is any trouble.

Before we get to our stopping place, four white teenagers drive up and stop to get leaflets and talk with us. They are from the church into which the two white men had retreated when Barbara had wanted to give them a leaflet. In the next few days, they come back two more times to find out more about us and discuss at length the issues we have raised.

A Women's Strike Meeting in Florida

It is 1964. I have come to Miami to consult with the members of the Quebec-Guantánamo Walk who are trying to get to Cuba to help bridge the people-to-people gap between Cuba and the United States. They plan to picket the U.S. Naval Base at Guantánamo, just as they have picketed military bases in the United States.

I have been invited by the Miami chapter of Women's Strike for Peace to speak at a local hall. The meeting is chaired by Anne Allen (formerly known as Anne Allen Meerpol), who helped raise Ethel and Julius Rosenberg's boys, Michael and Robert, after the government murdered their parents. As the meeting is getting underway someone comes to the platform and whispers to me that the local Cuban radio station is announcing the meeting, giving the address and urging all patriotic Cubans to go there and shut it down. I look up to see a few of them coming through the front door. I am introduced and begin to speak.

I take my usual approach of trying to reach out to my antagonists, stressing points of potential agreement but not minimizing our differences. Being honest about both is important in such a situation, and besides I want to say things that the regular audience has a right to hear from me and the émigrés need to hear.

First, I say that during a recent visit to Cuba I observed things that I applauded and things that worried me. One thing that worried me was the one-party state, even though there seems to be more freedom within it than most people think. I say that every government needs to be challenged and freedom to do so is important. I found more freedom to criticize the Cuban government than I had expected but was told by some people who do so that they find it harder to get published or to get good jobs, even though they have not been arrested and thrown in jail for it. I hope that freedom will grow in Cuba, but meanwhile we need freedom right here in this hall now, freedom for me to speak for a while and freedom at the right time for everyone to express their agreements and disagreements. "I know that some of you are from Cuba and know things that I don't. In a moment I want to hear you."

While they are thinking about this (I hope), I mention my concern with the persistence of sexist stereotypes in Cuba, as indicated by the continued absence of males as workers in child-care centers and the elementary schools. Things like that take time, I say. Then I praise the gains I had observed, mentioning the new housing, low rents, the free, constantly improving health care and thriving literacy campaign. And I quote Fidel Castro's recent condemnation of "blind subservience to the Soviet Union," a development ignored by the U.S. press but important for both groups in the hall to know about.

Meanwhile, the hall has filled with noisy Cubans. The heckling gets louder, with hisses and threats, and I say that I am almost through. If they'll be quiet and listen for a few minutes more I will give them a chance to say what they know and think. I am anxious to hear it.

Before I can find out what effect if any this may have on the hecklers, the head of the local Woman's Strike chapter, who is not on the platform but in the audience, stands up, looks at a large group of angry Cubans across the aisle from her and says, "Since you are not acting like gentlemen, we are leaving." That is an exact quote—how could I ever forget it? Out march most of the non-Cubans, mostly women but a few husbands and other males. Anne Allen and I are left with sixty or seventy angry Cuban counterrevolutionaries. The only person in the audience who I know for sure is friendly is Marv Davidov, a brave and loyal friend from the Walk.

I get a little discussion going, but there are so many explosions of anger and threats about what should happen to me that it is difficult. Even so, I feel pleased that from time to time there appears to be some communication. As I encourage one of them to speak, he stands and the crowd quiets down long enough for him to do so and for me to listen and get in at least a few sentences in response. I begin to think that I may get out of there alive. At what seems like an appropriate moment, I finish the discussion and come down from the platform. Immediately I am surrounded by angry, threatening Cubans, but manage to get a couple of them to respond to questions I ask about their personal experiences in Cuba. Suddenly, I am staggered by a tremendous blow from the rear that reminds me of the time I was blindsided in New Haven by the townie. This time I do not fight back physically but turn to address the attacker positively and nonviolently, presenting my open right hand to him in an offer to shake hands.

He doesn't shake, but soon we are exploring the questions that inflamed him. Apparently he is responding partly to my stance and demeanor and partly to the attitude of the Cubans with whom I had been talking when he hit me. Perhaps they have been influenced by my manner of responding to their curses and threats and then to his blow. Angry as they still are, they are not about to beat me, or to let him beat me any further.

But what about the others? Between us and the door are other Cubans, obviously more belligerent and looking as if they are biding their time. There is a serious question about whether Anne, Marv and I will be allowed to leave when we want to.

After a while, I pick what appears to be a good moment, motion with my head to Anne and Marv that we should leave, and hold out my hand again to the man who had struck me. To my great pleasure, he takes it this time. I wish him well and we move toward the door and leave.

As we drive off, I look to see if we are being followed. We are. By two cars that slow down when we slow down to let them pass and pick up speed when we do. Both cars are full. Marv suggests that Anne drive not to her house or to where he and I are staying, but to the center of the city. An attack will be less likely there and perhaps we will be able to lose them in the traffic and lights. She does and after a few U-turns and other maneuvers to keep us in a well-lit area where there are lots of people on the streets, they give up and drive away.

V

Vietnam

31

The anti–Vietnam War movement did not start in a vacuum. It was the offspring of previous movements for justice and peace. And like a lot of children it had to fight its way against the efforts of its parents to prevent it from straying too far outside the compromises they themselves had made with conventional society. In some ways, I was cast in the role of being an older brother in these conflicts, someone who was old enough to be importuned to side with the parents but was more frequently drawn to stand with the rebellious kids.

In 1963 I was a speaker at the annual Easter peace and disarmament march and rally in New York City. It was sponsored by a wide coalition of groups whose leaders had agreed to limit the posters and banners at the rally to nuclear testing and nuclear war. Bayard Rustin, the executive secretary of the War Resisters League, was the master of ceremonies.

Just before my time to speak, some members of two groups, the Student Peace Union and a Trotskyist youth group, raised signs calling for a withdrawal of U.S. military forces from Vietnam. At the time most Americans hardly knew that there was a place called Vietnam, let alone that the United States had installed a puppet government and had a militarily active mission there to support it. For most of those who did know a little of this, Vietnam was a distinctly minor issue, of far less concern than strontium 90 in milk (from nuclear testing) and the dangers of annihilation in a nuclear war. And to the coordinator of the sponsoring coalition, the executive director of SANE (Committee for a Sane Nuclear Policy), raising the issue of Vietnam was an impudent, left-wing diversion from the antinuclear theme. The signs must go.

He mounted the platform and spoke angrily to Rustin, who consulted with me. My hurried response was that naturally we were opposed to U.S.

military intervention in Vietnam, the signs therefore did some good and no harm, and he should not get into the untenable position of ordering them removed. Bayard let me know that he agreed but was worried about offending the leadership of SANE, the largest and best known antiwar organization of the day. In the end he reluctantly decided to do as he had been told and ordered the signs to be lowered. When I followed him to the mike, I felt it necessary to say more than I had intended to in opposition to the intervention in Vietnam. To link Vietnam to the main theme of the event, I spoke of the similarity between what the United States was doing in Vietnam and what it was trying to accomplish with its nuclear arsenal, both being manifestations of a drive for global dominance and the power and profits that go with it. I got a good response from the crowd but when I finished I was told by the angry coordinator that I would never be allowed to speak at a coalition antiwar event again.

On second thought, age wasn't the major cause of the differences between my responses in such situations and those of some of the other adults. It's just that they made me *seem and feel* so much younger than they were. Actually, I was approaching forty-eight at the time, and I was almost fifty when I sided with the youth in a more widespread split in 1965 between the old-guard peace leadership and the youthful SDS (Students for a Democratic Society). The difference between our approaches had more to do with whether or not one thought there was an essentially well-intentioned, genuinely democratic government in Washington. If one did, one tried to play along with it, even while lobbying and demonstrating for reform on a particular issue of concern. But my experiences in the slums of New Haven, Harlem and Newark, in prison and the civil rights–era South, had convinced me that the government is dominated by a military-corporate complex that makes a sham of real democracy, aided by a Congress in which the personal ambitions of even its most liberal members usually outrank every other consideration. At Yale I had been taught that when the Supreme Court eventually responds, it is more to a sufficiently militant mood in the country than to what is written in the Constitution or in judicial precedents. Unlike the peace bureaucrats, my strategy was to work for the growth of a sufficiently militant grassroots, antiwar and prodemocracy movement that would compel not just the courts but the Congress and the executive branch to respond.

Writing about the Easter controversy in *Liberation*, I said:

> At one time the fight for integration was dominated by high-minded but non-revolutionary leaders . . . who thought that the Negro must win acceptance within the dominant white culture by confining his struggle to the respectable area of the courts and by projecting an acceptable image. "Always be cleaner, thriftier, more smiling, puritanical, legal and patriotic than the white folk."
>
> Now these leaders have been brushed aside—or in some cases are running at full speed in a desperate attempt to catch up with their "followers." But the peace groups, which were catapulted into a degree of prominence in the last five or six years by the explosive power of radical walks, sit-downs and "illegal" protest actions, are increasingly succumbing to the Madison Avenue marketing mentality. SANE, for instance, considered a display of opposition to the war in Vietnam too "controversial" for inclusion in . . . Easter peace walks this year.*

When SANE responded in the next issue with a letter that called the students' display of the signs "exhibitionism," I wrote:

> Rather than characterize this act as "exhibitionism," I would prefer to say that certain students felt so strongly about attacking the only war in which the United States is presently engaged that they decided to ignore the agreement that had been made by leaders and to present their signs to the seven or eight thousand peace-lovers (and the TV cameras) present. My friend Dr. Lucius Pitts, president of Miles college, near Birmingham, Alabama, has said that the Negro moderates can either go slow and be run over by the people or join the people in demanding Freedom Now. There may not be as many people demanding Peace Now, but students have lost confidence in—and are prepared to run over—those leaders who still believe that we can get peace by clinging to the coattails of a government which calls for peace, as Kennedy did in his American University speech, and wages war . . . in Vietnam.†

*Liberation, June 1963.
†Liberation, Summer 1963.

After the Easter event, Vietnam gradually became more of a public issue as the United States increased the scope and intensity of its military actions. All during the period, such increases were called "escalations," as in "the war keeps escalating." But when I used that phrase in a conversation with Edmund Wilson,* he said it was a misuse of words because it implied that the government was being carried along by an impersonal force that was beyond its control. In reality, he said, the government is willfully planning and executing outrageous acts that are causing more and more death and destruction.

He was right, of course, and I knew it, even as I knew, as Wilson did, that neither of us could know more than a small portion of the ugly things that the United States was doing, things that would come to light only years later, if ever. One such incident involved someone I knew at Yale, McGeorge Bundy, so I will tell it now. First, though, let me say that in contrast to my close relationship with W. W. Rostow, I had only a passing relationship with "McBundy," as we called him. But he and I had a few conversations during my senior year and more after I returned to Yale in the fall of 1937. I thought him likable, but sharper and quicker than he was reflective or deeply exploratory. Unlike Rostow, he did not consider himself a "revolutionary," but like Rostow his emphasis seemed to be on being a chess master, brilliantly moving the pieces (human beings) around and always being one of those in charge, rather than on helping people to make their own decisions and gain control of their own destinies. Ah, the temptations of being bright, likable and well-connected.

In 1963, during what turned out to be the closing months of the Kennedy administration, Bundy was preparing a White Paper to "prove" that outside Communist agitators were responsible for the conflict in South Vietnam. The problem was that he lacked evidence. To provide it, "CIA agents loaded a ship with over a hundred tons of weapons made in [Communist] Bloc countries, sunk it close to the coast, staged a firefight and

*Wilson's book *The Cold War and the Income Tax* was copyrighted in the name of *Liberation* and, if I remember correctly, the proceeds were donated to us. The December 1963 issue included two brief excerpts from the book, a scathing review by Milton Mayer and a more sympathetic review by Theodore Roszak.

then invited the press to the scene."* Max Frankel duly reported this "shipment" in the *New York Times* and called it "conclusive proof" of Communist guilt.

Even without knowing of this scandalous event, by 1965 it shouldn't have been hard for anyone in the antiwar movement to know enough to understand what Wilson was talking about. But it was almost as if some of the more conventional antiwar leaders didn't want to know. I had a series of further experiences similar to what had happened at the 1963 Easter event, which convinced me that most of the heads of the established peace organizations would be among the last to understand the policies and tactics that were necessary if the antiwar movement was to become as sound and vital as the war required.

But there was something else that had been driven home to me with equal force during this same period: if they were not competent to set the pace and prescribe the tactics for the rest of the movement, neither was I. Young people had been born at a different time than the peace bureaucrats and I had been, and therefore had a fresher perspective than we did, for they weren't laboring under some of the preconceptions that we had accumulated. Naturally, they were not infallible either, but it was important to listen seriously to them and their proposals for new ways of acting in the new period in which we were living. If I had at least a few things to learn from the bureaucrats, even while rejecting their main orientation, both of us had important things to learn from the youth, without automatically agreeing with everything they said, did or proposed.

*From George M. Kahin's *Intervention: How America Became Involved in Vietnam*, as quoted in *Monthly Review*, October 1986.

32

As parts of the truth about what the United States was doing in Vietnam became better known, protests erupted here and there around the country. But there was no coordinated national protest. Finally, Students for a Democratic Society (SDS) issued a Call for a National Anti–Vietnam War Demonstration in Washington, D.C., on April 17, 1965. Again the established peace bureaucracy objected.

The basic charge was that the call focused on the evils of the U.S. intervention in Vietnam and ignored the evils of Communism that the United States was combating there. SDS should have criticized Peking (as Beijing was called at the time), Moscow and Hanoi more than Washington (some said) or at least as much. My friend Bob Pickus, who was younger than me but had "aged" rapidly as chairman of the liberal Turn Toward Peace, issued a press release in which (referring to himself in the third person) he said:

> It is time that someone . . . challenged activity which is in fact more hostile to America than to war. One of the April 17th march's official slogans, "Get out of Vietnam," drew Pickus' criticism. "That is not," he said, "the way to end war in Southeast Asia or to help change America's mind about the use of national military power there. . . . America is involved in Vietnam. It should stay involved. The question is how."

A number of prominent pacifists emphasized that there was violence on both sides of the Vietnamese conflict and that therefore our slogan should be "a plague on both your houses." But the way I saw it, our country, the richest, most powerful country in the world, was brutally attacking a small, underdeveloped peasant country halfway around the world and the slogan provided a presumably "high moral ground" for failing to organize a nonviolent resistance movement to stop the tragedy at its source. It was pacifism at its worst.

On my own I would have had no problem accepting an SDS call that included a few words in criticism of Moscow and Peking, provided that the main thrust was against the policies and actions of the United States. But the SDS youth told me that while they had no more love for Moscow and Peking than I did* they did not want to do anything to encourage the type of anti-Communism that provided excuses for the invasion and a rationale for the major antiwar organizations to tone down their criticisms.

SDS added to its "sins" by accepting endorsements of the demonstration from any organization or individual who shared its opposition to the war, regardless of their position on other subjects. This meant that groups suspected of being soft on Communism—*even the Communist Party itself*—could be included. It was the beginning of a policy of "nonexclusion" that came to be a hallmark of the New Left.

In our conversations, the SDS leaders said that the American Communist Party was far too mild for them. They were offended by its opportunistic attempts to improve its tattered public image and rebuild its depleted forces by championing only "respectable" tactics in the struggle against the foreign-policy crimes of the United States. This coincided with my own experience of the Party at the time and throughout the Sixties. Later, when a broad national antiwar coalition had been formed, the Mobilization Committee to End the War in Vietnam (the Mobe), liberals criticized it because one of the 115 names on its sponsor list was that of Arnold Johnson, public relations director of the Communist Party. I used to laugh and respond that of all the people listed he was the one who always advocated the most conservative, cautious and law-abiding positions and was completely without influence in our discussions and debates. Ironically, both the Communists and the anti-Communist liberals tried to influence the anti–Vietnam War movement to adopt the same moderate

*As we shall see, some of them changed later, not in respect to Moscow but in respect to Peking and Maoism.

stance. They had opposing views of both the Soviet Union and the United States and mostly they despised each other. But they were united in trying to keep the antiwar movement law-abiding and respectable.

On the other hand, the truth about the Communist Party was never simple. In the early and middle Sixties, the Communists either permitted or encouraged its youth to operate in a more radical and relevant way through the Du Bois Clubs, a Communist front group. Bettina Aptheker, daughter of Party stalwart Herbert Aptheker and herself an open Communist, played a mostly positive role there and in a variety of other coalitions and committees. Because the Du Bois Clubs took good stands but were under constant attack, Staughton Lynd and some of my other friends joined as a gesture of solidarity with a besieged organization. But after wrestling with the question for a while I decided (rightly or wrongly) not to, given my conviction that it could not be trusted because it was being manipulated behind the scenes by the Party. I was worried about encouraging relatively inexperienced young people to join.

More significant, I separated myself from most of the national "peace leaders" of the day by sponsoring the SDS demonstration and organizing support for it. So did David McReynolds and Ralph DiGia of the WRL, Dagmar Wilson of Women's Strike for Peace, Norma Becker, Joan Baez and Staughton Lynd. But the opposition of the peace bureaucracy continued, coming to a head a few days before the demonstration was to take place. Twenty-two prominent adult peace leaders issued a statement condemning it. They included A. J. Muste, Robert Gilmore of the American Friends Service Committee, Al Hassler of the FOR, Homer Jack and Norman Cousins of SANE, Norman Thomas of the Socialist Party, H. Stuart Hughes, a prominent "peace candidate" for the Senate in 1964 (supported by Abbie Hoffman in Abbie's first venture into the peace movement), Robert Pickus and Bayard Rustin. To add to the outrageousness of the attack, a copy of the statement was hand-delivered to the *New York Post* by Gilmore. The *Post* responded with a prominent news story and a feature editorial that cited the prestige of the signers as proof that all true peace lovers would boycott the demonstration.

Besides making the criticisms that I have mentioned, the signers fell into a public relations trap laid by President Johnson. In a speech at Johns Hopkins University ten days before the demonstration, Johnson held forth the bait of wanting to resolve the problem in Vietnam through "unconditional discussions." But he specifically barred participation by one of the main Vietnamese parties to the conflict, the National Liberation Front (NLF) of South Vietnam and insisted on maintaining what he called "an independent South Vietnam." In other words, the United States would continue to violate the Geneva Agreements that ended the French war and provided for reunification of Vietnam under internationally supervised elections. President Eisenhower had refused to allow the elections because, as he explained later in his book *Mandate for Change*, "had elections been held . . . possibly 80 percent of the populace would have voted for the Communist Ho Chi Minh." Now the only discussions Johnson was open to would rule out reunification.

The "peace leaders" jumped into the trap. Like Pollyanna, they said in their statement that Johnson's speech "suggested the possibility of a healthy shift in American foreign policy." And like Pollyanna, they made no mention of the landing at Danang a month earlier of more than 3,500 Marines, the first publicly acknowledged U.S. combat troops in Vietnam. By the time of Kennedy's assassination there had already been more than 16,000 military "advisers" in Vietnam, participating in hundreds of armed confrontations, flying some 7,000 "air missions," and suffering 108 U.S. deaths, but the public knew almost nothing of this.* So the announcement that 3,500 Marines had landed in Vietnam had aroused considerable public concern, and Johnson had responded with some soothing, self-contradictory words for those naive enough to take them seriously. The irony was that the signers of the statement were, by other standards, sophisticated persons. With two glaring exceptions, their naiveté was to believe that the basic foreign policy orientation of "our democratic government" was sound and that a few wise words from a conformist peace movement would correct any "mistakes" it was making as it pursued the legitimate aim of stopping the spread of Communism.

The two exceptions were Muste and Rustin, both of whom knew better. Bayard was a special kind of exception, as I will explain later. As for A.J., the best I can say is that he temporarily reverted to his earlier predilection, doing something contrary to his own insights in order to

*See Robert Manning, "Development of a Vietnam Policy, 1952–1965," in *Vietnam Reconsidered*, edited by Harrison E. Salisbury (New York: Harper & Row, 1984).

protect his ties with influential "leaders" of liberal organizations whom he hoped to move *later* in a slightly more progressive direction.

When I confronted A.J. with what he had done, he admitted that he had made a bad mistake and offered to make amends in the next issue of *Liberation*. He did his best with a devastating analysis of the Johnson speech that left no room for thinking that it "suggested the possibility of a healthy shift in American foreign policy." But by then the SDS demonstration had come and gone, and for most of the youth active in 1965 his correction never caught up with the scandal of his having signed the statement. Shortly after A.J. died in February 1967, Greg Calvert, the executive secretary of SDS at the time, told me that he felt sad that this act, untypical of the A.J. whom he had come to know, admire and love, had alienated most of the younger New Left from A.J. and reduced the healthy influence he could have had on them.

The SDS protest turned out to be a huge success—for that early period—with around twenty thousand participants. Thousands of students carried signs which proclaimed I WON'T FIGHT IN VIETNAM. Paul Potter, the SDS president, said that "the incredible war in Vietnam has provided . . . the terrifying sharp cutting edge that has finally severed the last vestiges of illusion that morality and democracy are the guiding principles of American foreign policy." He called for a movement that will concentrate on building a decent society at home in which future Vietnams will be impossible. Staughton Lynd announced that he and his wife, Alice, were refusing to pay income taxes because of the war. Robert Moses of the Student Non-Violent Coordinating Committee (SNCC) said that the American killings in Vietnam were morally and politically on a par with the killings of civil rights workers in Mississippi. Beulah Sanders, a Black welfare mother with whom I worked closely afterwards through the National Welfare Rights Organization, described what it meant to be poor in a country devoting its resources to the military. Joan Baez and Judy Collins lifted people's spirits and expanded their vision with their songs and commentary. And Senator Ernest Gruening of Alaska, one of the two senators who had voted against the Gulf of Tonkin Resolution, said, "Don't think that when Mr. Diem [the U.S.-installed South Vietnamese head of state] requested President Eisenhower to come to his aid, the request hadn't been drafted for him in Washington."

So far as the charges leveled at SDS were concerned, I wrote in *Liberation* that

> The splinter groups left over from the Thirties were represented at the March but in no sense did they control or dominate it. The mood of the students (as I observed it at SDS's National Council meeting the [next] day . . .) tends to be a little scornful of both the Communists and the anti-Communists. *There is a heritage of ideological rigidity that they don't want to get bogged down in. . . . They don't think or talk or argue in the old terminology or thought concepts.* Like SNCC, they are confident that if their movement is dynamic enough and concentrates on its own legitimate goals and grass-roots objectives, it will not get trapped in the dead end of either sectarian Communism or sectarian anti-Communism. [Emphasis added.]

So the students had introduced a new spirit into the debate over Vietnam. They had refused to let the narrowness on both sides of the Cold War obscure the real issue. They had become a force to be reckoned with.

33

Even before SDS issued the call to its 1965 national antiwar demonstration, I had worked informally with it because of its work in areas that the conventional antiwar movement gave lip service to but rarely spelled out or implemented. Its involvement in the struggle against U.S. complicity in South African apartheid, which included a sit-in at the Chase Manhattan Bank, was quite likely the source of its adoption of a nonexclusion policy for endorsers of the antiwar action. Certainly my own agreement with this policy had been influenced by an article that we had published in *Liberation*, the full statement by Nelson Mandela when he was sentenced to life imprisonment on June 12, 1964. In it Mandela had defended himself against the charge of *being* a Communist by saying that in his choice of associates he didn't require "a complete community of interests," only "a common goal . . . the removal of white supremacy." For SDS and me the overriding common goals that didn't demand "a complete community of interests" were "the removal of white supremacy" and ending the U.S. aggression in Vietnam.

Another reason I worked with SDS was the Economic Research and Action Project (ERAP), which it announced in September 1963. As the first generation of SDS leaders graduated from college (or in some cases dropped out) they moved into poor, inner-city areas under the auspices of ERAP. There they worked with their neighbors for such things as community day care, community health centers, better schools and membership by the poor on the planning and decision-making boards of the much-heralded but heavily bureaucratic War on Poverty. In many ways, ERAP was a 1960s version of the community organizing project that I had been part of in Newark in the late Thirties and early Forties—in fact, as if to emphasize the similarity, one of the ten ERAP projects was established in Newark, under the name of the Newark Community Union Project (NCUP). In a further family connection, Betty's and my son Patchen worked closely with the ERAP group in Philadelphia—JOIN, Jobs or Income Now—while maintaining good standing at Swarthmore College. (He attended Swarthmore on full scholarship—since his parents couldn't pay for him.) After spending the summer of 1964 with ERAP, he wrote an article about it for *Liberation*.

SDS also called for "participatory democracy," a term that I had never heard before but quickly hailed as a contribution to the new spirit that was developing. To me it said in two words what I had long believed: First, that electing a centralized government to rule over us from Washington is a far cry from genuine democracy—rule by the people through decentralized participation in the decisions that affect their daily lives. And second, it said that representative democracy needs to be supplemented by grass-roots democracy in both the workplace and the community if there are to be *real* "checks and balances" in government, checks on selfish power and balances between the interests of different localities and areas.

Despite these accomplishments, SDS made its own mistakes during the Sixties. The most destructive was a gradually developing competitive sectarianism that spread like a virus until it finally caused the entire organization to break up into rival vanguard groups at its June 1969 national convention. But the most surprising, if less disastrous, mistake came right after the impressive April 1965 antiwar demonstration, and was mostly limited to a few of the top leaders who never succeeded in winning the bulk of the members to their viewpoint. Despite the success of the demonstration, Tom Hayden, Clark Kissinger, Rennie Davis, Todd Gitlin and some of their closest allies decided that serious revolutionaries should not waste time trying to stop the present war since that was impossible. A more productive course, they felt, was to expand their ERAP efforts to work at a grass-roots level for economic and political changes that would, in their own words, "stop the seventh war from now." Meanwhile, as Hayden used to tell me on my visits to NCUP, "The war is not a working-class issue" and trying to make it one would only interfere with their work with the working-class neighbors who were already somewhat suspicions of former college students who had moved into the inner city.

Fortunately, SDS as a whole never fully accepted this approach because newly energized antiwar students kept flooding into the organization in response to its national demonstration and other antiwar work. Personally, I hailed the concern for a fundamental revamping of the economic and political structure, with an emphasis on racial as well as economic justice, but was dismayed with the either/or approach that set activity against the war in opposition to this. Like the initiators of ERAP, I thought that the war was in large part a product of an undemocratic economic and political system, but unlike them I thought it important to work on both fronts, establishing the connection between the two as Potter, Moses, Sanders, Lynd and others had done in April 1965—and continued to do.

Despite these and other differences, I was mostly heartened and challenged by SDS (which was mostly white) as I had been earlier (and still was) by the young, mostly Black, youth of SNCC. Besides their restless energies and efforts to find their own way in the new period in which they were coming of age, they were not encumbered by some of the baggage that I and other members of the older generation carried. If ever I was tempted to forget that I had accumulated such baggage (without knowing what it was) I reminded myself of what Albert Camus, fresh from the French Resistance movement, had said to the post–World War II French youth: "Beware of all veterans." Naturally, I took that to include veterans of the antiwar and civil rights struggles, as well as war veterans. Veterans have insights based on their experience, but are also scarred and biased from them and need help from the youth.

A second lesson I knew earlier but had driven home to me again by some of the mistakes of SDS and SNCC is that if the veterans need the youth, the youth need the veterans, scars and all. Neither is complete without the other. I first learned this in the Thirties and Forties, when I was heavily influenced by older people such as E. Fay Campbell (the graduate secretary of Yale's Dwight Hall), Kirby Page (a radical clergyman who used to tour the colleges), Howard Thurman (a Black clergyman who inspired me when I was at Yale and afterward), Dorothy Day *(Catholic Worker)* and three World War I objectors with widely varying lifestyles and personalities: Ammon Hennacy (who worked as a migrant laborer), Evan Thomas (a medical doctor) and Julius Eichel (a small businessman). I also benefited, as did Betty, by observing how Julius and his wife, Esther, worked out their partnership as parents and radicals in the pressured times of World War II. And of course I learned a tremendous amount from A. J. Muste after he was artificially relieved of his duties with the FOR and began to recover from his years of bureaucratic entanglements and maneuvering. He became one of the most important influences on me, both through his wisdom and by his folly of signing the 1965 statement condemning SDS. This particular folly served as a close-to-home reminder that even the wisest, most beloved guru is subject to human error.

When SDS eventually abandoned most of its earlier insights and strengths, I concluded that one reason they did so was because they turned their backs on some of the "veterans" who had earlier turned their backs on them. But there was another important factor: a lot of Thirties veterans were more damaged than were some other generations of veterans, and they had less to offer the youth.

I noticed particularly the effect of World War II on many of the people I had worked with during the Great Depression. Most of them left for the war saying that "after we get rid of injustice and totalitarianism in Europe" (or Japan, though that was mentioned less often), "we will come back and keep on fighting against injustice and authoritarianism here." But most of them came back pale reflections of their former selves in this regard. They were exhausted from their participation in that deadly, all-demanding struggle and needed to focus on education, vocation, catching up with making a family and similar pursuits. Also, many of them were affected by having had their attention concentrated at a critical time in their lives on how good the United States was compared to Nazi Germany or fascist Japan. Then the Cold War came, with another emphasis on how much better this country was than its rivals, especially since it was a misleading period of relatively "good" times in which it was easy to overlook the plight of Blacks and other minorities and poor people. Some of my friends with whom I had participated in union struggles on behalf of industrial unionism and the fledgling CIO worked for unions and went along during this period with the co-optation of the national leadership of the AFL-CIO by the domestic and foreign policy wings of the capitalist establishment. Finally, growing numbers within another section of the Old Left were demoralized and debilitated by the collapse of their dream that the Soviet Union was a sparkling example of the kind of decent society that was possible for the United States and the rest of the world. When this demoralization climaxed in 1956 with the Soviet invasion of Hungary and Khrushchev's revelations about Stalin, it was the very year in which the first signs of "the Sixties" could be seen in the Montgomery Bus Boycott and in the effect it had on many of the country's youth.

For all these reasons, the SDS and SNCC generation were artificially isolated from most of the lessons of the Thirties that might have helped them. I am reminded of this loss today, when I speak at high schools and colleges, observe the quiet, useful role being played by teachers who are veterans of the Sixties and contrast it with the role too often played three decades earlier by veterans of the Thirties. The very fact that I get so many invitations from high schools is in itself an illustration of the contrast, for it was late in the Sixties when I first spoke at a high school. And when I speak today to a history or social studies class, teachers of biology, math, English and so on often bring their students to the class that has invited me. Clearly they do so not because I might touch on their academic subject but because they are veterans of the Sixties who, whatever uneasy compromises they may (or may not) have made, want their students to hear a firsthand analysis of that period.

The new perspective of the youth is not as evident in some years as others but whatever period it is, I try to encourage young people to believe in themselves and their historic mission. Typically, when the mail arrived today with a local newspaper's account of a visit I made to a Vermont high school, the article begins by saying: "The longtime proponent of nonviolent protest said he did not come to sell a specific political message but wanted to encourage students to think for themselves and 'follow their own instincts and impulses.' "

I speak of these lessons to older groups as well, in an effort to encourage them to listen to the young people and to learn from them. But, whether I am speaking to the young or to "veterans," I try to make clear that my own experience as a fallible white male who was once young and is now old has led me to believe that no generation or other category of humans is complete unto itself. We all need help from people whose age, sex, race, sexual orientation, class, degree of formal education or other aspects of their identity are different from ours, and often are used to divide us.

34

The peace bureaucrats did have reservations about the Vietnam War and were convinced that they were the best ones to lead the movement that was raising questions about it. Both inspired and challenged by the turnout at the SDS-initiated protest, SANE called for its own national protest for late November 1965 in Washington, D.C. But whatever their strengths, they still acted like unimaginative adults tied to the conventions of cultural and political respectability.

Unlike SDS's nonexclusion policy, SANE carefully screened potential sponsors. When Bob Moses and Staughton Lynd tried to effect a reconciliation with the more conservative side of the movement by offering to join the sponsor list, SANE rejected them. Yet both had given talks at the SDS event that electrified the audience and Moses (Black) and Lynd (white) had played key roles in the momentous Mississippi Summer project of 1964 during which James Cheney, Michael Schwerner and Andrew Goodman had been killed by white racists. SANE also refused to list scientist Linus Pauling, who had won the Nobel Peace Prize in 1962 (as well as the Nobel Prize in chemistry in 1954). Pauling was a pioneer in the battle for nuclear disarmament, the subject so important to SANE that it had opposed even a mention of Vietnam at the 1963 demonstration. But he had been publicly accused of being soft on Communism and that was all that mattered to SANE.

Second, SANE established a dress code. The men were asked to wear suits and ties, the women to wear dresses. Four years later I was frequently noted as the only member of the Chicago Eight who wore a jacket and tie during the trial, but when Betty and I participated with our kids in this event, I decided not to, because of my opposition to having a dress code imposed on the youth. And I was not alone. The march was crowded with women in pants and men in blue jeans, not all of them young. To make the image even "worse," a lot of the young men sported beards. Beards were thought by the leadership to be a sign of immature rebelliousness that would not look good to members of Congress and other "decision-makers." As late as our 1969 Chicago trial, Abbie Hoffman felt it necessary to point out that George Washington had worn a beard. But whether Washington was actually bearded or not, it was the youth who were being drafted and whom SANE was trying to keep beardless. If rebelliousness spread among them, with or without beards and blue jeans, it could lead to increased draft refusals and might eventually have an effect on restless young GIs. Developments like that would exert a more powerful influence on the government than the respectable, conformist dissent that SANE was trying to fit the kids into.

Finally, SANE urged everyone to bring and carry an American flag. Most of the young people (and lots of adults) did not do so and a tiny handful, led by Walter Teague, marched behind a Vietnamese NLF flag. (Teague was an ornery fellow who had recently formed a Committee to

Aid the NLF.) I carried neither. I thought that carrying an NLF flag was a senseless inflammatory gesture that gave a false message of who we were and why we opposed the war. My opposition did not depend on the virtues of the Vietnamese but on the evils of the U.S. efforts to subjugate them. Respect for self-determination does not require perfection in those who should be allowed to exercise it. For years I suspected Teague of being a government agent because governmental agents provocateurs were continually trying to drive a wedge between us and the American people by encouraging acts similar to his. Apparently he wasn't but some of his associates were. I hadn't gone to Vietnam yet and had no contact with any Vietnamese, North or South, but when I did get to know them a year later, they all said that they thought it was stupid for Americans to carry NLF flags. They said it would be better to carry U.S. flags to show that those Americans who stood for justice, peace and the rights of self-determination for all countries were the real patriots.

So in that respect they agreed with SANE. From a distance it probably made sense. But in the context of the debates within the U.S. antiwar movement of the time, carrying the U.S. flag suggested a politics à la Pickus, Gilmore and SANE, which I did not want to encourage. It represented an attempt to show the decision-makers that the assembled opponents of the war shared their view that the United States is basically free, democratic and virtuous, even though it had by accident, or at least contrary to its usual practice, gotten temporarily "off-course" in Vietnam. But the historic practice had involved slavery, genocide of Native Americans, the invasions of Mexico, Cuba, Puerto Rico, Nicaragua, Colombia, the Philippines and so on.

Politically, SANE followed the approach advocated in its earlier criticism of SDS. It took seriously President Johnson's talk about "negotiations." The following excerpt from a *Liberation* editorial by Staughton Lynd expressed both the appreciation by people like him and me that SANE was marching against the war and the reservations that we had about their failure to come to grips with the political realities.

> The SANE march . . . helped to keep dialogue about peace alive in the country. It showed that extreme acts of protest have not destroyed moderate forms of dissent but stimulated them. . . . But there is a problem which the program . . . didn't reach. In

> asking de-escalation leading to negotiations, SANE stayed away from the question of bringing American troops home. . . . A cease-fire without troop withdrawal would legitimize America's military presence, help to bring about a *de facto* partition of Vietnam. . . . Policy-makers . . . have said that after an end to hostilities, American troops might remain in Vietnam for years to "assist in the process of nation-building."*

There was a powerful additional reason why it was unfortunate not to call for a withdrawal of U.S. troops: the losses of life and limb, let alone the psychological torments that a growing number of GIs were undergoing. The conventional charge against the antiwar movement was that we were "stabbing our boys in the back." And oddly, for all their attempts to placate the public, the conventional peace leaders never came to grips with this question. For years, not just SANE but most of the established peace organizations opposed the slogans that some of us advocated from the beginnings of the anti–Vietnam War movement: "Bring the Troops Home!' "Bring the GIs Home Now!" "Bring the GIs Home Alive!" Crippled by their preoccupation with staying on good terms with the government, hailing periodic governmental hints of openness to negotiations and concentrating on this goal, they completely missed the deeper patriotism (and potential public appeal) of including that direct concern for the GIs. For some reason I could never understand, even Women's Strike for Peace (WSP), which mostly was far more relevant on the issues than the older male-dominated organizations and generally played a healthier, relatively militant role, insisted for a long time on calling for negotiations and opposed using the demand to bring the boys home. Besides early SDS and sections of the War Resisters League, the earliest, strongest support for the slogans came from the Trotskyist Socialist Workers Party, the Young Socialist Alliance (their youth branch) and other Trotskyist groups. But those who opposed the nonexclusion policy didn't think the Trotskyists even belonged in the antiwar movement.

For anyone who might wonder if I am exaggerating the differences

**Liberation*, December 1965.

between most of the established peace organizations and the youth, here are some excerpts from the *New York Times*' coverage of the SANE march* (with emphases added):

> For two hours, marchers carried placards that for the most part bore *cautiously phrased slogans*, such as "Stop the Bombing" or "Supervised Cease Fire." . . .
>
> [The marchers] went to the Washington monument to hear a series of *moderate appeals for the U.S. peace initiatives*. . . .
>
> There were small clusters of fired up youths . . . and the organized forces of Youth Against Fascism pressing upon the marchers signs that called for an immediate American withdrawal from Vietnam. *The organizers had tried to keep out such placards*. . . .
>
> For Washingtonians . . . the [march] today was *unusually sober and restrained*.

35

I have no reason to analyze all the activities that I had some connection with from those early days of growth in the anti–Vietnam War movement through the final days of the war. But two overlapping events between the April 1965 SDS-initiated demonstration and the November SANE

**New York Times*, November 28, 1965.

march indicate an increasing sense of urgency among people from a variety of traditions and the resulting formation of temporary alliances that culminated in two enduring coalitions that I was intimately associated with.

The first event, on August 6, 1965, was sponsored by the Committee for Nonviolent Action (CNVA), the *Catholic Worker*, the Student Peace Union and the War Resisters League. The second, on August 7, 8 and 9, was designated an Assembly of Unrepresented People and was called by an ad hoc group of individuals that included Lynd, Moses, Courtland Cox (also of SNCC), Barbara Deming, Donna Allen (WSP), Carl Oglesby (the new president of SDS), Norma Becker (N.Y. Teachers Committee against the War), Eric Weinberger (CNVA), Bob Swann and myself.*

Who spoke up? American Protest Against the War in Vietnam, 1963–75 by Nancy Zaroulis and Gerald Sullivan[†] gives an accurate description of the August 6th event but errs on the month and year that it took place—for reasons that I think I can explain. More seriously, in one of its sentences it ascribes power to me that I neither had nor wanted. Here is what it says:

*Other sponsors were Dena Clamager and Mel McDonald (both of SDS), Carl Bloise, Peter Kellman, Barry Weisberg, Steve Weissman, Stephen Amdur, Walter M. Tillow, Ed Hamlett, Jeffrey Gordon, Jimmy Garrett, Ray Raphael, Sandra Adickes, Francis Mitchell, John Porcelli, William Hartzog, Mack Smith, Dennis Sweeney, Russ Nixon, Florence Howe and Paul Lauter. Despite the support of the three SDSers, including its new National President, the SDS national office issued a statement that reflected the opposition of some of its early leaders (Hayden, Davis, Kissinger, Gitlin et al.) to "wasting" time and energy trying to stop the Vietnam war. It dissociated SDS from the Assembly and discouraged attendance. President Oglesby was on an extended trip to Europe when this happened. Neither the SDS National office nor the early leaders I have mentioned endorsed any subsequent national antiwar actions from then until the protests at the Democratic National Convention in August 1968. Even so, there were major numbers of grass-roots SDS members at all major events and Greg Calvert, executive secretary of SDS at the time, played a major role in the October 21–22, 1967, Siege of the Pentagon. Beginning with Gitlin's participation in a tumultuous antidraft week action in Oakland in October 1967 and Davis and Hayden's last-minute attendance at the October 21–22 event, those three became active again in antiwar efforts. SDS had a substantial (if from my point of view not very helpful) presence at the Chicago Convention but by the following June it had ceased to exist.

[†]Garden City, N.Y.: Doubleday, 1984.

> On July 3, 1964, President Johnson signed the Civil Rights Act. On the same day, David Dellinger called a demonstration against the Vietnam War to be held in Lafayette Square across from the White House. Present were A. J. Muste, folk-singer Joan Baez, Rabbi Abraham Feinberg, Rev. Daniel Berrigan and Rev. Philip Berrigan. The purpose of the demonstration was to publicize the "Declaration of Conscience," written a few weeks previously by Dellinger, Muste, Bayard Rustin and others at the *Liberation* office.
>
> The "Declaration of Conscience" was one of two statements in support of draft resistance that year. . . . It was a classic radical pacifist document, written in imitation of the French *Manifesto des 121* (1960), a "Declaration Concerning the Right of Insubordination in the Algerian War." The American version proclaimed a "conscientious refusal to cooperate with the United States government in the prosecution of the war in Vietnam." It called on its signers to "refuse to take part in the manufacture or transportation of military equipment or to work in the fields of military research and weapons development," and stated that "we shall encourage the development of other nonviolent activities, including acts which involve civil disobedience, in order to stop the flow of American soldiers and munitions to Vietnam.

As to the date, President Johnson signed separate Civil Rights acts on both July 3, 1964, and August 6, 1965, so that probably explains the error. But the *New York Times*, the *Liberation* issues of August and September 1965, and the Robinson biography of A. J. Muste all indicate that August 6, 1965, is the date when that particular demonstration took place.

A more serious inaccuracy is the statement that "David Dellinger called the demonstration." Never during the entire period did I call a demonstration on my own. Perhaps the authors were misled by my having drafted the Declaration of Conscience (in consultation with Muste, Rustin and Ralph DiGia) and having played an energetic role in helping to organize and recruit for the demonstration. Perhaps, even, I first proposed the demonstration in some small meeting or other. But a good organizer never issues a call on her or his own. If s/he thinks that the time is ripe for a particular form of action, s/he consults with others. If others agree, then a joint call is issued either by an organization, a group of organizations or a group of individuals. And on this occasion, the organizations I have mentioned called the demonstration.

I particularly remember this action, as well as the same weekend's Assembly of Unrepresented People. One reason was the participation on August 6 of a wide range of people (as is suggested by the names mentioned in the book), including a sizeable contingent of Southern Blacks. The Southerners included a delegation of thirty from the Mississippi Freedom Democratic Party; the delegation came primarily for the Assembly but a lot of them arrived in time for the rally in Lafayette Park. Another reason was the last-minute decision of Bayard Rustin not to participate, after he had played an active role in the advance planning. (That is a special sad story in its own right, which I will discuss in the next chapter.) First, though, a few words on the Berrigans, on the actions we took that day and on the Assembly.

It was the first time that Dan and Phil Berrigan had been with us on such an action, although I had met Dan a month or two earlier when he had presided at the marriage of two of my friends, Al and Barbara Uhrie. We had talked afterward, and I had been impressed with him. A Jesuit priest, he was a quiet and gentle poet, unobtrusive, sensitive and obviously a man with a lot of inner strength. When I told Dorothy Day how impressed I was by him, she said that he was a nice young priest who was pretty naive but had good instincts and would learn step by painful step what was required of us in these sorrowful days. By contrast, when I first met Dan's brother Phil, a member of the order of Saint Joseph, his strengths appeared to be more like those of some of the Hebrew prophets who were more noted for denouncing the evils of the world than for quiet conversations about the joys of life. When it came time for me to introduce them at the rally, I wondered about the appropriateness of what came to mind as I was standing at the microphone, but I said it anyway. It was something like this: "You all know about the DiMaggio brothers, Joe, Dominick, and Vince. Well here is another set of brothers whom you probably haven't heard of yet but about whom I predict you will hear a lot in the future, the Berrigan brothers." Appropriate as an introduction or not, they have been an inspiration ever since, to me and countless other people.

After the rally, we vigiled together on the sidewalk by the White House. Muste, Baez, Feinberg, the Berrigans and I (along with others who wanted to) knelt close to the fence, facing the White House, and prayed for peace. Personally, I prayed not to the White House and not to a distant God but to the deepest, most loving part of myself and all my fellows. Everyone was in violation of a law that required people to keep moving when adjacent to the White House, but unlike other times when people committed similar violations, we were not arrested. Probably it was because over a thousand people risked the arrest and someone decided that arresting a thousand people just then would be bad publicity. But the breadth of the leadership and the different racial, religious, secular and age groups they had roots in may have been a factor too.

We had designated the next three days as an Assembly of Unrepresented People for two reasons. One was in support of the current efforts in Mississippi to unseat its five congressional representatives because of the suppression of the right of the Black residents to vote. Naturally, we extended this to similar suppressions and efforts throughout the South. The other was to call attention to the limitations of the U.S. system of winner-take-all elections dominated by big money, the corporate press and the two branches of the basically single political party (Republicrats and Democans) that has undemocratic access to both.

We called for the Assembly to begin with two days of workshops that would probe these and other serious injustices. We listed some of them in advance and promised that others could be organized on the spot, according to the interests of those who came. As a result, we had the widest array of workshops of any Sixties gathering I know of. They included local-level organizing of the poor for a voice in the lives of their communities and in the administration of federal antipoverty funds, the school system, free universities, American Indians, children's issues, women's issues, Puerto Rican Independence, civil rights, crime and punishment, labor unions, the economic system, the electoral system, neocolonialism, South Africa and challenging HUAC and the antiunion Taft-Hartley Section 14B. We may have failed on the Middle East, but I'm not sure.

The workshops were amazingly successful, even though the collective follow-through on most of the issues was less substantial than I had hoped. For most people the urgency of the Vietnam War and the continuing struggle for Black rights took precedence. But for years I kept seeing specific examples of basic work being carried out in all these other areas by individuals who had been energized by the Assembly.

A National Coordinating Committee to End the War in Vietnam was formed at the Assembly itself and a month later the Fifth Avenue Peace Parade Committee was formed in New York at a meeting initiated by Norma Becker and myself. Subsequently the reorganized and expanded National Coordinating Committee became the Fall (1966) Mobilization Committee to End the War in Vietnam, the Spring (1967) Mobilization Committee and (in the fall of 1967) the National Mobe.

The exchanges at the Assembly added to the broadening of outlook on both coasts and elsewhere. Jerry Rubin played an active role in the formation of the National Committee, filled us in on the movement in the San Francisco Bay area and asked for ideas and help to strengthen Berkeley's plans for Vietnam Day observances in October. I had met Jerry for the first time in May, when I spoke at Berkeley's massive Vietnam Day teach-in, along with other speakers from outside the area, including Staughton Lynd, Norman Mailer, Isaac Deutscher and Dr. Benjamin Spock. At the Assembly, Jerry was the same energetic, fast-talking and persuasive self that I had observed in Berkeley but had not yet turned into the prankster practitioner of humorous, even ribald, guerilla theater that he later became.

For the final day, we had announced a plan to march to the Capitol to declare peace between the people of the United States and the people of Vietnam. We said that we wanted to do this from the balcony of the House of Representatives, but that if we were unable to gain access to the House, we would read a Declaration of Peace on the steps of the Capitol. (See Appendix for the text of the Declaration.)

When we marched toward the Capitol building, it was a workday, so a few hundred of our people had already left. Even so, over eight hundred marched. The march was led by Bob Moses,* Staughton Lynd and myself. Partway to the Capitol, the three of us were doused with red

*Like me, Bob did not consider hero-worship healthy for the movement. So he had recently taken the name Bob Parris, in an effort to get away from being identified as the legendary hero he had become for many people. As a result, he is identified in the publicity about the event as Bob Parris. For some years after that, Bob did most of his work in Africa and now, back in the United States, he uses the name Moses again. I have used it here so that those who know about his work in Mississippi will make the connection.

paint by some people wearing Nazi uniforms. A few blocks later, we were stopped by a double or triple line of police. When this happened, Moses and Lynd walked right up to the police and were immediately arrested but I held back and called for a continuation of our Assembly in the street. I facilitated it with one bullhorn while a second was passed from one speaker to another. It began with an elderly woman and a young girl reading successive halves of the Declaration of Peace. Then the whole Assembly, ringed by police, chanted the Declaration. After two hours and fifteen minutes of the best assembly of the weekend (although the police had originally given us ten minutes to disperse or be arrested), we made a group decision that those who were ready to face arrest should try to advance toward the Capitol by penetrating the police lines, nonviolently crawling between any two policemen or between their legs. Three hundred and fifty-six made the attempt. Naturally, we ended up beaten, bloodied and in jail.

Inside the lockup, I was isolated from the others and told that I was being charged with more serious crimes than the rest, "treason," one official said. I didn't know how seriously to take him, but when our lawyer, Phil Hirschkop, appeared he said that the district attorney had told him that they were planning special charges against me for having incited assaults on the police. Phil was working to prevent this but predicted that I would do serious time. By then quite a few of our people, including Moses and Lynd, had been bailed out or paid a fine, without realizing what was happening to me. But when Phil told the rest what I was threatened with, they refused to accept bail or pay fines or cooperate in any way unless the special charges were dropped. This was one of many instances, throughout the Sixties and continuing to the present, in which a group of arrested protestors saved me (or someone else) from being singled out and hit with heavier charges than the rest. In this case, I was reunited with the others after a few hours and heard nothing more of the threatened assault or treason charges.

According to news accounts that I have looked up, I was fined three hundred dollars, refused to pay the fine and was sentenced to either thirty days or (according to the *New York Times*) forty-five. Eighteen others got similar penalties when they refused to pay "ransom" even after the special charges was no longer an issue. The Nazis who threw the paint were fined ten dollars. A *Times* article five days after our arrest says that the nineteen of us were on a hunger strike, but I can't remember any of these details and have no idea how long the hunger strike lasted.

What I do remember is that the prison radio brought us news and regular reports of the Black riots in Watts. This not only emphasized for all of us the linkages between two of the struggles that had been stressed at the Assembly and in which we were all active—Black rights and anti-war—but also brought home to us the fact that we were entering a new period on the first of these issues. Something else I remember was more personal, but it served as a constant reminder to me of still another linkage. A lot of the red paint that had been thrown on us had landed on my face. Because of the sweltering heat during the long Assembly in the streets, as well as the long delay before the prison authorities let me scrub it off, my face was covered with itchy scabs that felt like the scabs from bedbugs and lice during and after my trips on the road in the Thirties. So I was also reminded that the struggle for a new economic system in which there would no longer be any homeless or other poor is a crucial part of the nonviolent struggle. Just being in prison amongst a population that overwhelmingly consists of the poor and racially oppressed always reaffirms these linkages. But even though this time we were segregated from the other prisoners in a large dormitory, I clearly felt how these issues are interrelated.

The next issue of *Life* magazine, which had a huge national and international circulation at the time, carried a dramatic picture of Moses, Lynd and myself, with the red paint prominent on our faces and clothes. I mention this because this somewhat accidental circumstance may have had something to do with my being invited to Japan the following year for the annual Hiroshima Day events and a conference of the Japanese anti–Vietnam War movement, Beheiren. And going to Japan led to my going to North and South Vietnam.

36

Bayard Rustin, apparently riding high after his role as coordinator of the complex forces that put on the massive August 28, 1963, civil rights march in Washington, sat in as always on the sessions in which "Dellinger, Muste, Bayard Rustin and others" finalized the Declaration of Conscience and plans for the August 6, 1965, demonstration. But when we were getting ready to release the Declaration publicly, he declined to sign it without offering any clear explanation. "Maybe later," he said. And a few days later he did sign it but also announced that he would not be going to Washington for the demonstration at which it was to be featured.

I was not surprised either by Bayard's initial refusal to sign, his signing later under pressure or his decision to stay away from the demonstration. For some time he had been torn by internal conflicts as he moved slowly away from his old politics. Increasingly, he showed signs of feeling less at home in the little group of friends who met weekly to work on *Liberation* and to exchange ideas on Movement strategy—A. J. Muste, Ralph DiGia, Barbara Deming, Paul Goodman, David McReynolds, Dick Gilpin and myself, with Sid Lens there periodically. Hitherto he had gone along with the things we were doing, even helping to plan them, while he did other things that we would not do. He did them with new associates and financial backers whose politics were different than the ones that he had held for years and the rest of us still adhered to, whatever our differences in detail or style. Now, his decision to remove himself from the August 6 action was the first substantial indication that his attempts to play a balancing act between two contradictory sets of politics and associates could not continue and that he was casting his lot with the more conventional approach.

As much as anything, it was the cumulative effect of two events that had broken his heart. In both he had felt abandoned and betrayed by people whom he loved and worked closely with. The first happened in January 1953, when A. J. Muste had agreed to fire him from his job as Youth Secretary of the FOR. The reason was that Bayard had been arrested in California for a homosexual act in the privacy of a parked car, arrested by police agents who Bayard thought were out to get him because of his radical politics. A.J., like everyone who worked closely with Bayard, had been fully aware of Bayard's sexual preference because Bayard used to flaunt it and make risqué jokes about it at all our small meetings together. But after the arrest, A.J. chose not to take a stand in favor of Bayard's continuation in his job but to go along with the more conventional religious pacifists who formed the bulk of the organization's membership and were key to its finances. Up to a point, Bayard understood the reasons for this, since he was somewhat of an organizational "realist" himself. But when some of us in the WRL got together and persuaded it to hire Bayard, A.J. resigned from the WRL board in an act of public protest. For Bayard that was an act that twisted a knife in an open wound, the pain made even worse because for years A.J. had been a much-loved father figure for him. It was one thing for A.J. to go along with the prejudices within his own organization, but he was not active in, or closely identified with, the WRL. Resigning from its board—it seemed to Bayard, as it did to me—went far beyond the bounds of understandable behavior.

Later that year, A.J. went back on the WRL board after he himself was relieved of his position as executive secretary of the FOR. From then on he worked more closely with the WRL than with the FOR, stipend and old relationships notwithstanding, and he and Bayard worked together again. But Bayard made clear to me that there was no way that the relationship could ever be what it once had been. The wound was covered over but not healed.

Then, in 1960, came the second blow that devastated Bayard beyond recovery and caused him to move slowly and painfully away from the radical nonviolent politics of which he had been by far the most creative and charismatic practitioner I have ever known. This time it was Martin Luther King, Jr., who broke his heart. King fired him from his position as staff secretary and chief adviser, a position that Bayard had been able to fill while working officially for the WRL, because we had seen development of the nonviolent civil rights movement as a key part of the WRL's work.

This time it was pressure from Congressman Adam Clayton Powell that forced the issue. Powell was inordinately jealous of King and knew, as we all did, that Rustin was the chief idea man on King's staff. In addition to his many talents, he had the years of experience in nonviolent movements and methods that King lacked and sorely needed. So Powell decided to undermine King by getting rid of Rustin. He told King that if he did not fire Rustin and dissociate himself from him altogether, he would expose King publicly for having a close relationship with a known homosexual. The implication was that King himself would be suspected of the "taint." King, whose freewheeling sex life made him susceptible to politically motivated "scandal" independently of Bayard (as J. Edgar Hoover later proved) apparently felt that he could not run this additional danger. So he fired Bayard. Again there was an extra factor that twisted a knife in the wound. Martin did not meet personally with Bayard to discuss it, but had a committee inform him that King was severing the relationship.

King, even more than Muste, needed Bayard so badly that the separation did not last, but from then on their relationship was more secretive. Once again the wound was partialy covered over without being healed.

Bayard served as chief organizer and sparkplug for the August 28, 1963, civil rights march in Washington, D.C., at which King delivered his famous "I Have a Dream" speech. But Bayard's position was unofficial (as assistant to A. Philip Randolph, the march's chairman) and King and the other civil rights leaders kept him as much in the background as they could. Even so, the march was attacked by Senator Strom Thurmond on the floor of the Senate because of Bayard's homosexuality. But Bayard's flair, magnetism and skills made it unlikely that he would be able to stay in the background for long. And from my own contacts with the seventy-five-year-old Randolph, whom I had known and admired since the Forties (without always agreeing with him), and from my frequent presence in the march's main office in New York and at some of the climactic meetings in Washington, I could see that he was physically and mentally incapable of supervising Rustin, even if he had wanted to. So Bayard clearly ran the show. At the march and afterward, Randolph with typical graciousness acknowledged this by calling Bayard "Mr. March himself."

On the day after King's committee informed Bayard of his fate, Bayard came to see me, cried, and said that from then on he was going to have to set up his own organization, with its own backers and a less controversial approach. "I can't stand it any longer," he said. "Twice now I have been betrayed by people I loved and trusted. I understand why they felt they had to do it, but if I weren't out in left field politically, no one would make a big issue of my sex life. I'm going to have to defend myself by turning my back on some of the things that I believe in and have always stood for. But don't worry, I'm not giving up the fight. I'll find other ways of being useful."

Not long afterward, I saw Bayard again and he told me that A.J. had said to him that he was ashamed of Martin for not standing up to Powell. But when Bayard tactfully reminded Muste of his own actions seven years earlier, A.J. offered no apologies but said, "Times have changed since then." I was surprised that A.J.'s refusal to apologize for what he himself had done—even while condemning King (and Powell)—hurt Bayard as much as he told me it did.

From then on, from my point of view, it was all downhill for Bayard, though it took a long time for him to get as near the bottom as he eventually did. One does not move easily away from something that has been one's lifeblood for twenty-five years and for which one has spent twenty-eight months in jail during World War II, done time on a Southern chain gang and been beaten and arrested innumerable times. First he worked out an agreement with A. Philip Randolph to found the A. Philip Randolph Foundation and to be its executive officer. And true to what he said to me, he did some good things through the foundation—for a while. But the founding grant came from the AFL-CIO through the active intervention of Lane Kirkland, a 100-percent procapitalist staff member (later its secretary treasurer and then president) who worked closely with the CIA in Europe and Central America.* Step by step the Randolph Foundation became a very different organization than the one that Bayard would have

*Promoting pro-U.S. labor organizations in Europe and Central America through the International Confederation of Free Trade Unions.

made it years earlier. Meanwhile, Bayard formed BASIC, Black Americans to Support Israel Committee, a rich source of funds for him and a committee that made excuses for all the ways in which Israel violated the political principles that he had held earlier.

By 1979, when white supremacist Ian Smith held an election in Rhodesia (now Zimbabwe) that the State Department, the Organization of African Unity and the entire civil rights leadership all considered fraudulent, Bayard attended as an observer and gave it his blessing. This was not the first time he had played that role. After the United States had landed troops in the Dominican Republic in 1965, Bayard had observed and endorsed the 1966 elections that installed a right-wing, pro-U.S. government. On that occasion, he said he could arrange for me to be one of the observers and urged me to agree for him to do it, saying that it would open up prestigious new contacts and channels for my work. But he made clear that he already knew that he would endorse the elections and stressed how important it would be for people like him and me to do so. So I declined.

From all these activities, many people are convinced that Bayard was employed—or at least subsidized—by the CIA. If so, perhaps this happened because of the logic of the politics he had adopted, or perhaps the CIA had threatened to make a public issue once again of his homosexuality if he did not act in accord with its wishes. To me whether he served them officially or unofficially didn't make that much difference.

Back on the morning of August 6, 1965, the day of the demonstrations in Lafayette Park and at the White House, Bayard had taken only his first tentative steps on the path I have described. And he had not as yet severed his old associations or renounced all of his old activities. So when I arrived at LaGuardia Airport to board the plane to Washington, I was excited to see him at the gate, preparing to get on the same plane. "Great," I said, "you've decided to go after all." "I'm not going to the demonstration," he replied. "President Johnson is signing the Voting Rights Act today and I have been invited to attend the ceremony in the White House." "Wonderful," I said, "be sure to get one of the pens he uses to sign it. You can come out, cross the street into Lafayette Park and use the pen to sign the Declaration of Conscience. As you know, I am chairing the rally and I will call you to the platform to sign it publicly.

Then you can say a few words linking Black rights and opposition to the war."

Because Bayard's heart was still in large part with us, and because he loved good nonviolent theater, he seemed tempted. But on the plane he explained with a sigh that his path was a different one now. He was in alliance with different forces and could not afford to antagonize them. "Besides," he said, obviously rationalizing, "the antiwar movement doesn't stand a chance. Lyndon Johnson is too smart for it. He has already begun to isolate Gruening and Morse [the only two Senators who had voted against the Gulf of Tonkin resolution] and he'll isolate you and A.J. too." I tried to convince Bayard otherwise, drawing on the ideas and experiences we had shared for nearly twenty-five years. But the hurts he had experienced and his need for refuge were too powerful for anything I could say to change his mind.

Sixteen years later, in 1981, I saw Bayard for the first time in several years. Robert Gilmore invited me, my wife, Bayard and his lover to dinner with him and his new wife. My guess was that Bayard had asked Bob to do it. As soon as I entered, Bayard took me aside, hugged me, cried once again, and, despite the nearby presence of Gilmore, who supported Bayard's current politics, said, "Oh, Dave, you stayed true all these years to the things that we held in common and I haven't been able to. I sold out." I couldn't be dishonest and say that he hadn't, but it hurt to know the reasons it had happened and how much it had violated who he had been and apparently wished, at least in part, he still was.

Even if I hadn't known the reasons, I would have done my best to comfort and console him. I tried, but I couldn't find the right words. The best I could do was to stammer that I loved him no matter what, hug him and cry with him.

37

I couldn't get to Japan for Hiroshima Day, 1966, because the Fifth Avenue Vietnam Peace Parade Committee was holding a demonstration that day. Besides wanting to speak at the rally and carry out my duties as one of the Committee's two coordinators, I was particularly conscious of the fragility of the relationships within the coalition. As A. J. Muste's biographer summarizes them:

> Bringing together such liberal-respectable groups as SANE and Women's Strike for Peace with such left-wing splinter elements as the DuBois Clubs and the May Second Movement; including both the Communist Party and the Socialist Workers' Party along with the New Left as represented by SDS; and also containing traditional pacifist organizations such as CNVA, WRL, AFSC and the Catholic Worker Movement, the Parade Committee was an achievement and a challenge for Muste.

And of course a challenge for me and Norma Becker as well, not only because of the Parade Committee's importance within the New York area, but also because it played a major role in the recently formed, nationally oriented Mobilization Committee to End the War in Vietnam. The Mobe had an even broader range of constitutents and potential contestants; I was first its vice-chairperson and then its chair. (When we finally got smart enough to include a woman and a person of color, I became the cochair.)

Everything went well at the demonstration and I left for Tokyo in time for the Beheiren Conference. There I met for the first time two persons, Makota Oda and my fellow American, the historian Howard

Zinn, who are among the most humane, thoughtful and creative workers for justice and peace that I know—as is Howard's wife, Roslyn. Oda, a former Fulbright scholar at Harvard, was already a well-known novelist in his own country and since then his work has been translated and published throughout much of the world, including a recent publication in this country of *The Bomb.** We have kept in touch ever since and through him I have made a series of trips to Japan for international conferences concerning Southeast Asia, Korea and the Middle East, with special attention to the roles of Japan and the United States in those areas.

Oda was one of several Japanese at the conference who compared the U.S. actions in Southeast Asia with the way their own country had acted throughout most of Asia from 1931 to 1945. Here in his own words is the historical context in which they came to think this way:

> During World War II we had the experience of being both aggressors and victims and it had a powerful effect on us. First we burned, destroyed and killed the people of other countries in blind obedience to the government's claims that it was building a "co-prosperity sphere" that would benefit all the people of Asia. Then the war turned against us and we were forced to suffer everything that we had imposed on other people. For years afterwards we saw ourselves as double victims, victims of our government's lies and victims of the death and destruction that rained down on us because we had believed and supported those lies.

Most of the older Japanese I talked with had hailed their American "deliverers" at the end of World War II and the ideals of democracy, freedom and peace that the United States claimed to represent. Everyone especially welcomed the Peace Constitution, with its ban on Japanese armaments. But then a strange thing happened to the United States (or at least its image in Japan) on its way to Vietnam. In 1947 it violated the ideals it had proclaimed by using its economic and political power to pressure Japan to rearm in violation of the Peace Constitution. In the

*Translated by D. H. Whittaker. Kodansha International/USA Ltd., Tokyo and New York, 1990.

words of Oda again, "The U.S. worked with reactionary Japanese business and cultural circles to reinstitute the values, attitudes and system of the hated past."

Oda himself had been only fourteen when the war ended, but he told me of an experience that was forever seared in his soul—and is now permanently burned into mine. It happened during a merciless bombing of Osaka (along with Tokyo) on August 14, 1945: "After what seemed an eternity of terror, I stumbled out of my shelter and through the corpses that lay all around. Scattered among them were leaflets which the American bombers had dropped. The leaflets proclaimed in Japanese: 'Your government has surrendered. The War is over.' "

In the United States, I had been continually reminded of the Day of Infamy on December 7, 1941, when Japan attacked Pearl Harbor. I had to go to Japan in 1966 to learn of the Day of Infamy, on August 14, 1945, when the United States engaged in one last orgasm of blood lust, *after Hiroshima and Nagasaki and after Japan had already surrendered*. When Oda told me this, he didn't use it to tell me how cruel and vindictive the U.S. *people* are, any more than I would have told him that the Japanese attack on Pearl Harbor proved how treacherous the Japanese *people* are. We both knew about the wartime atrocities of Japan that had fanned the American hatred and, along with the psychology created by every war, contributed to the United States' Day of Infamy. And we both had read the evidence that before the Japanese attack on Pearl Harbor the United States had been following a secret policy of shooting Japanese ships and aircraft—on sight and without warning. Also, we had both heard that long before Pearl Harbor the United States had broken the Japanese code, knew in advance when and where the Japanese attack would take place, and had deliberately permitted it to happen without alerting its defenses or heading off the Japanese ships and planes.

Most Americans would dispute these last two charges, both because the media and government have mostly passed over the evidence in silence and because people instinctively shy away from the pain they would experience if they allowed themselves to believe them. But there has been extensive documentation of both charges. Preliminary documentation of the first one was presented to Congress on the first anniversary of the Pearl Harbor attack by Congresswoman Jeannette Rankin and has been further implemented since. Documentation of the second charge has come from a series of reputable scholars, including Edmund Wilson and John Toland, the author of *Infamy, Pearl Harbor and Its Aftermath.* (See the Appendix.)

So Oda and I were drawn together by our common belief that it was not natural for either Americans or Japanese to engage in the kind of wars that the histories of both countries are full of. Both peoples had been prepared for them not only by propaganda and disinformation but also by violations of the best aspects of human nature that are entrenched in the institutions and mores of both societies. So we said to each other at the Beheiren Conference that to be real the antiwar movement must work to create the kind of society that nourishes and strengthens a better kind of "human nature" in the everyday relationships of "peacetime." That requires an economy and culture in which everyone will be able to earn a living in a manner that expresses their natural inclination to contribute to the well being of the community rather than to compete fratricidally in order to gain more power, prestige or affluence than their fellows. I felt a special bond with Oda because, unlike some who say that this is their goal, he was as concerned to free the victors in society's competitions from the harms they suffer as to free their victims. To me, that is the essence of genuine nonviolence. Finally, Oda stood for all this without losing the contagious sense of humor and warmth in everyday relationships without which even the seemingly most holistic movement can become self-righteous and boring.

In terms specifically related to Vietnam, another member of Beheiren said to me,

> Having undergone the merciless bombings of our own country helped the Japanese public to identify with the people of Vietnam. At the same time, having been sent to China and elsewhere ourselves—or having had family members or friends sent off to kill and die—helps us identify with the G.I.s. We understand their plight and do not condemn them personally. Instead we feel a strong sympathy for them.

Again, that was exactly what I had been fighting for inside the U.S. antiwar movement with respect to our attitude toward the GIs.

In concrete terms, the sympathies that Beheiren felt toward both the

Vietnamese and the GIs led them to befriend the American GIs during their stopovers in Japan and, as true friends would, to talk with them along the lines they had talked with me. The next time I heard from Oda, about a year later, was through the visit to Japan of Ernest Young, on his way home from a visit to North Vietnam that I had arranged for him and two other Asian specialists. Beheiren introduced Young to four members of the U.S. Navy who had recently "deserted" in Japan and asked for asylum. They asked it not of the Japanese government but of Beheiren. Beheiren provided it by arranging safe passage for them to Sweden in a Japanese fishing boat. When we published an account of this action, with statements by Young and each of the men, in the November 1967 issue of *Liberation*, we called them "patriotic deserters." But soon after that, I started calling such people "patriotic asserters" believing that they have refused to desert their consciences and have *asserted* their loyalty to a better United States than the one they had been drafted—or volunteered—to fight for.

The sense of humor and personal warmth that I first observed in Oda in 1966 came out dramatically fifteen years later, when he and I were part of a group that was under serious attack by Japanese and Korean Moonies. We were protesting U.S. and Japanese support for the South Korean dictatorship of Chun Doo Huan and the flagrant U.S. complicity in the 1980 massacre of hundreds of Koreans at Kwangchu for protesting the abuses they were suffering . The final event of the project was a public meeting in Kyoto. Just before my time to speak, a large group of Moonies arrived to attack the meeting. The project's security force shut and locked the doors, but when I walked to the microphone to begin talking, the doors adjacent to the platform were moving back and forth in an alarming fashion, pushed in a few inches by the Moonies and pushed back a few inches by the Japanese guards. Oda was my introducer and translator; somehow he managed to make it sound humorous that I had come all the way to Japan to be met with this kind of hospitality. I could hardly believe it, but with everyone's eyes (including mine) fixed on the doors to see if they would be forced open, locks, hinges and all, Oda came up with a series of jokes on that theme, which brought forth roars of nervous laughter from the audience—and me.

By the time the meeting had ended, a small contingent of police reinforcements had arrived and the Moonies were no longer trying to get in; they were still massed outside waiting for us, though. The police said there were too many Moonies for them to handle, and that the only thing to do was to wait them out. Eventually, most of the Moonies left and the police escorted the audience out a few at a time. But when Oda and I left with the final group, a large number of Moonies came out of nowhere and attacked us. In the confusion, I got separated from Oda and wound up in a car whose occupants spoke no English or any other language that I knew. After an hour or more of a dangerous high-speed chase, we eluded our pursuers and made it to a safe house, where I met up again with Oda and his wife, Hyon Sune—who is Korean.

It was well past midnight, but neither Sune, Oda nor I was ready to sleep after what had happened. So we drove to Nara, site of an ancient Buddhist monastery and its spacious holy grounds. There, we took in a sacred waterfall together and then separated for an hour, during which I walked in solitude except for the company of a full moon, hundreds of tame deer and other indescribable wonders of nature.

38

After leaving Japan, I spent three weeks alternating between Saigon (and vicinity) and Cambodia while waiting for an answer to the request I had made at the North Vietnamese embassy in Tokyo for a visa to visit North Vietnam.

At Tansonnhut Airport in Saigon, large numbers of young Vietnamese were leaving the country to study abroad, and large numbers of Americans of about the same age were arriving. Thinking with horror of how many of these Americans would be wounded or die in the jungles of Vietnam, I asked one of the departing Vietnamese, as gently as I could, if he felt any hesitation about leaving while Americans his age were coming to risk mutilation and death. His reply was: "As a human being, yes. But you must remember that it is the United States which insists on continuing the war."

Soon I was talking with other students inside the city, members of an underground student group. They told me that

> All the present collaborators [with the United States] were collaborators and hirelings of France. During the Japanese occupation they collaborated with the Japanese. This tiny oppressing minority collaborates with whatever foreign power is seeking to rule over us. They profit from colonialism so they don't want independence. They profit from the war, so they don't want peace. But the people are against the Americans, that is for sure. One hundred percent of the people are against the United States.

Next I met with a series of Buddhists. The Venerable Thich Thien Hoa, president of the United Buddhist Church, stressed the universal hostility toward Americans, explaining it in the following way:

> We realize that many Americans want to help us. We thank them for this. But the policy of the United States government is not to help the Vietnamese people, but to help a small group which oppresses the people. The American government has been here more than ten years and it has always supported dictator governments, so the Vietnamese people are against the American government.

Here are a few other journal notes from my visits to Saigon:

> At midnight I see a mother gather four little children around her, one at the breast, to catch what troubled sleep they can on a rain-drenched sidewalk. Nearby a group of youngsters whom I would judge to between the ages of eight and twelve, obviously without either homes or parents, tug at my sleeves for a *piastre,* victims of war who do not appear in the statistics or the military reports: children progressively hardened and corrupted in order to survive.
>
> A U.S. TV man who has been in Saigon for eighteen months tells me that there is a constant influx of such children

and a high turnover. Periodically, he says, the authorities "clean" the streets by having the homeless waifs arrested. Kids as young as ten are given sentences of ten to fifteen years on trumped-up charges, and then trained as suicide-squads. They gain their "freedom" by risking death or mutilation while betraying their countrymen to the hated foreign invader.

When I get to the entrance to my hotel, a little girl, perhaps eight years old, asks for money. I give her a little and she runs back a few steps and cries out defiantly: "*Ka Ka Do* Americans; *Ka Ka Do* Americans" ("Cut the Americans' throats. Cut the Americans' throats.") Just then, two American M.P.s ride slowly by in a jeep, guns protruding menacingly. The little girl turns from me and screams at the soldiers: "*Ka Ka Do* M.P.s; *Ka Ka Do* M.P.s." In the background I hear someone who is obviously half drunk complaining, "Nobody likes the Americans and I look like an American, but I'm not. I'm Canadian."

The next day, I wander into the street. Packages of American cigarettes catch my eye. There are strange white labels under the cellophane wrapping. Looking more closely, I read on a pack of Pall Malls:

FOR USE OUTSIDE U.S.
DONATED BY M & O CHEVROLET CO.
427 FRANKLIN ST.
FAYETTEVILLE, N.C.

A package of Lucky Strikes says:

FOR USE OUTSIDE U.S.
DONATED BY
COLONIA MEMORIAL POST 6061 V.F.W.
606 INMAN AVE.
COLONIA, N.J.
TAX EXEMPT
NOT TO BE SOLD

These cigarettes are for sale everywhere. Either they were intercepted at the dock by Vietnamese workers or sold by someone somewhere in the U.S. chain of command who has access to them. Despite the generosity of his would-be supporters back home, the ordinary GI who wants them may have to pay for them.

39

In mid-September 1966, I received word in Cambodia that my visa for North Vietnam had been approved. I expected to leave a few days later to make connections in Viangchan, Laos, for the weekly plane to Hanoi, but it was not to be.

The plane was operated by the International Control Commission that had been created by the Geneva Accords at the end of the French-Vietnamese war. Once a week it took members of the Control Commission to Hanoi—and occasionally a passenger such as myself. But while I was waiting for my visa, the plane had been shot down under mysterious circumstances. Now, after a delay, a successful flight had taken place and I wanted to take the next one. But the Vietnamese insisted that I not go on an ICC plane. "It might be shot down again," they said, "particularly if you are on it." Nobody knew who had shot down the earlier plane or why, but clearly the Vietnamese had their own opinion about it. I argued as forcefully as I could, but they absolutely refused to let me go that way. I was dependent on them for the visa, so in the end I had to accept their verdict.

I was only two short hops from Hanoi, but to get there I had to go thousands of miles in the opposite direction, to New Delhi, Cairo and Moscow, back through Southern Siberia, Mongolia, Beijing and Nanning. It was a particularly slow route because I had to wait in Cairo for my visa to Moscow and in Moscow for my visa to China, besides being delayed in Siberia by snowstorms that first stopped all traffic and then forced me to travel by train instead of by air. So my decision to go to Vietnam because Japan seemed so close turned out to have been based on an illusion. But even apart from the other countries, the visit to North Vietnam was so rewarding that I never regretted the decision.

One of the things I was concerned to find out was the real extent of U.S. bombing. The government insisted that it was bombing only "steel and concrete," never any civilian areas. At the time most Americans believed this and people like me who knew about other governmental lies didn't know what to believe. On the other hand, the Chinese government had announced that Hanoi was in ruins from the bombing. But I didn't trust the Chinese government either and, given the presence in Hanoi of a number of European embassies which hadn't made similar announcements, this didn't seem likely to me. But there was no reliable way of knowing.

When I got to Hanoi and its environs, I found out that neither was right. The United States was mercilessly bombing civilian enclaves all over North Vietnam, but central Hanoi had hardly been touched. One could even imagine that the occasional bomb that had fallen there was through pilot error (or personal anti-Communist exuberance) rather than by governmental design. But here is an excerpt from what I wrote after visiting Phuxa, on the very outskirts of Hanoi, perhaps a ten-minute drive from the center of the city:

> What can one say to a twenty-year-old girl, swathed in bandages and still in a state of shock because her mother, father, three brothers and sisters were all killed at their noonday meal when American bombers attacked the primitive agricultural village in which they lived?
>
> "Ask your President Johnson," she said to me, "if our straw huts were made of steel and concrete. Ask him if our Catholic church that they destroyed was a military target, with its 36 pictures of the virgin, whom we revere. Tell him that we will continue our life and struggle, no matter what future bombings there will be, because we know that without independence and freedom nothing is worthwhile."
>
> Meanwhile an American mother mourns the death of her son, shot down on a bombing raid over Vietnam. In the United States we are told that he was defending the Vietnamese people against Chinese aggression, but there are no Chinese soldiers in Vietnam. . . . The last Chinese soldiers to invade Vietnam were 180,000 U.S.-supported Chiang Kai-shek troops, in the winter

of 1945–46, after peace had supposedly come to the world. They helped the Allies suppress the Vietnamese independence which the United States had promised Vietnam when it needed her help during World War II.

My hosts in North Vietnam were determined not to let me take any chances by traveling through areas where the heaviest bombing was taking place. But after a series of extremely useful meetings in Hanoi, I began arguing that none of them would mean as much back in the United States as things that I could report from having traveled widely throughout the countryside, observing the nature and extent of the bombing and talking directly with the people. In the end I had to use a mild form of nonviolent resistance to get them to allow this, indicating as nicely as I could that I wouldn't go to any more meetings until they agreed to take me out where things were happening and I could see them with my own eyes.

When I finally did travel extensively east and south of Hanoi, it didn't take long to find out why they had been so afraid to let me go. We traveled mostly by night in a jeep camouflaged with tree branches. When the lights were turned on, which was only in a heavily wooded area, only the faintest pinpricks of light suggested the route through which the driver had to negotiate our way. An hour or so out of Hanoi, we had just turned from a barely traversable byway onto a real road when we heard the roar of planes. The jeep stopped and we got out and lay in a shallow drainage ditch by the side of the road. Suddenly, the darkest of nights became like midday as the planes released flares that seemed to have the power of a dozen midnight suns. We weren't strafed, as I half expected to be after the constant reports of strafing, but the bombs fell close enough to shake the earth and threaten my eardrums.

Even with the constant danger of this kind of attack, it was still safer to travel by night than by day. In daytime we slept, but still found time to confer with local inhabitants—in caves and crowded underground shelters, or walking hurriedly through devastated towns and villages and taking frequent refuge when planes came. Sleeping in the caves was by far the safest; I particularly remember one that I slept in on two or three of my visits. It was the only place I ever felt safe from the attacks because it was deep inside a small mountain and was protected by an overhanging cliff.

Thirty-five miles south of Hanoi, in what had once been Phu Ly, a city with a population of over ten thousand, not a building was standing. Survivors told me that after the heaviest bombings, low-flying planes had come back at intervals of twenty to thirty minutes to strafe anything that moved.

As if this were not gruesome enough, there was no mistaking the intentional bombing of isolated hospitals with huge red crosses still visible on their shattered roofs. And I talked with eyewitnesses from Europe who had seen the destruction of a huge, internationally famous leprosarium, which for obvious reasons was even more isolated and doubly identifiable—by its well-known location and markings.

And here is an excerpt from another day of my journeying:

> How does one greet a seventeen-year-old boy who limps painfully across the room, looking as if he were fifty (though he will never reach that age) because his face, neck, legs and arms are covered with welts and abscesses from napalm bombs? I don't know, but I remember protest meetings in the United States at which Christian clergymen have said: "It may be true that our tax money buys napalm but you can't expect Americans to refuse to pay their income taxes in protest. After all, whatever mistakes the United States may make, this is a democratic country and we must obey its laws."
>
> What does one say to a seven-year-old lad who (if he manages to survive future attacks) will have to go through life with only one arm, because his right arm was severed near the shoulder in a bombing raid? When I talked with him and a twelve-year-old friend, who had lost a leg in a different attack, I tried to get away from the horrors of war. I asked them about their school and told them about the daily life of my ten- and fourteen-year-olds in the United States.
>
> We had a good conversation. There were the beginnings of trust and affection. But there was no way we could get away from the war, as one can in the United States by turning off the news or changing the topic. School? Seven-year-old Dai had lost his arm when his kindergarten was bombed. Ten of his classmates and the teacher were killed; nine were wounded. Twelve-year-old Chinh had been on his way to school one morning with a

friend when "There was the explosion of bombs and I didn't know that my leg was cut but only that I couldn't stand up and couldn't walk any longer. . . . [While I was being carried to the first-aid station] I still could see everything all around, and I saw a number of my friends and some of the villagers lying dead on the ground. Then I lost consciousness and couldn't see anything.

It is amazing how simply and naturally he speaks, without a trace of self-consciousness or self-pity. I wonder if he will be able to preserve such a healthy attitude as he goes through life without a leg.

Suddenly American planes come upon us, roaring over the little complex of primitive shelters and the communal well at which women were washing their dishes and the three of us were talking.

A lot has been written about the use of tiny antipersonnel pellet bombs, which are useless against steel, concrete and even wood. In other words, they are useless against "military" targets but are lethal to people. So I will only say that no one in the general public knew about their use in Vietnam, and neither did I until I saw them all over the place. I brought one home with me and took it to my first press conference. The press wanted to see it more closely and the room was crowded, so I foolishly handed it to someone in the front row and said to pass it around. It never came back to me and no one owned up to having pocketed it. I assumed that it wound up in government hands, either directly through a government agent posing as a reporter, or indirectly through a reporter who was looking to score some brownie points that might give him privileged future access to some official or officials. Whoever it was knew what a dangerous weapon it was, not just for what it was doing to civilians in Vietnam but for what it would do to Americans, if they saw it and pondered its uses.

The Vietnamese concern for the lives of their American visitors was always present. Later, a plan I thought had considerable merit and wanted to be a part of met with an absolute *no.* The dikes were increasingly under attack, and we feared that a catastrophic flooding might be in the offing; Jim Bevel (of SNCC, SCLC and at the time project director for the Mobe) came up with the idea of having the antiwar movement send teams of

American volunteers to camp on them, hoping that would protect them. But when I proposed it to the Vietnamese, they were adamant in refusing to permit it. Somehow, in the midst of all their own losses, they went to extreme lengths to prevent any losses of life among American opponents of the war. In a way I hate to say it, but if some of us had been killed perhaps it would have speeded up the ending of the war, as well as serving as a beneficial reminder that nonviolent activists risk their lives too, even as soldiers do. In the absence of such risks, nonviolent action lacks the visible power it must have to convince people that it is a viable alternative to the military method of "defense." Certainly the lives lost by nonviolent civil rights workers in the South had a major educational impact of this kind as well as helping accomplish whatever gains were made in the lives of Black people.

During this first visit, I was so appalled by the destruction and weaponry, as well as by the contrast between the U.S. propaganda and the reality, that I urged the Vietnamese to invite observers from the United States who would have more credibility with the media than I would, given my identification with the antiwar cause. I knew that my reports would reverberate within the antiwar movement and in a gradually widening circle, but more than that was needed. So I urged the officials to invite American reporters to come, see for themselves and report what they had seen. I also suggested that they invite Senator William Fulbright, chairman of the Senate Foreign Relations Committee, a man of conservative politics whose fundamental honesty had impressed me when I had talked with him in his office.

They didn't invite Senator Fulbright and they showed a surprising amount of resistance to inviting a reporter from the pro-war, capitalist press. It was one of the disappointing blind spots I encountered during my visit. But logic was so much on my side, that they gradually softened and eventually read off to me a list of newsmen who had applied for visas. They asked me whom they should invite, but I didn't feel right about saying and replied that it was a decision I would not make for them. But I stressed that the politics of the reporter were less important than his honesty. I could not imagine that anyone who was the least bit honest could see even half of what I had seen and fail to report enough to give the American people a jolt.

In the end they invited Harrison Salisbury, of whom I had spoken highly without presuming to say that he was the one they should ask. His cables to the *New York Times* stunned the public—and the public relations liars in the administration—with their descriptions of the nature and extent of the devastation. They created a new dynamics in the antiwar movement's battle to turn the public against the government's terrorist policies. The government could no longer get away with its claim to be bombing only "steel and concrete"—of which, by the way, there was very little in Vietnam.

Salisbury's trip coincided with a period during which the United States was attempting to palliate the public, showing its devotion to the Christmas spirit by ordering a strictly temporary Christmas Day halt to the bombing. This was a fortuitous coincidence that enabled Salisbury to travel for one day more widely than he might otherwise have been able to (and less perilously than I had during the three weeks from October 28 through November 18). But, given the time change, it also resulted in having his first story appear in the *Times* on Christmas Day, 1966. Besides the other objections to his dispatches, some people said that it was not right to disturb the country's celebration of Christmas with such gruesome, "unpatriotic" material.

My response to this was to say, "Yes, Virginia, there is a Santa Claus and he gave us all a gift this Christmas. He put coal in the stockings of the government and gave at least a small portion of the truth to the American people. But there is also someone besides Santa Claus whom some of us celebrate on Christmas, the nonviolent revolutionary peasant of Galilee who urged us to love our enemies, beat our swords into plowshares and study war no more."

40

On my way to North Vietnam, I saw a magazine with a photograph of a downed U.S. pilot being driven through the streets of a Vietnamese city while angry residents jeered and spat at him. The story spoke of U.S. fears that the Vietnamese were planning to try the American prisoners for war crimes.

I was offended by this inexcusable treatment of the captured man and resolved to speak out against it when I got to Vietnam. Even if the bombing of civilian areas turned out to be extensive and indiscriminate and had caused widespread fear and hatred there was no valid excuse for this. I did think about what would have happened if a "little brown Jap" had floated down into an American city after bombing it during World War II (instead of a big white "longnose" parachuting into a ravaged Vietnam), and I concluded that he might have been lynched. But as surely as I would have opposed such treatment in the United States—as I had opposed the herding of U.S. citizens of Japanese descent into concentration camps—I was determined that when I got to Vietnam I would oppose not just lynching and individual war crimes trials but also the clearly offensive treatment of the prisoner shown in the photograph.

I showed the picture to a series of Vietnamese authorities, pressing on them the necessity for humane treatment of all the POWs, arguing from basic human reasons more than from the Geneva Conventions. And I spoke strongly against war crimes trials, which I considered a travesty when they had been carried out by the United States and its allies after World War II. To my surprise, they all said that they agreed with me on both issues. When I told my interpreter, Do Xuan Oanh, how pleased I was with the response, he said, "Well, first of all it's in the best tradition of Vietnam. But also you must understand that when you speak of such things it has a different impact on us, coming from a spokesperson of the antiwar movement, than when it comes from a government that has planned and organized the war crimes that have caused so much suffering for our people." At that point, I had no idea that Oanh was no ordinary interpreter, but a close friend of Ho Chi Minh and a renowned poet and musician (he was author of Vietnam's national anthem).

By the time that I had a face-to-face meeting with Ho Chi Minh (which I shall describe later), he had heard reports of my protests, brought up the subject before I could and thanked me for my concern for the prisoners. He had heard not only through Oanh but, as he told me, by listening to a tape recording of a meeting I had with people who were described as "key leaders of specially organized sectors of Vietnam"—labor, youth, women, agriculture, education and others. He emphasized that it was not the intention of the North Vietnamese leadership to punish prisoners but to return them to their homes better informed and better citizens than when they came to rain death on the Vietnamese people.

His words were exemplary and I only wish that they had been lived up to. But they weren't—at least not consistently. Some of the POWs were beaten and tortured, though just how many no one knows, given the U.S. government's practice of exaggerating in order to emphasize Vietnamese depravity and justify past and current U.S. aggression. But for even one POW to be treated that way is too many.

Usually overlooked in discussions of this emotional subject is the initial burden the United States laid on the men when it ordered them to commit acts that constituted war crimes under the Nuremberg Principles that it had helped formulate after World War II. For perspective, two of the accusations at Nuremberg against Hermann Goering, head of the Nazi air force, were that he set fire to British cities and that he bombed civilians, crimes for which he was hanged. Of course Goering did these things in a bad cause and many Americans thought they were doing them in Vietnam in a "good cause." But the cause didn't seem all that good to the Vietnamese prison guards and it was hard for them to live up to Ho Chi Minh's principles.

Meanwhile, the United States used the supposed danger of war crimes trials as a means of winning popular support for the ferocity of its attacks rather than as a reason to start conforming to the Nuremberg Principles, whereas the Vietnamese held out the promise of immediate postwar releases without trials as an inducement for the United States to end the war. But the United States continued to talk as if such trials might take place, with an insensitive disregard for the pain such talk caused the POW families for whom it supposedly was expressing sympathy.

From time to time the North Vietnamese released three POWs as a sign of their readiness to release them all. The first release came after one of my other trips in which I had lobbied again in favor of their treating the prisoners with respect and sensitivity. On my return to the United States, the Vietnam Peace Committee sent me a teletype message asking me to come back to Vietnam to facilitate a prisoner release. Anxious for others to have a firsthand experience of North Vietnam, I consulted with other antiwar leaders and we selected Howard Zinn and Father Daniel Berrigan as two ideal persons for such a mission.

The spirit of this first release of prisoners held by North Vietnam was violated when the United States intercepted the ex-POWs before they could get closer to home than Viangchan, about 125 miles from the Vietnam border. It took them to the air force base in Thailand from which they had originally attacked Vietnam, flew them back to the United States on a military plane (for debriefing and to see their families) and then returned them to the Thai base. There it reassigned at least one of them to new bombing missions. Even the interception in Laos was in violation of an agreement I had with the State Department that the men would be allowed to return to the United States on civilian airliners. An official had contacted me immediately after my receipt of the teletype from Hanoi, and I had explained that any interference with the return trip would endanger future releases. The plan had been that the men would report to the military as soon as they landed in the United States, but this was not good enough for the government. If it couldn't rescue them from the Vietnamese, it would at least rescue them from Zinn and Berrigan.

No one knows how many POWs this arrogant and duplicitous act caused to be kept in prison for how many unnecessary months or years. But after a delay, the Vietnamese government resumed the practice of limited releases, continuing to release the prisoners not to the government but to the antiwar movement. In all, four groups of three prisoners were released, with Cora Weiss, Reverend William Sloane Coffin, Richard Falk and I escorting the last three home in the fall of 1972. We secured Vietnamese permission to bring along a family member of each of the prisoners, so the wife of one and the mother of another took the trip with us. The family of the third prisoner refused to go. We also took Peter Arnett, an AP reporter in South Vietnam whose dispatches had seemed more balanced and fairer than those of many U.S. reporters—the same Arnett who stayed in Baghdad during the 1991 Gulf War and reported from there for CNN. To avoid interception we traveled home by way of China, Moscow and Denmark.

Cora and I tried unsuccessfully to convince either Congressman Father Richard Drinan or Congressman Ron Dellums to be part of the 1972 trip. At first, Dellums enthusiastically accepted the invitation, but he changed his mind after consulting with his senior advisers. He told us that they had convinced him that going would hurt him in a difficult election that was coming up. This sorely disappointed us. Besides thinking that his personal stature and his membership in Congress would have made a significant contribution to the public debate, I had learned, from a hasty visit to the Vietnamese negotiators at the Paris peace talks, that one of the released prisoners would be an African-American from Dellums's home district. I thought that his bringing home one of his own constituents would have set a good example as well as helping to offset whatever negative uses his electoral opponents would have tried to make of his action.

To add to my disappointment, I remembered a conversation Ron and I had when he was first elected to Congress. Significantly, we had met at an anti–Vietnam War conference in Stockholm. "I know what you are probably thinking, Dave," he had said. "That now that I'm a congressman I'll begin to play along with the system in order to keep getting elected. But I feel too deeply about these matters to get caught in that trap. I'll be a different kind of congressman than most. I don't care if I am never elected again if winning an election means compromising my principles." After his decision not to go with us to Vietnam, I had to wonder whether the daily compromises every congressperson makes in the effort to be a successful player in the game of congressional tradeoffs—while simultaneously keeping a vigilant eye on powerful lobbyists and their effects on future elections—had not changed him more than he had thought it would.

I tell this story not to condemn Ron Dellums, whom I admire and who *is* at least a somewhat "different kind of congressman than most."

But it indicates the realities of that body as I have observed them through the years, and it explains why I have repeatedly refused to take that route myself, even though there have been many times when I was urged to run. Usually I wouldn't have had a chance, but there came a period when I was asked to run by people whose clout, connections and access to money, combined with the mood of the country and the publicity and contacts that came from my role in the antiwar movement and the Chicago trial, might have produced a respectable, if not necessarily victorious, campaign.

Vietnamese confirmation that at least a few of the POWs were tortured came to me in 1985 when I returned to Vietnam for the tenth anniversary of the military ending of the U.S.–Vietnam war. My friend Oanh and a few others said to me that there had been "a few" such cases. But they all insisted that this was in clear violation of government policy and determined official efforts to prevent it. They said that given the cruelty of the bombings and strafing, some guards took out their anger and resentments on the prisoners.

Impressive confirmation of this human reality comes from a 1985 article by columnists Jack Anderson and Dale Van Atta. Writing retrospectively about a spectacular Rambo-type raid on a POW camp at Son Tay, they said:

> On Nov. 21, 1970, a force of 60 elilte commandos landed in a secluded compound 23 miles west of Hanoi, deep inside North Vietnam. The men were told their mission was to liberate as many as 80 American POWs being held there.
>
> Not a single POW was found.
>
> The chief planner of the raid, Gen. Donald T. Blackburn, told our associate . . . years later: "We knew they had been moved . . . but . . . the real purpose of the raid was to show the North Vietnamese how vulnerable they were.

As a result, according to General Blackburn,

> The treatment of American POWs was improved dramatically as they were moved into Hanoi for security. *It was "less likely that some sadistic sergeant in the sticks" would mistreat them.* [Emphasis added]

During the 1985 visit, I spoke of the prison abuses once again to Le Duc Tho, Vietnam's chief negotiator at the Paris peace talks. He said,

> If some did suffer abuses, we regret it. We don't condone such things. But none of them were killed. But on Phu Quoc Island [a South Vietnamese prison supervised by American "advisers"] our prisoners were tortured and mistreated to death. Today there are five thousand graves of such victims on Phu Quoc island.

41

I usually visited some U.S. POWs when I was in Hanoi, hoping to communicate a little solidarity and support and offer to contact their families on my return, tell them that their son, husband or brother was alive and give them any messages he might send to them. Also, it served to emphasize to the Vietnamese my concern for the prisoners and provided an opportunity to express that concern directly to the prison authorities.

In 1967, I traveled to Vietnam with Nick Egleson, the president of SDS at the time, and together we visited Lt. Richard Stratton and Douglas Hegdahl of the U.S. Navy in the Hanoi Hilton, as the POWs called the prison in Hanoi. Hegdahl told us that he had fallen undetected off his ship in North Vietnamese waters and been rescued by the Vietnamese. Writing about the visit in *Liberation*, I said this:

> I have been a prisoner long and often enough myself to realize that one is never completely free as a prisoner but under a great deal of psychological pressure, no matter who the captor or guarding authority may be. Therefore I explained to the Vietnamese that although I would like to see some prisoners, I wanted to do

> so primarily as an American seeing fellow Americans who were in an extremely difficult situation and that I would not want any recording made and would not expect to use the interview for political purposes.
>
> Nick and I made it clear [to Stratton] that, because of the circumstances, we did not think it would be desirable for us to publish any statement that Stratton might make about the war, and he said, "Well, let's just talk off the record then." I simply want to say about that part of the conversation that he seemed to speak very freely . . .

I will add now, years later, that a lot of what he said would have been useful in challenging U.S. propaganda—if we were sure that he was speaking truthfully rather than to impress his Vietnamese captors, and if we had been willing to violate our commitment not to make it public.

> All in all, we spent at least three hours in unhurried rambling conversation with the two prisoners. . . . Toward the end of our visit, Hegdahl said several times things like "I wish you could stay longer." "How long are you going to be in Vietnam, do you think you can visit me again?"*

Here is the closest to a "positive report" that I ever wrote, after one of my other prison visits:

> I was favorably impressed by the conditions I observed in the Hanoi prison, by my interviews with prisoners and with the Vietnamese officials, but I . . . remember too well how visitors who toured the Federal prisons in Danbury, Conn., and Lewisburg, Pa., when I was there, failed to detect the abuses to which the prisoners were subject. . . . It must be extremely difficult for prison guards and officials always to live up to Ho's ideal of not responding with "individual enmity and rancor" and of showing the world that they are "more civilized than the homicidal invaders."†

Liberation, May–June 1967.

†*Liberation*, October 1969.

Meanwhile, it took the revelation of the My Lai massacre in late 1969 to expose the U.S. public to some of the atrocities *on the ground* by our own troops in Vietnam. But I had heard innumerable eyewitness accounts of them at the Bertrand Russell War Crimes Tribunal in Stockholm (May 1967) and Copenhagen (November 1967). I joined *that* war crimes tribunal because it was agreed beforehand that its purpose was to save lives, not to destroy them. We felt it important to conduct a careful investigation of what was going on and to bring it to the attention of a wider public, but we agreed not to call for the punishment of anyone. Some people were impressed that I served on the tribunal at the invitation of Bertrand Russell and worked intimately with Simone de Beauvoir, Jean-Paul Sartre, Vladimir Dedijer of Yugoslavia (and Harvard), Swedish playwright Peter Weiss and other famous people. (Weiss's award-winning play, *Marat/Sade*, had recently created a sensation in London and New York.) But even apart from my disappointment at the fawning way in which de Beauvoir treated Sartre and tried to influence everyone else to do the same (in complete contradiction to her views in *The Second Sex*) it was not the famous people who impressed me the most. Rather it was the Vietnamese victims who testified to the tortures they had gone through and three U.S. GIs who testified to the tortures they had inflicted and seen inflicted—not at Phu Quoc Island but at a variety of U.S. Army bases.

As for the Vietnamese, if you looked at their scars or listened to what they had experienced—snakes and sticks forced up their vaginas, water poured into their lungs, electric shocks to their genitals, napalm welding their limbs or chins to their bodies, babies torn from their arms and dashed to the ground, their children strafed from the air—you would think they were heroes and heroines, not ordinary persons like you and me. You and I couldn't go through what they did and come out as human and humane as they were. But after a while I learned that they were ordinary people like you and me—and heroic. There were too many of them from every age and station of life for it to be otherwise.

As for the three GIs, it was disturbing enough to hear incident after incident such as the following from the testimony of Private David Tuck.

When speaking of "a VC being tortured by the South Vietnamese under the direction of U.S. forces," a prisoner who Tuck thinks was later executed, he reported:

> They were using a knife to sort of pry under his toenails and the soles of his feet. When this got no results they went on to more sensitive parts of his body. Well . . . evidently this man was . . . a tough nut to crack. So then . . . they put the knife under his eyeball.

And after Tuck told about having been in a Huey helicopter from which a tied and bound Vietnamese prisoner had been thrown out in mid-flight, he said that when he "got back to base camp . . . you know, such a thing is an everyday thing—you know we did not think too much about it."

And while Special Forces Sergeant Donald Duncan was telling about other instances of senseless cruelty to hapless Vietnamese, all the famous people in attendance were crying. But it was the testimony of Peter Martinsen that disturbed me the most and raised questions of a special nature. Martinsen was a former Prisoner of War Interrogator with the 541st Military Intelligence Detachment in Vietnam, who had been trained at the U.S. Army Intelligence School in Fort Holabird, Maryland. He described brutal prisoner interrogations that he had conducted and observed, saying that in some of them the prisoner had survived and in others he had not. I thought that his testimony had climaxed with the following words:

> I can't think of an interrogation that I saw in Vietnam during which a war crime, as defined by the Geneva Conventions, was not committed. . . . All of our interrogators had participated in actual torture.

But then he said something that was even more frightening:

> Then you realize, because everybody participates in the torture—unless we have a special group of sadists working as interrogators, which I don't believe: I believe they are just normal people—you realize that there is an innate capability to do harm to your fellow man in proper circumstances, and these circumstances are provided by the war in Vietnam. It's so horrifying to recall an interrogation where you beat the fellow to get an effect, and then you beat him out of anger, and then you beat him out of pleasure.

When Martinsen said this, I felt first horror at what had happened to him and then a surge of admiration for him for being so honest. But now, I will just say that his words provide, I think, a proper background for me to try to answer a question that the media have been asking me over and over for the last fifteen to twenty years. Invariably it comes whenever I am arrested for nonviolent civil resistance activities of one kind or another—and it is not only the media that asks it: "Why do you keep going, doing the things you do? How do you keep going, after all these years?"

Apart from saying that I don't do nearly enough, which has to be an important part of any honest answer, I feel as if I rarely answer the question well. But in the context of reliving Martinsen's testimony, perhaps I can answer a little more clearly than usual.

I continue because I hate to see "just normal people" suffering from the illness of getting "pleasure" by harming people. Sometimes I see the illness when they endorse, cheer on or participate in the beatings, torture and murder that is carried on through certain institutions of our society—the prison system, the death penalty and war. But equally I see the illness when people take pleasure in beating out their fellow humans in the competitive pursuit of private success that produces winners and losers, victors and victims. So it is not just the suffering of the victims that upsets and moves me, but also the illness of the victors.

On a more positive note, I continue because of something I have learned, in prison, in struggles for human rights and in the antiwar movement. It is that there is nothing more fulfilling than to work in a Beloved Community of people who are laboring to cure that illness, in ourselves and in the society, and do not demand a sterile conformity of ideology and action among those who share that goal. In such a community, the members are working, each in her or his own way, to create the "proper circumstances" in which "just normal people" will develop their "innate capability" of living as sisters and brothers in a world in which everyone will be equal—a world in which people are *really* born equal and will never cease to be treated as equal, whatever their individual diversities and failings; a world that will not make a mockery of the U.S. claim that we live "with liberty and justice for all."

Of course, the members of such a community are limited by a host of human failings that slow down the process of achieving that world. None of us is as sensitive or wise as we want to be, or knows adequately how to combine new truths with old truths, other people's insights with our own insights. But that is no reason not to keep working to become less and less a part of the problem and more and more a part of the solution. It makes it all the more important to learn from our mistakes, lapses and failings, while we "keep on keeping on"—struggling, learning and growing through participation in a Beloved Community of persons who are helping one another to struggle, learn and grow.

For me, the Beloved Community includes everyone who is working—or did work when they were alive—for that kind of transformation of themselves and the society. I am inspired by them whether I know them personally or not. It's what we used to call, in my Student Christian Movement days, "the Church Invisible." But it is not limited to people who identify with a particular religion or spiritual tradition.

42

As my first visit to Vietnam was drawing to a close, Do Xuan Oanh told me that besides my scheduled appointment next day with Prime Minister Pham Van Dong, there was someone else who says he has been impressed by what he has been told of your frankness during the visit and the challenges you have raised, and has asked to see you." When I asked who it was, Oanh smiled, took on an air of mystery and refused to say anything more than that. I had no idea whom he meant and it never occurred to me that he might be speaking of Ho Chi Minh, the legendary and much-loved president of Vietnam.

The next day I had a wonderful visit with Pham Van Dong. I was impressed by the exploratory nature of our conversation, its depth, and the feeling that he and I were on an almost identical wavelength as to the kind of society we wanted, however different the paths we had taken in our differing situations to work toward it. It was a case of discovering when

I least expected it someone who belonged to the same Invisible Church or Beloved Community that I did. While we were talking and I was drinking that in, a curtain parted at the edge of the room and a gentle, elderly man with a humble demeanor walked in. Dong and I both looked at him and I started to rise, but he indicated that I should stay seated and we should keep talking because he wanted to hear what we were saying. He stood quietly for at least five or ten minutes and then, when Dong and I had finished a lengthy interchange, walked over to me with his hand outstretched and a friendly little smile on his face. It was Ho Chi Minh.

Ho spoke warmly of the joy he felt to meet me (words that struck me as sincere and not in the least artificial) and asked if I was feeling all right after the exactions of my most recent trip through the areas under attack. Then he spoke of the tape he had listened to from my meeting with Vietnam's key leaders and the gratitude he felt for the questions I had raised and my concern for my fellow Americans whom his country held as prisoners. Here are his opening words on the prisoners. He spoke them in English and I wrote them down immediately afterward:

> I don't have to tell you of the terrible things they have done. You have seen with your own eyes the death and destruction that they have rained down on our people, on our towns and villages, schools, hospitals and churches. But we feel sorry for them because they have come thinking that they are helping the Vietnamese people, saving them from some terrible thing called Communism. . . . After they have been here a while, they find out that even the anti-Communist Vietnamese don't want them here. We don't want to punish them and we don't want to keep them here. We want only that they be able to return to their homes better informed and better citizens of their own community and the world than when they did those things.

When he said the words "some terrible evil called Communism," he paused momentarily and uttered a strange, barely audible little suggestion of a laugh that I did not know how to interpret. It didn't seem to imply scorn of the people who thought that way, though I did consider that possibility. Instead, something in his manner made me more inclined to believe that he was thinking, as I was, of how much easier it was for people to believe this because the crimes of the Soviet Union had given Communism such a bad name. But when it came to his statement about "even the anti-Communists don't want them here," there was no confusion in my mind about what he meant. Not only because I had observed that in South Vietnam myself, but because he went on to say that in the beginning a lot of people in the South had thought that "it was possible to have an independent anti-Communist regime that was aided by the United States but not dominated by it." However, he said, they soon learned "that was not what the American government had in mind and they turned against the American occupiers."

Ho chuckled about how baffled the U.S. rulers must be "at the failure of the great and wealthy United States to conquer the poor peasant country of Vietnam. They are used to getting anything they want," he said, "but in Vietnam, the harder they try, the deeper the trouble they get into." He explained this by saying that "an attack on a heavily industrialized European country similar to the attack on Vietnam would have brought it to its knees in a few months." Vietnam, he said, was saved from collapsing because "it is a poor peasant country lacking in industrial might and not dependent for survival on vulnerable concentrations of factories, transportation centers and cities." At that point, I thought of what Nguyen Van Hieu, an NLF official I had met in Phnom Penh, had said to me: "You see that bamboo bridge over there? A barefoot guerrilla can cross it, but a heavy U.S. tank cannot."

"Here our strength is our people," Ho said, "and the more they suffer, the more determined they are not to give up." He also said that another reason that Vietnamese forces often defeated larger, more heavily armed U.S. forces, even in an occasional classic military encounter, was that "the Vietnamese are defending their homes and families but the Americans are not. But," he quickly added, "Americans have fought very bravely in the past and if San Francisco or New York were ever invaded, they would fight just as bravely again."

When Ho spoke of how rich a country the United States was, he came back to the POWs again and said that "Americans are used to more food than the people of a poor country like ours, so we give the prisoners larger daily allowances of food than those allotted to our own soldiers."

When Ho talked about the time he had lived in the United States after World War I, he had nothing but praise for the family in Brooklyn for whom he had worked. "They were fine people," he said, "and were very nice to me." Even though he had been their "houseboy" (a word he used without any apparent annoyance) he never succumbed to generalizing about them as exploiters, class enemies or people corrupted by the power of money. "I didn't have to work very hard," he said. "I used to have a lot of free time to study and to take trips to other sections of the city. When you get back to the United States, you can say that when I worked as a domestic servant in Brooklyn I earned forty dollars a month and now that I am president of Vietnam, I get paid forty-four dollars a month." And it was true that unlike so many officials in other Communist countries, he was noted for the simplicity of his lifestyle.

The thing that had disturbed him most during his stay in the United States was the shocking poverty of the Black people in Harlem. He said that he traveled there frequently on the subway, to be near them and learn from them. But apparently the family he worked for had not succumbed to the temptations of conspicuous consumption, class and race prejudice; and, typical of his whole approach, Ho told the truth about them rather than using them to make dishonest propaganda about "the bourgeoisie."

In fact, Ho never spoke harshly of any Americans. When he said "it is a shame how many Americans think they can buy anything with money—people, land, governments and the right to destroy other people's culture and traditions," it was a harsh (if accurate) judgment. But even there he seemed to speak with compassion and sorrow, much as a warm-hearted person speaks of friends who are ill with an addiction (alcoholism, for example) and hopes that they will recover. And when he referred to what others had called "the arrogance of the American invaders," he called it "unconscious arrogance."

In a similar vein, one of the last things Ho said to me was, "We do not want to humiliate the Americans or make it difficult for them to return home. If they finally decide to let us live in peace and to take their soldiers home where they can lead safe and honorable lives, we will have celebrations for them. Our girls will bring flowers to the boats as they get ready to sail away and our musicians will play songs for them."

Before I met Ho, I had wondered whether his image as a kindly and unpretentious leader of his people might be propaganda, aided by the accident of a photogenic appearance that resulted from his firm but gentle face, kindly eyes and wispy goatee. But I left captivated by qualities that cannot easily be faked and ran counter to characteristics that some of America's supermilitants of the period were claiming are necessary for true revolutionaries. As had happened with Pham Van Dong, I knew that Ho and I were members of the same Beloved Community, regardless again of the different situations in which we worked and the specific demands that those situations had made on us. His interpretation of the demands made on him were to organize a violent defense of his country, and my interpretation of mine was to work nonviolently against my country's attempt to subjugate his country and its people.

The day after this conversation I left on the long flight home. In Peking, my plane was met by a representative of the Vietnamese embassy who took me to the embassy for dinner with the ambassador from Vietnam to China. As soon as I met the ambassador, he offered a toast and I responded with one. Then he turned to me and said, "Dellinger, we know your heroic work against the Korean War, and we know of your heroic work against the present war. What were you doing in World War II against the fascists?"*

Holy shit, I said to myself: I've only just met the man and I have to explain to him that I was in prison for three years for refusing to fight in the war against the fascists. I had good discussions in North Vietnam about my belief in nonviolent principles and tactics, and was open to discussing them with the ambassador, *but in the first five minutes? And in response to a question phrased like that?*

I began by giving him a quick summary of my early opposition to the fascists, my visits to Nazi Germany and contacts with Jews and anti-Nazis. And I told him how the U.S. military-industrial complex had

*When I wrote about this incident in the introduction to my *Revolutionary Nonviolence*, a combination of false modesty and knowledge that I hadn't been that heroic led me to paraphrase the ambassador's words, leaving out his references to my "heroic work." But by now I think it is better to report this exactly as he said it. These words were so embarrassing that I have never forgotten them.

collaborated with the fascists for years until a combination of events had led it to decide that the Nazis had become a threat to its own imperial ambitions.

That was the easy part. It wasn't hard for him to understand that the country that was currently trying to further its imperial ambitions by bombing and bludgeoning Vietnam into submission hadn't been a reliable ally in the fight against fascism and colonialism. Also, he knew only too well what had happened on September 2, 1945, only seventeen days after the end of World War II. Vietnam had declared its independence and the Western Allies had responded by freeing their captured Japanese troops, giving them back their arms and using them to put down the Vietnamese.The ambassador may not have known what Gen. Douglas MacArthur said at the time, but he knew even better than MacArthur the reality that lay behind the words MacArthur used: "If there is anything that makes my blood boil, it is to see our allies in Indochina and Java deploying Japanese troops to conquer the little people we promised to liberate."*

But it would have been dishonest for me to have stopped with that history as the sole reason for my stand in World War II. So I took a deep breath and began to speak of my commitment to nonviolent action, both as a tactic and as a way of life. When I mentioned Gandhi, the ambassador interrupted me in the middle of my sentence, practically shouting from excitement: "Yes, yes! You remember how Gandhi announced a plan for the nonviolent defense of India when the Japanese were advancing in the Pacific and everyone thought they would land there and try to take it over."

I not only didn't remember, I didn't know anything about it. (I looked it up when I got home and I know about it now.) But from then on we had a searching discussion of something that I did know and place a lot of emphasis on. It was the necessity of developing the tactics, spirit and power of nonviolent action to the point at which people everywhere

*Quoted in Edgar Snow, *The Other Side of the River: Red China Today* (New York: Random House, 1962), p. 686. Also see *Vietnam History; Documents and Opinions on a Major Crisis*, edited by Marvin E. Gettleman. (New York: Fawcett, 1965), p. 46.

will be able to see that it could successfully resist all foreign invasions and domestic tyranny.

Clearly the ambassador was not about to say that Vietnam should lay down its arms and begin to defend itself nonviolently. Nor did I suggest it. (Should I have?) But he was so pained by the losses of life both countries were suffering that he knew that there had to be a better way and somehow the world had to find it. That was what had led him to do some research on Gandhi. From this research, he felt that a start had been made, but that more had to be done to develop and demonstrate the method in a wide variety of situations. That conversation sent me home more determined than ever to experiment imaginatively in an effort to help expand and demonstrate the powers of nonviolent action, both as a method of liberation for oppressed people and as a method of defense against foreign military invasion.

When I think of how little I have done to contribute to the evolution of nonviolent force into a more contagious source of loving power, no wonder I winced when the ambassador spoke of my "heroic work."

43

During my 1966 visit to North Vietnam, I secured an agreement that the Vietnamese would welcome as many visitors from the U.S. peace and justice movement as they found they could handle, given the extremities of the wartime situation. They suggested two trips right away, so I organized a women's trip that consisted of Diane Nash Bevel, an outstanding Black member of SNCC, Barbara Deming, a leading participant in the antiwar and civil rights movements, Pat Griffith, a Far Eastern specialist with a conscience, and Grace Mora Newman, sister of one of the Fort Hood Three—three GI "asserters of conscience" who had publicly refused assignment to Vietnam and were doing long prison sentences. The three

GIs had come to see me when they first decided to refuse, and I had organized a press conference as the opening step in a campaign to publicize their decision and support them in it. A. J. Muste, Stokely Carmichael, the chairman of SNCC at the time, Lincoln Lynch, public relations director of CORE, and myself participated, along with the three GIs.

The second trip was by three clergymen, A. J. Muste, Rabbi Abraham Feinberg (of the August 6, 1965, action) and Anglican Bishop Ambrose Reeves. It took place in January 1967, and there is not much question that the strains involved in it had a lot to do with Muste's death on February 11, at the age of eighty-two.

For the rest of the war I kept organizing visits by a wide range of honest, nonsectarian persons, working of course in conjunction with other members of the movement, including people who had been on previous trips. The visitors included Susan Sontag, Mary McCarthy, Cora Weiss (of Women's Strike), Nick Egleson (chairman of SDS at the time), Jay Craven, Sid Peck, Linda Evans, Grace Paley, James Johnson (of the Fort Hood Three who by then had completed his three-year prison sentence), Telford Taylor (the U.S. prosecutor at the Nuremberg Trials) and many others. Given the U.S. preoccupation with Vietnamese war crimes trials, when Taylor returned from his visit, he was pressed by Dick Cavett on Cavett's popular TV show to say whether under the Nuremberg statutes Walt Rostow and McGeorge Bundy, my erstwhile friends from Yale, would be adjudged guilty of war crimes. His answer was, "Yes, of course."

I also arranged trips by a film team of John Douglas, Norman Fruchter and Robert Kramer of Newsreel, and a group of eleven students, selected by the National Student Association, who went in November 1970 to work out the terms of a People's Peace Treaty. The U.S.-supported Thieu-Ky regime in South Vietnam refused them entrance to that part of Vietnam, but in anticipation of this a member of the delegation had made an advance trip to Saigon and worked out basic terms with the South Vietnam National Student Union, which turned out to be similar to those later agreed to in Hanoi. The People's Peace Treaty contained the proposed principles for a satisfactory ending of the war and was a binational follow-up to our efforts at the Assembly of Unrepresented People in August 1965 to declare peace at the Capitol between the people of the United States and the people of Vietnam.

After Cora Weiss's trip, she, Barbara Webster and I worked together in arranging trips. But of course everyone who went encouraged, and in many cases helped organize, other trips. One thing that Cora, Barbara and I never did was say that no one should go to Vietnam except under our auspices. But when Eldridge Cleaver, aided by us, made a trip in the company of four others, he returned and announced that the Vietnamese had told him that from then on he was in charge of all contacts between the Vietnamese and the American antiwar and Black rights movements. No one was allowed to visit the Vietnamese unless Cleaver authorized it. Of course, he had made it all up. I knew this even before the Vietnamese told me so.

Like most of the visitors, Cora Weiss pressed for the rights of the POWs and secured an agreement that the Vietnamese would cooperate with a committee that she and I would organize. It became the Committee of Liaison with Families of Servicemen Detained in North Vietnam, with Cora and I as chairpersons and Barbara Webster as full-time coordinator. The Committee of Liaison provided a conduit for the first large-scale exchanges of letters between the POWs and their families and for getting the first extensive North Vietnamese responses to the families' inquiries about their MIA relatives. Both functions continued until the signing of the Peace Treaty on January 27, 1973, and the return of all the POWs. From my work in this area I do not believe that the Vietnamese held—or to this day continue to hold—any POWs. I consider most claims that they do to be another case of shameless, unnecessary cruelty against the families whose loved ones were missing in action. The purpose, of course, is not to hurt the families but (1) to justify the war retroactively (see how treacherous the Vietnamese are!); (2) justify the U.S. failure to "contribute to healing the wounds of war and to postwar reconstruction," as specifically promised in the January 1973 Paris Peace Agreement; and (3) justify the vindictive economic and financial embargo that, as I write, has been going on for nearly twenty years.

During my second trip, in May 1967, the Vietnamese and I worked out a plan for a meeting between American antiwar activists and representatives of both the NLF and the DRV (Democratic Republic of [North] Vietnam), to be held in Europe. In September 1967, it was held in Bratislava, Czechoslovakia. Wanting to have as broad an American delegation as possible, I asked Tom Hayden, who had valuable contacts that I didn't, to work in conjunction with his associates to select a number of the delegates, while I would work out the rest in close cooperation with the National Mobilization Committee and other channels. Tom agreed and it was his first significant move back into the antiwar movement.

Besides the vitality of the meetings at Bratislava, I particularly enjoyed it—and the travel to and from it—because Elizabeth (as Betty now called herself) and our eleven-year-old daughter, Michele, made the trip with me. Madame Nguyen Thi Binh, the NLF's foreign minister and later the chief representative of the NLF at the Paris Peace talks, cochaired the sessions with me and Nguyen Vinh Vy of North Vietnam, who soon afterwards played an important role at the Paris negotiations. But I especially remember the natural friendship that developed between Betty and Madame Binh and the special attention all the Vietnamese gave Michele. She was the same age as their "Peace Babies," as they called their children who were born in 1955 and 1956 after the end of the French war and the signing of the Geneva Accords had led them to believe that peace had finally come to them.

At Bratislava we raised the question of the prisoners again and the NLF showed interest in releasing some of theirs. A team of first-generation SDS leaders, Tom Hayden, Carol McEldowney, Vivian Rothstein and Norman Fruchter, traveled directly from Bratislava to North Vietnam. On their way home, Tom stopped in Phnom Penh, where the NLF delivered three of their prisoners into his custody for the journey to the States.

VI

Martin Luther King, Jr.

44

The worse the war got, the more I wondered when Martin Luther King, Jr., could be persuaded to take a clear stand against it. From time to time he referred to it negatively but said nothing that would bother the authorities or encourage anyone to take action against it. The level of his political approach can be seen in an announcement he made in August 1965. It came four days after our Assembly of Unrepresented People, while many of us were still in jail, and conveyed a completely different message to the public and government than we were attempting to communicate. Harry Boyte from King's staff had played a positive role at the Assembly, so when some of the people who had participated in it heard that King was going to hold a press conference on the war they hailed it as additional proof of the impact of the Assembly. "Finally," they said, "it has smoked him out to say something." But when they learned what he actually said, they were severely disappointed.

King's announcement was that he was planning to appeal directly to Ho Chi Minh, President Johnson and the Saigon government to halt the war, with similar appeals to the leaders of Communist China and Aleksei Kosygin in the Soviet Union. He sounded like the conservative "peace leaders" who had argued that SDS should have criticized Moscow, Peking and Hanoi as much as it had Washington. But, like them, he failed to criticize Washington equally with the Communists. As the *New York Times* reported:

> The Nobel Prize winner said that his letters to the leaders of governments embroiled in the Vietnamese conflict would "make

> it clear that President Johnson has demonstrated a greater desire to negotiate than the Hanoi and Peking governments."*

No wonder the *Times* headlined the story, DR. KING TO SEND APPEAL TO HANOI. But having made his public relations gesture, King never sent the letters to any of the governments.

If King was genuflecting to President Johnson and endorsing the line that the government was promoting in its effort to undermine the antiwar movement, a lot of other Black leaders were either more astute, more principled or both. The Assembly itself had grown out of a meeting of Black SNCC activists with Staughton Lynd, Eric Weinberger and myself. James Farmer and other leaders of CORE had already spoken up against the war, and the McComb chapter of SNCC issued an unequivocal statement in the summer of 1965 in response to the death in Vietnam of one of its members. He had been drafted as a direct result of his participation in local civil rights struggles. When his body came home the chapter distributed a leaflet that said, "Negro boys should not honor the draft here in Mississippi. Mothers should encourage their sons not to go." This was followed in January 1966 by a resolution of National SNCC that called for U.S withdrawal from Vietnam, and another in August 1966 that specifically criticized King, linking him with conservative Black leaders like Roy Wilkins in not showing enough concern for "the colored peoples of Vietnam." In the midst of King's apparent lack of concern, Black GIs were suffering a disproportionate percentage of the U.S. combat deaths, 23.5 percent in 1965, even though they constituted only 11 percent of the population.

When I returned from Vietnam in November 1966, the time was clearly overdue for King to add his voice to the antiwar effort, even if it meant breaking with his conservative backers. And who knows, maybe he would drag some of them along with him. So the Spring Mobilization Committee decided to make a special effort to convince him to take a stand. As a first step, I traveled to Chicago to invite James Bevel to move to New York and join our staff. He and I would work together to persuade King to march and speak at our major demonstration in April 1967.

Bevel was a brilliant organizer, if somewhat quirky. During the

**New York Times*, August 13, 1965.

massive demonstrations in Birmingham in April and May of 1963 he had initiated a "Fill the Jails" campaign and had organized the children to leave their schools to participate. When King objected to Bevel's appealing to children young enough to be in elementary school, Bevel's response had been that anyone old enough to join the church was old enough to join a march for freedom. Since the custom of the local churches was for children to join as soon as they entered grade school, this gave him a lot of leeway. The children responded in great numbers and soon people all over the country were learning that the city had jailed over a thousand children for demanding their elementary rights. There were heart-rending stories about how some of them had defied Bull Connor's fire hoses by "leaping high above the spurting water" (Barbara Deming in *Liberation*) or dancing on top of it until they got knocked to the pavement by its force. This and other Bevel initiatives played a major role in turning the situation around and, despite their initial conflict, King was sufficiently impressed to hire Bevel as an SCLC organizer. After a while, though, Bevel had found the organization's conservatism frustrating, so he took a leave of absence.

Bevel accepted our invitation and for the next few months he and I went through a complicated struggle with King and his staff. King was clearly tempted but his top staff was opposed to his taking a step that they thought could be used against him in the civil rights struggle. To them, not supporting the government in wartime either was unpatriotic or would seem so to the individuals, groups and foundations on whose largess they relied in order to maintain lifestyles to which neither the Mobe's activists nor the members of SNCC were accustomed.

Meanwhile, I had been experiencing the same problem—from the opposite direction—inside the Mobilization Committee. A number of our members and supporters objected to the emphasis we were placing on Black speakers and Black rights. They thought that combining the issues of war and race was alienating a lot of people who otherwise might be ready to line up on "the primary issue," the Vietnam War.*

*To make matters "worse," we always had at least one Puerto Rican speaker who advocated independence, an end to the United States's military occupation of that country, and no more bombing exercises on the Puerto Rican island of Vieques or

These objections came to a head about the time we decided to ask Bevel to join our staff. After a full discussion and a grace period to try to resolve the conflict, most of the worriers went along with the decision to continue the policy of making clear the interconnections between the country's treatment of Black people and its assaults on the Vietnamese. But the Mobilization's treasurer, Otto Nathan, resigned his post in protest. Nathan, a close friend of Albert Einstein and executor of his estate, supported civil rights personally (much as King opposed the war personally), but thought that having so many Black speakers and so much emphasis on Black rights was alienating a lot of potential opponents of the war. Despite our differences on this point, he and I remained close friends and when he played a key role in organizing and sustaining a weekly antiwar vigil in Times Square, I made a special point of joining it as often as I could, both because of its value and because of our friendship.

But now I'll provide some background on King as I knew him, since it provided the context for Bevel's and my efforts. Also I think it is important to get rid of the less-than-real-life images that have turned King into a plaster of paris saint. That image denies him his true human greatness and distorts his influence on today's struggles for justice and peace. As is evident from the examples I have already given, Martin Luther King, Jr., was not born fully grown out of the heart of Jesus (or Gandhi or Sojourner Truth), as the goddess Pallas Athena was supposedly born out of the head of Zeus. He was fallible like everyone else, and subject to the temptations and corruptions of fame. And like most people he had ambivalent feelings on a lot of matters; sometimes his actions moved in one direction and sometimes in the opposite direction. But no matter how many wrong turns he took and dead-end roads he tried, by the time of his death at age thirty-nine, less than a year after the 1967 Mobe demonstration, he had shown himself capable of far greater growth and development than most people achieve in a full lifetime.

For a long time, I knew King more from my close involvement with his associates and through the telephone than from face-to-face contacts. From the first days of the 1955–56 Montgomery Boycott on, A. J. Muste,

---

use of Puerto Rico as a launching pad for U.S. military assaults on countries such as Cuba (in 1961) and the Dominican Republic (in 1965).

Bayard Rustin, Roy Finch, Ralph DiGia, Charlie Walker and I used to analyze the latest developments at our weekly *Liberation* meeting; A.J, Bayard and I did the same between meetings. We communicated our thoughts, questions and recommendations to King, either by telephone or through Rustin. Bayard spent considerable time in Montgomery during the early days and kept in constant touch with us by phone. Sometimes we called King and sometimes he called us, or more likely we called Bayard or Bayard called us and put King on. For A.J. and me, this continued until Muste's death in February 1967, and for me, until shortly before King's death. As to the merits, or possible lack of them, of our constant advice, the late Myles Horton of the Highlander Folk School told me in 1985, when he and I were in Nicaragua together with Witness for Peace, that King had said to him more than once that he "always loved to hear from Muste and Dellinger but usually took our recommendations with a grain of salt, despite our experience and insights in activities that he was new to." I am sure that this was true, and deservedly so, both because everyone has to follow one's own judgment and pace, and because both A.J. and I were white Northerners. But King encouraged the relationship by giving us his articles to be printed in *Liberation*, beginning with his first article on the Montgomery Boycott ("Our Struggle," April 1956), by having me write one article for him and by asking me to go to Bimini with him to write his first book.

Throughout this period, I was impressed with King's deeply spiritual commitment to nonviolence and by his eloquence. But I was much more impressed and inspired by the young Blacks in SNCC and by many in CORE than I was by the politically naive and somewhat lordly Martin Luther King, Jr.—"De Lawd," SNCC and most of the other activists called him, and justifiably so. Julian Bond, a balanced observer, told *Newsweek* in July of 1963 that Martin "sold the concept that one man will come to your town and save you." And E. D. Nixon, who with some difficulty had recruited King for the 1955–56 bus boycott, complained before the boycott was over that King treated him "as a child." But a lot of the fault lay in what the establishment media did to King during that struggle. His eloquent, deeply moving sermons on nonviolence played an important role in it, as did his ability to communicate with a politically important stratum of cautious Black clergymen and with the national media. But others had been the initiators and were far steadier organizers and better tacticians. No matter, the media hailed him as the originator, guiding light and dominating genius of an enterprise to which he made important contributions, but which he had originally resisted taking part in—and from which, to the dismay of many of his associates, he took untimely absences.

Here is a somewhat humorous account of King's original resistance to playing a role in the Montgomery Boycott and the circumstances under which he changed his mind, as I heard it from E. D. Nixon. E.D. was the person who bailed Rosa Parks out of jail and the first one to call for a boycott of the buses in response to her arrest. He was a sleeping car porter who traveled widely in his job, which was how I had gotten to know him and why I heard this story during the first few days of the boycott, before most of the country knew that there was a boycott. Nixon had a long history of leadership in the Black community of Montgomery, brought an important perspective to the activity and helped rally support for it within the city and on the road.

Nixon and a few others thought that getting King committed to the boycott was key, and that if he were designated president of the Montgomery Improvement Association, the boycott's sponsor, he would be a spokesperson to whom the media would pay attention and who could communicate with it in a way that others could not. King came from a distinguished, high-society Atlanta family, had graduate degrees from Northern colleges and was unusually eloquent. But he was skeptical and refused, saying that he was new in town, had a new baby and was preoccupied with problems within his church. Nixon refused to take no for an answer and told King that he was going to nominate him at the forthcoming organizing meeting to be president of the effort. King's response was that he wouldn't be able to come to the meeting because it was on a Sunday afternoon and he had to spend the afternoon visiting his parishioners. At this, E.D. said, "Well, you had better be there, Martin, because we've announced that it will be in your church." Whereupon King changed his plans, attended and was overwhelmingly pressed into accepting the post.

Nixon was right about King's background and charisma being attractive to the media, and after the boycott's success King was hailed by the media as the unparalleled leader of the exciting new Negro movement. Like anyone who would have been so designated, and more so than some, he had trouble handling the burdens automatically imposed on him by such a pretentious assessment. Besides the sycophancy it aroused in some quarters and the jealousy in others, he was deluged by partisan advocates of causes and tactics that they hoped to advance through his endorsement or participation. In that sense, in 1966 and 1967 Bevel and I were part of the throng, as I had been from the beginning.

After the success of the boycott, our little group of *Liberation* advisers was upset that King became obsessed with a top-down approach to social change. We said to ourselves that it stemmed in part from the fact that it's a national disease in our so-called democracy, and in part from the giddy position of national leadership to which he had been artificially elevated. But clearly his ambitions were focused more on being a spell-binding preacher and lecturer than on being a grass-roots activist. Although the Montgomery boycott had been a grass-roots triumph, for years afterward he had no feel for grass-roots activism. He strove instead to win the confidence and support of the White House and other elitist "decision-makers," working overtime for audiences with presidents Eisenhower, Kennedy and Johnson and vice presidents Nixon and Humphrey.

In one incident King had been working for months to arrange an appointment with Kennedy during the 1960 presidential campaign. Meanwhile students in Atlanta were planning a sit-in at Rich's, a fashionable department store, and were pressing King to join them, correctly assuming that his presence would be inspirational and that it would guarantee widespread publicity. King wasn't interested and went out of his way to try to set up the Kennedy appointment for the day of the sit-in so that he would have an excuse not to take part. But Kennedy failed to cooperate, deciding that meeting with King would hurt him in the election more than it would help. Rebuffed, Martin surprised the students by joining the sit-in at the last possible minute and was the first to be arrested. Once he became emotionally involved, he followed the Gandhian principle of refusing to pay bond while awaiting trial. As a result, he spent eight dangerous days and nights in jail—the first time he had ever spent any time there. Five years earlier, during the Montgomery boycott, he had been arrested and held briefly on a fake traffic violation; and far more seriously, his home had been bombed.

One other incident that happened around that time is not as well known as it should be since it shows the growing pains that King, like every human being, had to go through on his way to his later development. Despite his general tactical political commitment to nonviolence, he kept a gun in his home and office during the boycott and for some time afterward as a potential means of protecting himself and his family. But he renounced this method of defense after an incident that was described to me by one of the persons who had been present. At a strategy meeting in a house that was guarded by several people with guns, they noticed someone walking through the shrubbery outside one of the windows. Two of the guards pointed their rifles at the shadowy figure, ready to fire. Just in time he stepped out of the shrubbery and they saw that it was a Western Union delivery boy. It turned out that he had a telegram for King. King witnessed the incident, was shaken by it and said that he would never use or countenance such a dangerous method of defense again.

In 1963, after the climactic and mostly successful Birmingham struggles of April and May, King accepted a proposal from SNCC and CORE to "bring the methods of the South to Washington" in August. The plan was for massive civil resistance, with lie-downs on the runways of the National Airport, sit-ins at Congress, mass actions outside the White House and other nonviolent actions that would bring Washington to a standstill similar to the one in Birmingham. But on June 22 King got a long-sought White House meeting—in fact, five of them on one day.

First he met privately with Burke Marshall, head of the civil rights division of the Justice Department, later with Bobby Kennedy and then President Kennedy. Next he attended a larger meeting between the president and a group of civil rights leaders and finally, the president took him for a private walk in the Rose Garden. A few hours after these meetings, Bayard Rustin, who was back in close contact with King (but mostly on the sly, because of Congressman Powell's intervention), told me that Kennedy had said in the larger meeting that if the plan for August was adhered to, he would see to it that cars and buses bringing the troublemakers to Washington would be stopped before they got there and their occupants arrested. On the other hand, he had told the assembled leaders that he favored passage of a civil rights bill and would find substantial sums of money for the use of "responsible civil rights leaders who lobbied for it in a proper way." Bayard said that King told him he had been won over in the Rose Garden to Kennedy's "seriousness of intent."*

King accepted Kennedy's offer of money for SCLC, and so did a number of mainstream civil rights leaders, including Roy Wilkins for the NAACP and Whitney Young for the National Urban League. The money, it turned out, came from the Taconic Foundation, a CIA front.

King followed up by showing how responsible he could be. First, he fired Jack O'Dell, as Marshal and the Kennedys had insisted he must because of their claim that O'Dell was "a Communist." Then, siding with Wilkins and Young who had never been part of the original plan for the August events and had virtually no influence on most grass-roots activists, he used his prestige to put an end to the idea of bringing the civil-resistance methods of the South to the seat of the federal government. On King's insistence, the original program was replaced by a strictly legal march and rally, which became the massive August 1963 Civil Rights demonstration. Even within it, Kennedy ordered that the buses carrying demonstrators must not come into Washington until the day of the march

*Unaccountably, Taylor Branch, in his *Parting of the Waters* (New York: Simon and Schuster, 1988), does not mention either the bribe or any other pressures to change the nature of the demonstration. He makes it sound as if the only discussions were about the problems involved in holding an already planned legal march and rally, and efforts to get King to fire Jack O'Dell and dissociate himself from Stanley Levison, because of their alleged Communism.

Even Arthur Schlesinger, a close adviser of Kennedy, says in his book *A Thousand Days* (New York: Fawcett, 1965) that "The conference with the president did persuade the civil-rights leaders that they should not lay siege to Capitol Hill." And Malcolm X said that prior to the meeting, "The Negroes . . . were going to march on Washington, march on the Senate, march on the White House, march on the Congress, and tie it up, bring it to a halt, not let the government proceed. They even said they were going out to the airport and lay down on the runway and not let any airplanes land." Both Schlesinger and Malcolm are quoted in Howard Zinn's *A People's History of the United States* (New York: Harper & Row, 1980), pp. 448–51. I mention these independent verifications of what I knew at the time because for years there has been a strange conspiracy of silence on the subject, allowing the true facts to disappear down Orwell's Memory Hole of History. That's what happens when we turn wonderful but fallible human beings like King into sacred demigods.

and must leave the city by sundown—and King (and Rustin) accepted this prohibition.

Earlier, when it looked like King was going to go along with the plans to turn Washington into another Birmingham, Bayard had seemed like his old self for a while, but now he reverted to his newer persona and said that he agreed with the changes.

45

The day before the famous August 28, 1963, march and rally, I attended a Washington meeting of the national leadership of the event. King was not there but was represented by Walter Fauntroy. Apart from John Lewis and Jim Forman of SNCC the meeting was packed with pro-Kennedy, tactically conservative liberals, both Black and white. Bayard Rustin had said that I could sit in if I promised not to speak; besides feeling that I had to live up to my pledge, I knew that if I tried to speak Roy Wilkins would silence me as out of order. After a while, I got fed up with what was going on and my inability to do anything about it, so I left.

The meeting was in the Hilton Hotel, and the first thing I saw when I left the room was Malcolm X in the lobby spellbinding a rapidly growing group, mostly SNCC people and other activists. He was describing the "betrayal" of the movement's natural militancy that King, Wilkins, Whitney Young and others had engineered. Besides condemning the abandonment of the plans for sit-ins, lie-downs, etc., he talked about the pressures on John Lewis to alter the text of a speech that Lewis had planned to deliver at the rally. And it was true. Bayard Rustin, citing Martin, whom he said he had been in touch with by phone, and working closely with Kennedy officials and conservative Black leaders, had been leading a fight that eventually forced Lewis to remove or rewrite portions of his speech that were critical of Kennedy and the Kennedy administration. The final excisions and revisions did not take place until the next day's rally had actually begun, and that time King definitely played a vigorous role in bringing them about. Those passages would have spoken "truth to power"—and to the public—in a more directly political way than King's closing dream did. The country had a right and need to hear *both* what King said and what Lewis would have said. It was critical that both the dream and the nightmare be spelled out that day, since the nightmare of high-level political opportunism was a major factor in denying the fulfillment of the dream. To this day, there is a reason why King's dream is featured at pious conventional tributes to Martin Luther King, Jr., while his more pungent speeches and writings that include *both* the dream *and* the nightmare are usually overlooked. I think of the "Letter from Birmingham Jail," which predated his fateful meeting with Kennedy, the address at Riverside Church in April 1967 and some passages from the last months of his life.

Here are some parts of Lewis's original speech that were deleted (or modified).

> We cannot support the administration's civil rights bill, for it is too little and too late. There's not one thing in the bill that will protect our people from police brutality. We favorably call attention to the Kastenmeier Bill—H.R. 7702 instead.
>
> In Albany, Georgia, nine of our leaders have been indicted not by Dixiecrats but by the Federal Government for peaceful protest. But what did the Federal Government do, when Albany's Deputy Sheriff beat Attorney C. B. King and left him half dead? . . . [Or] when local police officials kicked and assaulted the pregnant wife of Slater King, and she lost her baby?
>
> Moreover, we have learned . . . that within the past ten days a spokesman for the administration appeared in secret session before the committee that's writing the civil rights bill and opposed . . . a provision that would have guaranteed, in voting suits for the first time, fair federal district judges.

> . . . This Administration's bill . . . will be totally worthless when administered by racist judges, many of whom have been consistently appointed by President Kennedy.
>
> We will march through the South, through the heart of Dixie, the way Sherman did. We will pursue our own "scorched earth" policy and burn Jim Crow to the ground—nonviolently. . . . We will take matters into our own hands and create a source of power outside any national structure that could and would assure us a victory.
>
> . . . The revolution is at hand and . . . the nonviolent revolution is saying, "we will not wait for the courts. . . . We will not wait for the President, the Justice Department, nor Congress, but we will take matters into our own hands and create a source of power outside [these agencies], for both the Democrats and the Republicans have betrayed the basic principles of the Declaration of Independence.

The censored Albany indictments had come less than three weeks before the August 28 events, during the period when King was working closely with the Kennedy operatives. Moreover, Robert Kennedy had gone out of his way to announce the indictments himself and to say that he would send a special assistant to Albany to help the prosecution. This was the same Bobby Kennedy who, as I had learned earlier from Jim Farmer and other members of CORE and SNCC, had made an invidious offer to those organizations: "If you'll cut out the Freedom Rides and sitting-in stuff, I'll get you a tax exemption."

A few months later, C. B. King served as our attorney when I and other interracial marchers were assaulted and jailed for entering the "whites only" section of town with signs calling for an end to racial persecution. And during my trips to Albany I grew to love and admire all three of the Kings (C.B., Slater and Slater's wife, Marion), as well as some of the others who had been indicted. Also, I heard a lot of complaints in Albany about Martin's having allowed himself to be released from jail in 1962 while those who had been arrested with him were not, and about his having followed this by urging compliance with a repressive court order that the local leaders thought should be resisted. It was a complicated story, and I didn't necessarily agree with all the criticism, particularly since Martin had come back and been rearrested after the court order had been overturned. But Lewis's proposed text had criticized only the Federal government, not Martin, and it was especially ironic for Martin to insist on deleting Lewis's particularly relevant remarks about a city whose Black population already had serious reservations about King's style of operating.

The next day's event, with its massive and diversified turnout and King's captivating but limited "I have a dream" climax had a powerful effect on the participants and the country. In retrospect, I cannot assert dogmatically that the original plan of sustained, large-scale nonviolent civil disobedience would have accomplished more in the long run, though I think it might have. From my own trips to the South, I had agreed with the reason given by John Lewis, Jim Forman, Bob Moses, Jim Farmer and dozens of others for the original tactic. It had become a cliché among just about everyone who worked for long in the South that "the federal government is the enemy." Despite occasional face-saving gestures, *always in response to immense pressures created by direct-action methods*, the Kennedy administration worked hand in hand with the White Citizens Councils, the Bull Connors and Laurie Pritchetts (repressive police chiefs), the Southern sheriffs and, of course, the pro-segregationist Democratic Senators and Congressmen. King himself had said earlier that the FBI were "influenced by the mores of the [white] community . . . friendly with the local police and people who are promoting segregation. Every time I saw FBI men in Albany, they were with the local police force." So most of the activists in the South had decided that the time had come when the tactics that had proved useful there must be used against the federal government in its own bailiwick.

As additional evidence of why Lewis's full speech would have added to the significance of the occasion, despite the magical aspects of the last part of what King said, let me offer this account of the scene when Martin spoke.

I was sitting on the platform with I. F. Stone, a few feet from King. After about five minutes of Martin's speech, "Izzie" said to me, "This is boring, Dave, let's go to the press tent and see what's happening there." I agreed with him that the speech was pedestrian and labored, a severe disappointment after the magnificent "Letter from Birmingham Jail." But

I refused to leave because I had been close enough to the disputes over tactics and over Lewis's speech that I wanted to follow every word to know exactly what King said. I wanted to hear what, if anything, he would say about the Kennedy administration, about the offensive actions of the FBI in the South and about the importance of continuing the militant nonviolent resistance campaigns. (He said nothing about any of them.) And another of my concerns, shared by a lot of civil rights activists, had to do with Jim Farmer. Farmer, one of the scheduled speakers, had refused on principle to have a $500 bail paid for him so that he—and he alone of two hundred thirty-two people arrested together in Plaquemine, Louisiana—could be released from the jail and be on hand. King had said that Farmer should accept the bail offer but Jim had refused and was still in jail, and I wanted to know whether or not King would say anything about him. It would have been especially appropriate, not just because Farmer's stand was critical to movement solidarity but also because his life had been threatened in Plaquemine by an angry lynch mob that was working in collaboration with the local FBI and police—and he was still in danger. King didn't refer to any of this, but Floyd McKissick of CORE had read a moving letter from Farmer so perhaps that excuses him. But I think it would have been particularly relevant—and shown truer greatness—if he had done so.

My memory is that a lot of people besides Stone and me were bored—or at least not moved—by most of King's speech. Certainly the crowd was relatively restrained. But then he threw aside the prepared text from which he had been reading and launched into his inspirational dream melody, a theme he had used in a couple of previous speeches and now brought to rhythmic heights. He came alive for the first time and so did everyone else.

My analysis has always been that King was so uneasy over the deal he had made with Kennedy and the role he had played regarding Lewis's speech that his full heart was not in him when he prepared his own talk and during the time he spoke from it. But the underlying magnificence of the occasion, with over two hundred thousand Black and white people marching, singing and cheering, got to him and he became something closer to his better self.

After years of almost never hearing anyone else say this, I began to wonder a few years ago if my biases had clouded my judgment. But then

I spoke at a crowded Martin Luther King birthday event at which the full video of King's 1963 speech was shown. As I watched and listened, I felt the same way about the early parts of the speech as I had when I first heard it. And when I looked around the room, I saw that most of the audience was relatively inattentive, even restless, as they had been in 1963 at a similar stage of King's talk. But once again everything changed when King set aside his prepared text and launched into his moving presentation of "I have a dream. . . ."

II

The next political crisis in which King and I took different approaches came during the presidential election year of 1964. He displayed the same tendencies to "trust the system" and the liberals among its leadership, much as SANE and a lot of the heads of national antiwar organizations were doing. It began when King, along with Roy Wilkins, Whitney Young, A. Philip Randolph and Bayard Rustin (but with Lewis and Farmer dissenting), called for a six-month moratorium on demonstrations in order to avoid a supposed backlash that might prevent the election of Lyndon Johnson. The irony was that except for the ambivalent and erratic Martin Luther King, Jr., the others (including by now Rustin) almost never favored demonstrations.

Like many others, I believed that demonstrations empower the participants, educate the public and pressure the "lesser evil" candidate to act in a slightly less evil manner than he otherwise would. So I did not observe the moratorium and demonstrated with a few hundred others outside the 1964 Atlantic City Democratic convention. I spent my time alternating between an antiwar protest organized by CNVA and WRL and a civil rights demonstration jointly organized by SNCC and the Mississippi Freedom Democratic Party (MFDP), regretting that the two actions were not united. The antiwar demonstration was particularly important because in Vietnam Buddhist monks had been immolating themselves and thousands of people were demonstrating in the streets. The U.S.-supported government had opened fire, killing many, and the U.S. response was to issue the following statement:

> We are informed that the [South Vietnamese] government is in the process of working out the details of a political solution which will enable it to continue the major task of defeating Communist aggression and subversion.*

In 1967, King told me that the power of his emotional response to the Buddhist immolations had played a major role in getting him to realize that he had to come out against the Vietnam War. But ironically it took more than two years for this to happen, so committed was he to the importance of working through presidents and presidential candidates.

The SNCC-MFDP demonstration was demanding seating at the convention for a biracial delegation elected by the MFDP. Regular Democratic delegates from Mississippi had been elected at racially segregated, all-white conventions, but the MFDP delegates had been elected at conventions open to people of any race or color. At that demonstration, I marched side by side with Bob Moses of that year's Mississippi Summer Project, Rita Schwerner, widow of Mickey Schwerner who had been slain there, Fannie Lou Hamer, John Lewis, Jim Forman, Charlie Cobb and other SNCC and CORE friends. It was the first time I had met Fannie Lou Hamer and I was so impressed by her that from then on I always proposed her as a speaker at the major national antiwar rallies. She always proved to be an inspiring, immensely popular participant.*

New York Times, August 26, 1964.

*Twenty-three years later, I was not surprised to find Fannie Lou Hamer's daughter at an international protest I attended in Libya. It was on the first anniversary of the Reagan administration's bombing of that country, a bombing in which it made an unsuccessful attempt to assassinate Muammar Qaddafi. The attack did kill his small daughter and caused brain damage to one of his small sons. I had no love for Qaddafi but knew that the bombing raid was inexcusable. It was supposed to be based on U.S. opposition to terrorism—at a time when, aside from the terrorism of the bombing itself, the United States was arming, training and financing pro-U.S. terrorists in the Middle East itself as well as in Indochina and all over Central America. For information on the series of lies issued by the CIA in order to make Qaddafi look even worse than he is, see the Afterword to my *Vietnam Revisited*, "From the Villages of Vietnam . . . to the Shores of Tripoli" (Boston: South End Press, 1986).

Meanwhile, King (and Rustin) worked on both sides of the Mississippi question. King made an impressive appearance before the convention's credentials committee, arguing that "If you value your party, if you value your nation, if you value the democratic process, you must recognize the Freedom Party delegation." But when the committee proposed a "compromise" that would seat the Freedom Party Delegates as honored guests without a vote, King accepted it even though the MFDP rejected it. King also urged those of us who were picketing (and at one point holding a sitdown on the boardwalk) to discontinue our protest—which we refused to do. In fairness to King, the compromise also called for "a special committee to aid the state Democratic parties in fully meeting the responsibilities and assurances [exclusion of racial bias] required [for] . . . the 1968 Democratic National convention."

While the battle was being fought out at Atlantic City, King and Rustin worked closely with Hubert Humphrey to work out the compromise and to gain acceptance for it. Even the newspapers said that Humphrey was trying to negotiate a resolution of the problem that would prove to the Party heads that he would be a "responsible and trustworthy" vice presidential nominee and office holder. So I felt that King was working, at least in part, to gain the vice presidential nomination for someone he thought would be more useful to him in the future than Richard Nixon had proven to be when he was vice president.

46

When I invited Bevel in December 1966 to help persuade King to come out against the war, his response was that it would be a waste of time. King would never do it because J. Edgar Hoover had tape recordings of some of his extramarital trysts and had threatened to use them to destroy

King if he got too far out of line. Adding opposition to the war to his other activities would cause Hoover to carry out the threat.

I had known of the tapes for a long time but didn't think that they would necessarily serve as a permanent restraint on King, given his political conscience, the increasingly horrendous nature of the war and the mounting popular opposition. And there were pragmatic reasons as well. Malcolm X had been assassinated, but Stokely Carmichael and other Black Power advocates were challenging King's nonviolence while speaking out on Vietnam with a clarity that made King's silence all the more perplexing to many who had admired him, and whom he wanted to continue leading.

After Bevel and I discussed all these considerations, he agreed to move to New York and "see if we can get anywhere with that strange, tormented man." When I said, "But don't forget how deeply compassionate and moral he is at the core," Bevel said something like this, in his usual salty language:

> You think I don't know that? But the sonofabitch keeps playing those motherfucking games with the government, thinking he can get more done that way. You know what happened after Birmingham, when Kennedy talked him into changing the August '63 protest. But they don't give a shit about anything he believes in. They've always gotten more from him than he gets from them, and now they've got him by the balls with those fucking tapes. But, okay, let's go to work and see what we can do."

My knowledge of the tapes had come in December of 1964 when J. Edgar Hoover had publicly accused King of being "the most notorious liar in the country." King was incensed and made an appointment with Hoover to demand an apology. Our little band of *Liberation* "advisers" (which by then included Paul Goodman) knew how angered and upset King was by this personal attack and hoped it would lead him to begin to see the political realities through more accurate eyes, whether he got the apology or not. But he went into the meeting breathing fire and smoke and came out thoroughly cowed. Lamely, he told the waiting press that the discussion had been "amicable." The reason, as I learned that same day, was that Hoover had confronted him with the tapes and his readiness to use them against him.

Bevel and I opened negotiations by sending King a formal letter on the Spring Mobilization Committee letterhead, outlining our plans for the April 15, 1967, demonstration and inviting him to march and speak at it. Then we followed up with a series of exchanges with King and key members of his staff (Andrew Young, Bernard Lee, Bernard Lafayette, Hosea Williams and Ralph Abernathy). I also talked with Fred Shuttlesworth, hoping that he and Martin had gotten back on good terms again; but, wishing us luck, he said that they had not, and that any attempts by him to raise the issue would probably have a negative effect. Bevel talked with Harry Belafonte and I probed the matter with Bayard Rustin. I had come to feel that Bayard was telling King to stay clear of the issue, even though he kept saying the opposite to me and Muste. "I'm working on him," he would say. "Stay out of it and leave it to me." But I felt that if I pressed Bayard in a one-to-one situation he might level with me. And he did, saying that he thought that it was not yet a politically appropriate time for King to do this. "Hold off," he said, "and I'll let you know when it is." But for him, unlike King, the time never came. Myles Horton, who attended the first SCLC conference after Martin came out against the war, reports that "Bayard Rustin . . . came down to the SCLC convention and made a long speech trying to persuade the delegates to keep the peace movement and the civil rights movement separate."*

Sometime in January, I got word from Andy Young that King had accepted our invitation and would take part in the forthcoming demonstration, but that we should not announce it publicly. Everyone on the inner committee was thrilled. After a week or so of euphoria, though, we got our first shock. A formal letter came from Andy saying that "Dr. King" had looked over our list of sponsors (115 of them) and would be unable to participate unless we removed the name of Arnold Johnson, who was known to be a Communist. We held an emergency meeting and it began with a lot of those present taking the position that King's participation was too important for us to insist on keeping Johnson on the list. Who is more

*Myles Horton, with Judith Kohl and Herbert Kohl, *The Long Haul* (New York: Anchor-Doubleday, 1990).

important to us, they said, Arnold Johnson or Martin Luther King? As I remember it, Bevel was out of town drumming up enthusiasm for the event and did not respond to messages we left for him to call, so he played no role at that time. A. J. Muste was equivocal, reminding me briefly of the A.J. I had known and struggled with in the Forties and early Fifties. This time I think it was because he had not been involved in the negotiations and was recently back from an exhausting trip to Hanoi. He told me privately beforehand why he thought that "perhaps" we should yield, but I had a feeling that he didn't really want to and was turning to me to convince him otherwise. True or not, I told him why I thought we shouldn't, and he kept silent during the meeting until after the outcome was clear.

Based on my sense of the unfolding personal and political realities, I felt there was some chance that King would stay with us regardless of our decision. There was no way of knowing, but if he didn't and was that close to joining us he would come around next time. In any case, we had to adhere to our long-standing, principled and sound policy of non-exclusion rather than yield to a star, no matter how important the star was from a temporary public relations point of view. Fred Halstead of the (Trotskyist) Socialist Workers Party and I led the fight to turn down King's demand, and in the end, we arrived at a consensus for doing so. When Muste finally spoke up in support of the position Halstead and I had been advocating, the remaining holdouts said that they would go along with the decision, even though they thought it was a mistake. I notified King, and he accepted the decision without a word of complaint.

The next shock came when King told us that he had learned that Stokely Carmichael was to be one of the speakers on April 15; he said that he would have to withdraw unless we removed Stokely from the speakers' list. This time, Bevel was there, said that time was short and we must thrash the matter out with Martin right away. We initiated a conference call that turned out to include King, Young and Abernathy from the SCLC office, Harry Belafonte, Bevel and myself. Thank God—I mean Bevel—for including Belafonte. The call began badly. Bevel opened up with words that not surprisingly seemed clear and convincing to me, but Young and Abernathy responded negatively. When Bevel tried again, King spoke up with all the reasons why he would under no circumstances

At an anti-war rally in New York City in 1970. (Photo by Michael Abramson, Black Star)

Dave and Elizabeth Dellinger at home in 1970. (Photo by Franklyn Peterson, Black Star)

Dellinger faces the press in Chicago after he was convicted of contempt charges in the 1969–1970 trial. Also convicted were Jerry Rubin, *left,* defense lawyer William Kunstler, *second from right,* and Abbie Hoffman (not present). Acquitted were Rennie Davis, *left, behind Dellinger,* lawyer David Weinglass, *left behind Kunstler,* and Tom Hayden, *right.* John Froines, partially hidden to Dellinger's right, was acquitted earlier. (AP/Worldwide Photos)

With Vietnamese negotiators in Paris in 1972. With Dellinger are, *left to right*, Do Zuan Oanh, Mme. Nguyen Thi Binh (negotiator for the National Liberation Front), Le Duc Tho, and Nguyen Minh Vy.

Dellinger with Le Duc Tho during the Paris negotiations in 1972.

Dellinger with Daniel Ellsberg, getting ready to commit civil disobedience at the CIA in 1987.

Left to right: Abbie Hoffman, Paul Krassner, David Dellinger, and Bobby Seale commemorating the turbulent events of 1968 twenty years later near a statue at Chicago's Grant Park. (AP/Worldwide Photos)

Addressing a memorial rally after Abbie Hoffman's death in 1989.

Carrying crosses on Pentagon grounds in 1988 to protest U.S. Central American policy. *Left to right:* Daniel Ellsberg, Brian Willson, and David Dellinger. (AP/Worldwide)

Left to right: Ralph DiGia, David Dellinger, Art Emery, and Bill Southerland in 1990 at a Celebration of Conscience to mark the passage of the 1940 Draft Law half a century earlier.

speak from the same platform as Carmichael; I thought we were lost. Until then I had been relatively silent, being the only white person on the call. But now I took a deep breath and let loose with every argument I had, half expecting one of the others to say that I was in no position to understand all the considerations involved. Ironically it was Stokely, not Martin, who was calling whites "Honkies" those days, but there were other sensitivities involved. I had never heard anyone, white or Black, speak to De Lawd quite as I did then. But when I finished, Belafonte, who hadn't spoken before, broke in by saying, "He's absolutely right, Martin." Then he argued just as strongly as I had and, I am sure, more influentially. When he finished, King and the others raised a few final questions that Bevel and I dealt with—and then they yielded. We agreed that King would speak before Carmichael, and that there would be space on the program before Stokely spoke. I felt that this was not a principled matter and was something that we probably would have done on our own.

To get the full picture of the efforts King was making to advance beyond his previous position on the war and the difficulties that he, Bevel and I were wrestling with in our different situations, here are some of the events that provided the background to King's waverings and our frequent attempts to reassure him.

Several times during the period, King made stronger statements about the war than he had done previously, but then equivocated when the press questioned him about them. Then, about two weeks before the April 15 demonstration, he gave an interview to the *New York Times* in which he said that he did not favor civil disobedience against the war at this time but that if the United States kept "escalating" its activities, the time might come when that would become necessary. This was followed by a magnificent speech at New York's Riverside Church on April 4: he had decided that

> No one who cares [either for the poor, for the Black descendants of slaves or] for the integrity of life of America today can ignore the present war. . . . As I have walked among the desperate, rejected and angry young men I have told them that Molotov cocktails and rifles would not solve their problem. . . . Their questions

> hit home and I knew that I could never again raise my voice against the violence of the oppressed in the ghettos without having first spoken clearly to the greatest purveyor of violence in the world today—my own government.

I wasn't as encouraged by the speech as I probably should have been—probably because of my preoccupation with getting King to take part in a *public demonstration*, and my knowledge that he had always preferred to speak in a church (or lecture hall) rather than participate in an action. I was afraid that it might be his method of testing the waters, while providing himself with a *conscience-saving substitute for having to participate with us if the political heat got too great*. But the speech clearly came from his heart and had more significance than I realized. For years, it has been an enduring part of the country's heritage, whereas almost no one, including me, remembers much of what he said at the rally, though at the time we all thought it was great.

If my response to his interview and Riverside Church speech was somewhat ambivalent, the response from the NAACP was not. It appeared in front-page headlines in the *New York Times:*

N.A.A.C.P. DECRIES STAND
OF DR. KING ON VIETNAM
Calls it a "Serious Tactical Mistake" to
Merge Rights and Peace Drives
Fears Harm to Both Causes*

This came after a bitter condemnation by the Jewish War Veterans of America that was given a four-column headline in the *Times:* JEWISH VETERANS ATTACK DR. KING'S STAND ON WAR. They called it "pandering to Ho Chi Minh and an insult to the intelligence of all Americans." And these two attacks were followed by a statement by Ralph Bunche, the United Nations' Under Secretary for Political Affairs, who, like King, had won the Nobel Prize for Peace:

**New York Times*, April 11, 1967.

> In my opinion, Dr. King should positively and publicly give up one role or the other [civil rights leader or opponent of the war in Vietnam]. The two efforts have too little in common. . . . I am convinced he is making a very serious tactical error which will do much harm to the civil rights struggle.

And the day after that, the *Times* carried an analytical article in which the writer said:

> The outspoken stand of the Rev. Dr. Martin Luther King on the war in Vietnam has dampened his prospects for becoming the Negro leader who might be able to get the nation "moving again" on civil rights.
>
> He now seems further removed than at any point in his career from leaders of the political establishment, the Urban League and the National Association for the Advancement of Colored People and also from the mass of voters and he needs the support of all these groups to win new gains for the Negro. . . . But until a few weeks ago . . . he held exactly the same position as Dr. Bunche.*

Finally, the *New York Times* published an editorial that appeared on the stands the night before the demonstration condemning it as "romantic posturing and empty words" that will have neither "moral impact [nor] political effect."

In the midst of this barrage, a long-planned reception was held in

*Ironically, our rally was to take place at the United Nations Plaza and we had announced plans for a delegation from the demonstration to carry a message to Dr. Bunche, asking for U.N. assistance in halting the war. Obviously we planned for King to be a member of the delegation, and when the time came he was. At the last minute, so many people were begging to be included in the delegation that I let a young grass-roots woman activist from the Midwest take my place. I thought the experience would mean more to her than it would for me. So I missed observing what happened between King and Bunche, but reports were that both were gracious without getting into a serious dialogue on the issue that had divided them publicly.

New York to honor King and raise funds for the Southern Christian Leadership Conference. I was too busy to go, but while it was still taking place one of King's aides sought me out and informed me that King was reconsidering his participation. A group of trusted associates and important financial backers had told him that if he went through with the demonstration they would cancel their financial contributions to SCLC. I was told a number of names, but the ones I remember now are Stanley Levisohn and Harry Wachtel. Levisohn was a key financial supporter, both in his own right and through his many contacts. I knew that he opposed the war and had spoken out personally against it. So I speculated that although with part of him he must have wanted King to march and speak, after years of tactical Communist opportunism he may have thought it wise for King to hold back for now.* Or perhaps it was Bayard Rustin's attitude that he was expressing, because Bayard had a lot of influence with Levisohn and, as I had found out, definitely opposed King's participation "at this time." Wachtel, a prestigious New York lawyer whom I knew only slightly, had told King that he had a check in his pocket for twenty thousand dollars but would not be able to give it to him until he promised not to march on April 15. For an idea of Wachtel's importance to King and the dilemma his opposition put him in, Taylor Branch has written, in an earlier connection, that "Wachtel opened new and larger worlds . . . Wachtel knew how to get high government officials on the phone and how to touch corporate officers for five-figure donations. . . ."†

Later that same night, there was an emergency meeting between Andrew Young, Martin's trusted senior lieutenant, Jim Bevel and myself. Also present were Ivanhoe Donaldson and John Wilson (both of SNCC and the Mobe), Bob Greenblatt (one of the Mobe's cochairs) and Bernard

*As late as 1989, Stanley Levisohn's name came up when I was talking with a good friend who had left the Party years ago. While he was in the Party and ever since he left, he had done invaluable work for civil rights and many other good causes. I mentioned that my associations with Levisohn had led me to believe that the latter had been a member of the Party. "Well," my friend said, "I suppose he might have been, but it's hard to know." "Robert," his wife said, "you're talking to Dave. How can you say such a thing?" It turned out that Robert (not my friend's real name) and Levisohn had been members of the same Communist Party cell.
†*Parting the Waters*, p. 582.

Lafayette of King's staff. Wilson, Donaldson Greenblatt and Lafayette were extremely helpful, but there came a point when it seemed to me that it all came down to a no-holds-barred struggle between Young and myself, with King's participation hanging in the balance. I say this because Andy had indicated to us that King had "more personal things" on his mind that night and, concerned and confused by what had happened at the reception, had left the decision to him. At that point, I dispensed with the moral arguments, which were important to all of us but which we had already explored exhaustively. Instead, I laid out what I thought was the political reality; namely, that with or without King there were going to be several hundred thousand people marching and rallying. "We want him and we need him for maximum impact, I said, "but with or without him, it will be the largest antiwar demonstration yet. If King withdraws, he will suffer even more than the antiwar cause will. He is long overdue on this question and if he fails to act now history will pass him by and from now on his influence will be minimized."

Correctly or not, I felt that it was this argument that removed Young's last hesitations, and that King would stay in. This is not to say that the only reason King marched and spoke was to avoid disillusioning his grass-roots supporters and being bypassed by other leaders. Up to a point, those were important factors for anyone seeking social change, but for all the ambivalence on such matters, which had plagued him for years, I believe from my personal conversations with him in the ensuing days that he was relieved to do what he knew was morally right in terms of his own convictions and expanded goals.

47

It turned out that our problems were not over—let alone Martin's. Two days before our march and rally, a top official of the Intelligence Division of the New York Police Department came to my office and informed me that there was a contract on King's life. There was danger that he would be killed during our march or at our rally. He wouldn't give me any details but said that the information came from reliable sources and that they were taking it very seriously.* He also told me to keep it as confidential as possible, which rightly or wrongly I did. About the same time, an official visited Andrew Young in Atlanta and said much the same to him.

For all his earlier ambivalence, King insisted on marching and speaking, whatever the dangers. I think that this time the nature of the challenge made him all the more determined to do so. We decided that the nonviolent marshals, a few of whom usually walked several paces ahead of the front line of marchers, would hang back a little and provide a rudimentary, but not too conspicuous, shield. And we decided that King

*In 1979 the House Select Committee on Assassinations reported that in 1967 an informant had reported to the FBI that there was a $50,000 bounty for the death of King. Apparently the House Committee concluded that the plot was associated with organized crime figures, but that leaves out the question of who offered the bounty to them. One has only to remember that in the Sixties (and afterwards) the CIA offered similar bounties to the Mafia if they succeeded in assassinating Fidel Castro. In fact the House Committee was formed in 1975 in response to public concerns about possible governmental involvement in the political assassinations of the Sixties. Unfortunately, the documents from this inquiry have been sealed and have never been made available to the public.

should stay off the platform before and after he gave his talk. We placed the speaker's rostrum well back on the platform and while Martin was talking, several of us lined up next to it and at least a little forward from it most of the time, leaving less of a passageway than usual between him and the audience (and potential assassin). His reception was tumultuous, his words well received, and he left to be whisked away to safety.

The next day several stories in the press noted the short time King had spent on the platform and attributed it to his dissatisfaction with the radicalism of the organizers and some of the speakers. James Wechsler, former Communist, friend and biographer of Mrs. Roosevelt, and friendly to me on the few occasions that we had met, wrote in his column in the *New York Post* that one of King's objections was undoubtedly to one of my comments. Whether appropriately or not, I had said that if a person was raping someone, the solution was not to negotiate but to withdraw, and that is what the United States should do in respect to Vietnam, stop raping it and withdraw. Wechsler implied that this crude sexual analogy had offended King's sensibilities, a suggestion that those of us who knew King found amusing.

As Martin left the platform that day, he turned to me and said, "It was great, greater than the '63 civil rights rally; see you at Harry's [Belafonte's]." But I didn't go to Harry's. I had been absent from home too much, and thought it more important to take Elizabeth and our kids out to dinner and drive home with them. After dinner, I suggested to Betty that we stop by Harry's for a brief look-in, but she said that she and the kids were too tired. For once I did what was right from a family perspective and we went directly home.

Zaroulis and Sullivan write in *Who Spoke Up?* that "Dellinger remembers . . . 'Martin Luther King turned to me on the platform and said 'It's more [people] than the August '63 civil rights march.' " King and I both knew that it was more people, and he did say that at one point. And he complained to the press a day or two later about the police and media estimate of a hundred thousand participants, saying that "when there is an issue that the police or press are against, they play down the numbers involved. When it is an issue they favor, they add to the total number." Then he added that he had "more experience than the New York police," and declared that "there were fully three hundred thousand and perhaps four hundred thousand people in the demonstration." But the numbers wasn't what he emphasized to me when he was leaving. He compared the *political* relevance of the two events, and indicated that this event had gone further than the 1963 march and rally in the political and tactical directions that he now knew were right.

Less than a year later, King was dead from an assassin's bullet and the investigation was shabby, pinning it on a single racially prejudiced individual and ignoring, among other things, the statement by three people, including reporter Earl Caldwell, that they heard shots that came from the bushes across from the rooming house from which James Earl Ray supposedly fired the fatal shot.*

I had believed what the police official told me about the contract on Martin's life, both from the earnestness with which he spoke and because it made sense, given the directions in which King was moving at the time. But if he had become so dangerous to the existing racial, military, political and economic status quo by April 15, 1967, that some sinister forces within it, whoever they were, had issued a contract on his life, how much more dangerous he became between then and April 4, 1968.

My opinion is that taking part in that April 1967 demonstration was a psychological turning point for Martin Luther King, Jr. Despite the pressures, public attacks and message about the contract on his life, he had publicly solidified the break with his past. I believe that it freed him to do other things that he had been feeling for some time the call to do. He stopped speaking as if the sufferings of Blacks are an anomaly within a society that stands for human rights. He stopped trying to woo the White House and other establishment figures. He began organizing a Poor People's Campaign to take to Washington the "methods of the South" that he had forced out of the August 1963 events. He adopted the position that John Lewis had taken at that time:

*In 1991 Caldwell wrote in a column in the *New York Daily News* that he was present, heard the shots and told the FBI, but that they showed no interest and as far as he knows never investigated them. In 1988 a British filmmaker produced a film *Who Killed Martin Luther King*, funded by BBC Television, which raises questions about U.S. government complicity in the assassination. He and his associate John Sergeant provide a lot of evidence for government complicity while arguing the case in the Summer 1990 issue of *Covert Action*.

> We will not wait for the President, the Justice Department, or Congress, but we will take matters into our own hands and create a source of power outside [these agencies], for both the Democrats and the Republicans have betrayed the basic principles of the Declaration of Independence.*

From then on, he was working with Appalachian whites, Puerto Ricans, Mexican Americans, American Indians, inner-city residents of every color and ethnic group and whomever else he could among the supposed "least" of his brothers and sisters. He was killed while supporting the striking sanitation workers in Memphis.

Here are some statements that were made on different occasions during that last period of his life, observations that have mostly dropped down the Orwellian Memory Hole of History. They have done so because they are anathema to the corporate-owned media, to the political opportunists who run the country the way the military-corporate elite want it run and to those who think, as King himself once thought, that the best hope is to work through centralized mainstream leadership rather than through independent grass-roots campaigns of community-building and resistance.

> For years I labored with the idea of reforming the existing institutions . . . , a little change here, a little change there. Now I feel quite differently. I think you've got to have a reconstruction of the entire society, a revolution of values.

> The evils of capitalism are as real as the evils of militarism and evils of racism.

> We can't have a system where some people live in super-

*Ironically Lewis gradually departed from that position—at least partially—and adopted a politics that was much closer to Martin's 1963 position of looking for social change to come from the top down. Thus, early in the 1992 Democratic primaries, when most grass-roots and national activists were extremely negative about the presidential candidacy of Governor William Clinton, Lewis, now a Congressman, joined Andrew Young in endorsing him.

> fluous, inordinate wealth, while others live in abject, deadening poverty . . . from now on our movement must take on basic class issues between the privileged and the underprivileged.
>
> Negroes . . . must . . . fashion new tactics which do not depend on government good will. [We must] compel unwilling authorities to yield to the mandate of justice.
>
> Nonviolent protest must now mature to a new level . . . mass civil disobedience. . . . There must be more than a statement to the larger society, there must be a force that interrupts its functioning at some key point.

After King's death, the Poor People's Campaign and the planned Resurrection City in Washington that summer fizzled. I participated for a couple of days in Washington, but the plans had been whittled down in advance, the turnout was minimal, the leadership was in the hands of King's former staff and the spirit in which King had called for the venture was lacking. Most of the leaders slept in hotels while the rest of us slept in the tents, jerry-built, crowded shacks and mud of Resurrection City. Given the overall situation, a few of us who had hoped for more decided that to press for it would have been disruptive without accomplishing much. Accordingly, we confined ourselves to playing as positive a role as we could in workshops and interpersonal relationships.

None of this surprised me for a number of reasons. King's assassination was devastating for those who loved him and worked on a day-to-day basis with him, and they needed a longer period to adjust to the loss and to reestablish a sense of where they were going to try to go without him. Second, most of them had not grown politically and tactically in the direction he had grown and therefore lacked the conviction and imagination to act and lead as he would have acted and led. Finally, their need to rethink and readjust was accentuated and influenced by the nature of the relationship between King and most of his closest associates. He was the maximum leader on whom they depended more than was healthy for either him or them.

Of course, this type of relationship did not come about in a vacuum. It developed with an assist from the way the media, a lot of the country's political and religious leaders and many within the movement treated King from the Montgomery boycott on. I myself, I am ashamed to say, met him at the airport the day before our April 1967 event in a big, black chauffeur-driven limousine. That is what his office had told me to do. He and I sat alone in the back seat as we were driven to his hotel, while Young and his staff companions from the airplane took taxis, even though the limousine with its jumpseats and front seat could have accommodated several of them.

Today King is still exalted and sanctified in ways that are unfair to the King he eventually became, to the causes for which he sacrificed his life, to the beliefs that he came to hold about the nature of our society's military and economic wars and to the ways he was working and asking others to work when he was killed.

VII

From Protest to Resistance

48

Early in March 1967 a group of students at Cornell issued "A Call to Burn Draft Cards." It was to take place on the same day as our April 15 march and rally, but the call made no reference to the Mobe or the activities we had planned for that day. When they consulted with me, it was clear that the burning was to be a separate activity and I had no hesitations about endorsing it, both on principle and because I knew and admired several of the students, including Bruce Dancis (son of World War II objector Winston Dancis), Matty Goodman (Paul's son), Tom Bell and Burton Weiss. Besides my own acts of nonviolent civil disobedience, I had helped officiate at an earlier draft card burning at the Arlington Street church in Boston, where I had been surprised and pleased to have Patchen, our oldest son, come forward and hand me his card to hold until he lit it. Originally he had registered, after considerable soul-searching, in order to get into Harvard Medical School, but now both the extent of the war and its intensity had reached the point where he decided to burn his card, come what may.

Nobody suggested on that occasion that it was inappropriate for me as an officer of the Mobe to officiate. But this time the issue became embroiled in internal Mobe politics. In early April the Cornell students asked me if they could burn the cards as part of the Mobe demonstration. I explained that this would require approval by our steering committee, and that I doubted this was possible to get. Many of our constituent groups were horrified by draft card burning, time was short, things were hectic and the Mobe was having enough problems over what to do about King's various demands, everyone's requests for speakers and other issues without introducing such a controversial matter into our last-minute deliberations. Whenever there was a serious division, we always discussed the matter thoroughly at one meeting and then arranged for mediation, if necessary, in order to find a formula that could be accepted by everyone at a future meeting. This time there was neither time nor energy for it.

This approach had a history. When I was first asked to chair the meetings, I had said that if I were to do so, we would not operate under Robert's Rules of Order but as friendly colleagues who had no interest in using technicalities to outmaneuver those with whom we had tactical disagreements. I would welcome challenge whenever anyone felt that I was not handling the discussion and decision-making fairly. Everyone had agreed and that was how we operated. At a subsequent meeting, we split on an important question by a vote in the vicinity of 64 to 35 and—perhaps somewhat arbitrarily—I said that I would not allow an important decision to be made with so many people opposed. If the group did not agree, it would have to find a new chair. They declined, and we proceeded by my asking those who opposed the motion to say what changes they would want in it to make it acceptable, and asking those who favored the motion if they would accept the changes or had some other way of resolving the conflict. This procedure brought the two groups closer together, but in the end we had postponed the decision until after mediation.*

So by precedent as well as on principle, I was not about to ask the Mobe for a hurried last-minute endorsement of the draft card burning, whether a sizeable majority might vote for it or not. Instead, I proposed that they should burn their cards ahead of time, not far from where our march would take off a short while later. That way, those of us who supported them could be present without involving those who did not.

The students who had talked with me agreed to this, but as the number of potential card burners increased and the day for both activities drew near, others began lobbying to burn the cards on the platform of our rally. Unfortunately, they used the personal endorsements of the burning by Norma Becker and myself as an argument to support their

*Earlier, A. J. Muste had always played a creative role in mediating issues on which we were pretty much split down the middle, usually working with Norma Becker and myself. But so far as I can remember, this was the first time we had mediated a disagreement when the vote was nearly two to one.

plea. This upset some of the Mobe members, and at one of our last steering committee meetings before the demonstration, Sidney Peck, a stalwart organizer, speaker and idea person, surprised me by calling for my replacement as chair. He said that I had violated the trust of the members and brought scandal on the Mobe on the eve of one of its most important events. What would Martin Luther King, Jr., think of it? Perhaps he would even withdraw from the march and rally. I explained exactly what I had done and why, and that far from promising Mobe support, I had worked with Norma to organize a separate Support in Action group, independent of the Mobe, that would stand with the burners in a nonviolent circle of protection before our march. In the end, no one supported Sid's motion, not even representatives of groups far more cautious and conservative than Sid, and I think that Sid himself was satisfied when he learned all the facts. But meanwhile the discussion had made it clear that both Sid and I had judged correctly that there was a lot of opposition to direct involvement by the Mobe in draft card burning and in civil disobedience generally. Also—as we found out a day or two after our march and rally—Sid had gauged King's sentiments on draft card burning correctly. Martin spoke on CBS and said that the Spring Mobilization Committee to End the War in Vietnam could not "condone such actions." Unwisely, I think, he linked the burning of the draft cards with the burning of an American flag that someone had done later the same day in an isolated and completely separate incident.*

An estimated 175 persons burned their cards before the Mobe began its activities, some of them last-minute converts who were swept up in the dynamics of the occasion. Norma Becker and I did stand with them, along with a sizeable crowd of other supporters, and then I rushed over to where I was to meet King and start the march.

Despite this background, a lot of us were hopeful that after the success of the high-spirited April 15 events and the enthusiastic responses to its mostly militant rhetoric, the Mobe might be ready to endorse some form of civil disobedience that had an official connection with its next demonstration. Sit-ins, nonviolent blockages and other protests had been taking place increasingly on a local level all over the country, particularly

**New York Times*, April 19, 1967.

in the colleges but also at recruitment stations, draft-induction centers and places like Dow Chemical Corporation, a manufacturer of napalm. Moreover, there were signs that without such outlets the significance of mass demonstrations had begun to pale.

Originally, liberal organizations such as SANE, the American Friends Service Committee, Clergy and Laity Concerned about Vietnam and the Fellowship of Reconciliation had stayed aloof from the Mobe, because of our nonexclusion policy, radical criticisms of the government and unequivocal demands for bringing the troops home without delaying for lengthy negotiations. More and more of their members participated, but the leadership held back. However, as the war intensified and the number of demonstrators increased, some of the leaders began to adopt a more radical point of view. Others felt compelled to adjust and join the Mobe because so many of their members demanded it, and because that was the only way their organization could be part of a massive antiwar demonstration on a national level.

For a long time, the demonstrations played a crucial role, not just in showing the public, the traditional peace organizations, the government—and the Mobe—how widespread and serious the opposition was but also in giving heart to the demonstrators. Early in the Sixties, most "respectable" middle-class citizens thought that marching in the streets for any cause was "making a public spectacle of oneself," something they would never do. And to do so against one's own government in time of war made it even more unthinkable. Consequently, when they became so upset over the war that they finally set aside this conditioning and marched in their first demonstration, it frequently led to an unmistakable psychological breakthrough, one that I observed in a number of people whom I knew personally. And there was an additional factor: people who were under attack for their antiwar views—at work, in their neighborhood or hometown, often in their own families—tended to feel politically and personally isolated and sometimes wondered about the patriotism or general legitimacy of their views. But they could come to a national demonstration, march, sing, listen to persuasive speakers, interact with a diverse crowd of tens of thousands—later hundreds of thousands—and be reassured that they were not crazy after all. Participants were heckled, harassed and—mostly around the fringes of the activity—subject to physical attack by police, angry right-wingers or both. But the main effect of participating was energizing and empowering. They went back to their local communities ready to play a more confident and active role.

After a while, though, the demonstrations tended less and less to work that way. Periodic demonstrations began to take on a life of their own as the be-all and end-all of the movement. The line got blurred between participating to end the war and participating in order to enjoy the exhilarating experience of expressing one's antiwar views in solidarity with thousands of like-minded people. There were indications that some people were going to a demonstration much as some people go to a church, synagogue or meditation center. For them, the marches and rallies had become periodic self-satisfying rituals that weren't consistent enough in leading to follow-up activities elsewhere. Instead of helping people to gain new insights and the energy to go home and express them in new relationships and practices, they were becoming almost a substitute for doing so.

On the other end of the spectrum, some people were getting discouraged after a couple of years of demonstrations had shown no visible effect on the government. Ironically, these feelings came to a head around the time that the government had decided that it had to respond to the growing opposition by cutting the number of U.S. troops being sent to Vietnam and seriously considering some face-saving way to bring the war to an end. But the government consistently lied about this, and it was hard for people to know how effective their antiwar activities were. (It remained so until the Pentagon Papers were published in 1971.) Even then, as Nicholas von Hoffman wrote as late as 1973,

> [I]n the White House . . . they . . . continue to repeat that the movement had no effect on them, that while the peaceniks marched, they watched the Washington Redskins, but don't you believe it. They were peeking through the curtains.*

Under the circumstances, and with active egging on by governmental agents provocateurs, some people began "trashing" around the edges of the marches—breaking windows, overturning garbage cans, taunting the

*_Washington Post_, January 26, 1973.

police and so on. The first time I saw rocks thrown at a demonstration, they were handed out to the demonstrators by plainclothes members of the New York Police Department, some of whom a number of us recognized immediately. In my mind, succumbing to this temptation was a short-sighted form of self-indulgence that interfered with the purpose and spirit of the marches. Apparently it made the trashers feel good (for a while!) to vent their frustration and anger, but it focused attention on the rightness or wrongness of intentional, often indiscriminate, property destruction by opponents of the war rather than on the rightness or wrongness of the war itself. For a typical example, I think of the counterinauguration of 1969 when a demonstrator proudly showed me, afterwards, the huge plate-glass window of the National Geographic Society that he had smashed. There never was a time at the Mobe's demonstrations when the trashers made up as much as one percent of the participants, but the media and the pro-war forces—and therefore lots of the public—paid more attention to them than to the message intended by the other 99 percent.

So an additional reason for wanting nonviolent civil disobedience to be added to the plans for a *national* march and rally was to provide a more constructive way for such people to express their anger and determination to end the war. And for others who had not succumbed to trashing, taking part in a civil disobedience action could be a way of achieving another psychological breakthrough: if their first experience of marching in the streets had done something for them spiritually, for most people openly breaking even a minor law in a good cause, let alone their first arrest and first jail (or station house) experience, had even more profound effects.

I wanted the demonstrations to become more like some of the meetings I had attended in Black churches in the South. They had been marvelous examples of both individual and communal self-expression. The singing, praying, talking and enthusiastic shouts of "Amen," "Tell it Brother," "Teach Sister" were even more inspiring for me than our best antiwar rallies. But when the meetings climaxed, no one said, "That was wonderful, when do we do it again?" The words one heard were "*Let's go!*" and they opened the doors and marched into the streets to face the clubs, police dogs and jailings that stood between them and their goal of racial justice. And the impact of what they did was heightened by the nonviolent spirit and practice with which they did it. In my mind, we had reached—or should reach—the stage in which our antiwar marches and rallies should climax in similar fashion. And that was what I and others proposed.

Initially, a lot of voices were raised against advancing to that stage. To my surprise, both Women's Strike for Peace and Dr. Spock, the beloved baby doctor, argued that it wouldn't be fair to the women and children who came to such an event. We had no right, they said, to expose them to the violence that would inevitably ensue. As one who, I knew, had fallen into the trap of sexism even more times than I recognized, I thought that this reflected obvious, if also unrecognized, sexism—plus a touch of adultism as well—in two places where I would have least expected it. But we followed our usual procedures in a division of this kind and, step by step, reached a working consensus, first in a steering committee meeting and then in a larger meeting of about seven hundred people. By then, everyone understood that the civil disobedience action would be separated in space and time from the mass rally that preceded it. Dr. Spock then committed himself to participating in the civil disobedience and so did a number of members of Women's Strike, including Dagmar Wilson, one of its founders and best-known leaders.

All through these discussions the Socialist Workers Party opposed the addition of civil disobedience, whether separated from the first rally or not. As Fred Halstead, one of its leaders and an indefatigable and basically sensitive worker within the Mobe, wrote later, "We supported increasing the influence of the moderates in the general publicity and tone of the event because we agreed with them that this was the best approach to turn out the largest numbers."

But this time, they could see that the inclusion of the civil disobedience had become the will of the largest number of organizers and for their own reasons they tolerated it without being disruptive.

The plan finally agreed upon was for the day (October 21, 1967), to begin with a mass rally at the Lincoln Memorial. This would be followed, for those who wished to take part, by a march across the Potomac to the Pentagon. At the Pentagon there would be a brief rally to serve as a cut-off point for those who did not want to participate in the civil disobedience. Finally, there would be an attempted blockade of the Pentagon by those who wanted to join it. The slogan for this final action would be "Shut Down the Pentagon!"

The overall slogan for the demonstration was "From Protest to Resistance." Thinking about it now, I wonder if a better slogan might not have been "Both Protest *and* Resistance." But we were trying to emphasize moving forward to a new stage of more active, large-scale resistance. Also, we were formulating our answer to a much-trumpeted article by Bayard Rustin that the media and the liberals were using against us. It was entitled "From Protest to Politics," and advocated moving from mass marches and rallies into conventional politics—which was the opposite direction from the one we were proposing.

Much as I had recruited Bevel to play a key role in wooing Martin Luther King, Jr., for the April 15 demonstration, I recruited Jerry Rubin to join our staff and play a key role in organizing this event. Jerry had flair, had helped organize activities on the West Coast that moved from mass rallies to civil disobedience and had worked well with others at Berkeley's Vietnam Day and at the Assembly of Unrepresented People. But this time, it didn't work as well as recruiting Bevel had. After a short while, I kept getting complaints from other staff members that Jerry did no work and was no help. Surprised and puzzled, I investigated.

The problem was that something else had come along that was far more exciting to him, and that he thought would make a greater contribution to ending the war and to developing a new spirit in the country, particularly among the youth. He was captivated by the action that Abbie Hoffman, Jim Fourat and about a dozen other hippies had engaged in at the New York Stock Exchange in late August. They had gone to the third-floor gallery and thrown a large number of dollar bills onto the floor below. About a thousand dollars' worth, they said. Accurately or not (one could never tell with them), they reported that the stockbrokers had stopped their trading and fought among themselves for the bills. One way or another, that was the image that went out across the country, through the grapevine more than in the media. It proclaimed the ugliness of a society of greed in which the object of life is to get more money (and the things that money buys) than one's fellows. The *New York Times* said nothing about stockbrokers fighting each other for the bills, but reported that Fourat said, "It's the death of money," while a blond girl who accompanied him hummed a dirge and said, "This is a paradise earth. There's enough for all." A third said "We just want to make a loving gesture to these people."*

I don't know if Jerry, like the people who had stopped going to demonstrations, thought beforehand that he had grown tired of the same old routine, straight political actions, with or without civil disobedience. That didn't seem to be behind his decision to accept our invitation. But that's how he felt after he learned about the Wall Street action and followed up by getting to know Abbie Hoffman, Jim Fourat, Paul Krassner, Keith Lampe (Ponderosa Pine), Bob Fass and others of their group. Abbie and Paul were natural comics, but Jerry never was. Jerry was bright and quick, though, and often came up with odd twists and turns that made the group more effective in their chosen field of endeavor than they would have been without him. Perhaps he had moved across the country hoping that a change of scenery and associates would reinvigorate him. If so, it was another group of associates who did it for him, rather than those of us who had invited him.

So it wasn't that Jerry stopped working, but that he didn't do the work he had come to do. Instead of getting out mailings for the forthcoming Siege of the Pentagon, he was working with his new friends to plan and recruit for a Levitation of the Pentagon. A group of "Holy Men" (known to the government as crazy hippies) would encircle the Pentagon and conduct a ritual of drum beating, chants, incantations and incense that would raise it a hundred feet from the group and exorcise its evil spirits. They carried out their plan and from that time on Abbie Hoffman used to tell people that they had been "only partially successful. We raised it only ten feet." Too bad!

New York Times, August 25, 1967.

49

On October 20, 1967, the day before the rally, march and attempt to shut down the Pentagon, President Johnson called out the National Guard to deal with the emergency. It was the first time the troops had been called out to defend the government against us. So far as I knew, nothing like that had happened since 1932, when, as a seventeen-year-old, I had been shocked when Herbert Hoover called out troops headed by General MacArthur to defend Washington against impoverished World War I veterans who were demanding their long deferred bonus payments. I doubt if many others made that connection, but I did. After all, my antiwar convictions had been formulated around my memories and studies of World War I. Even so, little did I know that two years later (in November 1969) a new set of veterans, under the leadership of Vietnam Veterans Against the War (VVAW), would be marching in Washington, allied with us and calling for an end to the war. But the way we responded to the troops in 1967 played at least a small part in bringing about that alliance.

Getting agreement on how we would respond was not easy. The night before we were due to face the troops, we discussed it at an expanded Steering Committee meeting at the old Willard Hotel. A small but noisy and determined group offended me and many others by calling the soldiers "fascists" and "the enemies." (The unfortunate word "pig," which contradicts everything I and other nonviolent activists stand for, had not come into such persons' vocabulary yet.) They demanded that we treat the soldiers in accord with these descriptions of who they were. Undoubtedly, some speaking that way were short-sighted fed-up activists who were disgusted that the war kept getting more and more brutal, with more and more troops sent to Vietnam, more and more chemicals (including "new improved napalm") and heavier and heavier bombings. They were disillusioned by the government's apparent failure to pay any attention to our protests, and now were doubly offended by its bringing out the troops against us. So they wanted us to respond angrily against these visible agents of the government. When I (and of course others) disagreed, they responded by saying that we were trying to defend people who by our own principles should never have gone into the army in the first place, whether as volunteers or conscripts. In addition to these short-sighted and self-righteous members of the movement, at least two people who pushed this line were later publicly unveiled as paid operatives for the FBI—and I don't have much doubt that there were others too. "Divide and rule," was always the government's approach to the movement, and the best way to cut off any movement from its potential reservoir of emotionally stable supporters is to introduce violence into its ranks, not just physical violence but violence of spirit as well.

Because of the dispute and the constant late arrivals of new people from all over the country, we didn't arrive at any final agreement—and confirm it with the late arrivals, so that we felt confident that it would dominate the day's approach—until long after midnight. Then there were technical matters for some of us to go over and I didn't get to bed until four in the morning. The agreement was to add a "teach-in for the troops" during all the activities. We would address them as brothers who were being victimized by the war. Our slogans would be: "You are our brothers, join us" and "You are victims too, join us." And we would encourage everyone to reflect this understanding in their individual contacts with the GIs.

The rally took place at the Lincoln Memorial and everyone was thrilled by the spirit and numbers, well over two hundred thousand. Quite early, those of us on the platform were attacked, not by soldiers but by members of the American Nazi Party. Three of them broke through our nonviolent marshals and, from a couple of steps above the microphones, one of them jumped on top of me. Bill Coffin, whom I had been about to introduce as the next speaker, had to pull him off me. Bill embraced him in a bear hug and got him off the platform while I picked myself up and made the introduction. First, though, I tried in my usual (not always successful) manner to inject an element of humor into a tense situation by saying that someone had just handed me a Mobe check for me to sign for the sound system (true) and that was what the guy was after (false).

At some point in the program, I used my role as M.C. to thank everyone for coming, explained the plan for a teach-in to the troops, and told of the planned March to the Pentagon. I let them know that the police were insisting on a route that we thought would make it easier for them to prevent us from getting to the Pentagon and we had refused to accept it. This meant that we might have to sit down on the bridge when the first line reached Virginia. I said that anyone who wished to was welcome to join those of us who would be marching, but instead of urging people to do so, I encouraged them not to if it didn't seem right to them or if they had personal reasons for not doing so (family obligations, for example). Then I explained that if we got as far as the Pentagon, we were going to have a brief cut-off rally in the parking lot, so that all those who, for whatever reason, didn't want to participate in the planned civil disobedience on the Pentagon grounds could leave—or stay in the parking lot and observe as much as they could from there. (Later we found that having people watch such actions from nearby often led to their participating in the next civil disobedience—or even joining that one on the spot. And contrary to what might conventionally be expected, we found that, as happened that day, they were more apt to join if the police were brutal.)

Earlier, we had gone through many lengthy, difficult negotiations to get the permit for the rally at the Pentagon's parking lot. On October 6, the government had told us that unless we canceled the plan for civil disobedience there would be no permits at all, not even for the Lincoln Memorial. Our buses would not even be allowed to unload passengers in Washington. (Shades of Kennedy's threat before the August '63 civil rights events.) Finally we got permission for the Lincoln Memorial but not for the parking lot. But the power of our numbers (as demonstrated by our April rally and by actions all over the country), the support of people who defended our constitutional right to hold a public rally regardless of what some people might do afterwards and the government's embarrassment after we publicized their threats to bar the buses all worked in our favor. We finally got a permit for the parking lot as well.

First, though, the government's negotiators tried to persuade us to set up a purely formal and ritualistic form of civil disobedience in which "those who want to be arrested" would cross an agreed-on boundary line at the edge of the parking lot, sit down and submit to arrest or removal from the area. But we wanted something with more teeth in it, a clearer effort to shut down the Pentagon and a real confrontation rather than a legitimized one. So we refused to negotiate the manner of the civil disobedience and in the end (contrary to those who felt that the movement was powerless) we got the permit.

Because of the permits and the publicity about our difficulties getting them, more people came than otherwise would have. And although SDS had refused from the beginning to endorse the event, its executive secretary, Greg Calvert (who favored the action), had joined me, Barbara Deming, Arthur Kinoy—and usually Brad Lyttle, Norma Becker and Fred Halstead—in the negotiations with the government's General Services Administration. Greg's reports of our meetings put a little fire under a lot of SDS members and they came. I mention these factors because I think that without the expected numbers we would not have gotten either permit and certainly would not have reached the Pentagon.

We did have to sit down on the bridge before the police yielded on the route, and they probably did so only because so many tens of thousands marched that the whole bridge was occupied, all the way back into Washington. When we got to the Pentagon, we started the transition rally, but a group that included Norman Mailer and Walter Teague (the perennial carrier of the Vietcong flag) rushed ahead and stormed the nearest entrance. My heart sank, but I continued explaining our nonviolent plan. We had set up a number of group leaders, with bullhorns, and everyone who wished to participate should join one of them and set out to try to block a designated entrance to the Pentagon.

The group I was leading—with Maris Cakars of the New York Workshop on Nonviolence, Dr. Spock and Monsignor Charles O. Rice of Pittsburgh—was approaching its assigned entrance when the door opened and a contingent of troops marched out and took a position barring the way. We hailed them through the bullhorns and spoke friendly words to them in accord with our slogans. When the commanding officer had enough of this, he gave them an order to attack us, we sat down and kept talking to them. As they got closer, everyone went prone, in the old SNCC defense tactic, with hands or bodies protecting their heads and genitals. But Spock, Father Rice, Maris Cakars and I, who were sharing the bullhorn, merely dropped to our knees and kept talking. I don't know how to explain what happened next. I had never before been hit and kicked by so many people so many times, but only by symbolic blows that I am tempted to call "love taps." I don't know whether this was the commanding officer's plan for reminding us what the troops could and would do if we did not leave, or a spontaneous response by the GIs to the way we had talked to them when they first appeared and after they got the order.

In any case, this peaceful encounter was soon replaced by something very different. A swarm of government marshals rushed us from the opposite direction, flailing and beating us with clubs. Then they escorted us (or carried those like me who would not walk) to dormitories inside the Pentagon that had been set up as holding centers until we could be taken to jail. I shall never forget being carried off by two or three marshals and suddenly realizing that Ben Spock was running beside me, practically crying, and saying, "Dave, they won't arrest me, Dave, Dave, they won't arrest me." Apparently he was too popular a figure to be included in the list of disreputable people who would appear in the next day's news accounts. It didn't last beyond that day, though, because a few weeks later he committed civil disobedience at the Whitehall recruiting station in New York and was arrested like everyone else. From then on he was almost as disreputable as the rest of us.

In the end, well over a thousand were arrested, with 780 of us held and several hundred released. Perhaps double that number were beaten or gassed. Meanwhile, the largest single group, most of whom had not planned to commit civil disobedience, were engaged in a confrontation with the troops who were lined up at the top of steps that led to the main entrance of the Pentagon. That encounter lasted thirty-three hours, all through the first night, the next day and until after midnight of the second night. At the beginning, some of the angry demonstrators (and agents provocateurs) threw things from the rear of the protesting group (and over their heads) toward the soldiers, but eventually Greg Calvert and others prevailed on them to stop. Then someone (Super Joel I believe, who was fresh from the levitation of the Pentagon) performed an inspired act that was "heard" around the world. He stepped forward and placed a flower in the bayonetted gunbarrel of one of the soldiers. Soon others followed his example, and before long the demonstrators were sharing not only flowers but cigarettes, coffee and friendly words with the soldiers.

When I got out of jail, the Mobe held a press conference to give our version of what had happened. Earlier, two paratroopers had gone to our Washington office and reported that several of their number had left the line, in the confrontation at the main entrance, gone inside, thrown down their guns and declared that they would stand guard duty against the friendly demonstrators no longer. They were being held in the stockade. Now the paratroopers came to the press conference and told us (and the press) that, like themselves, a large number of their fellow GIs were "on your side." For years afterward, I kept meeting veterans who said they were on duty that day and had been affected by our friendly teach-in. And to this day, I keep meeting other veterans who didn't necessarily know of the teach-in but tell me that when they were on duty in Vietnam they were heartened by learning of this and other protests and the demands to bring the troops home.

50

Despite the support from the paratroopers, the symbolism of protestors placing flowers in soldiers' gun barrels and the successful linking of mass protest with massive nonviolent civil disobedience, not all the participants were encouraged by the results of our action. We had failed to shut down the Pentagon. Cathy Wilkerson of our Washington office was one of several I knew who were disappointed. She and I had long discussions before and after the press conference, but nothing I said—or that the paratroopers had said—would change her mind. From then on, she moved steadily in the direction that a number of key members of SDS moved, until in June 1969 they formed an underground group called the Weathermen.

I knew most of the original Weathermen well. They were fine, compassionate people, sincerely dedicated both to immediate steps to relieve the sufferings of the oppressed and to the long-range goal of creating a new society. They were working in their own way for a society that would eliminate domestic oppression and prejudice even as it renounced imperialist interventions such as the U.S. invasions of the Dominican Republic (1965) and Indochina. But from 1965 on, SDS was under constant sectarian attack by the Maoist Progressive Labor Federation (PL) first from the outside and later through infiltration as well. PL attacked them for their "middle-class, liberal, Social Democratic politics" even after SDS had clearly moved away from any illusions that some of its leaders originally held along these lines. This conflict, along with exclusion of SDS's largely white membership from SNCC (on the basis of "Black Power"), the rise of the Black Panther Party and its guns (but only for self-defense), the ghetto riots and their impatience with the apparent failure of nonviolent resistance to stop the war, led this group to adopt a Leninist, semi-Maoist, "vanguard" approach. Essentially it was a self-righteous sectarianism of their own, which they described as an advance from middle-class to working-class politics.* First they turned to baiting and fighting "the pigs" (police) and trashing, then to an underground espousal of more serious violence. This came to a temporary climax in the premature explosion on March 2, 1970, of one of their bombs in the Greenwich Village (NYC) townhouse of Cathy Wilkerson's parents. Cathy barely escaped death, along with Cathy Boudin, but my friends Terry Robbins and Diana Oughton (along with Ted Gold, whom I did not know) were killed. In an earlier account of that tragic event, I wrote:

> Terry Robbins, who had shyly kissed me on the cheek a few weeks earlier when our discussion of violence had come to an impasse, as if (it seemed to me at the time) to assure me that he was still

*Greg Calvert says, in *Democracy from the Heart*, "In reaction to the ghetto riots and the increasing menace from PL, activists in SDS began to adopt . . . that peculiar form of [Che] Guevarism which became the Weather Underground." He also reports that "Cathy Wilkerson experienced the Pentagon as a missed opportunity 'to fight,' which was thwarted because of the lack of leadership. My move to stop . . . a charge through the line of federal marshals was for her an example of a leader unwilling or afraid 'to fight.' " *Democracy From the Heart: Spiritual Values, Decentralism and Democratic Idealism in the Movement of the 1960s* (Eugene, Oreg.: Communitas Press, 1991). It is a superb book.

> a warm, loving human being, was so blown apart that he never could be identified. Only a message from his underground comrades named him as one of the victims. Shortly after the event, a private message from one of my underground Weathermen friends told me that Ted Gold . . . was only killed because he had been traumatized by a sudden realization of the horror they were preparing for their enemies and had come back to the house to try to persuade his associates to abandon the project.*

The message explained that they were making an antipersonnel bomb in the Town House, an imitation of the kind the United States was using in Vietnam. That was what had upset Gold. After that tragedy hit home, all the Weathermen whom I saw during a series of underground visits told me that they had fallen into what they called "the military trap." From then on their bombs were directed at symbolic structures, including the Capitol and various military or corporate installations, and they went to great lengths to be sure that no one was injured.

Meanwhile *Ramparts*, a West Coast magazine that earlier had made invaluable contributions to informing and enlightening people, had carried an article on the Pentagon action that called it a costly failure. Instead of bringing more than two hundred thousand people to Washington, we should have burned an automobile in each of the roadways used by people coming to work at the Pentagon. That would have shut it down more effectively. Sometimes I wonder if David Horowitz and Peter Collier, who became editors of *Ramparts* shortly afterward, fell temporarily into the ridiculous attitude expressed by that article. If so, that might help explain why they have been acting in recent years like reformed sinners, writing and lecturing on what they see as the crimes and failures of the Sixties movement.†

What saddened me was that *Ramparts*, along with Cathy and others, missed the humane spirit ("You are our brothers, join us") and new

**More Power Than We Know*, in which I write at greater length about the Weathermen.

†Earlier, David Horowitz had written an excellent book, *The Free World Colossus*, which made a first-rate survey and analysis of the imperialist background and activities of the United States. (New York: Hill and Wang, 1965.)

seriousness ("From Protest to Resistance") that was communicated by our activity and did more to restrict the Pentagon's future activities than if we had physically shut it down for a few hours without significant human participation. Dozens, maybe hundreds, were disappointed and discouraged, but for everyone who had that reaction there were thousands who were energized by having been there. And for everyone who dropped out of the active movement (or adopted what they called "stronger methods") at least a hundred new people were encouraged to join the movement. Even greater numbers of people who did not get personally involved began to conclude that the war was not worth the price it was costing in terms of domestic division and conflict.

I first found out the effect of the Pentagon activity on the government when I was invited to speak in Santa Barbara, California, at the Center for Democratic Studies (headed at the time by Robert Hutchins and W. H. Ferry). One of the people present was a recently retired general who had been inside the Pentagon during our action. After my presentation, he took me aside and told me that the military had been panicked by what had happened on that day and knew that the days that it could continue the war in Vietnam were numbered. When I asked him if he would make a public statement to that effect, he declined.

Some of the military may have been panicked, but this did not stop generals Wheeler and Westmoreland from making an urgent request (February 1968) for 206,000 additional U.S. troops—in order to reach the "light" that they always saw "at the end of the tunnel." For the first time in the history of such requests, and even after the fright created by the recent Vietnamese Tet Offensive, the government refused to send a single additional soldier.* A year later, the information and reasons came out in the *New York Times*:

> If tolerance of the war had worn thin, so had the nation's military resources, so thin indeed that there was almost nothing more to send to Vietnam without either mobilizing the reserves, enlarging

*Some would say this refusal was partly in response to the Tet Offensive. I agree insofar as Tet showed that the war would have to go longer than the public would stand for.

> draft calls, lengthening the twelve-month combat tour, or sending Vietnam veterans back for a second tour of duty, *all extremely unappealing*. [Emphasis added.]*

There was no shortage of *potential* military resources, but through actions like our "failed" October 21–22 event, and others that were stimulated or strengthened by it, "tolerance of the war had worn thin" and there was a shortage of *available* manpower, young men willing to be mobilized, drafted, subjected to lengthened combat or sent back for a second tour of duty.

The decision not to send the additional troops was followed in short order by Lyndon Johnson's poor showing in the New Hampshire primaries and announcement that he would not run in the 1968 election, and the government's decision to begin peace negotiations in Paris. It was followed as well by the defeat of Hubert Humphrey, because he wasn't principled enough to oppose the war, and the election of the unpopular Richard Nixon, because he was wily enough to announce that he had a plan for ending it.

When the secret Pentagon Papers were released by Daniel Ellsberg in 1971, one could read a half-dozen references to the restraining influence of the "massive march on the Pentagon" and the risk of "a domestic crisis of unprecedented proportions" for which there would not be "sufficient forces . . . available for civil disorder control."†

To add to this impressive list of accomplishments, the October 1967 nonviolent siege of the Pentagon played a major role in influencing Daniel Ellsberg to release these papers. Ellsberg told me this a few days after he did so. And in 1987 he testified to this in a trial of myself and twenty others (including Elizabeth) for having committed civil disobedience in the Capitol Rotunda against U.S. sponsorship of the terrorist Nicaraguan Contras. (Unfortunately, the judge heard the proffered testimony outside the presence of the jury and then refused to let Ellsworth testify in front

**New York Times*, March 6, 1969.

†See the *Pentagon Papers*, Senator Gravel, ed. (Boston: Beacon Press, 1971), vol. 4, pp. 197, 217, 478, 492, 541, 564. Or Noam Chomsky's *For Reasons of State* (New York: Vintage, 1973).

of the jury.) Ellsberg said that on October 21, 1967, he was in Robert McNamara's office, where the two of them were drafting plans for a U.S. invasion of North Vietnam. Hearing a commotion outside, he and McNamara went to the window and saw us being clubbed and carried off by the marshals. Ellsberg looked down on us and said to himself, "Those people are living by their consciences. They are putting their bodies where their hearts and minds are. What would happen if I did that?"*

Like a lot of people in the army and government, Ellsberg had come to know by then that the war was a lie, fought for reasons different than those told to the American people and by genocidal methods. But, like most of them, he wasn't expecting to endanger his career or get himself in "trouble" by doing anything about it. But step by step he began to act in accord with *his* conscience, finally reaching the point at which he released the papers. Releasing them had a profound effect on speeding up the inevitable—but perpetually postponed—ending of the war.

Besides these results of national significance, the Pentagon action had significant personal repercussions in my own life and for my family. During it, I marched from the Lincoln Memorial to the Pentagon with Rennie Davis and Tom Hayden, both of whom had stayed aloof from the antiwar movement for almost two years and were just beginning to come back in. They had helped produce SDS's line that contesting the war was a diversion from more fundamental attempts to change the society through ERAP and other long-range activities. From then until July 1967, when I asked Tom to play an important role in the Bratislava conference with the Vietnamese (and Tom in turn invited Rennie), whenever I visited

*Ellsberg has also spoken of the influence on him of Randolph Kehler, a Vietnam war resister who was on his way to prison for twenty-two months when Ellsberg met him at a War Resisters League conference. Kehler and his wife, Betsy Corner, are war tax refusers and in December 1991, the IRS seized their house for nonpayment of war taxes. The response of a significant number of his antiwar colleagues was to risk arrest by occupying the house, with a new group replacing a former group each week. As I write, I have occupied the house twice. Once was a brief stay with Brian Willson, the Vietnam Veteran who lost his legs when a train deliberately ran over him while he was sitting on the tracks protesting its cargo of war materials for El Salvador and the Nicaraguan Contras. The second time was for a week, with my wife, Elizabeth, and some of our colleagues from northern Vermont.

the Newark, New Jersey, ERAP project (NCUP), Tom always argued that we had no hope of stopping the present war and should concentrate all our efforts on projects like ERAP that would eventually make it possible for people to "stop the seventh war from now." But the plan to meet with the Vietnamese in Bratislava intrigued him, and his experiences there plus a follow-up trip to Vietnam had helped crystallize a new perspective (which was probably gestating inside him anyway). He and Rennie were barely back from Vietnam when they turned up at the Lincoln Memorial, and as we talked en route to the Pentagon, I welcomed them back into the activist antiwar movement and the three of us formed an alliance for planning and carrying out a major action at the Chicago Democratic Convention the following August. Both of them, in line with the concerns that had led them to participate in ERAP, were pleased that the plan would join the antiwar activities to a counterconvention that would analyze the nature of American society and propose alternative methods of handling the whole range of problems that beset it and led to war.

The connection of the Pentagon action with another event that had a powerful effect on my life and on my family is more conjectural. But a month or so after it, bombs started exploding in the sorting station for my mail and two months and ten days after October 21, 1967, one of them reached my home. To my mind, my active involvement at the Pentagon in the new stage of national antiwar protest, which so worried the government, had a lot to do with this.

51

A Snapshot

This is my address to the jury in February 1987, in the trial at which Daniel Ellsberg testified that observing our 1967 Siege of the Pentagon from McNamara's office window had been a major influence in his later decision to release the Pentagon Papers.

Good morning! The trial has been going on a long time and I regret the inconvenience it must have been in your lives. That is one reason that I decided not to take the stand and stretch it out even longer, especially since I wanted from the beginning to make a closing statement.

Every night I have reported on the phone to my wife, Elizabeth Peterson, who is ill and is being tried *in absentia*. I have reported to her what the testimony has been and who has been prevented from testifying [Ramsey Clark, Daniel Ellsberg and former CIA agent David MacMichael]. My statement today reflects her input and basically I speak for both of us.

The evidence has shown that we have tried to the best of our ability to tell you the truth, the whole truth and nothing but the truth, so help us God. But it has not been easy. In the Rotunda, we were denied our constitutional right to speak the truth. We were arrested, fingerprinted and put on trial for having tried to do so. All this even though Lieutenant Hill made it clear in his testimony that we were not blocking, impeding or threatening anyone. We were even denied part of our audience when the police closed the Rotunda [a public section of the Capitol building] and ushered out the tourists and the TV cameras through which we might have reached a nationwide audience. As you saw in the video, CBS News left in protest, knowing that the demonstration did not threaten security, as the prosecution has falsely claimed.

Other evidence has shown that those whom the government says we *might* have been blocking did not feel interfered with in any way. In fact, the evidence has shown that they clapped and cheered us. If we did not block or obstruct anyone, we are clearly not guilty of "blocking and impeding."

And if we did not block or impede anyone, then our demonstration was clearly legal and we are not guilty of that charge.

And if we did not block anyone and participated in a perfectly legal demonstration, then the order to close the Rotunda and the order for us to leave was illegal and we are not guilty of "unlawful entry." The government has not denied that we entered lawfully, but the government, in its twisted logic, accuses us of unlawful entry because we refused to obey an unlawful and unconstitutional order to leave.

The fact is that the government planned to arrest us no matter what we did, whether we stood, sat or lay down. The evidence shows that it planned to arrest us however we exercised our constitutional right to symbolic free speech in order to dramatize the torture, mutilation and murder of civilians at the hands of the Contras.

As you have seen, the same government that could not tolerate our speaking the truth in the Rotunda has not wanted us to tell you the whole truth in this trial. That is why they have objected to the testimony of a former attorney general, a former CIA agent and a former high official in the Vietnam War.

The testimony has shown that our demonstration was both religiously and politically motivated. That we acted in the tradition of the nonviolent civil rights movement and the movement to stop the Vietnam War, a war in which 58,000 GIs were killed and nearly 300,000 others wounded. Our banner showed that we linked the evils of racism and terrorist war by saying that aid to apartheid and aid to the Contras equal U.S.-sponsored terrorism. The testimony has shown that we were not only concerned over the innocent civilians being raped, tortured, mutilated and killed by the Contras, but also for the American GIs who are in danger of being sent to fight and die in Nicaragua.

The government has claimed that we are guilty because we acted in the Rotunda differently than ordinary tourists. We did indeed act differently than Joan Arnold [one of the defendants] did when, as she told you, she took her Girl Scout troop to the Rotunda. But the evidence has shown that we acted in accord with our constitutional rights in an emergency situation. We acted the way I hope I would act if I were walking down the street one night and saw that your house was on fire. I hope I would not act as an ordinary passer-by. But if I broke a window or a lock in order to save you and your children or parents, does anyone think I would be on trial for unlawful entry? If I were, I would expect the jury to find me not guilty. In the present case, we broke no windows, forced open no doors. And I expect you to find us not guilty.

> I say this not only because the facts are clear and justify, nay demand, such a verdict. I say it also because the strength of our country rests in the conscience of its people. If it did not, we would still have slavery; the government would still not permit Blacks or women of any color to vote. And our GIs would already be dying in Central America, as they died in Vietnam until the aroused conscience of the American people finally put an end to that slaughter.
>
> The defendants have testified that there are times when all citizens have a right—a duty even—to strike a blow for freedom. We have shown why this is such a time. The government is not the master; the people are. The government is not the master, not the president, not Lieutenant Hill, not the prosecutor, not the judge; the people are.
>
> Soon you will be the sole judge of the rightness or wrongness of what we did. Rather, your common sense and your consciences will be. I am glad that it is that way. And when you render your verdict and the case is finally put to rest and you can go home to your families and your normal lives, I think that you will be glad too, and proud of what you have done. You will be proud that you have followed your own consciences, rather than the dictates of any government.

We were found guilty, but three of the jurors told us later that the judge had left them no alternative by the way he phrased the guidelines for the verdict they must render. Basically, it was that if they thought we had done the things that both the government and we said that we had done, they must find us guilty. These three jurors told us that they would not sleep that night, and maybe for a lot of nights. That is how they felt about having finally agreed with the other jurors that, having been given these guidelines, they had no choice but to convict us, even though by their standards we were not guilty of any crime.

As I saw it, the judge, who had been accused of being a "liberal," tried to appease his critics by the way he excluded our witnesses and charged the jury. Then he tried to appease his conscience by the nature of the sentence he imposed. It was to perform one hundred hours of "community service." When he imposed that sentence on the others, I was in jail in Virginia for having committed civil obedience (community service) by blockading the CIA, so I was not on hand and was sentenced separately later. But he gave me the same sentence as the others. When I asked him what community service meant, he said, "Just keep on doing the things that you are doing every day anyway." Not surprisingly, I agreed to do so.

VIII

The Chicago Trial

52

Sometime around April 1, 1968, I received a phone call from Averell Harriman, who had just been appointed chief U.S. negotiator for the forthcoming Peace Talks with the Vietnamese. He said he wanted to consult with me about them and we made an appointment for April 5 in Washington. I soon realized that while I was in Washington it would be a good idea for me to talk with Sargent Shriver, director of the War on Poverty, who had recently been appointed ambassador to France and would be on duty when the negotiations began. I had known Sarge slightly at Yale but had not seen him for years. I called him and he readily agreed to see me.

Then I had a second thought. As usual in such situations, there should be *two* representatives of the Movement present, and after some consideration I decided to ask Tom Hayden. The National Mobilization Committee had approved—after considerable debate and delay—our plan for a week of demonstrations and counterconvention at the Democratic Party's Convention in August, and on my recommendation Tom and Rennie Davis had been made Project Directors. Moreover, Tom had made two trips to Vietnam, so it made sense for him to be the second person. He accepted the invitation and I checked with Harriman and Shriver; both agreed.

On April 4, Martin Luther King, Jr., was assassinated. With some hesitation, Tom and I decided to keep the Harriman and Shriver appointments for the following day. My only concern was to be able to get to Atlanta, see Coretta and some of Martin's closest associates and to attend the funeral. And after our meetings, I did so, spending a couple of days there and staying with Julian Bond. Martin had been scheduled to speak at the Mobe's April 27 demonstration in New York and while I was visiting with Coretta, she was brave enough to offer to speak in his place. She did, movingly, only eighteen days after the funeral.*

The conversations with Harriman probably had some value, but what I particularly remember about them is that they took place while sections of Washington were burning in Black riots in response to King's murder. Harriman sat with his back to the open window and I could see the smoke and flames over his shoulder, even though he dismissed them with a wave of his hand when I mentioned them. After a while, his secretary came in, said something to Harriman and then, with her back to him—he was hard of hearing—spoke softly to Tom and me. She said that everyone was leaving the building because of the danger, and please do not keep Mr. Harriman any longer. But Harriman was anxious to continue our discussion and kept insisting that we stay, which we did long enough to frighten the secretary even more. She finally left before the three of us did.

The plan had been for Shriver to pick us up at Harriman's office, but he called to say that it was not safe for him to drive there. A taxi would not be safe, so the best he could suggest was that we walk, carefully, to his office and talk with him while he was riding to his home in Virginia. If we were not there by a certain time, he would have to leave without us, to be sure that he got out of the city safely.

We got there in time, even though we had to go out of the direct route a couple of times in order to avoid a block filled with rioters and police. After we left Sarge's office, so many people were fleeing the city that it took a long time for his chauffeur to drive us across the bridge. As with Harriman, I suppose our discussions had some minor value, but what I remember best is Sarge talking with his wife from the phone in

*Shortly before I introduced Coretta to speak, I learned that a large group of Columbia students had occupied some university buildings in protest against plans to erect a university gymnasium on land that traditionally was used by Blacks from Harlem. I announced the occupation from the platform and, after the rally, led a contingent that marched from Central Park to Columbia in solidarity and support. Not being a student and wanting them to work out their own dynamics, I resisted the temptation to sit in with them. Tom Hayden had not been involved in the Mobe's demonstration, but he flew into town and joined them. He was a lot closer to his student days than I was.

his limousine. His end of the conversation went something like this: "Yes, I know, dear, I know I'm late. Yes dear, I know they're coming and I should be there to greet them. Yes dear, but Washington is burning. There was no way I could get there any earlier." Shriver was late for a dinner party. When we got to his house, we said hurried goodbyes in the courtyard and the chauffeur drove Tom and me to the airport.*

Between those appointments and the signing of the Peace Treaty on January 27, 1973, I made several trips to Paris (usually as part of a multipurpose trip) and met frequently with both U.S. and Vietnamese negotiators, shuttling back and forth between them. Besides Harriman and Shriver again and their top advisers, I met with Henry Cabot Lodge, Jr., and his associates (Lodge was Nixon's replacement for Harriman), but I never met with Henry Kissinger. The first time I met with Lodge, he told me what a fine man my father was; it gave me pleasure to report this to my father, even though I was hardly an admirer of Lodge. I wasn't sure how important it was to be involved this way, but both sides asked me and I decided that I would do it, so long as it did not take too much time away from being with groups that I considered more important—grass-roots and national opponents, real and potential, of war and injustice.

If my first appointments with Harriman and Shriver were complicated by the response of some Blacks to King's assassination, it can be argued that our plans for the Democratic Convention four months later were even more complicated by the same factor. The Black riots in Chicago were even more substantial and lengthy than those in Washington, and at a press conference on April 15, Mayor Daley harshly criticized the police for having been lenient (relatively intelligent and humane) with the rioters:

*Hayden seems to have forgotten how the appointments with Harriman and Shriver came about and who was there. In his book *Reunion* (New York: Random House, 1988) he writes that he called Harriman and Shriver for the appointments, sat by himself watching the smoke and flames through Harriman's window and rode with Shriver and his chauffeur to Shriver's home. In his account, I wasn't there. I hope my memory hasn't played too many similar tricks on me.

> I have conferred with the superintendent of police this morning and I . . . said to him very emphatically and very definitely that an order be issued by him immediately . . . to shoot to kill any arsonist or anyone with a Molotov cocktail . . . and to issue a police order to shoot to maim or cripple anyone looting any stores in our city. . . . I was most disappointed to know that every policeman out on his beat was supposed to use his own discretion. In my opinion, policemen should have instructions to shoot arsonists and looters—arsonists to kill, and looters to maim and detain.*

Originally aimed at Black rioters, these words were used again and again to warn prospective demonstrators of the fate they were risking if they answered the Mobilization's call (or later the Yippies' call) to come to the Convention. Our demonstrations would be nonviolent, so technically the orders to shoot to kill or maim didn't apply to us, but everyone from Daley officials to people who knew Chicago and the series of brutal police assaults on peace demonstrators and hippies in May, June and July used his words to describe the kind of treatment we should expect. And after it was announced that six thousand National Guardsmen and seventy-five hundred members of the U.S. Army would be there to support the police, Brig. Gen. Richard T. Dunn, commander of the Guard troops, announced that his men would "shoot to kill . . . if there is no other way of preventing the commission of a forcible felony. The troops will be carrying . . . 30 caliber ball ammunition. This kind of ammunition is made to kill." Whatever the technicalities of his statement, word went out around the country that even the National Guard was threatening to "shoot to kill" protestors.

*Reprinted in *The Reader* (Chicago's free weekly newspaper), April 26, 1988, in a special "Chicago 20 Years Later" edition. In August 1988, I participated with Abbie Hoffman and Bobby Seale in several days of meetings organized by the "68 Plus 20" committee, some of which took place in the amphitheater that we had not been allowed to march within four miles of in 1968. I also spoke at a separate meeting in the main library of the City of Chicago. Those who invited me to that event made a point of saying, "This time you don't need to apply for a permit, the City of Chicago is inviting you and will sponsor your talk."

On the other side of the political street, Senator Eugene McCarthy, "the peace candidate," and his assistant Allard Lowenstein canceled a previously announced pro-McCarthy rally and urged *all* antiwar demonstrators to stay home in order to avoid bloodshed. Both before and after that, they criticized our plans for antiwar demonstrations, saying that we would cause a backlash that would hurt McCarthy's chances and interfere with ending the war as quickly as possible. And of course a number of antiwar people thought this on their own. Here is more of what Nicholas von Hoffman wrote in 1973, which accurately sums up the approach taken in 1968 by a lot of "conventional antiwar sorts"—and not just the late-joiners:

> Likewise, the late-joining, more conventional antiwar sorts will say that it was your Eugene McCarthys . . . who made the difference. McCarthy lent the movement respectability is how the thought is usually phrased. Actually, it was the other way around. The only respectability in politics is power; and men like McCarthy got it by hitching on to the peace movement.

Of course, it was my view that the power von Hoffman was referring to came mostly from the mass demonstrations and civil resistance actions.

Finally, the city stalled and stalled on issuing permits for marches or rallies of any kind—and refused to let the Yippies camp in Lincoln Park, as the Boy Scouts, the Elks and other groups were regularly permitted to do.

For all these reasons, the turnout for the Mobe was the smallest of any demonstration we had ever had, not more than a few thousand at the beginning of the week and perhaps twenty to twenty-five thousand attending the one rally (four miles from the site of the convention) for which we finally got a last-minute permit. But I felt—and apparently by the end of the week twenty to twenty-five thousand others did—that it was important for us to be there. Otherwise we would be allowing the government to set a precedent that would encourage similar threats and crackdowns all over the country to prevent demonstrations from taking place. The way I put it was that if we stayed away because of the threats, we would be allowing the creation of a police state by default.

In a sense, I did take one personal precaution though. I accepted my wife's pleas, and my son Ray's offer, for him to go with me and be at my side at every moment. The way I looked at it was that Ray wanted to go anyway, in accord with his own convictions; as a proud father, I was pleased that we would share the experience, whatever it turned out to be. But it developed that Elizabeth was right, because on at least two occasions, quick actions on his part did save me from being injured. Both times, he physically pulled me out from under a policeman's descending club.

Between the smaller numbers and the problem of surviving physically while maintaining a presence in the streets and visibly standing up to the police violence—in order once again to avoid the dangerous precedent of seeming to yield to it—the counterconvention didn't accomplish much. We had set up a number of centers, most of them devoted to discussing an issue other than the Vietnam War and all of them expected to come up with resolutions for consideration at plenary sessions attended by people from all the centers. A few of the centers did function some, but in a more limited way than we had planned, and there were no plenary meetings. In retrospect, I have never been completely sure that we were right in letting the need to show our resolve in the face of police attacks divert us as much as it did from the counterconvention. But my additional worry was that the somewhat short-sighted SDS types who later became Weathermen—and other angry, "pig-baiting" demonstrators—would dominate the outdoor scene if we absented ourselves for long.

Only one demonstrator was shot and killed that week (shot in the back while fleeing a police attack). The police claimed that he had pulled a gun on them. This was refuted by eyewitnesses, but after the first headlined report the media played the story down, emphasizing the police version and describing the young man as an unemployed drifter (as if that made the killing less serious). He was one of the "hippie" protesters—even "worse," a "hippie Indian"—who had come in from South Dakota to take part in the demonstrations and the Yippie's Festival of Life. Besides being a tragedy in its own right, his murder the day before the first formal activities were to begin caused some pacifists I knew (not my kind of nonviolent warrior) to cancel their plans for coming. It also added to the tension that week and to the hostility of some of the demonstrators toward the police.

I wanted the demonstrators to act as they had in our teach-in for the troops at the Pentagon, and a number of us worked hard to make that happen. Along with others, I spoke with a number of police officials beforehand, including James D. Riordan, Deputy Chief of Police, trying to establish good relations with them and the men under their command. (I'll tell you more about Riordan when I discuss the Chicago Eight trial that resulted from the convention activities.) We also prepared some leaflets to distribute to "the policeman out on his beat," to communicate our concern for him and, we hoped, to establish some rapport on a basic human level. By then we had learned that forty-three GIs at Ford Hood had collectively refused to be flown to Chicago to perform riot duty against the demonstrators (they were court-martialed), but we didn't ask the police to take a similar stand. All we asked of them was for as many as possible to use their "own discretion" and refrain from violent attacks on peaceful demonstrators. Later, Renault A. Robinson, head of the Afro-American Patrolman's Association, told us that a lot of Black patrolmen were kept off the beat because of their grumblings about the type of police actions that were planned—or had begun to take place.

Sometimes a few of us used bullhorns to address a large group of police directly, much as we had done at the Pentagon. On one of the occasions when this happened in front of the Hilton Hotel, where the Democratic Party delegates stayed and near which some ugly police violence had already taken place, Phil Ochs, Fred Gardner and I took turns climbing to the roof of a car, with Phil singing and talking to them and Fred and I speaking to them, while others were handing out the leaflets. Phil was one of the most popular folksingers of the time ("I Ain't Marching Anymore"); Fred had been organizing coffeehouses for GIs near military installations, an initiative that I applauded and participated in. Later, when we had our one legally permitted rally at Grant Park, Vivien Rothstein and others handed out leaflets to the police. Here is what the leaflets said:

> Our argument in Chicago is not with you.
>
> We have come to confront the rich men of power who led America into a war she voted against, the men who have brought our country to the point where the police can no longer serve and protect the people—only themselves.
>
> We know you're underpaid.

> We know you have to buy your own uniforms.
>
> You often get the blame and rarely get the credit.
>
> Now you're on 12-hour shifts and not being paid overtime.
>
> You should realize that we aren't the ones who created the terrible conditions in which you work. This nightmare week was arranged by Richard Daley and Lyndon Johnson, who decided we should not have the right to express ourselves as free people.
>
> As we march, as we stand before the Amphitheater, we will be looking forward to the day when your job is easier, when you can perform your traditional tasks, and no one orders you to deprive your fellow Americans of their rights of free speech and assembly.

Not all the demonstrators took the same approach. I can remember a few times when I came across a small group who were taunting the police by saying "Oink, Oink" at them. But mostly it was more in line with what Phil, Fred, Vivien, myself and most of the Mobe leadership advocated—difficult as it was after the brutality of some of the police attacks. So let me tell you what happened at the rally on nomination day, and shortly afterwards.

53

The official police estimate was that fifteen thousand people attended our rally in Grant Park during the afternoon of Wednesday, August 18, nomination day at the Convention. Early in the rally, someone lowered the American flag on the park's flagpole to half mast and the police responded by viciously attacking the small group of people who were nearby. (The flagpole was not on the platform but off to the side and at some distance from most of the crowd.) Afterwards, someone pulled down the flag altogether and raised a bloody shirt in its place. My opinion is that he couldn't have done this unless the police were more intent on beating demonstrators than on protecting the flag. Given the presence and habits of the police, some people argued that the second "desecration" was the work of one of their agents, but a year or two later a young fellow came up to me when I was speaking somewhere in the Midwest and said that he had pulled down the flag and raised his shirt as a more accurate symbol of what the real America was like that week.

This individual act far from most of the spectators became a signal for the police to charge the crowd, shouting the slogan they had been trained to use, "Kill, Kill, Kill," and beating everyone they could with their clubs. A sizeable part of the crowd had overflowed from the stands onto the ground below, and they were the ones the police got to first. But the ones in the stands stood and at least a few of them started throwing things. I was too far away to see what was thrown but everyone I talked with later said it was things like lunchbags, tomatoes, eggs and so on, perhaps an occasional lunchbox. The police have always claimed chunks of concrete, rocks, bags of urine, bags of feces. Based on the flagrant lies testified to by Chicago police officials at our subsequent Chicago trial and after the murder of Fred Hampton (see Chapter 60) and my inability ever to find anyone present who saw anyone throw the items claimed by the police, my guess is that either no such items were thrown or they were thrown by two or three people at most who violated our nonviolent discipline and my pleadings from the microphone.

I responded to the attack in the following manner—as recorded and transcribed by the government: "Everybody stay where you are. The marshals are at the site. . . . Everybody please sit down. Everybody please sit down and leave it to the marshals. Stay where you are and leave it to the marshals. . . . This is being done for the whole world to see. Let them see who is committing the violence here."*

I'm not sure, but I think that my use of the words "for the whole

*The transcription was by Richard Schaller, an intelligence analyst with the United States Naval Investigative Service.

world to see" was what led later in the day to the chant "the whole world is watching." It was used to give heart to the demonstrators and to warn the police that their actions would not go unnoticed.

After a while, the police violence temporarily stopped, but when it flared again, my words were:

> I have a report from the marshals. They say, word-for-word, there are only about fifty police. They are side-by-side, double armed and they are moving people out of that area but not advancing . . . Don't listen to rumors. Wait until you hear from the marshals. Stay in your seat, it must not be a panic situation. What the police want is to create a disturbance here. Our marshals are handling it. We will not allow the police to create a riot here. Hold your places.

I used similar words when the police violence resumed as I was introducing Carl Oglesby. According to the government transcript, I finally was able to say, "Brother Oglesby, rap to us and *rap to the police.*" It was my attempt to continue the teach-in effort to reach out to the police for better understanding and a better relationship.

Mostly people did restrain themselves, and one way or another the attacks eventually stopped. But sometime during them Rennie Davis, the head of the nonviolent marshals, was clubbed unconscious from behind while he was trying to calm the crowd and the police. He was taken to a hospital by our medical crew, and while he was there the police came and arrested him for assault of a police officer.

A half hour or more later, after everything had settled into a series of speeches uninterrupted by police attacks, Tom Hayden strode up and onto the platform with a group of four or five others. "We're taking over the microphone," he said angrily. "The police attacked us and you called for nonviolence. They beat Rennie bloody and you said to sit down and ignore it. Nonviolence is dead and you're telling the crowd to be nonviolent. We're taking over the microphone for the rest of the rally. From now on there will be no calls for nonviolence."

I looked around and behind me to see who else was on the platform. Never had I wished so much that a larger number of principled (not just temporarily tactical) nonviolent activists had come to the week's events instead of staying away because of the expected violence by the police—and uncertainty as to the depth of the nonviolent commitment of the project's codirectors, Tom and Rennie. After a while I myself had become especially nervous about Tom. In a series of personal confrontations that took place on and off in the months and days before the convention, though, both Rennie and Tom had sworn to me that they would remain nonviolent and would always work to keep the demonstrations nonviolent. Tom had walked a thin line for several days; now he had crossed over to the other side.

I wasn't about to give up the microphone and longed for support, but I didn't see any in the vicinity. In particular, I wished that Tom's and my friend Staughton Lynd had been there. Staughton is a creative nonviolent powerhouse who would have been of immeasurable help. But staying aloof from the major activities, he had come to Chicago one day, taken part in a small nonviolent march that headed for the Amphitheater, gotten arrested with about two dozen others and left. I was as deeply committed to nonviolence as Staughton was and could hardly fault him for his tactical decision. But I wished he had believed, as I did, that it was more important for people like him and me to be in the midst of the more tumultuous activities, acting as a nonviolent influence among overwrought leaders and the mass of demonstrators. That was in line with something I had written about A. J. Muste after his death in February 1967:

> A. J. was not one to stand aside or condemn a serious movement because some of its tactics might seem to him short-sighted or otherwise flawed. His approach was to penetrate to the heart of the tumult and there, without equivocation or self-righteousness, to help guide it into constructive channels. If he did not succeed, he quietly moved on, without bitterness or denunciation, and soon became the center of another tumult.

Seeing no support, I had to face down Tom and his gang alone. "That's not the way we operate," I said, in a manner that allowed for no contradiction. "We're a coalition and when we have a division we present both positions. I'm not giving up the microphone, but it's nearing time for the program to end, so when the speaker has finished I'll put you on to tell people what you propose that they should do when it's over, and I'll explain what the Mobe has planned and I am inviting them to do."

Tom backed down, but for whatever reason he said: "I don't want to speak, Tom Newmann will do it." Newmann was the stepson of Herbert Marcuse, a writer popular among the New Left and elsewhere. So I explained to the crowd that we were going to suggest three possible paths for them to follow when the rally ended. One would be for them to go home or to wherever it was they were staying, knowing that they had already made an important contribution and would have other opportunities to act again before the Convention was over. Second, there would be a nonviolent march in which we would set out for the area outside the Amphitheater where the Convention was taking place, knowing that we had a right both to march there and to be there. And then I turned the microphone over to Newmann, saying that he had a third option to propose.

I didn't hear much of what Newmann said because I was distracted by the Yippie's candidate for president, whom I was supposed to have introduced by then but had not been able to because of the challenge by Hayden. Now the candidate was threatening to bolt and run. The government's transcript has Newmann saying:

> Pigs smashed into our space this afternoon. Pigs smashed in and people resisted and yet from this speaker's rostrum Dave only called "Sit, be quiet! be still!" Many of us feel that we are going to have to liberate our space, we are going to have to fight for it. If they take over our space, we will take over their space. . . . Rennie Davis had his head smashed and there was not a mass move . . . to defend this park and to show our anger at them.

From the little I did hear, I thought that he was expressing the attitude Hayden wanted presented to the crowd, but before he finished Hayden abruptly grabbed the mike from him and said, "That's not good enough, I'll do it." However, telling Tom to wait until we dealt with the restless candidate, I introduced Jerry Rubin who introduced Pegasus, a pig whom the Yippies were running for president. They had bought it at a farm and brought it in for the occasion. Despite some hesitations based on my opposition to the practice of calling policemen "pigs," I had agreed to introduce him, both in implementation of our alliance with the Y and for the addition of a little humor to a bleak situation. Jerry's words were:

> The Republican Party has nominated a pig for President and a pig for Vice-President. The Democratic Party is going to nominate a pig for President and a pig for Vice-President. And our campaign slogan is "Why take half a hog when you can have the whole hog." And so we're nominating a pig for President. We're requesting Secret Service protection. Our pig promises to run on the following principles, the same principle this country has always been governed on—garbage.

Then Hayden spoke, and his key words were:

> Rennie Davis is in the hospital with a split head. He's going to be all right, but he would want you to do for him what he is unable to do . . . and that is make sure that if blood is going to flow, it will flow all over the city. . . . If we are going to be disrupted and violated, let this whole stinking city be disrupted and violated. . . . Don't get trapped in some kind of large organized march which can be surrounded. Begin to find your way out of here. I'll see you in the streets.

In view of the confrontation with Hayden and his gang, I had asked, before turning the microphone over to Newmann, for Allen Ginsberg, Jean Genet (the French poet whom Jean-Paul Sartre had called "Saint Jean") and Robert Lowell to come to the platform. They had all spoken the previous evening at our unbirthday party for Lyndon Johnson and I had enjoyed a long talk on another day with Lowell and Norman Mailer in Mailer's hotel room. Mailer had said that he was working on a deadline and would not be marching with us; partly because of this, but more because I remembered his impulsiveness at the Pentagon, I decided not to ask him to come forward. Ginsberg, Genet and Lowell had all come, accompanied by William Burroughs, author of *Naked Lunch*, and, if I remember correctly, Terry Southern, scriptwriter for Stanley Kubrick's film *Dr. Strangelove*. I explained the situation and asked if I could announce that they would join me in leading the nonviolent march. They agreed and I did, adding that the march would also be led by "Veterans of the Vietnam War and people from the Poor People's Campaign."

Thousands of people joined the march, but we didn't get far. After a few blocks, and still within one of the park's walkways, we were stopped by police lines that were closely backed by National Guardsmen in what we called Daley bulldozers—jeeps covered with barbed wire (supposedly protecting them from violent demonstrators)—and armed with automatic rifles. A few of us in the front line, including Sid Peck, argued and negotiated to no avail while everyone sat down. After perhaps an hour, and as it was beginning to get dark, we spied a long line of men trying to look casual as they walked in twos and threes on the other side of the bushes that lined the path, a few at a time crossing through the bushes and mingling with the would-be marchers. None of us in the front had any question but that they were plainclothesmen who, when it got darker, would attack from inside our lines while the other police attacked from outside. After consultations, we decided that there was no way we could go forward through the police lines, and that it wasn't fair to the marchers to subject them to such a slaughter. So we called off the march and urged people to proceed to the area of the Hilton Hotel and to regroup there. Standing a few feet from Deputy Chief Riordan, I announced this on my bullhorn and asked the person with a bullhorn down the line to pass on the word to the next one, and so on.

At that point I felt that I had led people into a trap that could turn out disastrously for them, so I decided that the only honorable thing to do was to stay until the last would-be marcher had left. Then with my son Ray and one or two others who had stayed with us, I set out for the Hilton. The importance of my staying until the area was completely cleared—and of the announcement I had made on the bullhorn—will be obvious when I tell about James Riordan's testimony at our trial.

Getting to the Hilton was a problem, since the police had blocked all the nearby bridges leading in its direction. On the way I had a rewarding experience with some National Guardsmen who were preventing all automobiles and pedestrians from crossing the bridge that Ray and I had just come to. Some of them were friendly in a way none of the police had been, and I persuaded them to permit one car to cross, explaining that it held a number of elderly women who had been scared to death when one of the guardsmen had thrust a gun barrel through the open window and threatened them. After I had seen this happen and observed the looks on the women's faces, I had spoken to them and they had appealed to me for help. I had a more mixed experience after we finally got to Michigan Avenue. First, I felt good about my son when he jerked me aside just as a policeman was bringing his club down on my head. (It glanced off my lower body.) Then I felt sad that another policeman felt it necessary to spit at Ray and whack first him and then me.

After that I called Elizabeth at home to reassure her that Ray and I were okay, and we proceeded to the Hilton. We got there just in time to see several bus loads of policemen drive up to join those already there. I felt like a complete failure. Besides Tom Hayden, others were saying things like: "Nonviolence doesn't work. We're getting the shit beaten out of us and getting nowhere. Martin Luther King was the most nonviolent man in the world and they killed him. Nonviolence is dead."

When I reminded these people that soldiers and people who revolt violently also get killed, they didn't want to hear it. Now I had led people into a trap, "a large organized (nonviolent) march" that had failed. The crowd was frustrated and leaderless, an undisciplined throng, and here came the police again, getting ready to attack.

The police got out of the buses, lined up and marched toward the crowd, goose-stepping and shouting their favorite slogan: "Kill, kill, kill." To my amazement and joy, the demonstrators universally responded with a spontaneous, more creative and forceful nonviolent resistance than I had thought possible. "O ye of little faith"—"O *me of so little faith!*" I thought. Every time the police attacked and beat the front lines of demonstrators, those who could still stand retreated a little. Then when the police were occupied carrying off their bloodied victims, the crowd surged forward again to regain their ground. Meanwhile everyone was chanting "the whole world is watching," not yielding to the violence and pressing closer to the TV cameras (and police) to be sure that the world did see what was happening. Even more inspiring to me, some of them rescued their fallen comrades, carrying them away before the police could. Some even snatched a few out of the policemen's arms without attacking the police. This went on for some time, and I knew that for the mass of the demonstrators, the spirit and practice of active nonviolent resistance were not dead.

But what of the police? To blame the police for the events in Chicago is like blaming the GIs for the war in Vietnam. Yes it would have been better for some of them to refuse the orders to charge, as a few GIs at the Pentagon and more recently the forty-three Fort Hood soldiers had refused to obey orders that violated their consciences. But police assaults, like wars, do not take place in a vacuum. In Chicago in 1968 a lot of the police had been led to believe that the demonstrators were either "Commie scum," "spoiled rich kids" or both, unpatriotic no-goods who were "stabbing our boys in the back," "our boys" who were risking their lives to defend freedom, democracy and all the other good things that the United States stands for.

"Spoiled rich kids?" Some of them had been, but by their presence there they were revolting against the system that had spoiled them. "Commie scum"? On August 21, Warsaw Pact forces invaded Czechoslovakia and I, already in Chicago with an advance delegation, personally led a protest delegation and picket line outside the Polish Travel agency, the only office of a Warsaw Pact country that we could locate. Besides maintaining that protest off and on during Convention week, we posted and carried signs that said WELCOME TO PRAGUE, U.S.A. or CHICAGO IS PRAGUE, U.S.A. For the most part the media ignored this part of our activities.

For three days we couldn't believe that the brutal police assaults were getting so little attention in the mass media. But as more and more newsmen (including Dan Rather and Mike Wallace) got assaulted, gradually the whole country began to see or hear what was happening. Public consciousness of just how brutal the police riot was finally spread throughout the country in a way that hadn't happened on many previous occasions when the police assaults had been just as brutal but more limited to the demonstrators, or had lasted only a few hours instead of the six or seven days they lasted in Chicago.

And there was another reason why the media blackout finally ended. One of the unwritten policies of the country is that people of color can be treated more brutally than white people if they revolt in defiance of the authorities—and sometimes even if they don't. For that reason, people like Dick Gregory and Jesse Jackson, who supported what we were doing—and in Dick's case, participated toward the end of the week—advised Afro-Americans to stay away. Here is what Jackson testified during our trial:

> I told him [Rennie Davis] that I hoped he got the legal permit, but even if he didn't it would be consistent with Dr. King's teaching that we then got a moral permit. Rather than getting permission from the city, we'd have to get a commission from our consciences and just have an extralegal demonstration, but that probably Blacks shouldn't participate, that if Blacks got whipped nobody would pay any attention, it would just be history. But if whites got whipped, it would make the newspapers.

And that is what eventually happened. As Tom Wicker of the *New York Times* wrote in a book that came out shortly after the Convention,*

> These were not Negroes . . . there were few Black faces among the demonstrators. . . . The marchers were political dissidents, many of them radical, most of them idealistic, demonstrably brave, concerned for their country and their fellow man. . . . . They did not threaten law and order in Chicago, not if ordinary police prudence, common sense and legal procedure had been exercised. The truth is that these were our children in the streets, and the Chicago police beat them up.

So there were a lot of reasons why that police riot against unarmed demonstrators got more public attention and quickened more consciences than had some of the other police riots in which I had been beaten up—and also why the city and the federal government were anxious to indict the "leaders" of the protest so that the public would have radical scapegoats for what had offended them.

***Telling It Like It Was: The Chicago Riots*, edited by Walter Schneier (New York: Signet, 1969). I wrote an article in this book as well.

54

On March 20, 1969, Rennie Davis, Tom Hayden, Abbie Hoffman, Jerry Rubin, Bobby Seale (chairman of the Black Panther Party), John Froines, Lee Weiner and I were indicted by a federal grand jury for our participation in the Chicago activities. The delay of seven months was caused by the refusal of Attorney General Ramsey Clark to go against his own knowledge and judgment by convening a federal grand jury for the purpose of issuing the indictments. Meanwhile, the city of Chicago was at least partially frustrated in its attempts to blame "outside agitators" for the rioting of its police. And the national power elite were somewhat stymied in their desire to utilize this media-featured event—and the horror induced by the violence that "the whole world" had watched on its TV sets—to demonstrate that democracy means voting, lobbying and working through the established (and controllable) political parties, *not* carrying one's grievances and demands into the streets. In particular, they wanted to use the scare tactics of disgrace and imprisonment to reduce the public appeal of the varied movements that some of us were considered leaders of—the New Left, the youth counterculture, the Black militants, and the national antiwar coalition. But as often happens, there were some people of conscience, even in high government circles, who had been aroused by the events of the Sixties and didn't go along with the government's tactics.

During the weeks before the Convention, Clark had sent two top assistants, Deputy Attorney General Warren Christopher and Roger Wilkins, head of the Justice Department's Community Relations Service, to Chicago to find out why the city was denying us permits to engage in constitutionally protected marches and rallies. They reported favorably on those of us who were trying to negotiate with the city and negatively on the city's rigid and belligerent stance. These two were joined during convention week by Wesley Pomeroy, the official Justice Department liaison between federal, state and local law enforcement officials for both the Republican and Democratic 1968 conventions. All three made reports to Clark, and from these and other sources he concluded that there was no reason to indict us. By November 18 the Presidential Commission on the Causes and Prevention of Violence had come to the same conclusion. It appointed a special commission headed by Daniel Walker (a conservative Chicago businessman who was also head of the Chicago Crime Commission) to investigate the nature and causes of the violence during Convention week; it ruled unanimously that most of it had been "a police riot."

When the Nixon administration took office in March 1969, none of this mattered to Attorney General John Mitchell (who was later imprisoned for perjury concerning the administration's illegal activities at Watergate). Besides being anxious to smash the activist antiwar movement, he openly advocated preventive detention of people the government thought *might* commit crimes if they were free. And he announced that "there's a difference between my philosophy and Ramsey Clark's. I think this is an institution for law enforcement, not social improvement." Similarly, his assistant attorney general, Will Wilson, said: "Clark's trouble was that he was philosophically concerned with the rights of the individual."*

So we were indicted.

The basic charges in the indictment were:

> a) traveling "in interstate commerce . . . with the intent to incite, organize, promote, encourage, participate in, and carry on a riot . . . .
>
> b) to teach and demonstrate to other persons the use, application and making of incendiary devices, and intending that such incendiary devices would be unlawfully employed . . . in furtherance of civil disorders.

**Atlantic*, May 1969, and the *New York Times Magazine*, August 10, 1969.

The only "overt act" the government could dream up to charge me with was that "David T. Dellinger . . . on about August 28, 1968, at Grant Park, Chicago, Illinois . . . did speak to an assemblage of persons for the purpose of inciting, organizing, promoting and encouraging a riot. . . ."*

In its opening statement to the jury the prosecution expanded my "overt act" of violence by declaring that

> Dellinger was the principal architect. He was the principal architect especially of the riots which occurred on Wednesday, the twenty-eighth of August, 1968. . . . The defendant Dellinger planned with some of his codefendants to present two alternatives to the people whom he massed at the Bandshell on Wednesday afternoon. The first alternative was to leave the Bandshell area and have a peaceful march—that is what they called it. . . . And the second was to have the remaining people invade the Loop in small groups for the purpose of guerilla action. . . . Dellinger said that the police and the Guards stopping this march would require a number of troops and police, taking them away from other areas so that people who planned the guerilla action in the Loop would not be prevented from invading the Loop . . . Dellinger introduced a number of speakers who gave speeches to the crowd urging them to move out of the park in guerilla bands and to fight the police. The defendant Hayden gave one of the speeches.

The second charge in the indictment was that the eight of us had "conspired together" to do these things. One problem about this charge (from our point of view and, we hoped, the jury's) was that we did not

*David *T*. Dellinger? Where did the "T" come from? At age thirteen, being a good golfer and desiring to become a world champion, I had adopted the middle name of Bobby Jones (Robert Tyre Jones), the world's greatest golfer of the period. By 1970, I had discarded the middle name more than thirty years earlier. But the FBI, with characteristically inefficient "efficiency" had dug it up and reintroduced it to my name.

all know one another. And of those who did know one another, as Abbie Hoffman used to say, "We couldn't agree on lunch."

Only one of us, Jerry Rubin, had ever seen Bobby Seale, the sole Black defendant. Bobby had flown into Chicago to make a speech during the night when the rest of us were at the unbirthday party for Lyndon Johnson. Before he left at noon the next day, he had made an impromptu talk in Lincoln Park, but none of the defendants were there except Jerry. Jerry spoke with him briefly before Bobby flew back to Oakland.

I knew Rennie Davis, Tom Hayden, Jerry Rubin and Abbie Hoffman well, whatever our differences in personality and politics. And I had met John Froines briefly a few years earlier when I had spoken at Yale while he was teaching there. I had probably met Lee Weiner (and definitely had seen Froines again) at the hectic, crowded sessions at Mobe headquarters during convention week, but I wasn't sure who Lee was or what he looked like until I was introduced to him at our first defendants' meeting.

Since I didn't really know either Froines or Weiner, I thought for some time that they had probably taught and demonstrated "the use, application and making of an incendiary device," the overt act they were charged with. As the prosecution put it in its opening: "The defendants Froines and Weiner . . . arranged to make and to explode Molotov cocktails." Pretty foolhardy of them, I thought, given Mayor Daley's much-publicized order for the police to shoot to kill anyone with a Molotov cocktail. But since, to my knowledge, neither was a prominent leader during the Convention or in some particular section of the movement that the government wanted to smash, I figured that they were included in the "conspiracy" because they had done something stupid that the government would use to implicate the rest of us and get us convicted. It had indicted all of us for intent to "teach and demonstrate . . . the use . . . and making of incendiary devices," but there was no way that they could claim that any of the other six had done that.

It turned out that the government had absolutely no evidence against either Froines or Weiner, and in the end the city's agent on the jury, of whom more later, used them as bargaining chips during the last grueling sessions in which four of the jurors were holding out for not-guilty verdicts for all of us. At that point, we decided that was why they had been indicted, to be available to use in any compromise verdict that might turn out to be necessary. Their inclusion made it possible for the government to persuade unconvinced jurors that a suitable package would be to acquit two of the defendants while finding the other five of us not guilty of one charge and guilty of the other. It was clear to most people from the beginning that Hoffman, Rubin, Hayden, Davis and I were the ones that the government really wanted to get (once Seale's case had been severed from ours). But of course the agent didn't say that to the hold-out jurors.

At the time of the indictment, Seale was in jail in California on another charge—a trumped-up conspiracy-to-commit-murder charge that alleged he had given a secret order for the murder of a police agent who had infiltrated the New Haven, Connecticut, chapter of the Black Panther Party. That charge was eventually dropped after two hung juries, with the last one voting eleven to one for acquittal. We were not allowed to visit him in jail, but we all journeyed to San Francisco to meet with Charlie Garry, the Black Panthers' lawyer.

Charlie opened the meeting by saying that the stakes were life or death for Bobby on the murder charge, and that our trial could affect the outcome of that trial. Therefore, we must stop all our antiwar activities for the duration and would have to submit for his approval advance copies of any speeches we intended to make or articles we wrote and wanted published. When he came up with this ultimatum, there was a long silence. None of us wanted to make things difficult for Bobby, and none of us knew Charlie, but what he was demanding sounded too much like the tactics of the Boston Five trial of about a year earlier.

In that trial, Dr. Spock, Bill Coffin (the Yale chaplain for whose kids Ray regularly babysat), Michael Ferber (Patch's college roommate), Marcus Raskin (a former top assistant to McGeorge Bundy) and Mitchell Goodman (author of an excellent antiwar novel, *The End of It*)—good men all and all valued friends of mine—had been charged with conspiracy to promote draft resistance. Their lawyers had dominated their defense and it tended to skirt substance and concentrate on technicalities. Or at least that is the way it seemed to us. And like Garry now, the lawyers had demanded that the defendants stop their antiwar activities from the time of the indictment until the end of the trial. Not everyone complied completely, but some did and others were more restrained and cautious than they would have been on their own. The seven of us thought that the intensity of the crisis in the country and in Vietnam demanded a more forthright and aggressive stance. *We wanted to put the government on trial, not win our freedom on a technicality.* Over two hundred GIs were being killed every week and many times that many Vietnamese, so going to jail for a few years, if that was the result, didn't seem like that much of a price to pay if it would make a significant contribution to ending the slaughter. If the whole world might not be watching the trial, a lot of people would be, and we would concentrate on getting out to them the message that the times called for active resistance.

That is the how we conducted the trial, despite Charlie. And to this day I always remember this when I am asked my views of those of the defendants who afterward adopted drastically different politics and lifestyles than I have. However forthright I may be on such occasions about my own politics and lifestyle, I point out that everyone of them decided to pursue tactics during the trial that they knew (or, perhaps short-sightedly, we all *thought we knew*) increased the likelihood of spending the next ten years of our lives in prison. So I say that I thank them for that and don't want to get into public criticism of what they are doing now.

To go back to the meeting with Garry, during the silence that followed his demand, every time I looked at one of the other defendants, he was motioning to me to speak. So finally I did, laying out for Charlie the reasons we could not curtail our activities or submit our speeches and writings to him, and why we wanted to have our defense concentrate on substance rather than technicalities. Charlie's response was immediate. Rearing himself up, he glared at me and said something like this: "Who the hell are you? I never saw you before. I don't know anything about you. But I was sure that one of the seven had to be a government agent and now I know who it is. No one except an agent would spout crap like that."

Abbie Hoffman immediately rose to my defense, and once the ice had been broken by my original comments and Abbie's forceful follow-up, others spoke up too. In the end a lot was worked out amicably with Charlie (who became my good friend and remained so until his death in 1991). We would not stop our activities and would not submit our speeches to him for approval. At the same time, we had agreed, for Bobby's sake, that Garry would be our chief attorney, with Bill Kunstler, Lennie Weinglass and Gerald Lefcourt* as his assistants—if they agreed to that arrangement. I left feeling a little nervous about what would happen in the courtroom under Charlie, but determined to stand up to him again if necessary. And I couldn't help admiring him for having fought for what he thought was best for Bobby and yet having yielded on the points that were crucial for the rest of us, after we had mostly convinced him that continuing our antiwar work and concentrating on substance rather than technicalities would not be harmful to Bobby's other case.

55

When it came to choosing our other attorneys neither of my first choices was available. They were Jeremiah Gutman and Arthur Kinoy. Gutman had impressed me when he was my counsel in hearings before the House Un-American Activities Committee (HUAC), after the 1968 convention and before the indictments. I had worked closely with Kinoy in negotiations with the government concerning the 1967 Pentagon action and had confidence in his skills and dedication to most of the fundamental principles that I held. But he was a full-time teacher at Rutgers Law School, worked mostly on appeal briefs and does almost no trial work. He recommended his partner at the time, William Kunstler.

Hayden immediately objected to Kunstler as a "liberal" who was not committed to the politics that we stood for and wanted at the forefront of our trial. He proposed Leonard Weinglass, a Newark attorney who was a close friend, whom Tom had gotten to know through NCUP. I agreed

*Lefcourt had to withdraw from our case in order to help defend the "Panther Twenty-One" in a similarly contrived trial in New York. The trial ended with no convictions on any of the charges.

with Hayden that Kunstler was no radical, but from talking with him I was impressed that he had a compassionate heart, lots of courage—as demonstrated by his work in the South on civil rights cases—and was intrigued with the issues involved in our case. I thought that his background in civil rights cases indicated good instincts and would come in handy in our trial. We all knew that most of Weinglass's experience was limited to local cases very different than ours, but we liked him from the beginning and were impressed by his quiet, thoughtful, intelligent and no-nonsense manner.

As it turned out, Bill and Lennie formed an ideal legal team and Bill was dramatically radicalized by the events of the long, drawn-out trial. Besides having somewhat diverse skills, they quickly joined the defendants in forming a democratically operating collective in which neither defendants nor lawyers had the upper hand but all decisions were made by consensus. Kunstler had an amazing ability to think on his feet, immediately getting to the heart of an unfamiliar situation. But sometimes he spent so much time outside the court exploring the youth culture and the dynamics of the New Left that he didn't do the solid kind of preparatory work that Weinglass did. Lenny always did his homework and was there with the necessary cases and precedents when they were needed and, like Bill, was good at sizing up a courtroom situation. But he wasn't as flamboyant (or hyperactive) as Bill, so Bill was usually the first one on his feet when the prosecution and judge were dramatically out of line. I soon came to love them both.

As it turned out, Charlie Garry never became our chief attorney—or even Bobby's attorney—because the government went to great lengths to prevent his participation in the trial. Shortly before the trial was scheduled to open, he had to have surgery for a badly infected gallbladder. He had scared his doctors by continuing with a previous trial of some indigent Latino defendants longer than was medically wise and now his life was at risk. Armed with several medical documents, we asked for a postponement of our trial for six weeks. This would have been routine in most trials of national significance—and this one was destined to last almost five months and was not finally settled for four years. If there were valid legal reasons for denying the postponement, the government never presented them. Instead, the chief prosecutor, Thomas Foran, replied, "It's a cheap ploy, Your Honor. They just want six more weeks to run around the country stirring up trouble with their subversive speeches." And, foretaste of what was to come, Judge Julius Hoffman immediately agreed, without even reading the doctors' letters and medical certificates we had brought.

This refusal to wait six weeks for the lawyer with whom Bobby had worked for years, the only person in the case whom Bobby knew, created the most serious crises of the trial. But the story of how the government maneuvered to deprive Bobby of Garry's services is even more shocking than prosecutor Foran's objection and the judge's automatic ruling. As soon as word of the denial reached California, lawyers filed motions there for the trial to be delayed until Garry was well enough to defend Bobby. A companion motion requested a court order that Bobby could not be extradited from California until after that motion was argued and settled in court. They secured the court order barring his extradition, but as soon as the federal government learned this it illegally loaded Bobby into a car, in leg irons, body chains and handcuffs, and began the long drive to Chicago by a circuitous route and with frequent stopovers of several days. Meanwhile, no one knew where Bobby was, and the government refused to say.*

In the interim, Fred Hampton, chairman of the Illinois Black Panther Party, served as Bobby's representative in meetings with the other defendants, and when Bobby finally got to Chicago, Fred applied to visit him in jail. This would have been our only, if indirect, contact with our codefendant before the trial began, but Judge Hoffman denied Fred's application. At that point, Bill Kunstler filed papers as legal counsel for Bobby, that being the only way anyone connected with the defendants could see him and find out how he was and what he was thinking. From then on, Judge Hoffman insisted that Kunstler had filed to be his attorney and had to remain so, even after Bobby had "fired" Kunstler, both verbally and in writing, and Kunstler had formally withdrawn as his lawyer.

Before the jury was selected, four of our out-of-state pretrial lawyers

*When the government first spirited him away, it knew of the verdict but conceivably had not received official notification. But Bobby says that he was kept in another jail in California long enough for there to be no doubt that he was still in California when the government received the official notice.

notified the court by telegram that they had completed their pretrial work and were withdrawing from the case. Normally, this is a procedure that is routinely accepted for out-of-state lawyers rather than requiring them to make an unnecessary trip and personal appearance. But the prosecution and judge saw an opportunity to force these lawyers (and the defendants) to act as unwilling accomplices in their efforts to force Seale and Kunstler to accept the government's fiat that Kunstler was Seale's attorney. Here is a key sentence from the transcript of that day:

> MR. FORAN: If the defendants are prepared at this time to represent to this court that they are satisfied with their counsel who are present here in this court, and will waive any claim that their Sixth Amendment rights are abridged, then we would ask the court not to issue an order to have Mr. Lefcourt, Mr. Kennedy, Mr. Tigar and Mr. Roberts brought in before the court immediately.

Being satisfied with the counsel present meant satisfied with Garry's absence and with having Kunstler serve as his replacement, so we all refused. The judge then issued an order that the four pretrial lawyers should be arrested, held without bail and brought to Chicago and into the court.

Michael Kennedy and Dennis Roberts got the arrest order quashed in the San Francisco federal court, but Michael Tigar was arrested at his home in Los Angeles at 3 in the morning and brought to Chicago in chains. Tigar told us that when he was first brought to Chicago, Foran said to him: "If you don't convince Bobby Seale to drop his right-to-counsel claim, we're going to hold you in Cook County jail all weekend, where you can get your white asses raped." The plural reference to "white asses" apparently included Gerald Lefcourt, who had been contacted by Kunstler and was on his way to Chicago on his own.

A prestigious (and conscientious but by no means radical) Chicago lawyer, Thomas Sullivan, came to court on Friday and assured the judge that if he vacated the arrest order he, Sullivan, would produce the four lawyers in court on Monday morning. Hoffman refused but Sullivan persuaded a higher federal judge to grant his emergency motion for bail, and they did not have to spend the weekend in jail.

More than a hundred lawyers (including twelve members of the Harvard Law School faculty) responded to news of the bench warrants and arrests by picketing the Chicago court and another couple hundred lawyers picketed the federal court in San Francisco. These protests forced Foran and Judge Hoffman to change their tactic and excuse the four lawyers from the case. Since lawyers seldom, if ever, picket a court, let alone journey from out of state on overnight notice to do so, their actions give an idea of how outrageous the prosecution and judge were in their effort to force Kunstler against his will and against Bobby's will, to be Bobby's lawyer. *But this did not stop them from continuing to insist all through Seale's part of the trial that Kunstler was his lawyer. Step by step this produced the most serious conflicts of the trial.*

Despite the crude denial of his rights, Bobby sat silently in the courtroom for days at a time when no one testified against him. But when a witness did, Bobby stood up and quietly said, "I object to this man's testifying against me in the absence of my lawyer." (The trial opened on September 26 and the first time Bobby did this was on October 8.) When he said this, the judge said that Bobby had a lawyer, "Mr. Kunstler," and ordered the marshals to have Seale sit down. After a while Bobby made application, with proper citations, to be granted the right to defend himself. Mickey Leaner, a young Black law student whom we all grew to admire and love, did the research for him. (Later she worked on our appeals.) But the judge turned down his motion and after that, whenever someone testified against Bobby, he would stand up and ask to cross-examine the witness. Later, he would start to ask the witness a question. Eventually the voices on both sides got louder, and Seale's language stronger, as the marshals threw him back onto his chair even more violently than they had at the beginning, and as the judge became increasingly exacerbated at Seale's persistence in demanding his rights.

A description of what happened on October 29, more than a month into the trial, will give the picture. A number of Black Panthers attended the trial that day and their presence led to a doubling of heavily armed marshals in the courtroom. Before court opened, Bobby told the Panthers that no matter what happened to him, they should keep their cool. When Judge Hoffman came in, Richard Schultz, the assistant prosecutor, stood up and declared that "Bobby Seale . . . told those people in the audience . . . that if he's attacked, they know what to do. He was talking to these people about an attack by them."

Bobby responded by calling Schultz "a dirty liar, a fascist, pig liar," and in the exchange that followed he said, "Will you please tell the Court I told them to keep their cool because I didn't want a spontaneous response to any kind of activity that might go on. Would you please tell the Court that I said to keep cool."

I had heard his words to the Panthers and it was true. Moreover, during this interchange Bobby was physically attacked by the marshals and the Panthers did remain cool.

The jury was brought in and here are a few excerpts from what happened:

> MR. SEALE: Good morning, ladies and gentlemen of the jury.
> MR. DELLINGER: Good morning.
> MR. SEALE: I would like to request the right again to cross-examine this witness because my lawyer, Charles R. Garry is not here and because I have been denied the rights to defend myself in this courtroom. I am requesting and demanding, in fact, that I have a right to cross-examine this witness, sir, at this trial.
> THE COURT: Mr. Marshal, take the jury out.
> MR. DELLINGER: And all the defendants support Bobby Seale's right to have a counsel of his choice here and affirm that he has been denied that right.

For this remark I was sentenced to seven days in jail for "contempt of court."

> MR. SEALE: Why don't you recognize my constitutional rights? . . .
> THE COURT: All I want to tell you is this: if you speak once again while the jury is in the box, we will take steps as are indicated in the circumstances.

The steps that had been threatened were to bind and gag Bobby.

Weinglass cross-examined a witness, after which the following happened:

THE COURT: Is there any redirect examination?

MR. SEALE: Before the redirect, I would like to request again—demand—that I be able to cross-examine the witness. My lawyer is not here, I think I have a right to defend myself in this courtroom.

THE COURT: Take the jury out.

MR. SEALE: You have George Washington and Benjamin Franklin sitting in a picture behind you, and they were slave owners. That's what they were. They owned slaves. You are acting in the same manner, denying me my constitutional rights of being able to cross-examine the witness. . . .*

THE COURT: Mr. Seale, I have admonished you previously what might happen to you if you keep on talking.

MR. SEALE: Happen to me? What can happen to me more than what Benjamin Franklin and George Washington did to black people in slavery?

THE COURT: And I might add since it has been said here that all of the defendants support you in your position that I might include that they are bad risks for bail. . . . Have him sit down, Mr. Marshal. . . .

MR. SCHULTZ: May the record show, if the court please, that while the marshals were seating Bobby Seale, pushing him into his chair, the defendant Dellinger physically attempted to interfere with the marshals by pushing them out of the way.

That was a polite but inaccurate way of describing what had happened. My chair was next to Bobby's and the previous time that the marshals had "seated him," I had seen one of them knee him in the testicles and had heard Bobby's involuntary gasp of pain. So this time, as the marshals were "seating" him, I got between Bobby and them and I was the one who got kneed in the balls, not having been smart enough

*Seale was inaccurate so far as Benjamin Franklin was concerned. In 1775 Franklin, along with Benjamin Rush, organized the first colonial society for the abolition of slavery. I am a direct descendant of Benjamin Franklin's brother, John Franklin, but when Bobby made the charge I was surprised at his inclusion of Benjamin, but wasn't sure that he was wrong about my great uncle. I made a point of finding out later.

to protect myself in the manner I had learned from SNCC in the South. In addition to the blow, I received a month's sentence for contempt.

A few minutes later:

> MR. SEALE: I have a right to defend myself.
> THE COURT: Will you, Mr. Marshal, have that man sit down? . . .
> MR. SCHULTZ: May the record show that the defendant Dellinger did the same thing just now?
> THE COURT: I saw it myself.

The judge ordered us to rise for a recess and we all refused, in protest against what had been taking place. For this everyone received a sentence of one day for contempt.

> THE COURT: . . . I tell you that I will not retain on bail in this court men who defy the United States District Court and I will give them the noon hour, the noon recess, to think about it.
> MR. KUNSTLER: They are protesting, your Honor, and I think that is protective of the First Amendment.
> THE COURT: They will have to obey the law in the process of protesting, sir. Now if they prefer to sleep in the county jail, let them think on it.

As we were leaving for the recess, Abbie and Jerry ran up to me and said, "That's real nonviolence. That kind of nonviolence we believe in." Of course I had acted spontaneously in defense of Bobby, but one of the debates within the movement at the time revolved around the charge that pacifists were too passive in the face of injustice and more interested in preserving their own "purity" than in engaging in serious nonviolent struggles to change the society or to aid its victims. I felt that in too many cases the charge was true, but that acting in such a way was a misreading of the true nature of nonviolence—so I was especially pleased when Abbie and Jerry said this. And I can't resist adding that a Chicago reporter who attended the trial every day and interviewed the marshals from time to time wrote in his book on the trial* that "the marshals generally [even

*John Schultz, *Motion Will Be Denied* (New York: William Morrow, 1972).

'the most aggressively proper marshal'] said that they had great respect for 'that man, Dave Dellinger.' " How much this was because of—or despite—my interventions and how much a result of my continued attempts (without which nonviolence is also incomplete) to reach out to them as my brothers, Schultz does not say.

After the recess, there were some heated discussions among both sets of lawyers and the judge concerning Seale's conduct, ending as follows:

> MR. SEALE: . . . How come I can't say nothing? He has distorted everything and it relates to the fact I have a right to defend myself.
> THE COURT: Well, I have been called a racist, a fascist—he has pointed to the picture of George Washington behind me and called him a slave owner. . . .
> MR. SEALE: They were slave owners. You got them up there.
> THE COURT: He has been known as the father of this country, and I would think it is a pretty good picture to have in the United States District Court. . . .

When Judge Hoffman said that he drew himself up dramatically and spoke with conspicuous pride. Then he said: "We will take a recess. Take the defendant into the room in there and deal with him as he should be dealt with in this circumstance. . . . Let the record show none of the defendants have stood at this recess in response to the marshal's request."

Another day's contempt sentence for all of us.

This time it was clear to everyone that the judge was going to carry out his threat of having Bobby bound and gagged. Walking out, Abbie, Rennie, Jerry and I said to one another that we should refuse to go back into the courtroom to participate in a trial that had already flagrantly trampled on Bobby's rights and now was going to bind and gag him. But in our meeting room, crowded with defendants, lawyers, legal assistants, staff members, wives and girlfriends, it didn't turn out to be that simple. After some long, confused minutes in which it seemed as if everyone was talking at the same time, there was a sudden silence and I heard Tom Hayden saying with great earnestness:

> We have to go back in there. For us not to would be just what they want. They want an excuse to revoke our bail and stop us

> from preparing our defense. They want us in jail so that we can no longer travel around the country making speeches and rallying support. We have to be like the Vietnamese who do what they have to do and feel no pain. I may vomit when I see Bobby bound and gagged, but we can't do anything to let them revoke our bail.

It was a principled position, but one that went against my principle of on-the-spot solidarity with an obvious victim.

Meanwhile the marshals had been pounding on the locked door for some time, shouting that the judge was ready, we must get into the courtroom immediately. But we had no agreement on what to do and we kept discussing, with the discussion now limited to the defendants (and the lawyers if they had wanted to speak). By then, Tom and I were the only ones who held a definite position and spoke for it. Everyone else was ambivalent, except John Froines who supported Tom. Finally, Lee Weiner said, "We don't even know for sure that he will be bound and gagged. We should go in and find out. If he is, we can consult with him tonight in the lockup and then decide what we should do." So we went back.

Bobby was carried in bound and gagged, painfully so, with his ankles and wrists chained to the chair legs. But when we met with Bobby that night, he took the position Tom had advocated. So everyone endured six more painful days of such treatment, with Bobby not only bound, gagged and chained but frequently brutalized by the marshals. Usually it happened when he struggled with the gags because they were choking him, or with the manacles that were cutting off his circulation, or when he tried to say something through the gags. By then, others joined me in trying to protect him, but even so he was beaten and hit in the balls and stomach a number of times; some of us were slugged and mauled while trying to protect him.

Tom did not vomit, but he stood up twice and objected, something that by political conviction he almost never did. The first time, he said that "Bobby Seale should not be put in a position of slavery. He wants to defend himself." The second time, he said, "Now they are going to beat him. They are going to beat him." Schultz's response was to say that

". . . it was Mr. Hayden who was addressing the jury while they were walking out of here," and Tom responded as follows: "I was not addressing the jury. I was trying to protect Mr. Seale. A man is supposed to be silent when he sees another man's nose being smashed?" For these "outbursts," Tom received contempt sentences of three months and four months respectively.

On November 5, five weeks into a trial that lasted almost five months, the public scandal of Seale's treatment became so great that the judge severed his case from the rest of ours and that part of the daily torture was over. In the end the government dropped the charges against Bobby altogether.

On my own, I would not have gone back into the courtroom after Bobby was bound and gagged. I hesitated a long time before doing so, both on that first afternoon and after Bobby had asked us to. Rightly or wrongly, I did it in order to preserve the fragile and constantly threatened unity of the group. Among other things there was a bitter conflict between Hayden and Froines on one side and Abbie, Jerry and Lee Weiner on the other. Basically, Rennie Davis and I were working overtime to hold the group together—or at least that's the way he and I saw it. On top of this, in my own frequent disagreements with Tom he always said, "Dave's a pacifist and pacifists don't have much sense of reality. So he can do what he wants, but the rest of us have to act more responsibly."

This wasn't the first time that I and the others had acted contrary to our personal impulses, initially to create some degree of unity among eight quite disparate defendants, and later to maintain it. Before the trial began, I had wanted to defend myself, with the advice of legal counsel, and had hoped that some of the others would too. But no one else wanted to and no one wanted me to, so I had given up the idea. Three years later, after our contempt charges had been overturned by an appeals court and came up for retrial, I defended myself and it didn't cause any group problems.

I never have been sure that I did the right thing by going back into the court on the day Bobby was bound and gagged. The unity of the defendants was important, and I was afraid that given my absence, the group would fall apart. But perhaps it would have been more important to take a principled stand of refusing to sit in a courtroom when any human being was being treated as Bobby was. Moreover, Bobby was Black and I was white, so refusing would have expressed to a wider public another important unity. A fundamental human unity of Black and white that Bobby himself might have ultimately appreciated my having asserted, despite the different tactical views he and I held on how it was best for his codefendants to respond to the abuse he was experiencing. To this day, I occasionally meet a Black person who asks, "Why didn't you white guys support Bobby Seale when he was being bound and gagged in the courtroom?"

56

Whatever the appearances to the contrary, the decision to "put the government on trial" did not mean that we intended to disrupt the orderly flow of courtroom procedures. Instead, it applied to such things as the breadth of witnesses we intended to have testify on why we came to Chicago, how we had acted there, how the federal government, city and police had acted and how our own and others' rights were violated. We would call some witnesses who were more likely to hurt rather than help us with the jury, but who had something relevant and important to say to the public—through their testimony and in reports and press conferences afterwards. Finally, we planned to continue our antiwar, projustice and profreedom activities as best we could on evenings and weekends, as well as speaking as advocates of such activities at public gatherings all over the country.

As had happened with Bobby Seale, the gradual increase in the number of instances in which we spoke up inside the courtroom came in response to repeated violations by the prosecution, judge, marshals and government witnesses of anything we would have considered an even remotely honest trial. Later, our opinion that the conduct of the trial violated even conventional standards of fairness (never outstanding) was affirmed by the appeals court when it overturned the guilty verdict. By then, a distinguished Chicago law professor, Harry Kalven, had studied the transcript of the trial and written:

> I am impressed, *contrary to the impressions I had gotten from the press coverage*, by the sense that the interruptions were in no sense random events and that two or three triggering events, such as the handling of Seale and the revocation of Dellinger's bond, account for the major part of the troubles.* (emphasis added)

Kalven's reference to the false impressions he had gotten from the press coverage probably explains why from right after the trial to the present I keep meeting people who say things like "You're very different than I expected you to be" or "You certainly mellowed since the trial."

The first contempt charges for most of the defendants came after more than a month of trial. Then it was for refusing to stand for the entrance or departure of the judge on the three days during which the lies of the prosecution, brutality of the marshals and rulings of the judge—along with Bobby's refusal to be silent in the face of them—led step by step to Bobby's being carried into the courtroom bound, chained and gagged. My own first contempt occurred three weeks into the proceedings and was not sparked by an immediate courtroom abuse. However, some of what I said was influenced by earlier abuses—and I consider the sixth-month sentence I got for it an abuse. It was National Vietnam Moratorium Day, with observances all over the country, and before court opened the defendants held a little ceremony inside the courtroom. Here is the government's record of that contempt charge:

> Specification 1: On October 15 when the Judge entered the courtroom, Mr. Dellinger was standing and the following colloquy occurred:

**Contempt: Transcript of the Contempt Citations, Sentences, and Responses of the Chicago Conspiracy 10.* Foreword by Ramsey Clark, former Attorney General of the United States; Introduction by Harry Kalven, Professor of Law, University of Chicago. Chicago: Swallow Press, 1970.

MR. DELLINGER: Mr. Hoffman, we are observing the moratorium.
THE COURT: I am Judge Hoffman, sir.
MR. DELLINGER: I believe in equality, sir, so I prefer to call people mister or by their first name.

Court had not been called yet and moved by the ceremony, with its reading of the names of dead GIs and Vietnamese, I was struggling, however ineptly, to stay on a deeper level than calling another human being "Your Honor."

THE COURT: Sit down. The clerk is about to call my cases.
MR. DELLINGER: I wanted to explain to you we are reading the names of the war dead.
THE MARSHAL: Sit down.
MR. DELLINGER: We were just reading the names of the dead from both sides.
THE MARSHAL: Sit down.

Subsequently, the jury was brought into the room. When the jury was seated, the defendant Dellinger once more rose and the following colloquy occurred:

MR. DELLINGER: Before the witness resumes the stand, we would like to propose—
MR. SCHULTZ: If the Court please—
MR. FORAN: Your Honor. If the Court please, may the marshal take that man into custody?
MR. DELLINGER: A moment of silence . . .
THE COURT: Mr. Marshal, take out the jury.
MR. DELLINGER: We only wanted a moment of silence. . . .
THE COURT: . . . I forbid him to disrupt the proceedings. I note for the record that his name is—
MR. DELLINGER: David Dellinger is my name.
THE COURT: You needn't interrupt my sentences for me.
MR. DELLINGER: You have been interrupting ours. I thought I might finish that sentence.

> THE COURT: The name of this man who has attempted to disrupt the proceedings in this court is David Dellinger and the record will clearly show that, Miss Reporter.

The next contempt charge came a week later, on Bobby Seale's birthday, after another heated debate between him and the judge, with the judge again threatening him with dire punishments. I stood up and said, "I think you should understand that we support Bobby Seale in this—at least I do." The strange form of that sentence, ending after a pause with "at least I do," came about because except for my plea for a moment of silence, no one (except Bobby) had ever spoken out in court before. After I had said that "we support Bobby Seale in this" I looked at my fellow defendants and all of them were indicating astonishment and disapproval. Tom, put a finger to his lips that clearly said, "Be quiet," and a couple of the others motioned for me to sit down. Not wishing to implicate them in an action that they disapproved of, I somewhat incongruously added "at least I do."

Another of my early contempt charges came when a police agent who had infiltrated our planning meetings during the Convention told a series of absolute lies. Tom Foran, the prosecutor, was standing a few feet from me and in utter disbelief I spontaneously asked him, "Mr. Foran, do you believe one word of that?" I said it so quietly, as one human being to another, that Foran had to tell the judge that I had spoken. When the judge then objected to my having done so, I explained to him that "I asked Mr. Foran if he could possibly believe one word of that. I don't believe the witness believes it. I don't believe Mr. Foran believes it." By then, after a month of the trial, I had learned that whenever our lawyers tried to expose a flagrant lie by asking a relevant and legitimate question, the prosecution would automatically object and the judge would automatically sustain the objection. So when Foran and the judge gave me the opportunity, I spoke the second time loudly enough for the jury to hear my opinion of that testimony and of the lack of ethics with which the prosecution was conducting its case. The judge had already made it clear that such remarks would lead to jail sentences for contempt of court (I got three months for that one), but there are times when a person has to challenge crude dishonesty on the spot, whatever the conventions and penalties. I voiced this idea in open court nearly two months later, in another contempt, when the judge said, "Courtroom decorum must be observed," and I replied, "Decorum is more important than justice, I suppose."

Finally, four months into the trial, on February 4 (Elizabeth's and my twenty-eighth wedding anniversary) James D. Riordan, the Deputy Chief of Police, testified. From my previous contacts with him, before the convention and when he halted the nonviolent march from Grant Park, I had always considered him "an honest cop"—and likable too. When he walked through the door to testify against us, I found myself hoping, *for his sake,* that he would not lie as flagrantly as most of the other prosecution witnesses had done. But I also knew the pressures that he was under. The following excerpts from the transcript will show what happened:

> MR. SCHULTZ: And where were you in relation to this group who wanted to march?
> RIORDAN: I was in front of them. I stopped the march.
> SCHULTZ: . . . did you have occasion to see David Dellinger?
> RIORDAN: I did. He was confronting me at the head of the march. . . .
> SCHULTZ: What if anything did you hear on the bullhorn?
> RIORDAN: I heard this unidentified speaker announce to the group that inasmuch as the march had been stopped, to break up in small groups and to go over into the Loop, to penetrate into the hotels, the theaters, and stores and business establishments where the police could not get at them, and disrupt their normal activity . . .

No one made any such announcement. Already he had lied, but I kept silent.

> SCHULTZ: Did Dellinger say anything when this announcement was made?
> RIORDAN: I did not hear him say anything.
> SCHULTZ: Did you see where he went?
> RIORDAN: He left with the group carrying the ["Vietcong"] flags.
> DELLINGER: Oh, bullshit. That's an absolute lie.

THE JUDGE: Did you get that, Miss Reporter?
DELLINGER: Let's argue about what you stand for and what I stand for [and if they want to put me in jail for that, fine],* but let's not make up lies like that.
THE JUDGE: I have never heard in more than a half century of the bar a man using profanity in this court or in a courtroom.

Shortly afterward, the judge dismissed the jury and revoked my bail. I spent the rest of the trial, except for court sessions, in Cook County Jail. I also was sentenced to five months in jail for this particular contempt charge.

As I was being led away, long-repressed emotions were expressed in the courtroom by defendants and spectators—in response to my bail revocation but equally, I believe, in protest against everything else that had happened during the preceding four months of the trial. Among other things, Davis and Rubin both said, "This Court is bullshit." Davis said, "I associate myself with Dave Dellinger completely, 100 percent. This is the most obscene court I have ever seen." Abbie Hoffman said, "You are a disgrace to the Jews. You would have served Hitler better." The judge's only response, other than later citing them for contempt of court, was to adjourn court for the rest of the day. The sentences he imposed were Abbie Hoffman, five days; Jerry Rubin, five months; Rennie Davis, six months.†

Abbie's comment was recorded in the transcript, so I suppose that he said it, but if so he didn't waste much time on it. While everyone else

*I distinctly remember saying the words in brackets but in the confusion and disorder that descended on the courtroom, the court reporter apparently missed it.

†The sentences imposed for contempt provide an interesting but somewhat fruitless field for speculation. Thus Tom (who spoke up less than any of the other defendants except for Froines and Weiner) received a total of one year, two months and thirteen days for eleven contempts (four of them refusal to rise), but Abbie Hoffman got only eight months for twenty-four contempts. Moreover, Abbie insulted the judge in a far more personal way than Tom or anyone else ever did. I had the most charges of contempt of all the defendants (thirty-two) and the longest sentence (two years, five months and sixteen days), but this pales in comparison with Bill Kunstler's sentence of four years and thirteen days for only twenty-four charges.

was acting out their frustrations, Abbie went over to my thirteen-year-old daughter Michele in the spectator section, put his arm around her and comforted her. "Your daddy's going to be all right," he kept saying to her. She has never forgotten that and neither have I.

At the beginning of the next day's session, Jerry and Abbie informed me that the defendants had met that night over what had happened to me and that, along with Rennie Davis, they had declared that it was a terrible mistake for them not to have listened to me and refused to go into the courtroom when Seale was bound and gagged. They told the other defendants that this time, they were not going to be passive after what had happened to me. So here is what Abbie said to the judge before the jury had come in:

> Your idea of justice is the only obscenity in the room. You *schtunk. Schande vor de goyim,* huh [a Jew who does the dirty work for the Gentiles] . . . That's why it has gone on here today because you threatened him [Dellinger] with cutting off his freedom of speech in the speech he gave in Milwaukee.

Abbie was referring to an incident two court days before my bail revocation. The judge had announced that

> It has been brought to my attention that there was a speech given in Milwaukee discussing this case by one of the defendants. I want to say that if such a speech as was given is brought to my attention again, I will give serious consideration to the termination of bail of the person who makes the speech. I think he would be a bad risk to continue on bail. The one who made it knows it, I won't go any further than this.

At this, I stood up and said:

> I made the speech. Was there anything in the speech that suggested I won't show up for trial the next day or simply that I criticized your conduct of the trial?
> THE COURT: I didn't ask you to rise, sir, and I am certainly not going to be interrogated.

> DELLINGER: Why are you threatening me with revocation of my bail for exercising my freedom of speech? What has that got to do with it? I am here, aren't I?

Perhaps Judge Hoffman would have revoked my bail anyway, for the "obscenity"* I uttered, but we all knew that he had been threatening to do it for some time.

Before Abbie was through, he spoke up several times, with the following excerpts typical of his attitude and language:

> You know you can't win the fucking case. The only way you can is to put us away for contempt. . . . You put him in jail because you lost faith in the jury system. . . . Contempt is a tyranny of the court, and you are a tyrant. . . . The judges in Nazi Germany ordered sterilization. Why don't you do that, Judge Hoffman? . . . We should have done this long ago when you chained and gagged Bobby Seale. . . . Best friend the Blacks ever had, huh? [This was a reference to a boast the judge had made during one of his arguments with Bobby Seale]. How many Blacks are in the Drake Towers [where the judge lived]? How many are in the Standard Club? How many own stock in Brunswick Corporation [the judge had reputedly become a millionaire by marrying the Brunswick heiress.]

The judge made no verbal response to any of these insults, but, without explanation, adjourned court early, with only half a page of testimony by one witness. Even stranger, when he sentenced Abbie for contempt of court, he combined seven separate interruptions that day, all

*Apparently the *New York Times* considered it an obscenity, or at least "unfit to print." Referring to the whole episode, reporter John Schultz wrote in *Motion Will Be Denied*: "It was marvelous to believe that all this resulted from the use of the word 'bullshit' once and once only and quietly. But by nightfall, . . . the news media of the nation convened editorial conferences from coast-to-coast to determine whether to treat explicitly, or euphemistically, what both the *New York Times* and Judge Hoffman called 'a barnyard epithet.' "

along the above lines, into one charge and gave him a sentence of six days.

On the following morning, I was brought as usual into the courtroom before any of the other defendants had arrived. First Jerry and then Abbie came in and sat down, one on each side of me. Each of them was wearing judge's robes. This time, they did not insult the judge verbally, but they showed their contempt by taking off their robes as the court session was ending and trampling on them. Under the robes were shirts proclaiming them members of the Chicago Police Department.

That day, Bill Kunstler made a motion for me to be able to sum up my own case when the time came for final arguments to the jury. This had been planned before my bail revocation and was the last remnant of my original desire to serve as my own lawyer. Kunstler cited a case of a few weeks earlier in which Roy M. Cohn (the former aide to Senator Joseph McCarthy) had been allowed to do so. The judge rejected the motion, with Schultz speaking about the obscenities I had "screamed" at the judge and I responding that I had never screamed and had "not used repeated vile or obscene language" as he and the judge had claimed. In actual fact, when I had challenged Riordan, I hadn't even risen from my chair and, according to several of the reporters present (and at least the one news account I saw while in jail) had spoken in a quiet, natural voice. After five months of observing how courtroom procedures separated people from their true selves, I was talking heart-to-heart with someone whom I had wanted to trust but who had disappointed me. The court transcript has me saying, during the disorder that followed, "You're a snake, we have to try to put you in jail for ten years for telling lies about us, Dick Schultz." And "Dick Schultz is a Nazi if I ever knew one." I know who said this, but it wasn't me. Not only wouldn't I say it but I was offended when I heard it, for I believe that it violated the spirit in which I had spoken and always want to speak. I don't believe in putting anyone in jail, let alone for ten years. Perhaps the prosecutors, who regularly went over the record with the stenographer before it was made official, were trying to add evidence as to why I deserved to have my bail revoked, or perhaps it was an honest error by the stenographer because so many people were speaking at once. But reporter John Schultz reports that "throughout the disorder David Dellinger sat with an appearance of release, or peace."

To give you one final example of the nature of the conflict between us and the prosecution (I include the judge as part of the prosecution), a man by the name of Irving Bock testified as a rebuttal witness on the day that Abbie and Jerry wore the judge's robes into court. Bock had represented Chicago's Veterans for Peace on the Mobilization's Steering Committee. Shortly before the August 1968 Convention opened, he had sought out Rennie and me and had shown us a balloon that was attached to a tube, saying that it was a device he had learned about in the air force for locating and assisting downed planes. He told us it could be inflated with helium and made to land wherever we wanted it to and offered to show us how to use it to land "objects" on the roof of the Amphitheater while the Convention was in progress. It was clear that the objects he had in mind were bombs, so my satirical response was, "What kind of objects would we land on the roof, leaflets?" Rennie and I immediately decided that Bock was an agent; besides rejecting his offer, as we would have done whoever proposed it, we warned a few key people of his identity, hoping to limit any damage he might create. When he testified against us, he identified himself to the Court as a member of the Red Squad of the Chicago police department. Later, we were told by Chicagoans that he also worked for the FBI.

On the stand, Bock denied the whole incident. Earlier, in his original testimony, Bock told a lot of other lies, such as that the defendants had announced plans for "the breaking of windows, pulling of fire alarm boxes, the setting of small fires," and that the nonviolent march I announced in Grant Park was planned as a diversionary tactic to tie up the police while the others engaged in guerrilla actions elsewhere. This was the lie about me that was sworn to by one police infiltrator after another. I don't believe for a moment that any one of them could possibly have believed it, or that either Richard Schultz or Thomas Foran, the two government prosecutors who coached them, could have believed it. Anyone who attended any of our meetings or listened to the tapes secretly made at them by the infiltrators had to have known of my constant insistence on nonviolent methods of protest.

57

For our defense, we had a range of people who testified that they had been mercilessly clubbed, maced or mauled by the police when they were involved in no illegal or violent actions, and/or that they had seen others similarly abused. They included demonstrators, nondemonstrating passers-by and bystanders, newspeople, doctors and nurses. Additionally, POW Interrogator Peter Martinsen and Special Forces Sergeant Donald Duncan from the Bertrand Russell War Crimes Tribunal came to testify that I knew of U.S. war crimes in Vietnam and felt an urgent human and patriotic need to demonstrate for an end to the war. We also drew on a number of government officials, members of public investigative bodies, civic leaders and others who had information about our nonviolent plans and actions, the city's denial of our constitutional rights and the violence of the police.

A number of our witnesses (some of whom were not allowed to testify before the jury) were major or minor celebrities of the time. These included Anne Kerr (a member of the British parliament who was a nondemonstrator but had been brutally arrested and then maced inside the arrest wagon), Dr. Edward Sparling (President Emeritus of Chicago's Roosevelt University), Phil Ochs, Allen Ginsberg, William Styron (1967 Pulitzer Prize–winning novelist), Dick Gregory, Jacques Levy (Broadway director of *Oh! Calcutta!* and other hits), Timothy Leary (one of those who we thought would not help with the jury), Ed Sanders (leader of the rock and roll group the Fugs, always full of good politics but a far-out spoof artist who was sure to be anathema to most of the jury), Stuart Meacham (leading Quaker), Carl Oglesby (former president of SDS), Mark Lane (JFK's campaign manager for the New York City area), Julian Bond (state representative and 1968 delegate from Georgia who was nominated at the Convention for vice president but had to point out that he was ineligible because of his age), Arlo Guthrie, Cora Weiss, Thomas Paterson Alder (president of the Public Law Education Institute in Washington), Wesley Pomeroy (Justice Department liaison between federal, state and local law enforcement officials for the Republican and Democratic Conventions), Roger Wilkins (head of the Justice Department's Community Relations Service in 1968), Country Joe McDonald (rock and roll star), Sam Brown (from Senator Eugene McCarthy's presidential campaign staff), Judy Collins, Paul Potter (former president of SDS), Norman Mailer, Congressman John Conyers, Ramsey Clark (Attorney General in 1968), historian Staughton Lynd, Ralph Abernathy (Martin Luther King, Jr.'s designated successor as president of the Southern Christian Leadership Conference) and Jesse Jackson. Among others not apt to be appreciated by the jury were Paul Krassner and Linda Morse. Krassner, the creator of the title "yippie" and editor of *The Realist*, a far-out humor magazine, took a dose of LSD before testifying and was a disaster in our eyes as well as the jury's. Morse was a wonderful young woman I had worked with, who had been so disillusioned with the police violence at the Convention that she temporarily abandoned her nonviolence and was training for armed revolution at the time. It was a decision that I hated, and one that she soon thought better of, but the prosecution made the most of it. We had one policeman, Renault A. Robinson, president of the Afro-American Patrolmen's League, and we tried to subpoena Lyndon Johnson and Mayor Daley.

The judge denied our motion to subpoena Johnson and permitted us to subpoena the mayor but disallowed any significant questioning of him. The technicality on which he did this was to deny our motion to have the mayor classified as "a hostile witness," a legal category for a witness who has been subpoenaed by the defense but favors the prosecution. "Hostile witnesses" can be asked a wider range of questions than are permitted for a "friendly witness."

> THE COURT: Why, the mayor has been a most friendly witness. I deny the motion.

When Kunstler tried to argue the motion, quoting irreproachable legal citations, this was Judge Hoffman's response:

THE COURT: . . . The Court finds that there is nothing in the testimony of the witness that has indicated hostility. His manner has been that of a gentleman.

Some other interesting things happened during Daley's presence. In addition to the federal marshals, the courtroom was filled with armed security guards who were employees of the city. One of them knocked down one of our women staffpeople for no apparent reason, seriously injuring her. Second, Kunstler managed to ask, while being overruled,

MR. KUNSTLER: Mayor Daley, on the twenty-eighth of August, 1968, did you say to Senator Ribicoff—
MR. FORAN: Oh, Your Honor, I object.
MR. KUNSTLER: [Continuing] "Fuck you, you Jew son of a bitch, you lousy motherfucker, go home"?

It was true. When Ribicoff had begun to speak inside the Democratic Convention about the police violence against the demonstrators, city officials had cut off his microphone and a red-faced Daley had shouted this at him. We had a video of it.

The third, really amusing scene occurred before court had reconvened for its afternoon session. The judge had not come in yet, Daley was sitting in his chair waiting and Abbie Hoffman walked up to him. In a typical moment of spontaneous guerrilla theater, Abbie held out his clenched fist and said, "Why don't you and I settle this whole business right now, just the two of us." I give Daley credit for laughing when Abbie did it, and I was relieved when none of his armed guards jumped Abbie.

Ramsey Clark, Staughton Lynd and Ralph Abernathy were on a long list of intended witnesses who were not permitted to testify before the jury at all. Moreover, almost every time others began to get into something damning to the government and its case against us, the prosecution automatically objected and the judge automatically sustained the objection. Here is a typical objection but one in which, as sometimes happened, some information was recorded anyway:

THE WITNESS [Elizabeth Jean Snodgrass, a registered nurse]: We were treating people for some severe Mace burns, skin burns and also some gas burns of the eye. Those who had not been treated

> immediately . . . had already begun to show blisters on the face and severe eye injury.
> MR. WEINGLASS: Is that injury accompanied by pain?
> MR. SCHULTZ: I don't know how she would know unless she was maced.
> THE WITNESS: I was.
> THE COURT: I sustain the objection.

Later, as happened miraculously once in a while, Snodgrass was able to give testimony that had some important content:

> THE WITNESS: The police had stopped at the mouth of the alley, and had turned to the medical people standing there and had picked up some cement pieces (the sidewalk had been chipped up and there was construction), and turned toward the medical group, and began throwing the rocks, while saying some obscenities to the group.
> MR. WEINGLASS: Were you struck by a rock?
> THE WITNESS: Yes, I was.
> MR. WEINGLASS: And do you recall what the police said to the group?
> THE WITNESS: . . . "Medical aides, my ass. If it weren't for you fucking bastards, the rest of the group wouldn't be here."

The judge ruled that Ramsey Clark had "nothing material or relevant" that he could contribute to the case, and ordered us not to mention to the jury that he had come to testify and been excluded. Martinson's and Duncan's testimony on the nature of the war was ruled irrelevant, as was our effort to introduce information about the massacre at My Lai, which first became public during the trial. In a Necessity Defense, which judges occasionally permit, even if it is proven that a defendant broke a minor law s/he can be found not guilty if it can also be proven that s/he did it in the course of trying to prevent a greater harm, danger or violation of law. But Judge Hoffman didn't want any such considerations to come before the jury. In 1984, Ramsey Clark was allowed to testify in one of my trials, in which I was being charged with breaking the trespass laws by being one of forty-four persons who sat in at the Vermont office of

Senator Robert Stafford. We were protesting his consistent voting for funding the Nicaraguan Contras and the terrorist government of El Salvador. Given the witnesses who were allowed to testify, the jury unanimously found all forty-four of us not guilty of the trespassing charge.* Three years later, in February 1987, Ramsey tried to testify at my Capitol Rotunda trial but, as Judge Hoffman had done in 1970, the judge listened to his proffered testimony out of the presence of the jury and ruled it inadmissible.

President Sparling was prevented from testifying as to the findings of the Commission he had headed which had investigated allegations of police brutality during an earlier peace march that had served as a testing ground (for the city and for local peace demonstrators) for Convention activities. The Sparling Commission had found that

> Brutalizing demonstrators without provocation, they [the police] failed to live up to that difficult professionalism which we demand. Yet to place primary blame on the police would, in our view, be inappropriate. Administrative actions . . . were designed by City officials to communicate that "these people have no right to demonstrate or express their views . . ."

After Allen Ginsberg's impressive testimony, Tom Foran got him to talk about his religious and spiritual emphases, asked him about having kissed Abbie Hoffman at the Coliseum, and followed this by asking him to read three graphically homosexual poems that Foran had selected. After each poem, Foran asked Allen to "explain the religious significance of that poem," and each time Allen explained it beautifully. The last one was "Love Poem on Theme by Whitman" and Allen ended his explanation by saying:

*For a slightly condensed transcript of the 1984 trial of the Winooski 44, see *Por Amor al Pueblo: Not Guilty*. Besides the testimony of Ramsey Clark, it includes testimony by Salvadoran refugees, former CIA officials David MacMichael and John Stockwell, historian Howard Zinn, international law scholar Richard Falk and others. Abbie Hoffman ordered copies to help him, Amy Carter and others in their 1986 trial for sitting-in at the University of Massachusetts at Amherst. They used the necessity defense, and won their case.

> So he projected from his own desire and from his own unconsciousness a sexual urge he felt was normal to the unconscious of most people, though forbidden, for the most part, to take part.
>
> Walt Whitman is one of my spiritual teachers and I am following him in this poem . . . projecting my own . . . feelings, *of which I don't have shame, sir,* which I feel are basically charming, actually (emphasis by Allen).

That ended the cross-examination, but as Allen passed Foran on his way out of the courtroom, Foran said in a voice filled with contempt and loud enough for the jury to hear, "*Fag!*"

Despite the cruel, prejudiced and prejudicial nature of that real obscenity, Foran was not chided, let alone cited for contempt of court. His remark wasn't even recorded in the transcript, even though much quieter comments the defendants made to one another at the defense table were often put in the record, and the judge, who in most cases couldn't have heard them, used them for contempt citations. One of my thirty-two contempt charges was for having said something very quietly to a government witness when he walked over to the defense table to identify Tom Hayden. His name was Louis Salzberg, a press photographer who had been hired by the FBI to infiltrate our meetings and had gone to great lengths to ingratiate himself with me. I looked up at him and said, "Quite a letdown, Louis, I'm really disappointed in you." Even the *New York Times* said that I spoke "softly." For saying this, I was sentenced to a month in jail. Foran's being a lawyer was not what protected him from contempt because before the trial was over lawyers Kunstler and Weinglass were charged with twenty-three and fourteen contempts, respectively. Bill Kunstler was sentenced to six months in jail for asking Mayor Daley "questions that were objectionable."

As for patrolman Renault Robinson, as usual the government objected to everything he was asked or started to say and the judge sustained the objections. He was cut off in the middle of a sentence in which he was trying to say that a lot of the Black policemen had been transferred to other duties because they had disagreed with the Police Department's tactics during Convention week. When he was asked about a "victory party" the police held shortly after they had beaten up the demonstrators, the question was stricken and the jury excused. Out of the presence of the jury, he testified that about 150 policemen attended the victory party given by the captain of his district and that at first they chanted "Thundering Third District." Then a group of officers stood at attention, raised their arms and chanted "*Sieg Heil.*" The testimony was ruled inadmissible, so the jury never heard it. On a later visit to Chicago, I met with Robinson and found that he had been severely punished by the Police Department for having tried to testify.

The closing argument to the jury by Foran repeated and compounded most of the other lies and voiced the sentiment the government had tried to communicate to the jury all through the trial:

> These are highly sophisticated, highly educated men, every one of them. They are not kids. . . . These are highly sophisticated, educated men and they are evil men. . . . Evil is exciting and evil is interesting, and plenty of kids have a fascination for it. It is knowledge of kids like that that these sophisticated, educated psychology majors know about. They know about kids, and they know how to draw the kids together and maneuver them, and use them to accomplish their purposes. . . . You saw them excoriating the founders of the country whose pictures his Honor has on the wall behind you.
>
> MR. KUNSTLER: Your Honor, that is not true. That was Bobby Seale.
>
> FORAN: "Kill the pigs. Get 'em. Get 'em. . . ." The vision and ideals that our forefathers had just can't be corrupted by the haters, the violent anarchists. . . . Gandhi, Dr. King—"Truthful, pure, loving." Not liars and obscene haters like those men are. Can you imagine? You know the way they name-dropped—can you imagine—and it is almost blasphemous to say it. They have named Saint Matthew and they named Jesus and they named Abraham Lincoln. They named Martin Luther King. Can you imagine those men supporting these men if they—
>
> A SPECTATOR [My daughter Tasha]: Yes, I can imagine it because it's true.
>
> THE COURT: Remove those people, Mr. Marshal.
>
> MR. DELLINGER: That's my daughter.
>
> A SPECTATOR [Tasha, continuing as she is being dragged out]: I won't listen to any more of these disgusting lies.

DELLINGER [As Michele is being escorted out]: That's my other daughter. Thank you. Right on. Right on. Don't hit my daughter that way. I saw you. That man hit her on the head for saying the truth in here.

THE COURT: The marshals will maintain order.

MR. DELLINGER: Yes, but they don't have to hit thirteen-year-old girls who know that I was close to Martin Luther King.

THE COURT: Mr. Marshal, have that man sit down.

MR. FORAN: You see how it works? "Don't hit her."

MR. DELLINGER: He did hit her.

A SPECTATOR [As Frank Joyce of our staff was slugged while leaving to be with my daughter]: They hit him. He did hit her.

MR. FORAN: Oh, bunk.

MR. DELLINGER: I saw him hit her.

MR. FORAN: Can you imagine? Can you imagine those men supporting anybody—supporting anybody who would try to draw young kids to a park—

A SPECTATOR [Abbie's wife, Anita]: Why did Ramsey Clark come here? Why did Ramsey Clark come here?

THE COURT: Remove that woman. Remove her and don't let her return, Mr. Marshal.

I had clearly seen the marshal give Michele a tremendous clout on the side of her face, in the doorway. Michele wasn't even struggling with the marshal. Tasha did struggle when the marshal grabbed her, and she was hit also.

It's hard for me to write this twenty-two years later without crying. And at the time, I had to go right back to jail and couldn't even comfort them. Not even during a prison visit, since I wasn't allowed any. I couldn't even find out how badly Michele and Tasha were hurt. Once again the sins of the parents, *my sins*, were being visited on their children, *my children*.

58

Back when the jury was being selected, all the questions asked of the prospective jurors were asked by Judge Hoffman. We submitted a list of questions for his consideration, but he did not use any of them. I no longer have the list, but *Rolling Stone* of April 2, 1970, listed some of them:

> Do you believe that young men who refuse to participate in the Armed Forces because of their opposition to the war are cowards, slackers or unpatriotic?
>
> Have you ever moved from a neighborhood because of the influx of people of certain religious, ethnic or racial origins?

Here *Rolling Stone* commented: "This is a civil rights lawyers question; you'd be surprised how many 'yes' answers are turned up."

> Do you have any hostile feeling toward persons whose life styles differ considerably from your own?
>
> If your own children are male, do they have long hair or wear what you consider to be unorthodox clothing?
>
> Do you know who the Jefferson Airplane, Country Joe and the Fish, Phil Ochs or the Fugs are?
>
> Do you consider marijuana habit-forming?
>
> Do you admire the Rev. Billie Joe Hargis or Billy Graham?

Rolling Stone's comment was: "All 'irrelevant' the judge said. But those questions, of course—and not the nonsense about 'inciting to riot'—are what the trial was all about."

Early in the selection process, we surprised the government by accepting a panel of twelve prospective jurors who remained after a couple rounds of challenges by ourselves and the government. A number of them were obviously hostile to us and we still had a few peremptory challenges that could have removed them. But there were two or three on the panel who we thought would be relatively open-minded and we hoped through them to reach some of the others—or at least to get a hung jury. In particular, we were impressed by a young woman by the name of Kristi King, whose sister had once been a recruiter for Vista (the domestic Peace Corps), and by another woman named Jean Fritz. We thought it was a good sign that Fritz, a middle-aged white woman, was carrying a book by James Baldwin under her arm when she entered the room. And we felt sure that the government would eliminate these two if we kept the selection process open by challenging the hostile members. Meanwhile, we would have used up all our challenges, and the prosecution would be able to pack the jury to its heart's content.

Little did we know that by closing off the process when we did, we excluded someone the government had intended to be on the jury. It was a young woman by the name of Kay Richards whose fiancée was Mayor Daley's supervisor of personnel for Cook County. She had carefully concealed this in the preliminary examination and we didn't find it out until after the trial and verdict. Then we learned that she had given an incorrect home address, presumably to prevent being investigated by reporters (or our staff people) who might have discovered her Daley connections. We had actually wanted her on the jury, because she was younger than most of the others and because she kept waving and smiling at us, even blowing a kiss to one or two of us (carefully concealing it from the judge and prosecution with her other hand). But when we accepted the jury prematurely she just missed out and became the first alternate.

That happened on September 24. On September 30, Mr. Foran reported that the FBI had informed him that a threatening letter had been sent to two of the jurors, one of them Kristi King. The contents of the letter were "You are being watched. The Black Panthers."

It developed that Kristi King had never seen the letter. But the judge called her into the courtroom, separate from the rest of the jury, showed it to her, and after she said that she had never seen it insisted that she read it out loud. Afterwards, while she was still shaking, he asked her, "Having now seen it, will you please tell me whether, having seen and read that document, you can continue to be a fair and impartial juror in this case . . . ? Do you still think you can do that?" Not surprisingly, she said no, and was dismissed. Kay Richards took her place.

An identical letter was sent to Mrs. Ruth Peterson, but when queried by the judge she said that she had already read the letter and discussed it with another juror (against the rules, by the way) and could remain impartial. She turned out to be one of the two jurors most insistent on guilty verdicts for all the defendants on all counts.

I was sitting next to Bobby Seale when the letter was read and he immediately said, "That's a forgery. We never sign anything 'The Black Panthers.' It's always 'The Black Panther Party.' Or if we are being formal, 'The Black Panther Party for Self Defense.' " For our part, we never doubted that the letter was sent by someone connected with the prosecution—the FBI? Chicago Police? Mayor's office? Or all of them working together in conjunction with the prosecutor *and judge*, as they did all through the trial.

A second result of the letters was that the judge sequestered the jury. They were put under the supervision of U.S. marshals, housed at the Palmer House Hotel, cut off from their families and denied conjugal visits for nearly five months. We argued against this, for human reasons as well as knowing that sequestered juries usually blame the defendants (government-declared criminals) rather than the judge. After the trial, two jurors friendly to us said to me, "We were locked up, constrained and under constant supervision, while the defendants were free to do as they pleased outside court hours."

When Judge Hoffman issued the order, he said to the jurors:

> The purpose . . . is to preserve the integrity of the trial and to see to it that people don't talk to you who aren't entitled to speak to you; that you do not see newspapers or any other journals or listen to radio or television and look at television.

But, as John Schultz reported in *Motion Will Be Denied*, "they were permitted to watch endless James Bond movies, where they could compare the government's undercover agents with spying viewed in a favorable way." And after the verdict, two of the jurors who had fought for acquittal for all the defendants on all charges told me that if the other jurors had been able to hear or see accounts of the My Lai massacre, it might have changed their opinion of why we came to Chicago and what we were trying to accomplish.

These two events, the seating of Kay Richards on the jury and the confinement of the jurors under supervision of the marshals had a significant effect on the eventual verdict, which was reached on February 18, 1970.

Just how significant I found out shortly afterwards when I went back to Chicago to speak at a public meeting. Two of the jurors, Jean Fritz and Shirley Seaholm, came to the meeting, sought me out and we talked. After that, I saw them on some future visits as well. Despite having brought the Baldwin book to the jury selection room, Fritz had come that day convinced that we were disreputable, guilty people: "I was a typical victim of the Chicago media," she said. Even so, our instincts about the importance of her reading Baldwin were sound, because she had the kind of open, inquiring mind that soon led her to change her opinions of both us and the government.

Fritz and Seaholm told me that four of the jurors had been in favor of acquittal on all counts and, barring consensus on that, wanted to hold out for a hung jury—which would have meant acquittal unless the government went through the ardors of another lengthy, embarrassing trial. But they were eventually worn down, in part by Kay Richards and in part by the sequestration and pressures exerted by the marshals and the judge.

In his book *Motion Will Be Denied*, John Schultz writes what he observed as a courtroom reporter: "Everyone in the courtroom saw Kay Richards laugh outright on the side of the defense, earnestly and consistently, for five months of trial. For whatever purpose, she was . . . playing a game, and it was quite a game to play every day for five months."

Seaholm and Fritz told me that similarly, all during the trial Richards hung out with them and the other two acquittal jurors (Frieda Robbins and Mary Butler), pretending that she supported them and us. But for some reason they felt that they could not trust her. And when time came for the verdict, she told them that unfortunately the government had proven its case and there was no alternative but to find us guilty on all counts.

Schultz writes,

> The two jurors said: "From the beginning, we had a peculiar feeling about her." "She wanted a lot of information, but she never gave any." "She used people."
>
> When her boyfriend came to see her, the marshals did not monitor them as closely as the other jurors and visitors. Sometimes they even left Kay Richards and Tom Stevens alone.

When the acquittal jurors held out, Richards developed a compromise verdict and she brought pressure on them to accept it as the best that could be accomplished. For this, we have not only the words of Seaholm and Fritz but those of Kay Richards herself. She boasted to the press a few days later that she had engineered a compromise that had saved the government from a hung jury and subsequent dismissal of all charges.

It is important to understand the context in which Richards, the judge and the marshals "achieved" this:

> Shirley Seaholm asked . . . "Does the government have us on its lists now?" . . . "How long after we were home . . . were we careful about what we said on the phone?"
>
> They listened to what was said in court and they concluded that there was no restraint on the government. The government could do as it wished, make up its own rules, and then break them and make them again as it saw fit. . . . The conditions and restraints of the sequestered lives . . . would not encourage the feeling that they were safely free to deliver a verdict as they perceived it. They knew that their mail was being opened. Their phone calls were monitored by marshals who listened to every word. Their conversations with family visitors were conducted in the immediate presence of marshals.
>
> "When I was on jury duty," said Shirley Seaholm, "it was

> the first time I was afraid of our government. . . ." Mrs. Fritz agreed. . . . "I came to fear our government for the first time." The parade of undercover and plainclothes agents and their testimony meant to those four jurors that the government's operations were probably more underhanded and skulking and distorted than anything the defendants could do. It meant someone next door to you or nearby you, in trust and proximity, perhaps someone on this jury itself, could be posing as your friend and helpmate in order to do you grave harm.
>
> The "acquittal" jurors in general were overtaken by a feeling of defenseless terror. . . . Mrs. Fritz said that she was almost hysterical, weeping more than once during the deliberations, wanting desperately to get out of there.*

Twice the jurors sent a unanimous message to the judge that they were hopelessly divided, unable to reach a verdict, a hung jury. Twice the judge ordered them to "keep deliberating," he would not accept a hung jury. He never answered their notes in writing—or informed our lawyers of this development, as he is required to do—but sent word back by way of the marshal. To add to the pressure, the marshal told the jurors that "the judge can keep you here as long as he wants."

Mrs. Fritz told me that having seen the judge in operation and having observed how determined he was to get us convicted, this statement terrified her. Among other things, she had phlebitis, it had gotten worse from sitting in the narrow jury box and she had been in pain for some time. She also said that several of the other jurors were not well either and everyone was suffering from the long months of sequestration, the denial of conjugal visits and the around-the-clock surveillance.

So in the end the four acquittal jurors accepted the "compromise verdict" that Kay Richards had come up with. It was to find Froines and Weiner (the "bargaining chips," as we later called them) not guilty on all

*This is from Schultz again. I quote him because he is an outside source who sums up well a lot of what the two jurors said to me, and because I did not write down their words as we talked.

counts and to find us not guilty of conspiracy but guilty of inciting to riot. Each of us was sentenced to "imprisonment for a term of five years . . . fined the sum of $5,000 *and costs of prosecution, the defendants to stand committed until the fine and costs have been paid.*"

But there is more to the story of Kay Richards than the above episodes reveal. Here is something that I wrote about her—and us—in an earlier book:*

> It would be convenient to end the account there: "good guys" (the acquittal jurors) tricked and intimidated by the government; "bad guys" (the jurors for conviction), themselves victims of society's stifling authoritarianism; "worse guys," the government and its agents. All of this is true, but in real life people are always more complex than that, [capable of] moving . . . if given a chance to escape from their present roles and stereotypes. What is one to say about Kay Richards, linked to the Daley machine, self-proclaimed manipulator of the compromise that saved the government from bitter defeat and assigned five of the defendants to jail? She concluded her nationally syndicated account of the trial with the following comment:
>
> > That trial changed my life, as it changed their lives. If I helped to put these men in prison, they have in a sense helped to free me from another kind of prison. I think now that in many ways they were good men—not evil men as the prosecutor said.†
>
> Perhaps if we had been better men we would have been able not only to strengthen the four acquittal jurors but also to break through Kay Richards' defenses more thoroughly and more quickly. Perhaps like thousands of others . . . from former hawk Daniel Ellsberg to conscience-stricken bomber pilots to some FBI agents and ITT secretaries, she might have broken out of the destructive role assigned to her.

***More Power Than We Know*, p. 213.

†Chicago *Sun-Times*, February 22, 1970.

After the verdict, the other defendants joined me in jail, the judge having denied our attorneys' application for bail, ruling that "From the evidence and from their conduct in this trial, I find they are dangerous men to be at large . . ."

Ten days later, on February 28, 1970, a federal appeals court overturned the denial of bail.

In November 1972 a federal appeals court overturned our conviction of inciting to riot, ruling that we had been denied a fair trial.

In May 1972 a federal appeals court overturned the contempt convictions.

The government never brought us to trial again on the original charges, but a four-week retrial on the contempt charges took place in November–December 1973. Before it began, the government dropped 123 of the original charges, leaving a total of fifty-two, and asked that any jail sentences be limited to six months. Limiting the possible sentences was a way of preventing us from having a jury trial. The judge was Judge Gignoux from Maine, the father of a girlfriend of mine from college days. Since I defended myself, I saw him often during the consultations in judge's chambers and he brought loving greetings from her. He didn't disquality himself and we didn't ask him to.

In the end, Judge Gignoux convicted me of seven charges, Hoffman, Rubin and Bill Kunstler of two each. But when the time came for sentencing he ruled that in view of the time that all of us, except Kunstler, had already spent in jail and the late date, four years after the events, nothing was to be gained by sentencing us to prison.

Here is the concluding paragraph from my statement to Judge Gignoux before sentencing:

> I began by saying that I have learned things from you because you are courteous and decent and I have also said that you blew it, you failed. You came out on the side of injustice instead of justice. But just as I will take things away with me, I hope something is churning inside of you. And I would like very much to welcome you—I don't know if I dare say to our side; that may sound a little self-righteous or too narrow—but I look forward to the day when this trial will have the effect on you whereby some of those poor people and some of the Black people and some of

> those dissenting people [I had specifically called his attention to these three groups earlier in the statement] will end up vindicated because you will rise to the level of justice in the broadest and most historic sense of the word instead of staying at the level of justice in . . . the United States of America in a capitalist society.

59

This is the statement I made to the court before I was sentenced for incitement to riot:

> I would like to make four brief points.
>
> First, I think that every judge should be required to spend time in prison before sentencing other people so that he might become aware of the degrading antihuman conditions that persist, not only in Cook County Jail but in prisons generally of this country.
>
> I feel more compassion for you, sir, than I do any hostility. I feel that you are a man who has had too much power over the lives of too many people for too many years. You have sentenced them to those degrading conditions without being fully aware of what you are doing, and undoubtedly feeling correct and righteous, as often happens when people do the most abominable things.
>
> I think that in 1970 perhaps the American people will begin to discover something about the nature of the prison system, the system in which we are now confined and in which thousands of other political prisoners are confined.
>
> The Black Panthers have said that all Black prisoners are political prisoners, and I think that all people in prison are political

prisoners. They are in prison, most of them, because they have violated the property and power concepts of the society. The bankrobber I talked to yesterday was only trying to get his in the ways he thought were open to him, just as businessmen and others profiteer and try to advance their own economic cause at the expense of their fellows.

My second point is that whatever happens to us, however unjustified, will be slight compared to what has happened already to the Vietnamese people, to the Black people in this country, to the criminals with whom we are now spending our days in Cook County Jail.

I have already lived longer than the normal life expectancy of a Black person born when I was born or who is born now. I must have already lived longer, twenty years longer, than the normal life expectancy in the underdeveloped countries which this country is trying to profiteer from and keep under its domain and control.

Thirdly, I want to say that sending us to prison, any punishment the Government can impose upon us, will not solve the problems that have gotten us into trouble with the Government and the law in the first place, will not solve the problems of this country's rampant racism, will not solve the problems of economic justice. It will not solve the problem of the foreign policy and the attacks upon the underdeveloped people of the world.

The Government has misread the times in which we live. Just like there was a time when it was possible to keep Black people in slavery, and then it became impossible, so this country is growing out of the time when it is possible to keep young people, women, Black people, Mexican-Americans, antiwar people, people who believe in truth and justice and really believe in democracy, when it is going to be possible to keep them quiet or suppress them.

Finally, all the way through this I have been ambivalent toward you, because there is something spunky about you that one has to admire, however misguided and intolerant I believe you are. All the way through the trial, sort of without consciousness or almost against my own will, I keep comparing you to George III of England, perhaps because you are trying to hold back the tide of history, although you will not succeed, perhaps because you are trying to stem and forestall a second American revolution.

Our movement is not very strong today. It is not united, it is not well organized. But there is the beginning of an awakening in this country which has been going on for at least the last fifteen years, and it is an awakening that will not be denied. Tactics will change, people will err, people will die in the streets and die in prison. But I do not believe that this Movement can be denied, because however falsely applied the American ideal was from the beginning, when it excluded Black people and Indians and people without property, nonetheless there was a dream of justice and equality and freedom and brotherhood. And I think that dream is much closer to fulfillment today than it has been at any time in the history of this country.

I only wish that we were all not just more eloquent. I wish we were smarter, more dedicated, more united. I wish we could work together. I wish we could reach out to the Forans and Schultzes and the [Judge] Hoffmans of this world, and convince them of the necessity of this revolution.

I think I shall sleep better and happier and with a greater sense of fulfillment in whatever jails I am in for however many years than if I had compromised, if I had pretended the problems were any less real than they are, or if I had sat here passively in the courthouse while justice was being throttled and the truth was being denied.

I salute my brothers and sisters in Vietnam, in the ghetto, in the women's liberation movement, all the people all over the world who are struggling to make true and real for all people the ideals on which this country was supposed to be founded, but never, never lived up to.

60

Two events that happened outside the courtroom during the first months of the trial added to the stresses I was experiencing in the trial itself. One began with a threatening letter from the "Black United Front" of Washington, D.C. The other was the assassination of Fred Hampton, Chairman of the Illinois Black Panther Party.

The letter from the Black United Front was addressed to me as Chairman of the National Mobilization Committee and arrived in my courthouse mail a few weeks before a major demonstration the Mobe was organizing for November 15, 1969, in Washington, D.C., the March Against Death. It said that whenever antiwar demonstrators came to town the police let them off easy and took out their anger and frustration out of sight of the media by running wild in the Black community, injuring innocent people and causing considerable damage. This time the Black United Front was going to do something about it. It demanded that the Mobe pay it a dollar a head for every demonstrator, beginning with an immediate downpayment of ten thousand dollars. While we were still trying to find out who the Black United Front was, a second letter arrived: If we did not pay, they would meet arriving buses and break the kneecaps of demonstrators as they left the buses.

It was true that the Black community did suffer in the manner they said during our major demonstrations. We had been concerned and trying to take steps against it for some time. But the Front's method of responding to the problem was hardly one that we could accept. So after our Washington representatives reported that it appeared to be a legitimate new group, we set up a meeting for the following Saturday. I canceled my speaking engagements for that day and, along with three or four other Mobilization officers, met with about twenty representatives of the Front.

As soon as we entered the room, one of the Front's spokespersons ostentatiously locked the door and announced that we were not getting out until we gave them the first check. If I remember correctly the down-payment had now gone up to twenty thousand dollars, a sum far in excess of anything that we ever had in our account. In the end we didn't give them a check and we got out alive and unhurt, but it wasn't easy and for a long time we didn't know if it would turn out that way.

The best I can say in explanation is that we acted sensitively and sensibly, and so did a gradually growing number of the Blacks, despite the contrary behavior of those who had raised the issue and dominated the early stages of the confrontation. We readily agreed with the charges—that the police acted as the Front said they did, that the Mobilization had not done enough to counteract it, and that the problem was aggravated by the inbred racism and insensitivity of many of the white demonstrators. We asked them for more information on these problems and offered to work together to improve the situation. And of course we said that breaking the kneecaps of arriving demonstrators would only add to the racism and provide the police with an additional reason for beating up on Blacks and the Black community.

Fortunately, there were some thoroughly admirable, clear-thinking Blacks present and, thanks to them, we worked things out. Besides planning for some immediate (and continuing) educational work within the Mobe, we added another Black speaker to talk about the need for D.C. statehood. The speaker agreed to was Julius Hobson, a leader of the fight for statehood whom I was fortunate enough to know as a comrade and friend. He wasn't present in that locked room and wouldn't for a moment have had anything to do with the Front's threats and proposed methods of dealing with the problem. But we should have included him, and the subject of D.C. statehood, on the program anyway.

I wonder, did you guess that the FBI had set up the whole confrontation? They did, but we didn't know it at the time or for some time afterward, whatever our suspicions. A year or so later a disillusioned Black ex-FBI agent by the name of Robert Wall confessed that he and other FBI personnel had instigated it, typing the letter to me in the FBI office and acting as chief provocateurs from the beginning. He wrote about it in the *New York Review of Books* (January 27, 1972), saying, among other things, that "The letter we composed was approved by the bureau's counterintelligence desk and was signed with the forged signature of a leader of the black group." Fortunately for us, they had to work through some honest Blacks in order to have any hope that their scheme would succeed, and it was the presence of these non-FBI members in our meeting that eventually overwhelmed them and led to a positive resolution.

I have to add one negative word, though. I don't believe that I or other leading members of the Mobe ever did enough to get at the roots of the insensitivity and subconscious racism that provided the context in which the FBI was able to launch its nefarious plot, a plot that obviously was potentially as harmful to Blacks as to whites. And we have not done enough to this day, in the successor organization to the Mobe or elsewhere. By this, I do not mean that we should automatically agree with our Black sisters and brothers, whatever they say or demand—far from it. Like whites, Blacks can be wrong too, as the instigators of this plot demonstrated. For insecure, guilty or fearful whites to lump all Blacks together and to be afraid to listen to them honestly, to consider honestly what they say or advocate and to respond honestly to it from the depths of their own being is in itself a sign of disrespect and of failure to treat Blacks as equals. Not to do so is an unproductive, unintentionally racist approach that I first observed among some white civil rights workers in the early days of the movement in the South. It became more common during the early Black Power days, and, sad to say, I observed it inside the National Board of the Rainbow Coalition from 1984 on. Not universally in the Rainbow Coalition but enough to be harmful, both for the whites who succumbed to it and for Jesse Jackson.

Now to Fred Hampton. When the Chicago defendants were not allowed to see Bobby Seale until the trial began, Fred acted as Bobby's surrogate in the meetings to discuss our plans for the trial. I have rarely been so impressed with anyone as I was with Fred at our first meeting. I remember thinking strange thoughts that I felt uneasy about, as if they might reflect a tinge of the unconscious racism that I don't believe in. My god, I thought, this twenty-year-old Black has a depth, understanding and sensitivity that I don't have and that just about every white person I know lacks. Maybe whites are the underprivileged members of our society, since at least some Blacks learn more from their persecution than any of us have learned from our privileged status. Eventually, of course, I settled for reminding myself once again never to forget that Blacks (and other oppressed groups, including other peoples of color) *are* able to see and understand things that their oppressors and would-be white supporters don't. And they are able to contribute insights and forms of leadership in our *joint* struggles for justice and peace that we can't. The trick is to understand this and act accordingly without falling into the kind of unnatural and unhealthy subservience I have mentioned.

Anyway, I was inspired by Fred from the beginning, more than I am ordinarily inspired by anyone I meet. And the feeling persisted as we became close friends and coworkers during the few remaining months that he was allowed to live. Besides our working together on the trial, he and I spoke quite a few times at the same public events, sometimes traveling together outside Chicago to do so. And when a problem arose because the Weathermen planned a violent demonstration in Chicago during our trial, he and I worked together, along with Bill Kunstler, to try to persuade them to change their plans.

Technically, Bill Kunstler and I were brought in by both groups, the Panthers and the Weathermen, to mediate a bitter conflict between them. But the closest Bill and I came to speaking up on behalf of the Weathermen was to try to persuade the Panthers that the Weathermen were sincerely dedicated revolutionaries who might be temporarily on a counterproductive path but should be respected for their seriousness of purpose and spared the humiliation of a public attack by Fred in advance of their demonstration. We also argued that such an attack would give the police an excuse to brutalize the demonstrators, on the pretext that they were even more violent than the Panthers (that is, than the police accused the Panthers of being). Fred agreed and lived up to it. But, wisely and correctly, I believe, he did condemn their action publicly after the event, which took place on October 8 and which the Weathermen called the Days of Rage.

The "mediators" spent most of the time supporting Fred and his three colleagues in their attempts to persuade the Weathermen to abandon the violence in their planned action. Fred called their plan "stupid," "adventuristic" and "Custeristic." He complained that they would expose their followers to useless beatings and jail sentences while giving the police the excuse they were looking for to increase their violence against the entire movement, including the Panthers. Moreover, they would convince the public that such police actions were justified, and they would turn off potential allies, preventing the expansion of the movement into newly aroused sections of the populace.

"Bobby Seale's life is at stake," Fred said at one point, "and you motherfuckers don't give a damn because you want to be motherfucking martyrs yourselves. Revolution is no motherfucking game with us. The Black community has too many martyrs already."

By the end of the meeting, I thought that we (mostly Fred) had made headway with the four Weathermen leaders present, and that it might affect the nature of their demonstration. They had promised that they would avoid the dangers we had pointed out, and it seemed that they would tone down the Days of Rage. But they didn't. Whether the four who had seemed to bend a little thought better (worse) of it later, or were not strong enough to stand up to those who were not present and accused them of "middle-class inhibitions against violence" (one of the Weathermen's favorite phrases), I do not know. But I watched part of the event as a disgusted observer and was revolted by what I saw.

I saw Bernadine Dohrn, Mark Rudd and a couple of the others in Winnetka later that evening in the "safe house" where I stayed during the trial and where I had arranged for them to stay while they were in Chicago. Unlike many of the others, they had escaped arrest and when they arrived they started telling me triumphantly about a Rolls-Royce they had smashed, a fancy restaurant whose windows they had broken, the windshield of a police car they had shattered and so on. I wouldn't have approved of any of that anyway, but I confronted them with what I had seen: the police had guarded the swankier neighborhoods and establishments on the area's main street and the Weathermen had responded by sweeping down a couple of unguarded side streets, attacking small shops, proletarian beerhalls, lower-middle-class housing and every car on the block. When shopkeepers or car owners had tried to protect their stores or cars, some of the Weathermen had attacked them with lead pipes, brass knuckles and clubs.* When I confronted Bernadine and Mark with these

*I found out the next day that one of my friends, an impecunious law student, was holding a meeting in his flat to organize support for me and my codefendants. His old jalopy and the car of one of the people who had come to the meeting were both

things, the glow left their faces and they admitted that some things had "gone wrong." This showed me how close to the surface was the conflict between their long-held but frustrated, humanist aspirations and their recent escape into the artificial intoxication that they called the "ecstasy of violence."

So the Weathermen helped bring down on themselves and some of the rest of the movement some of the unfortunate results that Fred had talked about. I have often wondered if they did not help create an atmosphere that made it easier for the police to get high-level approval for assassinating Fred Hampton less than six weeks later.

At 4:45 A.M. on December 4, 1969, the police blitzed the apartment in which Fred and a number of other Panthers lived. Fred Hampton and Mark Clark were killed and four others were seriously wounded. State's Attorney Edward Hanrahan, who (in conjunction with someone from the civil rights division of the Justice Department) had planned the raid, announced that the police had gone to the apartment with a search warrant to seize illegal weapons. As soon as they identified themselves, he said, they were met with a barrage of fire by the Panthers. He also said that during the ensuing gun battle, the police had twice called for a cease-fire and the Panthers refused it. It took years of insistent public pressure to expose these and other lies, including faked crime-lab reports. But eventually it was conclusively proven that about ninety-nine shots were fired in the initial gun battle and that only one of them was from the inside of the apartment toward the outside. The origin of that one is unclear, since the police continued firing after they got into the apartment, but it could have been fired by a Panther. All the rest came from the outside in, fired by the police.

Fred Hampton never woke up because he had been drugged by an FBI infiltrator earlier that evening. He was murdered while lying unconscious in the bed where he had been lying next to his pregnant friend, Deborah Johnson. When the firing first began from outside the apartment, she shook and shook him in an effort to wake him, but could not. After

---

smashed. Luckily his apartment was in back, they did not know what was happening outside and none of them were hurt because no one went out during the assaults.

the police shot their way into the apartment, they entered Fred and Deborah's bedroom and fired four shots into Fred's head, two of them from close range.

We asked for a day's postponement of the trial the day that Fred was killed, but the judge refused. Meanwhile, some of our staff members visited the apartment (which strangely was not sealed off until that night) and discovered some evidence as to the nature of the shooting—evidence that was later confirmed by the second grand jury to investigate the case and even, to my amazement, by the FBI, which had been in on the original planning.* My daughter Tasha was one of those who walked in grief through that apartment that day, while I was confined to the courtroom.

That night, most of the defendants gathered with a dozen or so Black Panthers in their office. It, too, had been raided, a week or two before Fred's murder. The mimeograph machine and all the furniture had been smashed and the card files and other papers seized. We sat on the floor, with our backs to the wall, commiserating. After a while, the Panther's Security Chief, William O'Neill who was sitting directly opposite me, looked at me and said, "Now, Dave, you understand why we had to pick up the gun, why *everyone* has to pick up the gun. Now you can see *why even you, Dave, have to pick up the gun.*"

I didn't answer. My heart was too full. My only thoughts were that I knew, loved and worked with Martin Luther King, Jr. He had been totally nonviolent, but had become so dangerous that he was dead, killed by an assassin's bullet. And I knew, loved and worked with Fred Hampton, who believed in picking up the gun for self-defense but opposed aggressive violence, even in a good cause. He too had become so dangerous that he was dead, killed by an assassin's bullet. It was one of the saddest moments of my life.

*Most of the story of the various investigations and trials, coverups and lies is told by Michael J. Arlen in his book *An American Verdict* (Garden City, N.Y.: Doubleday, 1973). The main element I find missing is the complicity of the civil rights division of the Justice Department. Also, Fred Hampton's brother, Bill, told me that more evidence came out after the book had been published, in the course of a multimillion-dollar lawsuit by survivors and relatives. The suit failed in 1977 but was reinstated and settled in 1982, thirteen years after the murder, for $1.85 million.

Sometime the following year, the Security Chief of the Chicago Black Panther Party, the William O'Neill who had told me that now I could see why I had to pick up the gun, was revealed to have been an FBI infiltrator who worked closely with the police. Probably he was the one who put the drug in Fred Hampton's coffee that night, so that he would not be able to wake up when the police came to execute him.

61

A Snapshot

Brief excerpts from my twenty-three pages of testimony before the House Un-American Activities Committee on December 5, 1968, after the Chicago Convention and before our indictment:*

> MR. CONLEY [Special Counsel to the Committee]: Now, Mr. Dellinger, are you appearing here today in response to a subpoena served on you by United States [Deputy] Marshall John Brophy . . . ?
>
> MR. DELLINGER: I did receive a subpoena, and I considered not coming because I think that one does not have to obey illegal and immoral orders. However, since I am anxious to tell everything that I know involving myself, the plans, the actions and so forth at Chicago, and since I consider the Committee largely ineffective, I am perfectly happy to be here and to discuss with you everything that I can about myself. So without necessarily recognizing the validity of the subpoena, I came in response and of my own volition.

*The full text appears in *Thirty Years of Treason: Excerpts from Hearings before the House Committee on Un-American Activities, 1938–1968*, selected and edited by Eric Bentley (New York: Viking, 1971).

MR. ICHORD [Chairman of HUAC]: At that point, Mr. Dellinger, I think you have adequately expressed your contempt for the Committee, and we will let the record show that, and in order to expedite things—

MR. DELLINGER: I don't know what your word "contempt"—

MR. ICHORD: If you want to express contempt against anybody else, go ahead.

MR. DELLINGER: I don't know where the word "contempt" is; I certainly did not use it. I consider it undemocratic for a man [Committee member Albert W. Watson of South Carolina] to represent a Congressional district in which 60 percent of the residents are Black and, by the last figures I saw, only 6 percent of the Black people vote. That is the type of thing that I mean. . . .

REP. WATSON: . . . Did I understand you correctly to say that it is not your business to give advice to people?

MR. DELLINGER: . . . I said that I give a certain type of advice all the time; that is, I speak generally. I myself, for example, think that American soldiers should refuse to commit war crimes in Vietnam.

MR. WATSON: Oh, certainly.

MR. DELLINGER: I think that young men should refuse to go into the armed forces, and I will say that publicly.

MR. WATSON: And you urge them to do that?

MR. DELLINGER: But I never [do] to an individual. Even when I am sought out by an individual [who asks,] "Should I do this or that?" I never say, because . . . if people take actions without having come to what I will call spiritually and psychologically and mentally—intellectually—to an understanding of why they do it . . . it becomes very difficult for them. I saw men crack in prison because they were there on a more shallow emotion than was able to sustain them, and so I never advise anybody and say, "You drop out of the Army," or "You refuse to register for the draft" or "You lay down your arms." But obviously that's my general position, and I try to shout it from the housetops. . . .

. . . If you come to me and say, "Now I am wondering," I might be tempted to suggest you resign from the House Un-American Activities Committee. But I would rather call for its

abolition. . . . "You have to wrestle with your own conscience, you have to decide what you are prepared to do."
MR. WATSON: Of course, it wouldn't be difficult for you to suggest that I resign from this Committee, would it?
MR. DELLINGER: . . . I say that might be a temptation. . . . But what I would rather do . . . is to have South Carolina turned into a democracy, which would elect people with all the citizens' votes. [Applause.] [The chair admonishes the audience.]
MR. WATSON: . . . It is a compliment down my way to be opposed by certain individuals, so I take no personal offense to the outcry against me. . . . [Rep. Watson questions me about the kind of literature I might take to a meeting of Americans with Vietnamese.]
MR. DELLINGER: It would vary, but naturally, I being editor of *Liberation,* what would come first to mind would be . . . issues of *Liberation*.
MR. WATSON: It would be anti-American literature?
MR. DELLINGER: I don't consider *Liberation* to be anti-American. I consider the House Un-American Activities Committee to be anti-American. There are two Americas, you know. I think I speak for the best interests of the best America.

About a month after these hearings, I passed Mr. Watson in the Washington airport. He reversed directions, came back to speak to me (warmly) and urged me to stop in and talk with him in his office when I could. Unfortunately, I never found the time to do it. In some ways, my inability to follow up on such openings is the story of my life. And perhaps it is the story of anyone's life who is as busy as I am and travels widely. Especially if she or he doesn't wear the self-defensive, self-hiding masks of conventional life and keeps meeting people on a sufficiently deep, or at least honest, level to make further contact seem desirable. Even so, I feel that I should have done a much better job of finding time for such follow-ups than I have.

62

There were some compensations for Michele and Tasha during the trial. Besides observing Bobby Seale close-up, getting to know his wife and their three-year-old son, Malik, and mingling with the defendants and their womenfriends (Abbie and Anita loved Michele and she loved them), they spent time with a lot of fine young people who served on our staff or came to the trial to support us. Bob Lamb, Susan Hathaway, Donna Gripe and Frank Joyce come right to mind, and there were others too who became their friends and companions. Also there were the "celebrities" who dropped in for a day or week or to act as witnesses, especially the rock stars and theater people. Besides those already mentioned, Nicholas Ray, a film director, shot a surrealistic film version of the trial that Michele acted in. And Dustin Hoffman visited for a week and hung out with her, both in the courtroom and outside. My bail had been revoked by then, so I didn't get to meet Dustin until later, though he sent me a flattering note that I answered. Anyway, I thought it was more important for her to spend time with him than for me to, and I appreciated the way he supported and helped sustain her.

Because of the bail revocation, I was unable to speak as planned at a support rally in the Hollywood Bowl, so Tasha flew out in my place, meeting all kinds of film stars. She reported afterward that she had been so nervous that she couldn't stand when it came time for her to talk, so she spoke while sitting on a chair. Similarly, she sat on the edge of Shirley Magidson's pool, in Beverly Hills, with her feet dangling in the water (Touch the Earth!) doing her best to explain the trial to the assembled guests. Later Shirley, a much-admired businesswoman who has always been active in campaigns for justice and peace, told me that everyone had probably been more moved than if I had been able to attend.

After that, Tasha spoke on other occasions too (even getting so that she could stand while doing so), and Betty spoke to a lot of gatherings, including a major protest rally in New York. So one of the benefits to having my bail revoked was that it took some of the emphasis on such occasions away from one of the male "stars" (or "villains," take your pick) and replaced him with a woman. There were a number of women who had played important roles in the activities in Chicago and who "deserved" fully as much as we males did to have been honored with indictments. But since they weren't indicted, we were the ones who were invited everywhere, and things were getting even more out of balance than usual. Also, I was glad that having Tasha and Betty speak helped focus some of the attention on the critical family dimensions of any serious struggle for justice and peace—sometimes joint and positive, sometimes unshared and divisive, but always complicated.

On the negative side, the most serious problem was that the Weathermen, who spent a lot of time at the trial seeking to win converts, made a special attempt to recruit Tasha, Michele and Danny. Maybe I was wrong, but I thought that besides their desire to win over every young person they could, some of them thought it would be a powerful sign of the changing times if the children of nonviolent Dave Dellinger joined them. The climax came a couple months after their Days of Rage, when they held a national conference in Flint, Michigan. By then Danny was thoroughly disgusted with them, but Michele asked me if she could go, with Tasha and Susan Hathaway. It was a crisis for me, but I decided that she had already seen so much and been exposed to so much that it was better for her to go and judge for herself. I also thought that to deny her the right to go might make the Weathermen attractive as "forbidden fruit."

Tasha and Michele both went, and ultimately they were revolted by the senseless calls to violence that they heard. Initially, Tasha had been so overwhelmed by the sufferings of Black people, as well as those of both Vietnamese and Americans in the seemingly endless war, that she felt some attraction to the Weathermen's advocacy of "stronger methods" for breaking out of the stalemate in which nonviolent protestors went through the same old routines without having any apparent effect on the government. But when they told Tasha that to work with them she would have to leave her three-year-old daughter, she was offended and examined their words more closely; her sounder instincts prevailed. Meanwhile, Michele, at age thirteen, turned out to be more "mature" than the Weathermen; she had recoiled from most of what she heard.

For all my disgust with the Weathermen's emphasis on violence, I had no idea that they had become as drunk as they were with the idea of "kicking ass," one of their favorite phrases (Hi, George Bush!). This was before the townhouse explosion had brought them back closer to their senses. Nor did I realize that in their case (as in Bush's) it had become a cover for far worse atrocities. But here are two of the statements that Tasha and Michele heard at that conference. The first one referred to the recent Tate–LaBianca murders by Charles Manson and his gang. It was made by Bernadine Dohrn, a woman who had been compassionate and sensitive when I first met her three years earlier—*and still was, but only for the oppressed, not for those who practiced oppression or went along with it.* "Dig it; first they killed those pigs, then they ate dinner in the room with them, then they even shoved a fork into pig Tate's stomach. Wild!" And, by one of the men: "It's a wonderful feeling to hit a pig. It must be a really wonderful feeling to kill a pig or blow up a building."

Thus my daughters observed firsthand the truth of the claim by advocates of nonviolent resistance, including their father, that violent revolt often harms the practitioners as much as it harms those who stand in their way.

Some time after the trial, Tennessee Williams offered to let me spend a few weeks at his place in Key West to work on a book, *More Power Than We Know*, which I was having difficulty finding quiet time for. Michele and her friend Lisa Mamis went with me, and although Tennessee had said he would not be there, he flew down the next day and spent two weeks with us. When time came for Michele and Lisa to return to school, they flew back with him while I stayed on. Tennessee's driver dropped them off at Lisa's house before taking a nervous Tennessee to his doctor for the "shot" he told them he needed for his appearance on the Merv Griffin show. Naturally, they watched the show and told me afterward he would have done better without the shot, which they thought had dulled his mind. At the very least, it was an interesting two weeks for them.

There was a lot more on the same order for both Michele and Tasha, including one hectic event at the Cathedral of St. John the Divine, where they observed at close hand Charlie Mingus, the progressive jazz pioneer, Norman Mailer and Tennessee, all of whom were on the program. Tennessee became offended by the "pornography" in a play by Norman Mailer and stomped out. I followed him briefly in an unsuccessful attempt to talk him into coming back; I calmed him down a little, and he invited me to meet him afterwards in a bar where he would be with some of his friends. I took Michele with me, but both of us were bored and we didn't stay long.

I will skip most of these periodic compensations for my daughters to say that Michele also went to Miami with me in 1972 for the Democratic Convention. There, again, she met both fascinating and wonderful young people, including Ron Kovic who later wrote the book *Born on the Fourth of July*, and other veterans associated with Vietnam Veterans Against the War (VVAW). And I introduced her to Germaine Greer, Warren Beatty, Jack Nicholson and Jon Voight. But by taking her to the Democratic Convention, I had unintentionally exposed her to danger again, emotional danger to her through physical danger to me.

A half hour before we were scheduled to leave for the New York airport to fly to Miami, I learned from a disenchanted, recently resigned FBI agent that Rennie Davis and I were to be assassinated there. The circumstances were such that it wasn't practical to have Michele not go with me, worried though I was for her. I thought it better not to tell her of the threat. For that matter I told almost no one, not wanting to create a distracting panic situation that would have unnecessarily complicated our planning and actions. Fortunately, my trusted friend Dan Weiner was there for the protests; I confided in him and he made a point of spending time with Michele when I was otherwise occupied.

At the first steering committee meeting of the loose Miami Conventions Coalition, some representatives of a Red Star Collective from New Orleans, Jill and Gai Schaeffer, said that unlike the Chicago Convention of four years earlier, this time the demonstrators must be armed. Their argument was that in Chicago we had the shit beaten out of us (so far as I knew, they hadn't even been there) and we must not allow that to happen again. I was chairing the meeting and of course I argued against this. Whereupon the Schaeffers came forth with the argument I frequently heard: I was a pacifist and had no right to cause people who were not pacifists to be killed because of my personal views.* One of them sneered that I was so far behind the times that I wasn't even a Leninist. Most of the others present (even those who were not as universally committed to nonviolence as I was) defended me personally and insisted that arming ourselves would be both contrary to our principles and suicidal.

After that meeting, I thought that things were under control. But at the next meeting, which was in the basement of a church, there were more members of Red Star Collectives, from Tampa and Gainesville, Florida. They announced that they had backed a van up to the entrance and had guns in it. They would distribute them to any demonstrators sensible enough and brave enough to carry them. Again, everyone rejected their arguments and no one took a gun. But soon the mass of demonstrators would be arriving and I didn't know how some of them would respond. I was afraid that we were in trouble.

Fortunately, a delegation of Vietnam Veterans Against the War arrived the next day, having been delayed by a trial of some of their members in Gainesville—a trial that grew out of the success of Joseph Burton, a Red Star Collective member, in persuading one of the Veterans to buy a gun. I told a couple of trusted friends among them of the projected assassinations of Rennie and me, and from then until they left, the Vets formed a protective "honor guard" for us. Everywhere I went, I had a circle of them around me so that no one could take a pot shot at me

*For years, I had not called myself a pacifist, because there was so much that I disagreed with in the traditional pacifist organizations. Most of them had a tendency to concentrate on the formal violence of weapons and of personal physical violence to the neglect of the everyday institutional violence of the society. And sometimes it seemed as if the emphasis was more on being "pure" oneself than on developing nonviolent force as a method for liberating the oppressed and for national defense. There have been some real improvements since those days, particularly in the F.O.R., but these tendencies still persist. Since first writing this, I have come across some quotes from my early mentor and later antagonist, Reinhold Niebuhr, that make the same point: "Pacifism of really the classical kind is where you are concerned about your own purity and not responsibility. And the great ethical divide is between those who want to be pure and those who want to be responsible" (Taylor Branch, *Parting the Waters* [New York: Simon and Schuster, 1988], p. 896).

without hitting one of them. It reminded me of the guard we had put around Martin King at the April 15, 1967, demonstration, when we knew that there was a contract on his life. Perhaps more important, at the first meeting of the Convention Coalition after their arrival, Al Hubbard, a Black veteran, announced that anyone who proposed that the demonstrators carry guns would be automatically assumed to be a government agent. From that time on, there were no such proposals.

Naturally, a year or two later first one and then a second disillusioned member of the Red Star Collectives confessed that all the four or five Red Star Collectives (or Red Star Cadres, as they were sometimes called), had been organized and staffed by FBI agents. And, in connection with the investigations that developed around the Watergate scandal, it was revealed that when the Democratic Party Convention had been scheduled to be in San Diego, as it had been originally, the plan had been to kidnap Rennie, myself and other projected leaders and take us to Mexico. Whether we would have survived the kidnapping is anyone's guess—as it is anyone's guess whether the plan in Miami was to persuade some of the protestors to carry guns, use this as an excuse to begin a gun battle and in the course of it dispose of Rennie and me.

On the last morning of the convention, the members of VVAW left to fulfill another commitment. They offered to leave a small contingent to protect me and Rennie, but we said that it was not necessary. On that day, I wasn't shot with a bullet and neither was Rennie, but both of us were hit hard in the stomach with tear gas canisters fired at close range. We were leading a protest march at the time. If the police had been satisfied to disperse the march by tear gas, they could have fired it long before they did. But they waited until Rennie and I were a few yards from them and shot us point-blank. The blows hurt a lot, and laid up Rennie for the rest of the day, but they weren't fatal.

During the Convention, the government tried to pacify the demonstrators by flooding them with Quaaludes, a recently developed drug that, among other things, was supposed to increase male sexual prowess. One of the chief middlemen who received the Quaaludes from the government and distributed them to demonstrators was a Zippie whom I knew. The Zippies were successors to the Yippies and were scornful of Abbie Hoffman, Jerry Rubin and Ed Sanders, who had endorsed McGovern in April, taking an optimistic view of the possibilities for achieving electorally the antiwar objectives for which they had demonstrated in Chicago four years earlier. This time, they were welcomed on the floor of the Democratic Convention, Jerry in a suit and tie.

Before the convention was over, the Zippie distributor of Quaaludes had been arrested for some particularly flagrant "malicious destruction of public property," and Rocky Pomeranz, the Miami police chief, had sworn that he had the goods on him. But, given the distributor's connections with the government and what he could have brought out in a trial (or around it), the Justice Department forced the city to drop the charges, much to the displeasure of Pomeranz.

Abbie and Jerry may have had hopes for McGovern's antiwar position, but while I was in Miami I received a message from the Vietnamese negotiators in Paris, asking me to tell McGovern that they wanted to invite him to North Vietnam and talk with them in Paris and on the way to and from Hanoi. If it was impractical for him to go to Vietnam, then he should meet with them in Paris and hold a press conference on how his administration would end the war by bringing the negotiations to a successful conclusion. When I went to see George, he was tied up in a meeting and sent Germaine Greer and Warren Beatty to find out what I wanted to see him about. Since Michele went with me, she met them.

I had known McGovern since 1960 or earlier, when we both spoke at a Quaker conference in the Midwest. And we had renewed our acquaintance from time to time, including on the platform of the August 28, 1963, Civil Rights Rally in Washington, D.C. I had always been favorably impressed with him, but the closer he got to being nominated as the Democratic presidential candidate, the more I observed a change for the worse in him. So perhaps the reason that he was "tied up" when I went to see him was that he wanted to distance himself from a leader of the antiwar demonstrations. Perhaps not. In any case, though, he rejected both invitations from the Vietnamese. Later he told me that Pierre Salinger had particularly advised against accepting them because of the negative effect it would have on his campaign.

In recent years, McGovern's resounding defeat by Nixon in the elections has been cited frequently as proof that no one to the left of center has a chance in presidential elections. But what I observed at the time was his desperate attempts to prove that he was *not* left of center. Besides his timid refusal to take advantage of the opportunity presented to him by the Vietnamese to dramatize his unambiguous opposition to the war, here are some other examples that offended me during the convention and that severely disillusioned his former supporters, Hoffman and Rubin. We compared notes and this is how they expressed our combined knowledge in their book *Vote:**

> Militants were "pissed off" that McGovern people deliberately "threw" the Alabama Black and South Carolina women's challenges to aid in winning the California credentials fight.
>
> Gay people were double-crossed by the McGovern organization. Privately the gay delegates . . . were told "we agree with you but . . ." When it came time for the public debate on TV, the speaker against equal rights for homosexuals, a McGovern spokeswoman, said freedom for gays would encourage "child molesting."
>
> Women were again furious that McGovern pressured delegates to vote against abortion reforms on the platform. It was another of those "We agree with you privately, but . . ."
>
> The young McGovern delegates felt manipulated by the organization. Attempts to weld all the youth delegates into a self-conscious "youth caucus" were foiled. . . . "They don't want the youth to come together as an organized power bloc," complained one McGovern delegate.
>
> McGovern used his floor whips, delegation leaders and an elaborate communications hookup from an outside trailer to the floor to successfully pressure supporters to vote against the $6,500 guaranteed minimum income proposed by the National Welfare Rights Organization and originally backed by McGovern.

After his nomination McGovern published a full-page advertisement in the *Wall Street Journal* in which he went to great lengths to prove to the financial/corporate power elite that he was not "left of center" but their friend and supporter. Then, when it was made public that six to twelve years earlier his vice-presidential running mate, Thomas Eagleton,

**Vote* (New York: Warner, 1972) was by Rubin, Hoffman and Ed Sanders, with the first two coauthoring the section on McGovern and Sanders writing on Nixon.

had been treated three times for exhaustion and depression, McGovern disappointed me again. First he announced that he supported Eagleton "one hundred percent," and then he buckled and insisted on a replacement. In 1988 George Bush treated Dan Quayle better than that after real scandals about Quayle were made public.

Besides Abbie Hoffman, Jerry Rubin and Ed Sanders, most of the other Movement people I knew who had been planning to campaign and vote for McGovern decided not to. And don't forget that the numbers of such people in 1972 were tremendous. Clearly, he robbed himself of the kind of enthusiastic grass-roots work that had been so important for Eugene McCarthy in the 1968 New Hampshire primary. So my opinion is that this turned out *not* to be a fair test of how far one can go in opposing imperialist wars and advocating basic changes in the society and still have popular support. It was more of a revelation of what the heads of the Democratic Party and the corporate funders who have ties to both parties demand of the candidates. Knowing McGovern as I did, I don't think he *wanted* to betray his own principles as much as he did, any more than I think that in that same year Congressman Ron Dellums *wanted* not to go to Vietnam, when Cora Weiss and I invited him to, to bring home a POW who was one of his own constituents.

So maybe the cliché that no one left of center can win the presidency is right after all. Not because the public is not ready to support such a candidate, if he is well grounded, personable and properly presented to them, but because the Party heads, their financial backers and the media won't allow it. When we were demonstrating in Chicago in 1968, the section of the power elite who controlled the Democratic Party nominated Hubert Humphrey, *even though 80 percent of the votes in the Democratic primaries had gone for antiwar candidates.* (Arthur Miller, another friend from those days whom I haven't kept up with, first pointed this out to me at the time.)

These realities tell more about the nature of our "democratic elections" than it is comfortable for most people to face up to. So in 1968 a lot of people who were desperate to believe in a candidate kept telling me that Humphrey was really a progressive at heart but had felt that as vice president it was his duty to support the president by going along with him on the war. And as late as 1986, when Home Box Office produced a film on the Chicago Eight trial* and held a press conference to launch it, the most persistent questions that the media asked the defendants centered on this: "Don't you regret that the actions you took in Chicago in 1968 helped cause the defeat of Hubert Humphrey?" But way back in 1964, when Humphrey was the vice-presidential candidate, I had written the following passage about him, in an article entitled "The 1964 Elections: A Trap":

> Not only did he vote for the Communist Control Act, but he offered an amendment to outlaw the Communist Party completely, making it illegal even to be a member. His amendment had been too McCarthyite for his more experienced colleagues and was rejected, but he was more successful with an amendment to the McCarran Act, which . . . became part of the law. It provided for the erection of concentration camps (they have been built and are ready for use) and gave the attorney general power in time of "National Emergency" to apprehend and detain, indefinitely and without trial, "persons as to whom there are reasonable grounds to believe [that they] will conspire with others to engage in acts of espionage or sabotage."†

So apparently McGovern, who was in Chicago in 1968 trying to get the nomination for himself, saw what I saw, and knew that despite some changes in the Party's Convention rules (Mayor Daley's delegation was refused seating in Miami) he had to prove to the heads of the Party that he wasn't a left-of-center candidate—and wouldn't be a left-of-center president. He made the effort, but it didn't work. Unlike Humphrey, who began to betray his early progressivism twelve years before his vice-presidential nomination and sixteen years before his presidential nomination, McGovern made his move too late. As I observed it at the time, the center-right people knew his history as an opponent of the war and as a

Conspiracy: The Trial of the Chicago 8. Written, directed and produced by Jeremy Kagan, based on the trial transcripts.

†*Liberation*, October 1964. Also reprinted in my *Revolutionary Nonviolence* (Indianapolis, New York: Bobbs-Merrill, 1970).

slightly left-of-center advocate for the elementary rights of the deprived persons of our culture, and they weren't about to forgive or trust him, no matter how many gyrations he went through to prove that he had become their friend. So they left him twisting in the wind.

I felt sad for McGovern, not for his failure to win the presidency but for what that insane ambition had done to him. Over the years, I had seen how even the finest men are corrupted once they have set their hearts on becoming president. And now I had seen it happen once again to one of the finest men in conventional politics. It confirmed and strengthened my conviction that the most productive path for me was to concentrate on working outside the electoral arena.

63

On August 5, 1972, eleven of us began a fast that we hoped would add to the pressure to stop the Vietnam War. We thought it was a good time to do so, because public support for the war had largely evaporated, thanks to revolts within the troops, the dramatic protests by returned veterans, the revelations of the Pentagon Papers and public exposure to the atrocities at My Lai. Even the wiser imperialists had been arguing for some time that the price of the domestic strife and disorder caused by the war was more than it was worth. But the government was stubbornly refusing to take the last necessary steps to end it.

We didn't expect the government to pay any direct attention to the fast, but we hoped that it might stimulate some people to do a little more than they were doing to increase the pressures to come to terms with the Vietnamese. Some of the people we had in mind were long-time antiwar people who had grown tired of "doing the same old things over and over again," while others had turned more recently against the war but, like most Americans, were reluctant to get involved in public demonstrations, let alone in more serious acts of resistance.

In some ways it was an ideal fast for me, because nine of the fasters set up communal headquarters in the New York Theological Seminary in midtown Manhattan. I had so many other responsibilities that I left frequently to carry them out and, unlike most of the others, didn't sleep there because of family considerations. But the fellowship of the group, the varied spiritual exercises we engaged in, the searching discussions and the frequent, well-attended press conferences were all extremely rewarding. I even enjoyed a meeting with Norma Becker, Cora Weiss, Sid Peck, Dave McReynolds and other respected antiwar comrades who called the meeting in order to persuade some of us to give up the fast. We had not announced it as a "fast to the death," and didn't expect it to end that way, but we had said that we would fast indefinitely and, when pressed, said we were willing to risk death. This frightened them; hence the meeting. I think that fasters and nonfasters felt better afterward and closer to one another.

Despite these positive factors, it was the only fast (or hunger strike) I have engaged in that nagged at my conscience. At the request of the group, I had consulted Dick Gregory, a frequent long-term faster, and he responded by coming with his doctor to meet with us before we started. They gave us a lot of advice, some of which I liked and some of which I didn't. It made sense to install filters in the faucets from which we got our drinking water, but I didn't like the idea of adding anything to the water we drank. I have looked it up recently and found that we added a tablespoon of honey and the juice of a small lemon to each gallon of water—"to reduce the toxicity," as Dick put it. We always mentioned this in our press conferences and elsewhere, and unlike some highly publicized fasters we took no vitamins or medicines of any kind, although Dick and his doctor had urged us to. Even so, I didn't feel right about the honey and lemon juice. Perhaps I had become a fanatic, a narrow fundamentalist of fasting. Maybe I was foolishly influenced by the standards set in my prison hunger strikes, where such safeguards were impossible—and by the other fasts I had engaged in outside prison, when I had followed the same regimen. I can't judge now. But in the interests of group unity I went along with the offensive honey and lemon juice.

Mitch Snyder, whose subsequent strikes on behalf of the homeless and for other good causes are well known, and John Bach, his erstwhile fellow convict at Danbury Federal Prison, met with us to plan the fast. I had gotten to know them a few months earlier after they completed their long sentences. While still in Danbury they had sent *Liberation* magazine a perceptive article about a strike they had been involved in against prison abuses. What I learned now was that although both were extremely dedicated, Mitch wasn't good at group process. He came into that meeting (and others I participated in with him) with his own set ideas and wasn't a good listener. In the end, Mitch and John started the fast with us and continued it for eight days while leading a march from Danbury, Connecticut, to New York City. Then they stopped fasting and went to Harrisburg, Pennsylvania, to support Elizabeth McAllister and her husband, Philip Berrigan, who were about to be sentenced for having smuggled letters out of their respective prisons—much as Bach and Snyder had smuggled the *Liberation* article out of Danbury.

After fifteen days, Rennie Davis and I flew to Miami, still fasting, for a week of demonstrations outside the Republican Convention. There we were joined in the fasting by Carol Kitchens, Shari Whitehead and Jeff (Shero) Nightbird. On the twenty-seventh day of the fast, I flew to Paris in response to a message from the North Vietnamese negotiators that their government was considering releasing three U.S. POWs and wanted to discuss the matter with me. The day I arrived in Paris, I met with Madame Nguyen Thi Binh and two other NLF delegates to the peace talks—at lunch! When the time came to order the food, they all said that they would not eat unless I did. After a while they tried to resolve the impasse by ordering something simple for me to eat. It was a difficult situation but after what seemed like a long time, they finally yielded and ate without my breaking the fast.

When I got back to New York, I made a public announcement that as soon as I received word from Hanoi to fly to Vietnam to get the POWs, I would end the fast, saying that I did not want to be in a "weakened condition" while carrying out that mission. But I did not live up to it. Once again I was either foolish, fanatical or both. I waited until a few hours before our flight to stop fasting, at the end of the fortieth day. Rennie and perhaps one other (the Reverend Paul Mayer) were still fasting and said they would continue until I stopped. So I was thinking about the effect of not just one person's continuing a little longer but of three of us. And forty days was a nice round number.

Mostly I held up fairly well on the trip, but was embarrassed when at a couple of key meetings with the Vietnamese I was violently sick to my stomach and had to excuse myself to go to the toilet and vomit. But with Cora Weiss, Bill Coffin and Dick Falk there, I wasn't really needed for those few minutes. And we did manage to bring the POWs home safely, without having the government succeed in its attempted interference in any way. Not only that, but the mother of Marcus Gartley and the wife of Norris Charles traveled to Vietnam with us, and back to the United States with their loved one (and the rest of us). The government did "capture" the three POWs as soon as we landed in New York, but they were not put to work bombing Indochina, or training other people to bomb it, as had happened after some previous releases. Even more positively, two of the three, Gartley and Charles, took part in some subsequent antiwar activities.

Did the fast accomplish anything? I don't really know. But at the very least it didn't do any harm. And I like to think that besides sensitizing us a little, it had a positive effect on some of the people who knew us and on others who learned of the fast. Further, I was able to draw on it when four veterans, Brian Willson, Charlie Liteky and George Mizo from Vietnam and Duncan Murphy from World War II, were talking about a fast to the death in 1986 against U.S. aid to the Nicaraguan Contras. A couple of them came to me to discuss it and I was able to offer some advice I thought was sound: If the underlying purpose was to get results, not to kill themselves, why not announce it that way? Don't call it a fast to the death. Don't even say it is a fast until the United States ends all aid to the Contras, a position that some of them were proposing. That might require either a fast to death or an awkward termination. Say that it will continue until there is evidence of a sufficiently widespread positive response in terms of stepped-up efforts to do away with such U.S.-organized terrorism. They thought this was a good idea and that was what they did.

I wasn't tempted to fast with them and they didn't need me. But when the question came up as to whether the time had come to stop or not, and not surprisingly there was some division among them, they invited me to Washington to meet with them. I spent an inspiring week with them, at the end of which they ended the fast. But when they did so, they pledged themselves to continue with other actions in which they would risk their lives in other ways. Soon after that, some of them went to Nicaragua. There they risked life and limb by tramping paths that peasants needed to use but couldn't, at least not safely, for fear that they were mined by the Contras. And soon after that Brian lost his legs in California, when he was sitting in protest on the tracks used by trains carrying U.S. munitions to ships that would take them to Central America for use by the Contras, the government of El Salvador and other repressive regimes. The train speeded up and ran over him. It was not an "accident."

If I helped them a little, they have inspired and encouraged me to continue my own particular efforts of a similar nature, risking my freedom and sometimes perhaps my life, but not trying to die. So why do I continue my activities into old age? Because I keep being inspired by people like them, fellow members of a truly Beloved Community.*

*See the Appendix for a brief account of a 42-day fast that I participated in with Brian Willson (and eleven others) from September 1 through October 12, 1992.

IX

Behind the Politics

64

During the 1968 Democratic National Convention, scenes of the events that took place in the streets and parks of Chicago filled the TV screens for days and made headlines in the newspapers. My name, face or words were often included in the coverage. When I got home to New Jersey I was greeted by Betty and the two of our children who still lived with us, Danny and Michele. They sat me down in the living room and made the following announcement, firmly and lovingly: "We're moving. We want you to go with us, but whether you are ready to move or not, we're not staying here any longer. It hasn't been safe for a long time and now it's impossible after all the publicity about you on TV and in the papers."

Ever since the destruction of the printing equipment, Betty's blacklisting as a teacher, the death threats and the family's narrow escape from the bombs, we had been debating whether to move or stay. Chicago finished it for them—and therefore, of course, for me. Even before I had gotten home, the parents of a summer camp-mate of Michele had secured an apartment for them (or us) in the Canarsie section of Brooklyn. We moved there the next day.

Our move did not take us into a tranquil city. It catapulted us into the midst of a turbulent conflict over efforts, mostly by Black teachers and parents, to gain local community control of the schools. I supported the effort and we championed it with articles and editorials in *Liberation*, but it was Betty and the kids who were on the firing line.

The schools were closed, so she couldn't teach but she got a job with the Welfare Department. Meanwhile, I continued doing more than full-time work with the Mobe and *Liberation*. But my contributions to the family income came from speaking engagements and a small advance on my book, *Revolutionary Nonviolence;* I don't believe that I ever got ɔy either the Mobe or *Liberation*—except of course for the printing we had done before the shop was made inoperable.

When the schools reopened in January, Danny and Michele were confronted with even more difficult problems than the ones they had learned to deal with in the New Jersey schools. Busloads of Black students were brought from outside the area to attend the previously all-white schools in all-white, racially prejudiced Canarsie, and tensions were high. Michele came home from her first day saying that she had tried to be friendly with the Black girls, but they had rejected her as a honkie. When she went over to a group of white girls, they had seen her talking with the Black girls and beat her up as a "nigger-lover." Gradually she made her way; Danny, who had similar conflicts to deal with, had his sixteenth birthday on January 21, and he dropped out of school, never to return. He developed a business selling pretzels on a street corner but after a few months moved to Berkeley, where he lived on his own and worked at the Berkeley Free Clinic. Today, Danny is a living example that one does not necessarily have to have a formal education to be well educated and creative if one has an inquiring mind and takes advantage of alternative methods. Among other things, he writes good poetry and short stories and has been published in a couple of small magazines, with more public exposure to come I am sure. Tasha and Michele didn't attend college and are shining examples of the same principle. In her early forties, Tasha, while working, began taking courses to get a college degree—even as her mother had done in her forties. Now she is close to getting the certification she requires to work with her husband, Lenny Singer, as a counselor for alcoholics.

By the time that the Chicago Eight trial began (September 1969) Betty, Michele and I had moved to a slightly less prejudiced, interracial neighborhood on Brooklyn's Eastern Parkway, midway between Park Slope and East New York. But it was impossible for us to be together for long as a family. I was away for over five months at the trial. And when I was not in jail, I had a heavy speaking schedule all over the country, spreading our ideas and raising money for the trial. Betty had to work at her job in Manhattan. She, Michele and Danny all attended the first few days of the trial, but then Betty and Michele returned to Brooklyn, while Danny remained in Chicago. After a few weeks, Betty and I agreed that keeping Michele away from the trial, which was being extensively covered by the media and was much discussed at her school, was doing her no good and some harm. From then on, she attended several substantial sections of the trial, as did Tasha.

Danny attended the trial from September until just before Christmas, by which time, as he puts it now, he had had some profound experiences. Attending the trial every day showed him how corrupt, dishonest and repressive our system of justice can be. This effect was heightened by the murder of Fred Hampton on December 4 and the obvious lies the authorities used to justify it, lies similar to the ones he had observed day after day in the courtroom. Another traumatic experience for him was to see the Weathermen in their Days of Rage and in their efforts to win him and everyone else over to their espousal of violence as a "more effective way of gaining justice for the oppressed. " Dismayed by what he observed as their insensitivity to everyone else and the self-righteousness with which they patronized all members of the Movement who would not follow their path, he concluded that their idea of violent rebellion was a deluded way of trying to create a better society. By Christmas he could stand the scene no longer and left to get his head and heart together. But he returned from time to time to stand in solidarity with me.

Meanwhile, Ray and Patch attended the trial when they could, but, like Danny, had their own destinies to work out, with Ray working as director of a halfway house for mental patients and Patch working his way through Harvard Medical School without financial assistance from his parents. By then each of them had decided long since that one form or another of living a life of nonviolent service was to be their aim in life. Years earlier, each of the three boys in turn had come home from grade school at one time or another and announced that he wasn't a pacifist. Betty and I said that it was fine for them to be anything they wanted, according to their own sense of right and wrong. In a few years, all three of them had become strong advocates and practitioners of nonviolence and the struggles to do away with war and the racial, class, sexual and other sources of prejudice and oppression. Both of the girls arrived at the same place by other routes and at their own pace. None of the five children ever became close to a carbon copy of their parents, thank goodness. But all the four who are still living continue to work, each in her or his own way, for a fairer, more loving society. When Ray died, among the flood of letters of tribute to him that we received was an impressive one from the members of the Peace and Justice Committee of the city of Berkeley. In addition to his other efforts, he had been serving on it for some years.

Besides the prolonged physical separation that the trial imposed on Betty and me, it created new strains: she had become, more than ever, the wife of that famous (to some) and infamous (to others) antiwar leader and Chicago Seven defendant, Dave Dellinger. And, I'm happy to say, she didn't want to be "someone's wife"—she wanted to be a person in her own right. But the constant attention to me everywhere we went not only robbed us both of our privacy but also undermined our sense of self. To give just one typical example, one night we decided to get away from it all by driving out of town for dinner. When we stopped for gas, the attendant recognized us, called over a couple of others and they overwhelmed us with their attention and praises. When we got to a little restaurant, all throughout the meal people kept coming to our table and wanting to talk with me. All except one man who glowered at us the whole time and spat at me as we were leaving. The combination of these experiences was devastating. And to make things worse, all that temporary fame and adulation threw me off balance more than I knew.

I have to be honest and say that during that brief period (my "fifteen minutes" of fame) I didn't think it was affecting me negatively. Not the way I thought I saw it affecting some of my codefendants, for all the mostly good feelings I had about them. After all, I was nearly double their age and had been inoculated by smaller doses of hero worship by smaller groups of people off and on for years, beginning when I was a sports star. I hated the hero worship we were inundated by, not just from obvious groupies but even by some otherwise relatively sane supporters. I never doubted that I knew how to handle it, even though I didn't like it, and I was convinced that I was in no way succumbing to its corrosive effects. Didn't I love—and love to quote—the following poem by e.e. cummings, a friend whom Kenneth Patchen had introduced me to in 1945 or 1946, shortly after I got out of Lewisburg Penitentiary?

let them go—the
truthful liars and
the false fair friends

and the boths and
*neithers—you must let them go**

And hadn't we published the following in *Liberation*, typical of the attitude that kept me relatively untarnished (*I thought*)?

Not One Disciple

I have been writing what were once called novelties for twenty-five or thirty years and have not now one disciple. Why? . . . because it did not go out with any wish to bring men to me, but to themselves.

—Ralph Waldo Emerson

But in its own way, my perspective on how I handled the situation was probably comparable to that of an earlier period. Then, I had felt critical of Martin Luther King, Jr., for not doing a better job of tending to the needs of his family, but I myself wasn't meeting my own family's needs nearly as well as I thought. On both occasions Betty, who was in a better position to judge, saw my behavior differently than I did. So I have to believe, in retrospect, that she is right when she says that the fanfare of the trial and its aftermath corrupted and desensitized me more than I knew.

For that reason—and perhaps for other reasons that crop up in many marriages—my relationship with Betty was more severely threatened than at any time before or since.

In our own way, we limped along and made efforts to correct the problems. To get away from the attention and to work at the problems, we took a trip with Michele to Mexico for a couple of weeks. Intermittently we had some wonderful times, but it ended in a conflict on our very last night and we returned in disarray. We spent the month of August 1970 together in Hawaii, on the island of Oahu, staying at the home of Walter

*Shortly before I met cummings, I read this poem in *1 × 1 (One Times One)*, which Elizabeth sent me in Lewisburg; it was first published in 1944. It was one of the poems I used to say out loud to myself when I was in solitary or the Hole.

and Bette Johnson, whom I had met during a trip to speak at the University of Hawaii. (They were traveling in Europe and left their son, Giff, probably fourteen or fifteen at the time, with us. Giff was a fine young man who is now a leader in the struggle for native rights in the Marshall Islands and elsewhere, and for a nuclear-free Pacific.)

Even in Hawaii we didn't get nearly as much privacy as we needed. And Betty's memory is that I spent too much time trying to get my book *More Power Than We Know* started, though the way I remember it is that we spent many wonderful hours together. In any case, we didn't succeed in eliminating the problems that made our relationship uneven. Our times together were only intermittently magical, and when we returned to Brooklyn we brought the problems back with us.

Finally, late in 1972, Betty said to me that she wanted us to live apart for a while. "I need to gain my independence from you," she said. "I need to find out who I am in my own right. I don't want to be someone's *wife*, I want to be *myself* for a change." I knew immediately that she was right, and we worked out the arrangements. She moved out and Michele stayed with me, though later she lived with Betty some too.

A funny thing happened, though. After we had been separated a few weeks, I began to realize that I, too, needed to gain *my* independence. On the one hand, I had not made the major adjustments that would have helped our marriage—such as spending less time away from home trying to fulfill my own drives, or being more sensitive to being really together and less preoccupied with other things when I was home (or when we were technically "together" in Hawaii). On the other hand, clinging in my own way to the marriage and desperate for our love to flower again, I had been overly governed by my desire to please, calm, placate and appease her. As a result, I too was not myself and needed to regain *my* independence.

We really did go through a definite, if erratic, healing process for the next year or so. And I won't attempt to explain it, particularly since I only partially understand it. But the heart of it, I think, was that gradually each of us was able to become more fully ourself again.

Until the last few months of our separation we were usually not completely separated. We spent Christmas together in Puerto Rico, taking Michele and one of her girlfriends with us. And after that we met occasionally for meals, to go to a concert, movie, park or museum, or to make love. But then everything fell apart.

Michele and I were going to spend a good part of the summer on Cape Cod, where I planned finally to finish my book. It was financially feasible through the combined help of a friend and the little that remained from my publisher's advance. This, I thought, was the time when Betty and I could spend a tentative, more complete time back together, during her month's vacation from her job. And I thought of it as the probable beginning of our permanent reunion and new life together. But for reasons that surprised me and that I never understood, she responded negatively. Perhaps she saw it as tagging after me again, fitting into *my* plans and returning to *my* environment instead of one chosen by her. Or perhaps it was just that if I was ready to enter this new stage, she hadn't quite reached that point yet. We got into a bitter argument and I gave up on the marriage.

I entered a relationship with another woman, someone with whom I had worked for years in the antiwar movement, had always liked and been attracted to, but had not felt free to be more than good friends with. Our times together were mutually rewarding and I reached the point where I thought that she and I would have a long-term relationship. I invited her to spend Christmas with me, Michele and Danny at my Eastern Parkway apartment. I intended to introduce her to the kids as the person with whom I was going to settle down. (Until then, we had kept separate apartments.)

Christmas came and the four of us were together. Before I had gotten to my "announcement," the doorbell rang; I answered, and it was Betty. She had found out from Michele and Danny about our little party. Crying, she said, "I thought that we both knew that we were only separating temporarily, that it was only a question of time until we would come back together again. Now I'm ready and you're acting as if it's all over between us." She handed me a letter and left. The letter said much the same thing, eloquently, convincingly. It spoke of the magic of our relationship and her belief that we were ready to relive it together.

I knew immediately what I wanted to do and had to do. But I was worried sick about the impact on the other woman. In essence, I told her that I had entered the relationship because for the first time since I knew her, I had thought I was free to do so. Now, I said, I am no longer free. And I either showed her the letter or told her of its contents. She must have been hurt, but she was as wonderful as I had found her to be earlier. We talked out as much as we could, then and for a few days. In a week or two Betty and I were back together.

Ever since, the old magic has flowered more wonderfully and more consistently than ever, even if we have to weed the garden once in a while.

Shortly after our reunion, Betty, the person with whom I first felt that magic back in 1941 and with whom I now feel it more wonderfully than ever, stopped calling herself by that name and started using the name Elizabeth. As far as I am concerned, a rose is a rose is a rose, no matter by what name she is called. And because of a beautiful flower, once called Betty and now called Elizabeth, I know the depth of meaning in something Albert Einstein once said: "There are only two ways to live your life. One is as though nothing is a miracle. The other is as though everything is a miracle." Guess which way Elizabeth and I are living our lives together, with every week, month and year becoming more so.

65

All through my childhood and youth, I was grateful that our home was more of a center of loving relationships than the homes of most of our neighbors and friends. And fourteen years after my father's death, which occurred in November 1971, I was temporarily shocked, on the day of the funeral of my brother-in-law, to hear one of the bereaved sons suddenly break into a paean of praise, not for his father but for mine: "Now there was a man who loved everyone and whom everyone loved." I quote this not to suggest that my nephew did not love his father, which he did, but that in his time of grief he consoled himself with his remembrance of his grandfather, my father. And in 1989, when my Wakefield friend Jean Wheeler Beebe organized a gathering of former childhood friends around a rare visit from California of our friend Miggie Fitz Kingsland, most of the people went out of their way to tell me what a wonderful man my father had been.

Similarly, when I was growing up the other adults clearly looked upon my father as someone special, someone they admired for his warmth and generosity, even as they teased him for his frequent, if minor, violations of the social codes around which their society was organized. More than once I heard him teased for his "old-fashioned" ethics of honesty and fair-play in situations where people said he was "overdoing it" or "not being practical."

One time I came home from grade school and repeated something the kids had said about lawyers: "the way to spell lawyer is l-i-a-r," since everyone knows that lawyers tell lies to defend their clients. My father was greatly upset and gave me a lecture, saying that anyone who did that should lose his license. I think it was typical of my father that he fervently believed this but wore blinders when it came to the ethical standards of some of the top Boston lawyers with whom he associated. When I was in high school, I worked in his office in summer. Many times I saw him turn down high-paying cases for wealthy clients that would have involved defending practices that he considered unethical. He was constantly on the verge of being appointed a judge, or so we kept hearing. But one of those summers, a Boston lawyer who was one of his close friends and associates told me that my father would never be appointed because he refused to "play ball with the right people." A year or two later this man, who obviously looked up to my father, became a judge himself.

For all the loving relationships in our family, my parents never completely succeeded in transcending the established principles of hierarchy—adult over child, male over female, early achievers (my older sister and I) over slower developers (my younger sister and brother, both of whom later developed wonderfully). And although my father valued loyalty to his high moral principles more than any personal "success" he might have attained by compromising them, he developed unhealthy ambitions for his children—particularly for me, his oldest son. I concluded, after I got old enough to understand it, that it was his way of resolving the conflict between his own egalitarian values and the emphasis on success that prevailed among the people whose respect and love he cherished. He substituted pride in his children's accomplishments for any overweening ambition of his own.

As the children grew older, my father's transferred ambitions became oppressive, causing painful ruptures at one time or another with each of us. My parents boasted so much of my supposed accomplishments that it was a constant embarrassment to me. When finally, as they saw it, I "threw my life away" by refusing to register for the draft and being sent to prison, the law of compensation set in and I became not just an embarrassment to them but a source of utter humiliation. My older sister told me, when I finished my first sentence, that some of their friends who had suffered for years under my parents' boasting about me took advantage of the opportunity to get back at them in a subtle but cruel way. For example, they constantly asked about me. Who knows? Perhaps they were genuinely concerned, but this is not how my sister interpreted it or how my parents responded. Anyway, by my second term in prison I had become a nonperson within the family as far as their friends were concerned. Neither of my parents would ever mention my name, and they changed the subject as quickly as possible if someone else did.

The night I made my decision not to register I talked to my father on the phone. Now that a long-feared catastrophe was coming to a head, he told me that he would commit suicide unless I registered. I did my best to comfort and reassure him, but he said that he would not hang up until I promised to register; if I hung up, he would kill himself immediately. We talked for what must have been an hour or more before the crisis passed. Finally he confided that he felt a little better and promised not to kill himself.

Step by step over the years, my parents and I recovered from this and other separations. But a rupture that developed between them and my younger brother, Fiske, was never healed. When he came home from World War II, in which he had served as an ambulance driver in the American Field Service, he had learned to drink. How much I don't know, because he was never close to drunk on any of the times I was with him. But any imbibing of alcoholic beverages was offensive to my parents, and mortifying, since they were notorious among their friends for their rigid views on the subject. To make matters worse, they had transferred their parental ambitions from me to him, their only remaining son. Now they were being humiliated a second time.

I don't know the details of how it happened, but one way or another he was driven from home at a time when he needed a quiet sanctuary of love and understanding in which to recover from his wartime experience. While he was still in exile, a stranger in a strange land, he was killed in a fight outside a bar where he had stopped after finishing his evening job as an airline ticket agent. To compound the tragedy for my parents, given their views about sex, the man who killed him said that my brother had made homosexual advances to him. I shall never forget seeing my mother for the first time afterwards, with her meeting me at the front door, crying and saying, "My son wasn't sick, was he."

The loss my parents suffered in this tragedy and the support I was able to provide them helped bring us back together. The strength of our underlying love asserted itself, though many of our disagreements and disappointments continued.

Through the years the disagreements gradually lessened, particularly as my parents came to admire what they called "the way you and Betty are bringing up the children." Ironically, they had always argued that I would come to understand the value of "success" and money when I had children of my own and saw how necessary these things were to give them a "good start in life." How else could I ensure that they were able to go to college, etc.? But in fact we were bringing them up in poverty in an interracial commune.

On the one hand, my parents were wary of our communal sharing of finances. On the other hand, not only were the kids "turning out wonderfully," but one of the reasons, apparently, was that they were sharing naturally in family activities that my father admired. Our life integrated forms of work that he had always believed in but had been unable to integrate fully into his own life as a rising lawyer who was striving to "make it"—mostly for the sake of his children, which was another irony. We were doing heavy physical labor, some of it "close to the soil": working an organic garden, caring for animals (a milk cow, chickens and sometimes pigs), making butter and baking bread, keeping open a hilly mile and two-tenths of dirt road that the townships considered private, building a house for a new community member and so on. We had already built a print shop and were doing the range of physical and mental work involved in operating a printing and publishing business. This integration of purposeful work of hand and brain was exactly what my father would have liked to have had in his life, but for the most part had to sacrifice to the requirements of his vocation, as organized in our society.

This partial coming together around the unexpected virtues and rewards of our lifestyle gradually influenced my parents to take a more open-minded look at some of my other activities that had previously offended them as inconsistent with the kind of lifestyle and ambitions they had coveted for me. When, beginning in 1955, I went into the South from time to time—to participate in activities of the kind I have mentioned earlier—they still urged me not to, but their tone had changed. After a while, they began to say things like, "We wish you wouldn't but we understand why you feel you have to. Please don't do anything foolish."

Finally, over eighty and near the end of his life, my father told me that he had decided that the way of life I had chosen was the right one.

Perhaps I should give one example to show that this was more than fatherly love—or just talk. About two years before my father's death, both my mother and father had severe physical problems. They decided to move to a nursing home owned by one of their grandsons, my older sister's son. In preparation, they made arrangements to sell their house to a young couple who lived nearby. (This was not the seven-bedroom, three-bathroom house I had grown up in but a smaller one into which they had moved about a dozen years after the last of their four children had moved away.) The price established was very low. When some of our family members objected that they were being taken advantage of, my mother and father would not hear of it. "They're a young family with two kids already and a third on the way," they said. "They need to move into a house that is more suitable to their family situation." Naturally I supported my parents, over the objections of those who told me that it would lessen my inheritance.

A few weeks after the sale was finalized, the "nice young couple" sold the house for double what they had paid for it. I was annoyed that they had misled my parents, and I heard some mild I-told-you-so's from one or two of my relatives. But I remained overjoyed at what my parents had done, and those in our family who had opposed it didn't seem all that upset either. I think we all realized that, nearing the end of their lives, my parents had made a simple but clear statement of how they had wished they had been able to live all along. In a way, they had tried, and it could be said that this action was merely a latter-day version on a larger scale of a lifetime of sporadic efforts. I think, for example, of the many times that my father provided his services free, or for a token charge, to persons who were in trouble and couldn't afford a lawyer. But there was something in his manner now, in conversation we had about other topics, and in the way that my mother supported him, that seemed to indicate that this time both of them wanted to act more decisively. They wanted to say something important—to themselves and to their children.

When my father heard the news of the sale of the house at a big profit, he simply said, "They'll use the money to get a more suitable place for their growing family." I couldn't tell whether he believed it or not, but it was clear that he wasn't about to let anything interfere with the joy he felt at his part in the transaction.

The time my father told me that he had decided the way of life I had chosen was the right one, his humility made me more humble than I usually was. I told him that I had made many mistakes trying to work out that way of life and was still making them. I particularly apologized for the times I had hurt him by my insensitivity. And I told him what I had always known, that I could not have chosen the way of life I was trying to live except for the example he had given me. I started to talk about the way he had treated waitresses, and how our eyes had met when he defended them. This was an experience that we had shared but had never talked about. I stopped in the middle of a sentence when he murmured, "Yes, I know. Of course, of course."

At the time, I did not know how close to death he was. A week later, he took to his bed and I flew back to see him. When I entered the room, he lay with his face to the wall, preparing to die.

"Raymond," my mother said, "David's here."

"Yes, I know."

After a few moments of silence: "Raymond, Raymond, David's here, don't you want to speak to him?"

"Why should I? We said it all last time."

I don't know how this sounds to anyone who wasn't there. But my father and I knew that we had already said everything there was to say.

As a sign of my mother's new attitude, she asked me to speak at his funeral, crowded as it was bound to be—and was—with conventional Republican civic and business leaders, as well as many of the poor people whom my father had befriended. My mother had become proud of me too, for all the "radicalism" of my life and the "disgrace" she once thought it had brought on him, her and me. I did speak, but my voice broke in the middle of what I was trying to say and I had to stop earlier than I had intended.

66

When people asked me during my early years what I was going to be when I grew up, there was no way I could answer. I didn't know and I couldn't force myself to say that I did, even though it made me feel guilty, as if I had forgotten to zip up my fly or had spilled hot chocolate on Mrs. Tuttle's Persian rug. How could I know what I would want to be after reading some of Robert Service's *Poems of the Yukon*, poems about a world of lifestyles and values that none of the questioners seemed to have in mind when they asked the question? My seventh-grade teacher said that Robert Service's poems weren't any good, but I didn't like the poet she told me to read instead. He didn't send a tingling up and down my spine the way the *Poems of the Yukon* did. Nor did it make my heart come alive with pain and love the way Amy Lowell did, early in high school, when I read her poem called "Patterns." In it Amy walked up and down "the patterned garden-paths" in her "stiff brocaded [patterned] gown" trying to deal with the news that her fiancé had just been killed "in a pattern called a war." Finally she cried out in words that turned me inside out, "Christ! What are patterns for?"

No wonder I couldn't choose one of the patterns that people said would provide me with a "good" living and assure me of being "a success."

Even apart from the poems, things were happening all the time that had nothing to do with those considerations, things that it is hard to explain even now. Things that were happening inside me when I looked into the fire in our fireplace; sat perched on a rock by the ocean, with the spray watering me outside and in; or woke up at night to the eerie music of a train's far-off horn as it reverberated in the silence of my room and inside every part of my being. Or lying awake at dawn, all summer long in Maine, listening to the chug-chug of the lobster boats as the men went out on the ocean—to earn a day's pay for sure, but just as surely for other reasons as well, reasons that I now call spiritual. And I'll never forget the time I was playing baseball in the cool of the evening on the shores of Lake Quanapowitt, with the smell of newly mown hay filling my senses, and how I tried to stretch a triple into a home run and got tagged for the last out. The score was tied and my teammates were arguing that I was safe and we had won the game, but it didn't matter to me, I felt as good as if I had made it. Running home with the peepers peeping, fireflies flitting and stars beginning to shine, I felt as if I would burst from happiness. So how could I answer the adults who wanted to know how I was going to be a winner in the grown-up game of rising to the top, with no concern for the losers, some of whose sons I had been playing with? "Getting ahead," they said. But getting ahead of whom? Why?

I couldn't explain it even this well then, particularly since they wanted me to answer in ten words or less, not caring what was happening inside me.

One time when I was in high school, my girlfriend Jean sounded as if she was beginning to grow up. She said I was too fussy and should be more polite. I should tell everyone that I was going to be a lawyer like my father so that he could be proud of me, as her father was proud of her brother who was going to go into business with him. I always got a hard-on when we danced together, and when we were dancing cheek-to-cheek at the Junior Prom I came in my pants. I still remember how good I felt, like waking up one morning and spring had arrived; or Beethoven's Hymn to Joy was playing loud and clear on the radio. And excusing myself to go to the boy's room to mop up. But the outside of my pants was still wet so I walked back in with my hands in front of me, even though I felt so good that I almost didn't care. But from things like her asking me to say I was going to be a lawyer I began to discover that the rest of us wasn't as much in love with each other as our bodies were, and I took someone else to the next dance.

If I stammered when people asked the question, or even managed to say that I didn't know, most of them rushed ahead and answered for me: "Oh you'll be a lawyer like your father." "Maybe," I'd say, "but I have no way of knowing." They would shake their heads and decide that I wasn't as smart as they had thought. Either that or I was very deep. It's good to be smart but dangerous to be deep. You have to be practical to get ahead in the world and being deep and being practical don't go together, not in America, which everyone knows is the richest country in the world and has democracy. If some people in a democracy are a lot richer than other people and run most everything, it's because they are smarter, work harder and know how to be practical about things like being thrifty and how to run a business that has a lot of people working for it—*for them!*

Besides my Aunt Neva, Mr. Beebe was the only one who didn't think I should be able to tell what I was going to be. He seemed pleased when I said how hard it is to know. I'll tell you more about Mr. Beebe in a minute. I don't think the rest cared what I was going to be. They just wanted to be sure that I was planning to be important enough to make my parents proud of me, paying them back for all the sacrifices they had made for me. Mothers didn't have much to be proud of except their successful husbands, pretty daughters and smart sons—unless you counted their cooking. But everyone knew that cooking wasn't as important as making money or most of the other things that men did. All the people who invited us to dinner had cooks, but after you took a few bites you were supposed to tell the lady of the house how delicious the food was so that she could feel important.

Anyway, most people were in a hurry to get through the question and the answer, so that they could finish with the kids and talk with the grown-ups—about things that matter. It was the same as how they always asked the grown-ups how they were, but people weren't supposed to tell them. If someone did, no one listened. And afterward they said, "What a bore he is."

After I had grown up and thought I had finally left questions like that behind me, people started asking me if I was a Marxist, a pacifist or a Leo—something, anything that would explain me. I still was supposed to be a *thing*. It wasn't enough to be myself. It wasn't even possible.

I shouldn't have been surprised, because if people don't know how to treat children as persons, how would they know how to treat adults as persons? Let alone how to treat themselves as persons. People like that are too busy, whether trying to "get ahead" in the world or trying to remake it in accord with some preset formula, whether "leftist," in accord with "the one true religion" or whatever.

Nowadays when people ask me if I am a this or a that, I still can't answer the way they want me to. They want to decide who I am without getting to know me or letting me get to know them. They are hiding and they want me to hide too. But they can't find anyone that way, not even themselves. Imagine a tiger getting to know itself in a cage. Imagine getting to know the full beauty of a flower by seeing it only when its petals are closed. Not even the bees are interested then. The only way to hide that doesn't shrivel you is to be alone for a while. That really isn't hiding, it's looking for yourself. Or looking for a different form of nourishment. It helps you find other people too.

Once I tried answering, "Who, me? I'm Dave Dellinger." It sounded silly because the person already knew my name. Immediately I began to backtrack and make explanations because I was afraid it sounded arrogant, as if I thought I was someone special. I did, because I think that everyone is. But I was afraid that it would seem that I thought that I was more special than the other person. If people haven't found out how special they are, they think that being special is having more talent, money, power or fame than other people. The kind of special I mean belongs to everyone, unless they lose it by trying to have more money or power, fame or beauty, than other people.

The first time I gave that answer was in college. I went on to say, "I don't think of you as a Christian, Bob, I think of you as Bob Cohen." He didn't like that. He thought I was saying, "You're nothing but a Jew, Bob Cohen, even if you are trying to hide it by becoming a Christian and going to church." I had been there only a short time and I didn't know how much anti-Semitism there was at Yale. I didn't even know Bob was Jewish. I don't think there were any Jews in Wakefield, Massachusetts, when I was growing up, only "Irish, Italians and Americans." Most people never mentioned Jews, not with all those Irish and "Eyetalians" to talk about.

Even when I didn't make mistakes like that it wasn't a good answer. It's just that sometimes I couldn't find anything better to say. But if they got it, it said, "I'm a little awkward but I'm trying. Stick around, let's not rush things and maybe we'll get to know one another."

I won't make excuses. Excuses are another way of hiding. Usually they don't fool anyone but yourself. So I'll just say that in our society it's hard not to hide and I hide a lot, even though I know it's bad for me. The best thing is to begin by being completely naked with one person. But it's easier to take your clothes off and "make love" than it is to be naked. Sometimes making love can prevent you from being naked, as going to church can prevent you from being religious, or giving to charities can stop you from being generous.

I hope that coming out of hiding by writing this book will help me handle the question better in the future. I didn't realize how much I have been hiding until I began to write it.

It's not only words like "chick" or "fag," "nigger" or "Pollack" that demean people by turning them into something less than themselves. Good labels are bad for human beings too. There's no way I can label you or you can label me without our missing each other. To take on a label in response to some exciting new area of discovery is to be in danger of killing the true self just as it is becoming more fully alive. Who wants to be someone else? Or a follower of someone else, which amounts to the same thing? Even if it's Karl Marx, Mohandas Gandhi, Jesus Christ or a wise old guru. They have a lot to teach, but I am me and you are you. If we don't know that, we won't even learn what it is that made them great. We'll be less like them and hardly ourselves at all.

There's no one to follow except the mysterious processes of life here and now as they unfold inside and outside us. For me that sometimes happens when I read an honest book, go to the toilet or hear the "honk honk" of geese as they follow the seasons home. Robert Frost said, "When I read a book I listen for the clean sound of the axe striking good wood." (Or was it Stephen Spender writing about Frost? I can't remember.) Sometimes when I read Alice Walker, Grace Paley, David Budbill, James Baldwin, Barbara Deming—or someone whose name is new to me—I hear the sound and sometimes I don't. Why should I pretend that one of them, or anyone, always struck good wood? Or that I don't strike it myself sometimes?

In the early Seventies I attended a political meeting at which someone asked Wabun-Inini (a.k.a. Vernon Bellecourt) of the American Indian Movement (AIM), if he was a Marxist-Leninist. He said that he didn't want to define who he is in European terms. He seemed to go down in the eyes of the questioner, but he went up in mine.

Once his ancestors had to wear European clothes, learn English, become Christian and use money, otherwise their oppressors called them savages. Christianity had been given us by God through Jesus Christ, so how could they refuse? For a while in the late Sixties and the Seventies, he had to become a Marxist-Leninist and let his would-be liberators lead him in preparing for armed struggle to establish the dictatorship of the proletariat. If he didn't, they would call him an enemy of the working class. Marxism-Leninism had been given us by science, through Marx and Lenin, so he had no business rejecting it. If he made a mistake and joined the wrong "correct vanguard party," it would have been as uncomfortable for him as it was for his forebears if they joined the Catholic church and the Baptists came to town—or vice versa.

My Native American friend said to my Marxist-Leninist friend, "We are all the glory of our ancestors and the spirit of the people still unborn." So why should I become someone's disciple instead of everyone's, including my own? Besides, you can't step into the same river twice, and a lot of water has gone down the stream since Jesus Christ and Karl Marx stepped into it. Not to forget all the pollution created by Christians and Marxists.

That doesn't mean that all water doesn't have a lot in common, or that all people don't. We are all different and we are all the same. That's something I don't understand, but it's true.

I used to quote George Meredith a lot. He said, "A truly cultivated man is one who understands that the things that seem to separate him from his fellows are as nothing compared to the things that unite him with all humanity."

There's more to it than that, but like a lot of things I can't put it into words. I can feel it, though—particularly when I am lying in the grass looking up at the sky and it takes my breath away. I melt into everything and everyone.

67

Here is something surprising, an area of my life that did as much as anything else to teach me that the things that seemed to separate me from some of my fellows were nothing compared to the things that united me not only with all humanity but with nature as well. Something that also drove home to me an early awareness of how our society is artificially organized on the opposite principle, a principle that causes daily suffering for most of society's losers and spiritual decay for most of society's winners.

To put it bluntly, from as early as I can remember I was a good athlete. Not good enough to deserve an honor that my hometown newspaper conferred on me in 1950, but good enough for them to stretch a point and select me as the town's "Best All Around Athlete" of the first half of the Twentieth Century. To be honest, I think the award may have had something to do with the family I grew up in and the relationship between my father and the publisher of the paper. Or it may have been an effort by someone to "rehabilitate me" a little in the eyes of the town's critics after my prison terms for draft refusal before and during World War II. Or maybe the reason was completely different. But whatever it was, I knew that the very concept of selecting the town's "best" athletes of the last fifty years was a typical example of trying to divide society into winners and losers, bigger winners and smaller winners. It fit in with society's division of people into those who deserve to live "high on the hog" and those who don't deserve to be treated significantly better than hogs are treated by their most cruel and insensitive commercial owners. Luckily, long before the 1950 selection had been made I had renounced that kind of divisive competitiveness. Here is the story, at least as I understand it.

From as early as I can remember, I played sports because they were fun. They came as naturally as climbing a tree, sliding down a bannister, wanting to kiss my best girl or jumping into the old swimming hole on a hot day. It was as natural to throw a ball or tackle a friend who was trying to make a touchdown as it was for a bird to fly, a brook to run downhill or the sun to shine. If there wasn't a game going, I would throw pebbles in the air and hit them with a bat or stick; or bounce a ball off a wall or a tree and try to catch it when it came rushing back.

By the time I got to high school, it was pretty clear that they weren't supposed to be games that I was playing, and that it wasn't enough to play them for fun. They were athletic contests and the object was to win. If you won often enough you were a hero, a star. You were praised by coaches, teachers and other adults, followed and courted by girls, treated with respect (and sometimes only partly hidden jealousy) by boys. Younger boys boasted that they knew you and waited for you to come out of the locker room so that they could say "Hi Dave" in front of their friends.

Of course I was affected by this. But at the same time, I never lost my love of sports for more communal reasons than the divisive glory of winning. I never stopped experiencing the joys that came, win or lose, from feeling fully alive and sharing those joys with the other players, *including my opponents*. This could only happen if I used whatever skill and strength I could in an effort to win and if they did too. For athletic excellence and beauty are best expressed through the interaction of two players (or teams) in friendly competition. I leap high to catch a pass, you try to leap even higher to knock it down or intercept it. But the higher and better-timed my leap is, the higher and better-timed yours must be—and will eventually become. And vice versa. Each player brings out the best in the other, and every true athlete shares the joys of the other's excellence as well as his or her own. No one enjoys tromping a poor player. And only the most corrupted have lost sight of the joys of helping a poor player get better.

I never lost this sense of shared bliss during the contest. But off the field things were not that simple. The best I can say now is that I did not always succeed in keeping the perspective I believed in and therefore in being the person I wanted to be. I did not always remember that more important than winning the athletic contests was winning the battle against being corrupted by the social seductions of athletics as a means to divisive kinds of fulfillment. I can still remember my ambivalent response walking down Main Street the day the newspapers featured my having scored the winning basket in a championship basketball game. I didn't know whether to be more proud or embarrassed, since I knew that I hadn't played a particularly good game. I had merely made a routine shot in the final seconds after someone else (unmentioned in the papers) had made a brilliant pass to make it possible. I tried to tell a few people what had happened, but they would have none of it. To them, I was "just being modest," as every sports star was supposed to pretend to be. I had been singled out in the papers and *that* was what counted.

As I remember it, I settled that time for hoping to play better in the future, so that I could enjoy the praise more by knowing that I deserved it. I think it is fair to say that most of my high school teammates shared these ambivalent feelings—loving the game for its own sake but also loving the praise; loving the praise for its own sake but also wanting to know that we had earned it by the quality of our performance and the quality of the opposition.

Even so, it got for a time so that after every contest I couldn't wait to see the story in the sports page of the next day's paper. I can still remember one banner headline: LAZZARO AND DELLINGER WIN FOURTH AND FIFTH STRAIGHT IN HALF MILE AND MILE. (Lazzaro was my best friend, Paul, whom I'll tell you about in a moment.) But I had mixed feelings about a full-page headline in the Boston paper after I won my division in the Harvard Scholastic Cross Country championships. Winning that race frightened me because the Harvard Scholastics was the big time, with runners from as far away as New York, New Jersey and Pennsylvania. Suddenly I felt very small, vulnerable and in danger of becoming someone I didn't want to be. Riding home in the coach's car, I had a moment of clarity: I knew that what I had done didn't add one jot to building the kind of world in which poor, looked-down-on people like Paul and Rena (my Irish girlfriend) would be created equal with me and everyone else—and would remain so throughout life, no matter what their ethnic heritage, athletic or other skills. Conceivably, it might help a little if it made people more ready to listen more seriously when I said that was what I believed in and wanted to work for. But I had learned by then that it was more apt to add a new group of embarrassing admirers and false friends who were more interested in hanging out with a "star" than in discussing such things. And I had seen what stardom had done to some other athletes I knew.

In track, Mr. Heavens, the coach, said that doing our best was the only important thing, not whether our best beat someone else's best. Probably it was his presence that helped me have that moment of clarity in his car. But he was the exception: the other coaches drilled, goaded, pushed and drove us. If we lagged, they raised questions about our manhood and challenged our fitness to survive in the Darwinian jungle of "tooth and claw" that our teachers were telling us about in their classes. Only the winners survive and only the "most highly motivated" win—now and later. Wanting to come fully alive in fun and games and to share a blissful sense of well-being with *all* the players, including one's opponents, wasn't accepted as high motivation, such joys not being relevant to the grim adult competitions for which athletics was preparing us.

But why should the natural joys of children "at play in the fields of the Lord"* (Mother Nature) have been corrupted to conform to the mistaken notions of adults? How much better if the influence were the other way around, from the children to the adults. Who do we think are closer to nature, which is the true fountainhead of human nature? Of course there are countless things that children must learn from adults, but why must the adults be such bad teachers? Why cannot grown-ups become mature enough to understand that there are important ways in which they (we) can and must learn from children, letting them reawaken the child in us?

One year my friend Roger Rand got the jump on me in golf by hitting golf balls into a net in his basement all winter, while I was enjoying myself—playing basketball and hockey, reading from the Harvard Classics and the New Testament (another surprise: see Chapter 70), having snowball fights or sledding and tobogganing. So he beat me for the junior championship at the Bear Hill Golf and Country Club and had first choice at the Saturday-night dances. The night after he won, Jean looked over my shoulder when I asked her to dance and didn't answer until Roger got

***At Play in the Fields of the Lord* is the title of a novel I love by Peter Matthiessen. (New York: Random House, 1965.)

there. All smiles, she accepted him. When I walked to the refreshment counter to think it over, Mr. Beebe started telling me what a fine boy Roger was. It was true, but it wasn't the best time for me to be hearing it—especially from Mr. Beebe.

So I followed Roger's example of playing less and practicing more. Instead of waltzing down the fairway like a deer frolicking in a meadow, savoring the joys of being alive in a world of green grass, blue sky and the sweet smells and sounds of nature, I worked long hours practicing the shots that gave me trouble.

One week I spent every evening blasting balls out of a sand trap. When it got dark, I turned the lights on in whatever car was facing the right direction and kept practicing. But that experiment ended when I got in trouble—with Mr. Beebe of all people. He had been drinking in the clubhouse (Prohibition having only limited application to the rich) and came out earlier than I had expected. His battery was run down and wouldn't turn over the motor in his big Pierce Arrow. I could see why he was upset, but even so I couldn't help thinking that he should have understood, since he was the one grown-up (other than my parents) who I thought wouldn't have switched to Roger as model youth just because he had beaten me in the championship. Anyway, by then I could blast a dozen balls out of a sand trap and land most of them within easy sinking distance of the cup, with some dropping in.

The truth is that I never lost my appreciation of the magical joys in sports, win or lose, star or not. But at the same time, I never fully escaped from the unnatural compulsions of a drive to win. I stopped drinking milk because one of my high school teammates had read that it was bad for our wind. I didn't eat my mother's homemade pies for four years because the freshman football coach told us to give up desserts. And when I ran against a top-flight competitor, I punished myself to the point where I coughed up blood occasionally for two or three days afterward. Most surprising of all, I stopped masturbating for a while—at least close to important races and games—because it was supposed to make you weak. Neither God nor my mother had been able to get me to do that.

Thinking about that reminds me of a sad, but humorous, example of the power of the mind to influence the body, especially a socially corrupted mind. I was asked at age fifteen to play in an exhibition match at a golf course at which I had broken the course record. Another junior "star" and I would play two champion adults. For some reason I was more nervous than usual and had troubled dreams all night. Just as it was getting light, I woke up with a mammoth wet dream. Still under the influence of lingering guilt feelings about masturbation, I was frightened that the loss of semen would harm my game. When I stood on the first tee, I was far more nervous from that than because of the crowd or the opposition. To my great relief, I got off a good drive and second shot, with the ball stopping a few feet from the cup on a par five hole. I sunk the put for an eagle three, amid the plaudits of the crowd. But on the next hole, a short one, I shanked my tee shot into an arm of the ocean that separated the tee from the green. My conviction that I was going to pay the price for my "self-abuse" returned, and for the rest of the game I intermittently hit spectacular shots that brought forth gasps of admiration from the crowd and spectacular flubs that were met with groans.

I never told anyone the reason, or what I thought was the reason, for my disappointing performance. But we were scheduled for a second match at another club two Saturdays later, and you can be sure that for two weeks I strictly observed the sexual rules that I had internalized from my surroundings. Fortunately this unaccustomed sexual rest didn't bring about another last-minute "enervating" dream, as well it might have. Brimming with virtue and confidence, I played much better and, unlike the first exhibition, we won handily. Oddly enough, by the time of these events I had mostly outgrown my belief in the debilitating (and morally offensive) aspects of solitary sex. But in a time of stress it returned to haunt me.

I write with mixed feelings about the hours I spent practicing the various sports. In the long run, it clearly added to the fun to be able to hole out from a sand trap, fake out a tackler, scoop up a grounder at the hot corner and throw out the runner by a step or slide a puck through a defense man's legs and pick it up again after eluding his attempted body check. It makes me feel good even now to remember such pleasures. And today I thrill at seeing miraculous acts of grace and skill that shine forth in the disgustingly commercialized world of professional "sports." I cannot believe that millions watch these events, on TV or at the scene, simply to see "their team" win or because they have a bet on the outcome—any more than I can believe that the stars should be paid anything close to the millions of dollars they get while millions of people are homeless or otherwise living in dire poverty.

I wrote about that years ago in an article entitled "The Glory of Baseball." Here is part of what I wrote:

> What movement in ballet can excel the sheer beauty of a man's running across the outfield at top speed and leaping into the air to snare a swiftly moving baseball on the tips of his outstretched fingers? Or the patterns of movement when the bases are loaded, two out, the count 3 and 2, and everyone is moving with the pitch? To the rhythmic grace of the performers in motion is added the unpredictable element of the trajectory of the ball.
>
> Ballet has its own beauty of which baseball fans are often not aware. But let the intellectual not be blinded by the snobbery of his particular cult into failing to recognize the aesthetic aspects of the ballet on the diamond. . . .
>
> The player who leaps like a fawn to snare a long fly may come down to the earth computing his chances of getting a raise. The radio announcer may respond by screaming that the catch has robbed the batter of a Ballentine Blast. But the instinct of the fan who worships the mental alertness and physical grace of the performer is as healthy as the instinct of the intellectual whose frustrated life is temporarily reassured by . . . a poem or painting.*

Sometimes I won the battle to keep the true beauty of competitive athletics in perspective and sometimes I lost it. But the only race I lost during my last two years as a high school miler was a race in which I slowed down on the stretch to let a senior who'd never won a race catch up and pass me so that he could finish his career with a win. Instead, a runner from the rival team slipped ahead of us both at the tape. And in 1990 I received a letter, dated May 9, from a fellow trackman at Yale, F. Allen Sherk, in which he wrote:

**Liberation*, August 1956.

> I vividly remember the freshman meet with Harvard. You were ahead in easy first place and I was behind you. You slowed down, held out your hand and we finished as a tie. That was one of the warmest human gestures ever extended to me. All my adult life I have tried to do the same thing for other people and thereby you have had more influence on me than any of the faculty.

But I can still hear the coach screaming at me, "Don't you ever do that again. It's a disgrace."

68

When I was in the second or third grade, I saw a picture in the *Boston Herald** of a sign that said "Nigger, don't let the sun go down on you in this town." After all these years, the picture is still alive inside me. It showed an attractive Southern town with classic white houses, big, well-kept lawns, a tree-shaded street, the sign at a turning in the road and a solitary Black man walking with his head down as he passed it.

When I showed the picture to my parents, they said it was a shame that some people in the South were so narrow-minded, but I was too young to worry about such things. When I wouldn't let the subject drop, they tried to end the conversation by saying that Negroes are happier living among their own kind. They wouldn't be happy in the white man's world. This was pretty much the same type of clincher my mother had supplied when I had asked for Nellie, our maid, to eat in the dining room with us rather than by herself in the kitchen: "She wouldn't like it and neither

*A conservative Republican paper at the time, it was delivered to our door every morning.

would we. We don't have enough in common." But this time I felt pretty sure that my parents were disgusted by the sign and what it represented but didn't want to think too much about it or have me think too much about it. That way danger lies: You will only make yourself unhappy or get in trouble. Anyway, things are better than they used to be, or are getting better or are better here than somewhere else. And you have more important things to do with your life.

I must have been upset enough to raise the subject in Greg Tuttle's house too, because I remember Greg's father explaining that even though it didn't seem right to us, everyone has their customs and we should respect their ways. To be fair, I think that he meant that we should respect the customs and ways of both the Southern whites *and* the Blacks. It was through people like him that I had thought, until I was jolted by the picture, that Negroes were happy, lovable darkies who lived down by the Swannee River. They were happy picking cotton, eating watermelon and singing spirituals on the old plantations.

When I was in the fourth grade, my family drove to North Carolina to visit my father's relatives. On the way, we ate in the patio of a Southern restaurant on a hot day. There were a lot of flies buzzing around and settling on the food, which was heaped high on our plates and on huge platters in the middle of the table. The white owner told two colored boys my age to stand, one on each side of the table, and shoo the flies away with palm branches while we ate. I whispered to my mother, but she said it was all right, they liked to do it. Anyway, it was their job and they wouldn't like it if we said that we didn't care about the flies so they didn't have to.

I didn't enjoy my food after that. When I tried to talk with the boy standing closest to me, all he would do is say "Yassuh, yassuh" and roll his eyes away from me. I can still remember how the whites of his eyes stood out against his black skin when he did it. My mother said I shouldn't speak to them because it embarrassed them.

Everyone was embarrassed, including me, after I stood up, said I was through, even though I wasn't, and would shoo the flies now so they didn't have to. I was embarrassed because the one closest to me, whose palm branch I reached out for, disappeared, taking it with him. In a minute the owner appeared and asked if everything was all right. "Fine," my father said. "Everything is delicious. My boy has never been in the South before, but he's a good boy. I hope we didn't cause any trouble."

"Why do you always have to do things like that, smartypants," my sister Lib hissed under her breath. Later, as we were driving away, she said that she didn't like it either, but that's the way things are down here and there's nothing we can do about it.

My parents were very gentle with me and didn't even give me a lecture. They said we should always live the way we think is right and let other people live the way they think is right. Besides, colored people did the things they were capable of and probably had more fun in life than we did. They were very religious and God loved them as much as he loved us.

After a while we stopped talking and I fell asleep, thinking how glad I would be when I grew up and could do the things I thought were right. The next thing I knew we had stopped at a gas station and I woke up feeling happy. I had been playing King of the Hill with a bunch of colored boys. We wrestled and laughed for a while and then one of them said, "Let's all be brothers of the hill." The one who had stood next to me in the restaurant and wouldn't talk to me kissed me. His cheek was smooth as silk against my cheek. I woke up happy and sad at the same time, and my cheeks were wet from crying. I never told anyone about the dream before, maybe because it was too deep. Or because when I was growing up boys didn't kiss boys and no one I knew thought that Black was Beautiful, except as darkies on the old plantation, singing spirituals, praying and eating watermelon.

A year or two later, we went to North Carolina again, this time by train. A Pullman porter and I became friends. (He was Black of course.) It was like me and my Aunt Neva, an adult and a child being friends and equals. I can still remember not wanting to leave him when we came to our stop. I told him and he said it would be all right, we would meet again on my way back. If we didn't meet then, we would when my family went to North Carolina again next year.

I remembered the two boys and my friend the porter when I read *Uncle Tom's Cabin* and cried. Sometimes I thought about them when I woke up early and played outside, alone, until my mother called me in for breakfast—the grass damp with dew, a white sliver of a moon overhead and the birds singing. And when I lay alone in my bed at night and a train whistle sounded a long way off, sending shivers up and down my spine. I always wondered if my friend was on it.

Since there weren't any colored people in town to set me straight, I half believed what my fifth-grade teacher said: "Now that they have their freedom like everyone else, they are working hard at the bottom, working their way up the American way. A few of the most ambitious ones have come North where they are treated fairly."

The men shined shoes, washed dishes or opened the doors at the best Boston hotels. The Black doormen wore white coats and red vests, or sometimes red coats and checkered vests. They grinned a lot. I was intrigued by them, but it wasn't possible for a kid like me, in town with his parents for dinner or a show, to get to know them. One time I tried by talking with the doorman in one of the hotels while my father was getting our car. My parents told me that I shouldn't do it again because it embarrassed him and interfered with his work.

The Black men's wives worked as maids for rich people in Brookline and on Beacon Hill. The rich people were good to them and gave them their old fur coats. When I was in the fifth or sixth grade, I was riding home through Brookline after a high school football game and we drove by some Black women in fur coats. My friends said, "Don't they look funny, walking down the street in fur coats." By that time, I had lived with the hurt from the picture in the *Boston Herald* for at least three or four years, but the boys who said it were older than me and didn't ordinarily let anyone my age ride in their car, so I didn't say anything. Then the driver did a U-turn so that we could drive past the woman a second time and laugh some more. I faked a little laugh myself, but I felt so ashamed that I vowed I would never do it again. I never did like Jimmy Dean who leaned out the window just then and yelled at them. Maybe that had something to do with why I fought him later that year, when he was beating up a little kid who had sassed him.

Where I lived, if you asked someone to get you a glass of water while they were up, he or she would say, "Who was your nigger last year?" The first time after we had gone South that I heard someone say that, I thought it was terrible. Then one day I said it myself. My sister and I were visiting a family at their summer home in Kennebunkport, Maine. They were richer than we were and even the youngest kids in the family were older than me and more worldly wise. Perhaps I was trying to act sophisticated too, I don't really know. But someone asked me to get something and all of a sudden it popped out. The oldest sister, who went to college, gave me a dirty look. "Oh, that's awful," she said. "How could you say such a thing?"

When I was in high school, I was invited by a family with a girl my age to go with them to a musical in Boston. After the show, Pearl Bailey, the Black singer who had starred in it, passed us in a huge convertible, riding with the top down. We came to a red light and her car was waiting for the light to change. Everyone laughed at her and the Black man who was driving, and said how funny they looked, acting "high and mighty" in their expensive car and fancy clothes. It reminded me of the way my friends had laughed at the women in the fur coats, except that everyone was more discreet this time. They were genteel adults and didn't want to be seen laughing. They had loved the way Pearl Bailey sang and acted in the show, but clearly they didn't think it was right for her and her friend to have risen quite so high in the American way.

This time I spoke up and got into an argument with my girlfriend's parents and older sister. The girl was embarrassed. She nudged me and whispered that I was spoiling the evening. I tried to defend Pearl Bailey's right to own a convertible, just like white people, but it was harder because she and the Black man *did* look out of place. I wished they wouldn't sit up so proudly, laughing and tossing their heads as if they thought they owned the world. Couldn't they be just a little less high and mighty so as not to offend the people I was trying to persuade to be less prejudiced?

69

The year I was in junior high school I tasted the joys and sorrows of my first love affair. The sorrows came because I fell in love with a girl who was not welcome in my home or in the homes of my neighborhood friends. Her name was Rena, and she was Irish and poor. My churchgoing neighbors called people like her "Micks" or "shanty Irish."

In the beginning, Jean and Miggie, two neighborhood girls, thought it was noble and exciting that I had fallen in love with a poor Irish girl, "just like in the novels." And after school one day Jean invited Rena and me home with her, when no one else was there except the housekeeper. That was the first time I kissed Rena, when Jean made a point of leaving us alone for a while. I'll never forget what that first early-puberty kiss of love did to me.

The support of the neighborhood girls didn't last. They didn't intend to be prejudiced, but they didn't know how to make Rena feel welcome or how to interact with her. And she didn't quite know how to relate to them. Pretty soon Jean began to hint that she and I were more suited to be girlfriend and boyfriend than Rena and I were.

My mother, who never used racial epithets and would have denied having anything against poor people, said simply and severely that Rena had a "bad reputation" and was a "bad girl." When I tearfully denied it, she said that it must be true, since she came from a bad neighborhood. A few days later, she "proved" her point: her friends at the bridge club had mortified her that afternoon by talking about me. Jean's mother had told everyone that I had gone home with an Irish girl after school one day, even though her mother couldn't have been there because she worked at Mr. Evans's shoe factory. A nice girl wouldn't invite me and a nice boy wouldn't go. So don't *ever* do it again. And why didn't I spend more time with Jean?

"You used to like Jean and she is such a nice girl from such a nice family," my mother said. "Her father and mother are people that everyone in town looks up to. And Jean is the kind of a girl who could help you lead an important, useful life."

"The right woman can mean a lot to a man's career," she continued. "Your father is a wonderful man, but he wouldn't be where he is today if I hadn't come from a good family and known how to help him." (In such conversations, his years at college and Yale Law School didn't count. It had taken my mother to civilize him.) "Even now I help him in little ways that you probably don't see. He has worked hard all his life in order to make it possible for you to accomplish even bigger things than he has. I'm sure that you don't want to disappoint him by throwing it all away over a girl who isn't worthy of you."

On another occasion, after my fierce attempts to defend Rena: "Maybe you are right that she is a nice girl, despite appearances. Maybe people *are* being unfair to her. But they will always be unfair to people like her who haven't been brought up right." (My mother hadn't even seen Rena yet, let alone her parents, and had no idea how Rena had been brought up—only where.) "She just doesn't have the background to do all the things for you that you are going to need." Then she reminded me how nice everything had been when President Coolidge came to dinner when he was governor, how the *Wakefield Daily Item* had a story about his visit, and how he had predicted a great future for me when we stopped to see him at the White House.

She gave me a lot to think about, but something inside me wouldn't let me promise that I would stop seeing Rena.

That same year, my closest friend also presented problems. His name was Paul Lazzaro and he was Italian and poor. We played side by side on football, basketball and baseball teams and discussed our innermost thoughts and feelings together. He was a Baptist and one day he invited me to go to the Italian American Baptist Church the next Sunday, but my mother didn't think it was a good idea and I never did. She said a family should all go to the same church together and, besides, I wouldn't feel comfortable. I can remember asking why not, and her replying that she was sure it was a nice church and the members were good Christians but they just were not "our kind of people."

I don't want to make things sound more simplistic than they were—or than life usually is. I had been excited at the prospect of going to Paul's church with him, and I argued strongly against my mother when she said what she did. But later, alone in my room, I began to think that maybe I *would* feel uncomfortable, sitting in a church in which everyone except me would be Italian. I could see, from brief forays into Little Italy and from having had supper at Paul's house with his parents, brothers, sisters and grandparents, that Italians did speak and act in ways that I was not accustomed to.

Having a friend from the wrong "race" and class wasn't as scandalous as having a girlfriend with similar failings. But my churchgoing friends couldn't quite make Paul comfortable, or feel comfortable themselves, when he and I dropped in on them in their homes, not even when one family was nice enough to invite us to stay for supper. It had something to do with things like not cutting your salad with a knife, even though it was harder with a fork. And not tipping your bowl when you got near the end of the soup, even though that was the only way to get it all. Also, you were supposed to leave a little food on the plate to show that you weren't "a starving Armenian." (It's hard for me to believe that my mother actually used to say that, but she did.) And you were supposed to stand when your friend's mother or father entered the room, shake hands with the father and say, "Good evening, Mr. Thayer, how are you today?" You asked the mother how she was, too, but you never shook hands with her. And you always answered the question, "Fine, thank you," even if you weren't.

When you left, you were supposed to say, "I hate to go now. It's been so nice, but I have to do my homework," or "I promised my mother that I'd be home by eight o'clock," whether either was true or not. The night we stayed for supper, Paul said after we had finished eating that he was going home to listen to the "Amos and Andy" show. After he left, my friend's kid brother said, "I bet he doesn't even have a radio," and the mother said, "Johnny, that's not nice." But the father said, "He probably does. They all have radios; that's the way they spend their money, whether they can afford it or not."

I left a little abruptly myself that time, with tears in my eyes, determined to defend my friend to the death if need be and to change the way the world is. But I was sorry that I had used the word "snobbish" because, after all, they *had* invited Paul to stay for supper. I was sure that they would tell my mother that I had been rude, even though in the end they had said they were glad that I had "stood up" for my friend and how nice the visit had been, really, and please bring him again sometime. But I knew they didn't mean it, and that he wouldn't want to and neither would I.

Almost everyone I knew called Italians "wops" or "Dagos," but my parents never did. They said it wasn't nice. Jimmy Dean said that Italians were "niggers in disguise." There were no "colored" people in our town, except maybe the Italians, since everyone called pink people like me and my neighbors white, or just Americans. There were no browns, yellows or blacks, except one old "Chinaman" on Main Street who did laundry and was called a "Chink." "No tickee, no shirtee," everyone used to say, but Nellie, our Irish maid, did our wash and ironing, so I never got to know him.

A few broad-minded people said it was very nice of me to be friends with an "Eyetalian" boy. My father said he was glad and he bet that Paul would "go places"—(he did)—but maybe I shouldn't bring him home again for a while, or "force him" on my friends? Didn't I see him enough at school and in athletics without having to do things with him other times? It was a shame that some people were narrow-minded (I believe he meant it), but after all they have a right to decide who they want to visit in their homes, and you want them to feel comfortable when they come to our house. My mother said, "Always be nice to everyone, but choose your friends from the very best." By my standards, Rena and Paul were the best, but that wasn't what she meant.

70

All through grade school I hated church, so I was shocked the year I met Rena and Paul to find myself reading the New Testament at home and loving it. At the time I thought it was totally by accident, but now it seems to have been almost inevitable, given the feelings that had been burgeoning inside me for some time, the tensions created by my friendships with Rena and Paul, as well as my need for a radical spiritual support that I wasn't getting from church or the adults I knew. Years later, after having read Carl Jung, I call it synchronicity.

For a year or two I had been browsing fairly often in the Harvard Classics, a fifty-volume work that filled a whole shelf in one of the family's big bookcases. Bit by bit I discovered Shelley and Sophocles, George Gordon Lord Byron, John Stuart Mill and John Milton. There was a lot I couldn't understand, even with the help of a dictionary and looking into the fire in our fireplace. But I was moved by the majesty of the language, and by things like the way Shelley reminded me of the skylark he wrote about, who "soaring ever singest."* My readings were like windows opening into worlds beyond anything I had dreamed existed, some of them worlds that I was determined to explore in person some day. After I read John Keats's "On First Looking into Chapman's Homer"—and looked up the word "ken"—they became new planets swimming into my ken.

One day I was alone in the house and looked up a passage in the New Testament that one of the writers had referred to, Shelley I think.

*For years I remembered the passage (and said it to myself) as "Who singing ever soarest and soaring every singest." My friend Michael Ferber read this chapter and corrected the memory—but I still like to say it to myself the other way.

The words came alive as something entirely different than anything I had heard intoned and used against us in church. Before long I looked up a reference by Jesus to one of the Hebrew prophets and fell in love with them as well.

All that year, the New Testament was my most treasured book—that and two of my mother's old books, Palgrave's *Golden Treasury*, which is probably where I read the "Ode to a Skylark," and Pancoast's *Standard English Poems*. To this day I can read on the flyleaf of Pancoast the words "Marie E. Fiske, 1907" in my mother's handwriting. My mother didn't find time to read poetry anymore, or anything in the Harvard Classics that she had eagerly bought when they first came out in 1910. Not with four children and a busy social life—but she encouraged me to. I have a poignant memory of occasionally reading one of my new discoveries to her and seeing the signs of pleasure and sadness on her face, sadness because reading such things had been crowded out of her life.

After I discovered the New Testament, I didn't have any choice. I became a "Christian." But try as hard as I could, I couldn't get to like church. I still liked best people like Mr. Beebe and our milkman neither of whom was a Christian in good standing.

Mr. Beebe laughed a lot and managed to look friendly even when he did go to church, which was mostly on Christmas Sunday and Easter. But the churchgoers complained that he drank and said "damn." I never saw him even close to drunk, or heard him say "shit," let alone "fuck," not even when he and his son Marcus, my father and I, were alone together on long weekends of fishing in Maine. People said that he neglected the family business, which could have made a lot of money if he weren't so busy enjoying himself. I was always puzzled when people said that because the Beebes seemed to be better off than most people, including us. I think that the real problem was that he "wasted" Saturday afternoons reading a book or spending time with his family when he should have been playing golf with his customers, or spent Sunday mornings that way when he should have been in church, communing with God *and his customers*.

One time when I was very young, I caught a fly inside our screened porch and pulled it apart, wing by wing, leg by leg, with all the fascination of a young scientist about to discover the secret of life. Mr. Beebe was there talking with my father and he shouted at me for being cruel—not too loudly but firmly enough for me to get the point: "Even flies have rights, you know." He stood up, opened the screen door, and shooed the rest of them out. I never forgot that.

Later, in college, I read *Tristram Shandy* by Laurence Sterne. As I remember it, Uncle Toby caught a fly in his room, opened the window and put it out. "Go, go, little fly," he said, "there's room enough in the world for you and for me."

I wish it were always that simple to respect the rights of other forms of life, but for me it isn't. Perhaps it would be more accurate to say that I'm not always sure what their rights are. I upset my father by giving up hunting when I was thirteen because killing animals wasn't my idea of sport—but I didn't become a vegetarian. And when my wife and I were bringing up a growing family in rural New Jersey, with very little food except what we raised, I killed a deer or two every year in order to be sure we had some other meat than our own chickens, especially for holidays. Before and after that I tried to be like the indigenous people of this country who give thanks to the animals who provide sustenance for us, promising in return to use the strength they give us to lead loving, unselfish lives in tune with nature.

When my wife and I lived in New Jersey she put poison out for rats, but neither she nor I felt good about it. At the time we had chickens, two cows and lots of rats in the barn and in our basement. After a while we ordered a record that was supposed to drive the rats away. We thought we would like that better than killing them. But when the record came it was a recording of rats screaming. That bothered us because we didn't like to think what someone must have done to some rats to make them scream. I kept hoping that the sound was faked by screeching violins or something else that didn't torture them. I'm not an absolutist about killing rats, insects and even animals that provide food, but they all have rights, even rats.

The milkman didn't believe in God, but that made him more interesting, given the kind of God they preached at us in church. When I was in grade school and rode with him in his milk wagon, he was fun and he let me hold the reins. The kids all knew that sometimes he went to the bathroom in an empty milk bottle. Even worse, he called it "pissing," instead of "going to the bathroom." But we made a pact never to tell that to our parents, or that he didn't believe in God. I don't know which would have been worse. They didn't like for us to spend time with him anyway, even if they didn't know those things.

After I got older, I still rode with him sometimes, to help him on holidays when his load was heavy—and because I liked to listen to his stories. One day when I was in high school,he told me that the nicest thing in the world was to make love to your girl in a cabin in the woods with a fire in the fireplace and the rain making music on the roof. He said "your girl," and my heart beat faster with a forbidden thought. But I knew that I had to translate what he said into terms I could live with in my own world. I could hardly wait until I was old enough to make love with my wife in a cabin in the woods by an open fire and the rain making music on the roof.

When I was twenty-six years old and finally got married, Elizabeth and I spent our honeymoon in a cabin with a fireplace and a metal roof. It was in the woods on the edge of Puget Sound where it rained a lot. Puget Sound is three thousand miles from where I lived and near where she lived, so she had chosen the place on her own. How do you like that for synchronicity?

I don't want you to think that my response to the milkman's words was all youthful prurience, extrapolated from what happened when I kissed Rena—and from masturbating. His words excited my sense of unity with the universe as well as my bodily juices. They united two powerful sets of emotions that I hadn't linked in the same way before. And although I may not have figured it all out at the time, linking them encouraged me to view sex in a new, more healthy way, even though it was an uphill battle and took years of marriage before I got rid of the poisons I had absorbed from church and my parents.

Despite the narrowness of church Christianity as I knew it, and the offense it was to most of my best impulses, the thrill of what I felt when I read the New Testament on my own was so great that I decided to become a minister and set about the task of making a part of the church a center of earthly and heavenly love. I wanted to spread the good news about how God notices even the fall of a sparrow—a poignant thought made even more poignant when I relived the pain I had felt a few years earlier when I had killed a sparrow with my new BB gun. The thrill of the hunt and the good shot had turned to grief when I held its warm and lifeless body in my hand. I wanted the world around me to follow the lead of Jesus, who loved sinners like Mary Magdalene and the woman taken in adultery; who livened up the wedding party by turning water into wine; and who said that those who take to the sword will perish by the sword but the peacemakers will *see God!*

Of course my readings in the New Testament were as selective as the minister's were. I skipped right over the sections that spoke about the eternal damnation of sinners. Years later I read scholars who argued that those sayings were falsely attributed to Jesus, added by later scribes whom I immediately identified with the leaders in my early church.*

One of the passages that I paid a lot of attention to, given my associations with Rena, Paul and others from their sections of town, led me to form an idea for a second American Revolution that I hoped would begin in my state, as I believed that the first one had. I wanted the State of Massachusetts, which was called a Commonwealth but was filled with private wealth and private poverty, to change, as the early Christians had changed. They "had all things in common, and sold their possessions and goods and parted them to all men as every man had need."

The words are from Acts 2:44–45, in the King James version (which is the one I read at the time). *The New Testament in Modern English*, as translated by J. B. Phillips, says: "All the believers shared everything in common; they sold their possessions and goods and divided the proceeds among the fellowship according to individual need" (Macmillan, New York, 1958). I prefer the King James version's "to all men [people] as every man [person] had need." But at St. Francis Acres, the intentional community to which I belonged for about twenty years, for the last fifteen years we "divided the proceeds among the fellowship [the members] according to individual needs," even as we tried to share outside the community as well.

*In some ways, the most helpful book to me in this area was Leo Tolstoy's translation of the New Testament, with his own introduction and commentary. Strangely, it is a book that almost no one seems to know, unless I have lent my copy to them.

71

My mother was right to worry about Rena and sex, even though her insight was colored by class prejudice. Rena did hold me tight and press her budding breasts against me when I kissed her, causing strange new sensations all through my body. For the first time I understood what my father had meant when he had talked to me before puberty about how a woman can make a man do things he doesn't want to by touching his stomach with her stomach (that's the way he put it), even when they have their clothes on. Something mysterious happens, he said, which he didn't understand, but I had better not get into that situation. If a woman invited me to her house or hotel room, I shouldn't go.

It was way beyond my experience at the time. Stomach? And a woman's inviting me to her hotel room? I was maybe ten or eleven when he said it, and I couldn't imagine such a thing happening to me. Maybe that's one of the reasons that the message I got seemed to be more about my father than about me. I was greatly impressed and have always remembered it, not just because it was the first and last time my father ever mentioned sex to me, but because I sensed awe and fear in his voice. And a need to tell me that even he had sinned once, so be careful.

It all came back to me the day I visited Rena in her house. I was faint with desire just from being alone with her in a house, waiting downstairs while she changed her dress in the bedroom. And if she had called to me, or had stayed there a minute longer, I would have gone to her, shedding my clothes as I went. But she didn't call, and when she came down I had gotten hold of myself. I didn't dare even kiss her, because I knew what would happen if I did.

Years later, I wondered what my life would have been like if I had made young, innocent love with the girl I loved at the age of twelve.

Since I didn't want my flight of fancy to be marred by a disastrous pregnancy, I mostly thought about having started a little later, when I would have known enough to use a condom. But the day that I visited Rena in her home is the day that has stuck in my mind as the pivotal time when it seemed so innocent and natural a thing to do that I almost did it. After that, my defenses were up and from then until I was married, I let the fears and inhibitions of a Puritan morality constrain me while waiting for the woman I would spend the rest of my life with, the only one I would ever make love to. I'll never know what my life would have been like if I had grown up in a society, environment or time that approached youthful sex more permissively. I don't care now, but there were times of stress and desire when I cared, both before and after I was married.

For months after I first kissed Rena, I desired her with all my young body and confused mind. In the end it was as much the power of this desire as the problems created by class that caused me to see less of her, until finally we drifted apart altogether. One more visit to her house and I knew what would happen. Sex outside marriage was the one thing (or so I thought at the time) that was forbidden by the church, my family and the New Testament. Jesus had forgiven the adulteress but he told her to go and sin no more. Saint Paul had said that it's better to marry than burn, but I burned and was too young to get married.

I had no sexual thoughts at all about Paul Lazzaro. But one night after we had played in a state basketball tournament away from home, we slept in the same bed. I woke up in the middle of the night to find him asleep with his arm around me. It made me nervous, because none of the boys I knew hugged or kissed another male after they got as old as Paul and I were, not even their brothers or fathers. After a while I remembered that at home Paul slept with his little brother and decided he had forgotten who was in bed with him. That made me feel better. Just then he woke up with a start, sat upright for a moment, looked at me (I had sat up too) silently hugged me and went back to sleep. Unlike my earlier feeling that it was okay for him to put his arm around me if he thought, in his sleep, that I was his little brother, this time my reaction was just the opposite. I felt good, without any nervousness, *because I knew that he knew it was me.* I was glad that he loved me enough to want to hug me. I squeezed his hand and went back to sleep.

I never had to reject the idea of having sexual contact with Paul because it never occurred to me, either before or after that episode. It never entered my mind that a deep friendship or love between members of the same sex could be expressed sexually. We were Damon and Phythias, David and Jonathan, two friends who refused to be separated by the fact that one was rich and one poor, one considered respectable and the other a social inferior because he was an Italian. But that had nothing to do with sex. I knew, from dirty stories and my parents' veiled warnings about accepting rides from strangers, that some men who were sick did disgusting things together, but that had nothing to do with me or anyone I would ever know. If premarital sex with girls was voluptuous but forbidden, sex at any age between members of the same sex was revolting.

Once, one of the older boys told a group of us that a few men had been born with their sexual glands in the wrong place, in their assholes, or, even more horrible, in their throats. That was why they did what they did. Isn't that awful, everyone said, and shivered a little, and we were all glad that we hadn't been born sick like that. But Jimmy Dean, who was both older and tougher, said that they should be beaten up and left to die. And Carl Walker, who couldn't catch a baseball and was afraid to fight, and who the kids didn't ordinarily allow to hang out with us, said he wished he could get his hands on one. He'd kick him right in the balls where it hurt, if they have balls.

Before puberty, all the kids in the neighborhood had done things we weren't supposed to, in furtive explorations and experiments. Boys and girls played doctor, with the boys being the doctor and the girls the patients whom we examined, if only for a hurried and fearful moment. But the girls never examined us. Later, the boys gathered a few times in houses under construction and masturbated. Everyone watched everyone else, but only a couple of times did anyone touch anyone other than himself, and then only for a moment. The one time that I did, in response to being called a "fraidy cat," it felt horrible and I drew my hand back right away. I didn't know that the sensation of physical disgust I experienced was psychological, caused by the unnatural homophobia of the world in which I grew up.

Unlike the assertions that everyone goes through a homosexual phase in his (or her) teens, I have no youthful memories of having felt any genital attraction to any male of any age. Even when my college roommate (Dave Swift) and I had a deep friendship and used to say that we loved each other (we did), I felt no specifically sexual attraction or desire. The first time that I felt sexually attracted to another male, if only for a moment, was after I had been in prison for several months. It came as a shock but was undeniable, even though it didn't last and I couldn't imagine myself doing any of the things that homosexuals do together. On the other hand, somewhere in my subconscious I must have remembered how good I felt when Paul broke the conventional barriers of the day by hugging me and I squeezed his hand in return. Because years later, long after marriage and three celibate years in prison (where it was considered "queer" *not* to engage in homosexual sex), it came back to reassure me in a fearful homosexual experiment with someone I loved.

We were on a peace walk and all day we had been hooted and physically attacked. And of course we had been called "fags" and "commies," "commies" and "fags." Finally, we were in bed trying to get some sleep to prepare for the next day's encounters in hostile territory. My friend hugged me as unexpectedly as Paul had and with the same honest affection. I think that made it a little easier for me to express my own affection in the way that he had in mind, mixed up and prone to guilt as I still tended to be.

Shortly afterward, my friend was killed on the Lower East Side of New York City by muggers. They demanded money from him, but he worked at the Catholic Worker house and had already given all his money away, so they killed him. In addition to my grief, I never found out what the long-run effects of our short-run sexual liaison would have been. But I have never regretted it or felt guilty about it. And perhaps because of it—and the apparent "normality" of homosexuality among long-term inmates in prison (where I saw truly loving couples as well as vicious rapes), I have come to hold a view that is not popular among most practicing heterosexuals and is currently opposed by most political activists in the Lesbian and Gay Men's movement.

It is that at some natural level everyone is bisexual, but that recognition of this has been limited by the false stereotypes that our society has imposed on both men and women.

If I am right, most heterosexuals succumb to the homophobic pressures of society and shut off their bisexual impulses, even when circumstances are such that fulfilling them naturally would be psychologically therapeutic and spiritually enlightening, as I feel that my experience was.

And most practicing homosexuals, desperate to have their form of sexual activity accepted as legitimate—and to gain the full civil and human rights that a prejudiced society usually denies them—argue that they have no choice in the matter but are "born" that way. In the end, of course, I don't know about anyone else. All I know for certain is what I found out about myself.*

72

I have written earlier about the problems I had as a child when grown-ups kept asking what I was going to be when I grew up. And how, later, I was upset when people tried to label me a pacifist, Christian, Marxist, Leo—or whatever. "Who, me? I'm Dave Dellinger and you're Bob Cohen." I have also reported how embarrassed and thrown off-base I was when, because of the Chicago trial, some people elevated me—and thereby reduced me—to being a hero, rather than a conscientious, flawed person who basically was not different than anyone else.

People still ask me to label myself and I still don't like it. At seventy-seven I look grown up, so they mostly ask what I *became*, what I *did*. Ironically, I'd like it better if they still asked what I am going to *become*, because I'm still learning and growing, and every year gets better. That, I think, provides a clue as to why during all those years I hated the questions I have mentioned. By turning persons into things they focused on a static approach to life and people. But, like everyone else who hasn't surrendered

*Months after I wrote this, I read that a student of Herbert Marcuse said, "You know Marcuse believes that after the revolution we'll all be bisexual." He said it to Gregory Nevala Calvert, a former executive secretary of the SDS. See Calvert's *Democracy from the Heart*.

I was a living, growing, changing person who didn't want to be put into a conventional cage—or an unconventional one.

Brave as that may sound, there's more to it than that. I lacked the courage (self-confidence) to breathe life into the questions by means of my answer. I shut myself off and prevented a true dialogue. I want to explore both aspects now, hoping perhaps finally to tell you who I think I really am.

So how should I have answered when people asked one variety or another of the conventional question? Should I have been less arrogant, rigid, shy (whatever it was), and given them a conventional answer? During these latter years I could have said, for example, that I'm a part-time writer and teacher, which is probably what they thought they wanted to know. Or should I have found a way of opening up an interchange in which we could have traveled together to the place where I might have told them something more important? Where I might have become foolish enough or brave enough to tell them that I look at people's faces on a subway or street—anywhere really—until I'm full. Full is what Buddhists call empty: emptied of separation, full of unity.

And, depending on their reaction, I might have found myself going on from there to say that sometimes I look at a tree, a bird, a child or a cloud—anything really, *or nothing*—until I levitate. If I got that far and they hadn't suddenly remembered that they were supposed to be somewhere else, I might have added that "levitate is too heavy a word for what happens, but people look heavy and they're the ones it happens to."

On second thought, I wouldn't have used the word "levitate," nor would I use it now. Not any more than I would say that I keep being "born again"—even though I do, in the midst of all my confusions and failures. Both expressions have been appropriated by follow-the-leader cults to mean something different than I mean. The kind of levitation I mean helps people to rise above their ego separations, not above other people. They become one with everyone else. When that happens, they really do take off, freed from the ordinary limitations of time and space, separation and enmity. And to me being born again is of much the same order, reentering a world in which all human beings and all nature are members of the same Family. It doesn't mean being told by an anthropomorphic male God that we should stop thinking for ourselves and believe literally in every contradictory sentence that "He" supposedly dictated, word for exact word, a few thousand years ago to a mixture of narrow-minded zealots and genuinely inspired prophets—and a lot of people in between.

People who use their spiritual experiences to exalt themselves above other people remind me of what George Bernard Shaw once said to a man who complained that Shaw wasn't a "100 percent patriot." Shaw said that anyone who says that he is 100 percent anything is usually 90 percent a fool. I say that any guru who claims to be a Fully Realized Being is at least partially a fraud, no matter how charismatic and wise s/he may be. And anyone who thinks s/he can believe in 100 percent of the Bible, with all its contradictions, is fooling her- or himself, often out of a desperate yearning to belong to a loving community. Too bad these people get stuck in such a narrow and self-righteous one.

To be up front about myself, one of the more sensible things that distracts me from saying what I do is that what most people do for a living rarely tells who they would want to be if they hadn't become desocialized—another word I had better explain. To me, getting desocialized is what some people call getting socialized: learning to fit in without causing any trouble, even though the conventions people fit themselves into cause a lot of trouble. That's like saying that peace is the air force's profession, or that arms control is the way to disarmament.

Where most people work and what they do there doesn't even tell where they would work if they had a free choice. A few huge corporations have a lot to say about what jobs are available at what pay to people of what sex, color, age, locality and nationality. Ask anyone who was working for a steel mill, General Motors or G.E. until the top managers and investors decided that they could make more money by transferring the plant to Taiwan, South Korea or elsewhere. "Buy American," Ford says, but most of their parts are made in Mexico. When I was growing up, it was shoe factories and textile mills moving from New England to the South in search of cheap labor. Now most of them have moved out of the country, for cheaper labor, even fewer ecological safeguards than this country has and the protection of dictators and death squads against attempts of the people to control their own destiny—or even improve their lot a little.

Ask someone who has just been levitating on top of a mountain or listening to Mozart anywhere how eager s/he is to get back to the job s/he will have to go to the next time the alarm clock rings. Thoreau refused to have a job like that, and the alarm clock that goes with it.

You can see how a rush of thoughts, feelings and linkages sometimes overcomes me when I try to explain what I do or who I am. I tell myself it's because I don't want to get trapped into playing masked and armored games that reflect and perpetuate our separations, but that's partly an excuse. Really it's a weakness, not having enough faith in myself or other people, not living up to my deepest intuitions of who everyone is underneath their pretenses and masks. My wife, Elizabeth Peterson, is better at communicating in conventional social situations than I am. She is less armored and therefore penetrates more naturally through other people's armor. With her help, I'm gradually learning to do a little better myself. Writing as honestly as I am trying to do now—and did earlier in the book—may help too. One way or another, all autobiographies are lies, but I'm trying to tell the truth.

Sometimes a conventional answer to a conventional question *does* slow down the process of finding out who either person is. The other day I sat next to a Black man on a bus. He asked me what kind of work I do and I told him. I said I taught in an adult degree program at Vermont College. Then I asked him what he does. He looked a little embarrassed and said, "Oh, I wash dishes in the kitchen at Vermont College." It wasn't a good beginning, even though between us we managed to overcome it and get to a lot more important indications of who each of us is.

The next time a Black man asked me what I do, I said that some people call me a "peace activist," but that I don't like the term because there can be no peace without justice and therefore I'm really a justice-and-peace activist. Given what Black people know about injustice, that got us to the heart of things faster.

In my case, I was a "well-born" "white" male with more equality of opportunity than most people. Step by step I made a series of relatively free choices to swim against the social current. But who knows what my choices might have been if I had been born into a free world instead of The Free World? I might have swum more freely with the flow of life and less against the currents of separation and death. If competition, inequality and racism had not been institutionalized and called democracy, I might be a flutist.

So how shall I answer? Shall I say that I love chamber music but stopped playing the flute when my life became unbalanced because I plunged headlong into the struggle against injustice and war? That my flute was stolen in 1939 by one of the unemployed Black men we fed and sheltered in our commune in the slums of Harlem? And that, painful as the loss was, I knew that I had been less wronged by him than he by the society that provided me with a silver flute and him with a drug habit?

Or shall I confide that from age twenty, when I first read Dostoyevsky, I wanted to become a novelist and spend half my time writing and half working at what Gandhi called "bread labor"? By "bread labor" Gandhi meant animating physical work to produce necessities such as food, shelter, clothing and cleanliness. But doing those things isn't animating if it isn't freely chosen. If it's the only way you can earn a living, like my Black friend on the bus, then it isn't what I mean. Nor is it bread labor if you're a woman and have to take care of house and children full-time, without having the opportunity for a fulfilling life outside the home—or can't escape from doing all the cooking and cleaning for husband and family, even with an outside job and interests. Then it's drudgery. Drudgery drains you, and it debases the people who profit from it, directly or indirectly, even though they may not know it and think there's some other reason why their profits and power, possessions and privilege, don't satisfy them. I'm talking about the ones who make profits that they don't earn, no matter what John Houseman used to say in the TV ads about Smith Barney, the Wall Street investment firm, that they "make money the old-fashioned way, they *earn* it."

I felt sorry for John, a talented sensitive artist, telling lies like that on national TV. I guessed that something important was missing in his life and he tried to make up for it by showing off his talents on TV and making money. I'm sure it didn't solve his problem. And if that tells us as much about the state of the nation as about John Houseman, what shall we say about Bill Cosby? He is such a "nice guy" that everyone loves him, even prejudiced white people. But after E. F. Hutton got caught stealing millions from the public till, Cosby used his clean, you-can-trust-me image to say what nice trustworthy people the thieves at E. F. Hutton were. From what I know, Bill Cosby *is* a nice guy. And I bet that in his way John Houseman was, too. That shows what a mess we're in. No one is safe, not unless we get socialized.

I know that none of this is a valid excuse for not being able to answer a simple question about what I do. I know that it's mostly my own fault. But when I go to a "social" gathering where a lot of the people are sampling the guests, grading and labeling them like wine, sometimes I feel like J. Alfred Prufrock. He's the one T. S. Eliot wrote about:

And I have known the eyes already, known them all—
The eyes that fix you in a formulated phrase,
And when I am formulated, sprawling on a pin,
When I am pinned and wriggling on the wall,
Then how should I begin
To spit out all the butt-ends of my days and ways?
. . .
And would it have been worth it after all,
. . .
To say: "I am Lazarus, come from the dead,
Come back to tell you all, I shall tell you all"—
. . .
Would it have been worth while,
If one, settling a pillow or throwing off a shawl,
And turning toward the window, should say:
"That is not it at all,
That is not what I meant, at all."

Anyway, I realize that sometimes my inability to respond intelligently is a product of my shyness, a shyness that you wouldn't expect if you looked at my political history. But at some level I do know that whatever world or combination of worlds people live in, they have to start with something brief and simple when they meet for the first time. So why shouldn't people start by asking what I do? I often ask people that question myself. And why can't I answer simply and directly, while waiting for the right time to raise the ante just a little in that strange game of strip poker in which the object is for both persons to win? The way for that to happen is for one of them to take off one of her or his masks—and then for the other person to do the same. But once it starts I have to remember not to raise the stakes so fast that the other person gets alarmed and throws in the hand. Or that I do, when I see the frightened look in her or his eyes.

If we don't begin with a simple, introductory question and answer, how can we find out, step by step, if there's anyone there? Someone who is looking out at us from behind the eyes, listening with more than the ears, speaking with questions inside the answers and answers inside the questions. Someone letting us in through her or his pores and simultaneously entering ours—all the ways in which two people can start to make love, if they haven't given up and are still inhabited—in other words, if there are persons inside their bodies.

Is there life on earth? Is there life in the midst of death? Is there a person behind the mask, a flicker of flame beneath the ashes? Am I still alive myself? How shall I find out? Not by hiding my nakedness, as Adam and Eve did when they drew back in fear from the prospect of sharing their ecstasy, ran trembling from the garden and blamed God for their cowardice. And not by rushing ahead pell-mell, enthusiastically telling neighbors and chance acquaintances more than they are ready to hear. It's no use trying to rise from the living dead, in the manner of Eliot's Lazarus, by impetuously telling all, "That is not it at all. That is not what I meant, at all."

Making love may be the purpose of life, but it's not easy in today's world. Usually we have to work our way, step by step, through a smog of convention to an honest word or touch before we can surmount the social emphysema that prevents us from breathing freely together. Like countries, we are paralyzed by our defenses and afraid to relax them. Even people like me who work to get the countries to lower their defenses find it hard to lower our personal defenses.

Even if we are not paralyzed, time and energy are not always available to both persons at the same time. One of us may have someone waiting for us somewhere and we need to make love to that person too—by not making her or him wait while we levitate elsewhere. I first learned that in 1940 in a commune, from some of its premature hippies who didn't know it. And it was driven home to me in the Sixties, by real hippies who didn't know it either. But even if we remember the person who is waiting for us and leave, it won't matter that much. If we have reached the place in us that is love, that's a lot. If we can't stay—or if we can but our new acquaintance isn't ready just then to go to that place in herself or himself—s/he will probably sense what came alive inside us, and will be more ready, another time, to take a step in the direction of a more open and fully human relationship, whether with us or someone else.

Sometimes it takes more love not to invade the other person's privacy. Everyone has to decide for themselves whether or not and when to open the door. It's okay to knock, but not too insistently. If we come alive with love ourself, what more can we ask? And if we begin slowly, we will find out soon enough whether there's anywhere further we both want to go, then or later. There's no sense in rushing, only to carry a reluctant mate over the threshold into a pseudo-union and quick divorce. Maybe we will be the one to say, "Nice meeting you, see you again sometime." There's nothing wrong with that. I often say it.

William Blake said that the trouble is that most people see with their eyes instead of through them. Marshall McLuhan said that we rely too much on the eyes and not enough on the rest of us. Sometimes I have tried to look out through my eyes and in through someone else's eyes, but that's dangerous. Perhaps the days when people may be able to look into and through one another's eyes are close at hand, I don't know. But such things have to come about naturally, not from frustration, impatience or boredom. And not at the command of a paid leader in an "encounter group" or New Age workshop—not for me anyway. Some people think they "loosen up" in such settings and who am I to judge? Be careful, though. It may be as artificial as taking LSD or sniffing coke—and may lead to dependency on a leader or a set program rather than to a freely flowing mutual trust and self-awareness that leads to genuine sharing and honest epiphanies.

Whatever the circumstances, don't rush. The other person might be a hustler. Or think that you want to have an affair. If you get distracted from making love and have an affair, you may not get to know one another. Even if the Bible does say, "And he knew her." Maybe he didn't. Maybe all he did was put one part of his body inside one part of hers and they never met. You can't trust the Bible. It says, "And he knew her" even when it was a case of the male prerogative or more obvious rape. It never says, "And she knew him." How could he know her if she didn't know him?

Another reason to start at the beginning and move slowly is that it might be important for the other person to go through winter for a while even if we are in spring or summer. If the seasons can be different at the same time in different parts of the earth, they can be different at the same time in people too. Anyone who doesn't lie fallow when her or his winter comes, letting the seeds do what they are supposed to do beneath the snow, won't bring forth a good harvest when the time for it comes. As surely it will, if we respect the seasons in us.

It's not healthy to force the seasons. Or to stay always in the same one. Be wary of anyone who does. That's one of the problems with being a public personality. People expect you to stay in whatever season of growth or decay you were in when they first heard of you. The media probably didn't get you right in the first place. But even if they did, if you stay there you'll stop being yourself. If you keep doing things that aren't you, there's no telling where you'll end up. With a lot of power or money maybe, or in some other kind of trouble. You may never meet anyone again.

I have to keep reminding myself that it's all right to begin with things like "I'm an editor, what do you do?" All words are lies, but if we use them honestly they can point in the direction of truth. They provide clues that can be used, along with more important things, to find out, little by little, if what "moves inside me moves inside you." Kabir calls it "the breath within the breath." He also says: "Something inside me has reached the place where the world is breathing."*

As far as I am concerned, that's what it's all about, getting to the place where the world is breathing. As long as we don't try to talk too much about it, or turn it into a cult or a stereotyped program. If we do that we may stop noticing that some people are hungry or in prison, working for someone else's profit or overwhelmed by all the other things, little and big, that make it hard for them to breathe freely, let alone reach the place where the world is breathing. But how can we get there fully ourselves if we leave them behind?

Sometimes it's easier to get there alone. But once we get there, we are not alone. I've been there contemplating my little finger. I learned that from Huey Newton, from a poem called "Ego," in a book of his poems that he gave me:

*From the fifteenth-century Indian poet Kabir, as translated by Robert Bly.

One day I suddenly realized I had forgotten
name
age
sex
address
race
I had found myself

What is greater than love or hate
I will tell you then
what is greater than love
is the relationship I have
*with the tip of my finger.**

And I've been there singing "Give Peace a Chance" with half a million people, outside the White House.† And in jail trying to get the tear gas out of my eyes and nursing my bruises.

Right now I was just introduced to you at a friend's house and am trying to find a way for us to take a few beginning breaths together.

Or I'm on an airplane, sitting next to a mystery who might be God but could turn out to be a terrible bore—with five hours ahead of us until we land in San Francisco. Am I up to it? Do I have the energy? How many layers of defenses does s/he have? How will I find out unless I am ready to surrender some of mine?

Luckily, while waiting for takeoff I read something that may help: "The practice of Zen mind is beginner's mind. The innocence of the first inquiry—what am I? is needed. . . . The mind of the beginner is empty,

**Insights and Poems*, Huey P. Newton and Erica Huggins. San Francisco: City Lights Books, 1975.

†The words seemed too mild, but the spirit of the people was strong and that was more important. At a 1980s Vermont sit-in to demand an end to U.S. military intervention in Nicaragua, El Salvador, Guatemala and Honduras, about seventy-five of us sang "Give Peace a Push," to the same tune.

free of the habits of the expert, ready to accept, to doubt, and open to all the possibilities."*

Can I answer from the innocence of a beginner's mind, open to all possibilities? If I can, there's no way that s/he will be a bore. We reap what we sow, and more than likely s/he will respond in kind, even if as haltingly and fallibly as me. But if s/he's not ready, or this isn't a good time for her or him, s/he'll reach for a magazine or look out the window. And I'll read some more.

Here goes:

> I'm (gulp) . . . I'm . . . sort of a writer.

Or:

> I'm active in the antinuclear movement and things like that. Right now I'm on my way to speak (humbly I hope) at a feminist conference for men that my son Ray helped organize.†

Or:

> I do a little of several things like writing, teaching and political organizing, but none of them as well as I would like.

Or:

> For twenty-three years I was a working printer, but I have worked in factories, on magazines, as a truck driver and as a farm laborer.

I never know what's going to come out. I have to wait to hear what my voice has said. It changes according to the season I'm in, the season the other person seems to be in and other messages.

*From Richard Baker's Introduction to Shunryu Suzuki, *Zen Mind, Beginner's Mind* (New York and Tokyo: Weatherhill, 1985.

†I wrote this, truthfully, while he was still alive.

At least I have some things I can say now. It's not like when I was a kid and didn't know how to answer in ways that I thought my grown-up neighbors were ready to hear. One of the reasons I'm a little more open now is that later I began to learn that some of the adults were more ready than I thought. That began when I got out of prison in April 1945 and went back to my old hometown to visit. Talking with people who had supported the war—and still did—I was surprised to hear them say that they respected me for having gone to prison for my beliefs. After that, we were able to talk together in ways that I had been afraid to try when I was growing up.

And that was before the atom bomb. And ozone depletion! Now, inside everyone alive—and inside every village, town and city all over the world—another kind of bomb is ticking, a Survival Bomb. I don't know whether to call it a Survival Bomb or a Love Bomb. But whatever name we call it by, it and the nuclear bomb and the environmental bomb are all telling us what the poet said the day World War II began: "We must love one another or die."*

Which will it be? Which bomb will explode first, the Love Bomb, the nuclear bomb or the environmental bomb?

It may seem like a small beginning, but how can we learn how to love one another if we don't talk honestly wherever we are and whatever the situation? If we aren't ready to move, however slowly, toward being naked? Even at a cocktail party. Even when we seem to be completely different from each other. Even when one of us is considered a hero and the other isn't. Even when we are opponents on different sides of sensitive issues in which we both have taken positions that mean a lot to us.

How else will we learn that the things that separate us from our fellows are nothing when compared to the things that unite us with all humanity? And the Universe.

*W. H. Auden, September 1, 1939.

Appendix

U.S. Communists and the Peace Movement

From reading Lenin and from some of the experiences I have described, it always puzzled me that I know dozens of wonderful people today who at one time or another joined the Party, worked through it and even called themselves "Leninists." It is hard for me to believe that they experienced at first hand, and with the intensity that I did, actions and attitudes such as I have mentioned. But from knowing them and observing the genuine concern of most of them for justice, I would have to say that if they did, and put up with them for a time, it was because of their anguish at the sufferings of millions of people under the only non-Communist system they knew—U.S. capitalism. And because they had a need, one I did not have, to believe that somewhere there was a country that gave hope to their dreams of a better world by being well on the road to putting them into practice. In the absence of any other examples, they had to believe in the Soviet Union.

Even so, the Party had a high turnover, except among its top officials. It attracted new members by the vitality of its grass-roots struggles for justice and by its glowing accounts of the internal triumphs of the Soviet Union, then lost them when they experienced some of the disillusioning realities of the Party's twists and turns or became convinced of the Soviet Union's more obvious failings. But having no other political home, some people hung in there longer than they otherwise would have. They thirsted so eagerly for justice that they thought it was necessary to fight "by any means necessary," and they put up with intra-Party methods and sudden reversals of the Party line even when they found them hard to swallow. Given the virulence and dishonesty of much of the "disinformation" circulated by the U.S. government and media *about things in the United States and elsewhere that they knew at first hand*, it was easy for them to dismiss disquieting stories about the Soviet reality as capitalist propaganda.

Here are some excerpts from an editorial I wrote in *Liberation* in 1968. Technically it was in response to governmental reactivation of HUAC and the McCarran Act. (One of the provisions of the McCarran Act was that all Communists must register with the government, with a penalty of five years in jail and a $10,000 fine for every day in which he or she failed to register.) But the editorial was also written as a challenge to the peace movement of the day, with its failure to understand the importance of empowering the diverse individuals and groups that make it up, without demanding sectarian loyalty oaths to its own official leaders, to anti-Communism or to a particular position on issues not critical to the immediate struggle.

> The House Un-American Activities Committee (HUAC) which appears unable (or unwilling) to distinguish between Communists and a fairly wide range of non-Communist and even anti-Communist non-conformists has aroused the ire of the entire liberal movement. But the opposition to the McCarran Act, which so far . . . has been used only against real, "red-blooded" Reds, has been tempered by the distaste many socialists and pacifists feel for Communists. We hope that the opposition will grow and make enforcement unthinkable—not merely because pacifists (or liberals or socialists) may be next, as the unfortunate phrase goes, but because tyranny is tyranny and can never be justified, no matter who the victim happens to be. To look the other way because the victim is a Communist ("who only believes in freedom for those on his side") is to succumb to the same double standard of values which does in fact characterize the Communist approach and must *in the end* keep all real humanists out of the Communist movement. [Emphasis added]
>
> Many pacifists and socialists argue that it is intolerable for

the government to police the peace movement, but that the peace movement does have an obligation to police itself, carefully screening its membership to eliminate Communists. In some organizations this is attempted directly by purges and loyalty oaths, and in others by what Paul Goodman calls the "Byzantine symmetry" with which they strain never to criticize the United States without being sure to lambaste the Soviet Union. . . .

Strange as it may seem, those most concerned with keeping Communists out of peace organizations are often those who, in one respect, are most like them—leaders who are most interested in selling a line to the public than in stimulating individuals to develop their own independent thoughts and actions in the interests of peace. Communist infiltration is chiefly a threat to those who are themselves trying to develop and control a rather pliable membership. True nonviolence calls for an alert and responsible rank-and-file who know their own minds and are not easily manipulated by anyone, whether government leaders, peace leaders or Communists . . .

What we need is a peace movement in which Communists . . . will be heeded when they talk sense and ignored when they do not. If, as has happened so many times . . . the Party line shifts and peace is no longer "progressive," the Communists will drop out of such a movement but no one else will follow them. Or if their experience in the peace movement is vital enough, they will leave the Party, not the peace movement. . . .

Unless the American peace movement thoroughly outgrows all partisanship toward *either* side in the Cold War, it will not develop the imagination and forthrightness to grapple with the root causes of war. Yet those . . . who insist on rigid exclusion of Communists never argue for a similar exclusion of pro-Americans. On the contrary, their emphasis on excluding Communists is usually hard to separate from their attempts to prove their respectability as loyal oppositionists, oppositionists loyal, that is, to the American nation-state. Historically, the peace movement, in this and other countries, has suffered most . . . from the disaffection, in times of crisis, of those who had not weaned themselves from loyalty to the country in which they lived. . . .

The power of a nonviolent movement stems from the actions

> it undertakes, not from . . . the private beliefs and associations of its participants. Most of those who praise Gandhi because of the campaigns he carried out would consider him a crank if they knew of him only through his writings on sex, diet, medicine, etc. Or would consider him politically confused if they read some of his statements on economics or socialism. . . . But when the unifying factor is the dynamic one of individual actions jointly undertaken, questions about political reliability and future loyalty recede into the background. It is not our business (any more than it is that of the government) to inquire into the motives or outside associations of those who challenge American and Soviet [nuclear] tests, commit nonviolent civil disobedience against missile bases or Civilian Defense drills, refuse to pay income taxes for war or to perform war work, eschew economic and power relationships which involve living off the labor or subservience of their fellows. Radical personal actions carry their own power and must always be the undergirding of an effective anti-war movement.

Some of the Uses—and Dangers—of Sabotage

Here are a few explanatory words about my attitude toward sabotage. In the statement I made before entering prison in 1943, I had written the following:

> True pacifists are uncompromising fighters against fascism, totalitarianism and every form of injustice and oppression. But we believe in fighting with methods that are successful. . . . Already the occupied countries show that there are ways of resisting an aggressor without huge armies and fleets. The noncooperation, the sabotage, the slowdown and the secret press of countries like Norway, Holland and Belgium have done more to insure the real defeat of Hitlerism than all the military might of the United States. [Note that I said "real defeat" and "of Hitlerism," not of Hitler the individual.] We need to go but one step further. We need a

> resistance that will renounce sabotage, sniping, deception, terrorism and all other essentially violent acts. We need to embrace a type of resistance that is equally unyielding to tyranny, but at the same time is humble, straightforward and loving.

When I got out of prison two years later I drew a more careful distinction between violence against people, which I continued (and continue) to oppose, and the physical destruction of property, which I had come to regard (and still regard) as a method that under some circumstances can be part of a loving nonviolent campaign. But it is a complicated issue.

In a society that exalts property rights above human rights, it is sometimes necessary to damage or destroy property, because property has no value except insofar as it contributes to human welfare, because sometimes it is necessary to challenge people to discover a new sense of priorities, and above all because sometimes that is the most efficient way of defending people. Thus, as fathers Philip and Daniel Berrigan and their associates said when they destroyed the draft files of a Baltimore draft board, there is some property, including concentration camps and draft files, that has no right to exist. And one could cite numerous other examples, from bombs, missiles and other instruments of destruction to a lock, door or window that bars entrance to a house whose sleeping inhabitants are in danger of being burned to death by a raging fire.

On the other hand, the use of violence against property presents many problems, not the least of them being the temptation to promiscuity, attended by a hardening of attitude toward the persons who protect property. During some periods, the anti-imperialist movement has tended to attract some people who are driven by despair, impatience or boredom to focus on property destruction and to neglect the building of enduring human relationships and institutions. Physical assaults on the primacy of property will not accomplish the legitimate purpose of exalting the rights of people unless they are part of a revolutionary nonviolence that expresses love, not contempt for those persons who, as brainwashed tools of the dominant society, happen to be one's opponents of the moment. The deplorable trend in some circles during the late Sixties and Seventies toward "pig-baiting," fanaticism and self-righteous coronation of one's little group as the revolutionary vanguard did not furnish a sound context in which to experiment with blowing up, burning down or trashing property. The combined excitement and drama of such actions can foster an illusion of revolutionary seriousness and effectiveness while actually discouraging hard organizing, critical analysis and tactical imagination.

English Version of Leaflet Distributed to Soviet Soldiers (and others) During 1951 World Citizens Peace Project

WE ARE FOUR AMERICANS WHO ARE BICYCLING FROM PARIS TO MOSCOW ASKING THE PEOPLE OF THE WORLD TO LAY DOWN THEIR ARMS

The United States you hear of most often is the United States of far-flung military bases, of atom bombs, of American dollars to bribe Europe into rearmament. We are from another United States, a United States of persons who want peace and friendship and economic equality throughout the world.

WE WANT TO ESTABLISH CONTACT WITH "ANOTHER EUROPE." WE WANT TO UNITE WITH PEOPLE OF BOTH BLOCS WHO KNOW THAT:

1. "Defensive armaments" on any side always lead to further rearmament on the other side—and to war.
2. Modern war cannot possibly defend anything—not "peace," not "democracy," not "socialism," not one's family or one's self.
3. If these things are true, we have a higher obligation than just to grumble about them privately. We must begin to act in accord with what we know by refusing to make or bear arms.

LET US JOIN TOGETHER IN NONVIOLENT RESISTANCE TO WAR AND INJUSTICE.

Nonviolent resistance is the carrying out in practice of the basic insight of all international working class movements and of all great religions—that all men are brothers who will eventually free themselves from artificial hostilities and divisions. Tolstoy in Russia, Gandhi in India and the American antislavery fighter William Lloyd Garrison are among the early pioneers of nonviolent resistance.

Nonviolent resistance uses strikes, boycotts, demonstrations and civil disobedience to attack militarism, totalitarianism and injustice. At the same time, those who embrace nonviolent resistance treat every individual as a friend. They steadfastly refuse to hate or kill anyone, including opponents both in their own country and in the so-called enemy countries.

For some the sacrifices will be great, but unlike the sacrifices of war they can help mankind to find a creative way out of the present hopelessness. Only the self-giving love of total nonviolence can sweep away the present fears and bring closer the day when all people will live together as brothers.

LET US SAY NO TO REARMAMENT AND WAR:

1. Refuse to serve in the armed forces.
2. Refuse to transport or make weapons of war.
3. Organize a collective nonviolent resistance movement.
4. Refuse to hate or kill anyone.

LET US SAY YES TO ECONOMIC EQUALITY AND BROTHERLY LOVE:

1. Work to equalize the standard of living throughout the world. In the United States we advocate contributing the 56 billion dollar arms budget to a world peace budget for this end.
2. Organize communal groups and enterprises in which people live and work together as equals. Work for communal ownership of existing enterprises.
3. Live and act as members of the world community whose first loyalty is to the people of the world rather than to any national government.

THE PEOPLE OF THE WORLD MUST REFUSE TO BE ENEMIES. LET US REACH ACROSS THE ARTIFICIAL BARRIERS AND MAKE PEACE.

David Dellinger, Printer, Member of a World Citizens Community.
Ralph DiGia, Bookkeeper, former union organizer, member of a World Citizens Community.
Arthur Emery, Dairy Farm worker, World Citizen.
Bill Sutherland, Writer, World Citizen.

PEACEMAKERS, 2013 Fifth Avenue, New York City, New York.

Declaration of Peace with the People of Vietnam

This was a separate document from the Declaration of Conscience that was featured at the beginning of the August 1965 weekend. The Declaration of Peace consisted of five paragraphs, each of which ended with the statement, "We declare peace with the people of Vietnam." It read in full as follows:

> Because for 20 years the people of Vietnam have been tortured, burned and killed; because their land and crops have been ruined and their culture is being destroyed; and because we refuse to have these things done in our name, we declare peace with the people of Vietnam.
>
> Because millions of Americans had hoped and expected that their votes in the 1964 elections would move our country away from war toward peace, and because these hopes and expectations have been betrayed in Vietnam, we declare peace with the people of Vietnam.
>
> Because the Congress of the United States, without adequate discussion, has permitted the declaration of an undeclared war, we symbolically assume its responsibility for this day in the name of those people of the United States and of the world who oppose this war and declare peace with the people of Vietnam.
>
> Because we believe that the steady escalation of the war in Vietnam threatens all people with nuclear death, we declare peace with the people of Vietnam.
>
> Because we believe that people all over the world must find ways of making peace with each other and to keep their governments from ever waging war, we declare peace with the people of Vietnam.

Appendix

Evidence Regarding Pearl Harbor

Here is some evidence for the charges that the United States helped provoke the attack on Pearl Harbor, and that the U.S. government knew the attack was imminent but failed to notify the Pearl Harbor command about it.

After building an impressive case that Roosevelt and Churchill conspired to induce Japan to attack us by imposing a deadly economic blockade on Japan, which is severely lacking in indigenous natural resources, Jeannette Rankin cited in her Congressional statement an article from the *Saturday Evening Post* of October 10, 1942. In it, Clarence E. Dickinson, U.S.N., said "we had sailed from Pearl Harbor on November 28, 1941 under absolute war orders. Vice Admiral William F. Halsey, Jr., had given instructions that the secrecy of our mission was to be protected at all costs. We were to shoot down anything we saw in the sky and to bomb anything we saw on the sea. . . . In other words . . . did not the President at least nine days before the Japanese attack on Pearl Harbor, without a declaration of war, authorize an identical attack upon the Japanese, also without a declaration of war?"

Sixteen years later Congresswoman Rankin reaffirmed in *Liberation* even more strongly the accuracy of her charge as I had heard her do privately and from lecture platforms as well.

Whereas Rankin placed the beginning of these attacks as "at least nine days before the Japanese attack on Pearl Harbor," other sources say it had been going on for months. And on July 18, 1991, the *New York Times* carried on its inside pages an inconspicuous story from AP saying that "until now 259 pilots and crew members of the Flying Tigers of World War II could not claim veteran status. For years the Pentagon did not acknowledge the Flying Tigers as anything but volunteers fighting independently of American controlled operations. But a special service review board recently ruled that the group had served on 'active duty' in their battles in 1941. . . . Fighter pilots for the elite team were recruited *early in 1941* from military bases across the country" (emphasis added).

Historian Harry Elmer Barnes, the author of several books on the duplicity with which FDR "lied the United States into war" (as he phrased it), wrote in *Liberation*, August 1958, that "Roosevelt . . . took steps to prevent the Pearl Harbor Commanders, General Short and Admiral Kimmel, from receiving the decoded Japanese intercepts that Washington picked up and [that] indicated that war might come at any moment, and ordered General Marshall and Admiral Stark not to send any warnings to Short and Kimmel before [the time] on December 7 when Roosevelt knew that any warning sent would be too late to avert the Japanese attack."

John Toland supplies some last-minute details of how the United States broke the code and withheld the information. Then he writes that "Army cryptoanalyst William P. Friedman found it hard to believe what happened. All he could do was pace back and forth, so his wife recalled, and mutter to himself repeatedly, 'But they knew, they knew, they knew.' "

And "Aboard a tramp steamer . . . Dusko Popov, a British double agent . . . heard the captain announce . . . the attack on Pearl Harbor. Popov was triumphant. That fall he had personally passed on to the FBI a detailed plan of the Japanese air raid which he had obtained from the Germans. . . . 'I was sure the American fleet had scored a great victory over the Japanese. I was very proud that I had been able to give the warning to the Americans four months in advance. What a reception the Japanese must have had!' " (*Infamy: Pearl Harbor and Its Aftermath*. New York: Berkeley, 1983.)

Hungering for Justice

From September 1 through October 12, 1992, I participated with Brian Willson and eleven others in a 42-day People's Fast for Justice and Peace in the Americas. September 1 was the fifth anniversary of the day Brian was run over by the naval munitions train in Concord, California. October 12 was, of course, Columbus Day, a day that traditionally has celebrated Columbus's "achievements."

Our headquarters were in Washington and we spent from two to seven every day except Sunday on the steps of the Capitol, answering a multitude of questions from passersby (who were responding to a sign on the steps that called attention to the fast) and others who came to visit and share ideas with us. These included indigenous peoples from most countries in the hemisphere, African Americans, Latinos, 1980 Nobel Peace Laureate Adolfo Perez Esquival from Argentina, Father Miguel D'Escoto from Nicaragua, Nelsa Curbelo from Ecuador (continental co-ordinator of the Peace and Justice Service or SERPAJ), Dolores Huerta of the Farm Workers and The 21st Century Party, Daniel Ellsberg, Martin Sheen, and other supporters from every country in Central and South America. Since I had a number of previous speaking commitments (and Elizabeth and I had agreed earlier to lead a four-day retreat in Minnesota), I travelled almost as much as I stayed in Washington, but continued to fast. After fasting on water only for three weeks, I drank fruit juices during the last three weeks. I didn't really want to drink the fruit juices but several doctors (including our son Patch) had said that at my age I would do serious, permanent damage to my body if I didn't. Because of these opinions, Elizabeth had serious initial reservations about my fasting, but gradually came to support it enthusiastically, spending the last five days with me in Washington and fasting on water only.

Other fasters included a former FBI agent, a woman from the Maryknoll Society Justice and Peace Office who is chairperson of Pax Christi USA, a "100-percent disabled" Vietnam veteran, a man who had served as contract administrator for the Rockwell Missile Systems Division for twenty-three years, a former stockbroker who now operates a soup kitchen, and a woman who had taught in public schools for twenty-two years and had decided that nonviolently achieved major changes in the society's institutions and philosophy would do more to bring out the best in our children than any amount of tinkering with the educational system. Bringing especial joy to me and Elizabeth, our foster son Howie Douglas fasted the first twelve days with us, before having to stop to fulfill risky obligations on a painter's ladder, and returned with his wife Betty for the last five days, with both of them fasting.

In some of my talks and writings, I quoted the following passages about Columbus:*

*From the quarterly newsletter of the Center for Global Education at Augsburg College, Summer 1991.

> Upon meeting the Arawak, Columbus wrote, "They do not know force. I showed them a sword, they took it by the edge and cut themselves out of ignorance. . . . Should your majesties command it, all the inhabitants could be taken away to Castile, or made slaves on the island. With fifty men we could subjugate them all and make them do whatever we want."
>
> Columbus proceeded to do just that. Eager to fill up the boats with treasures promised to the crown, the Spaniards forced every Arawk of 14 years and older to search for gold. Columbus had the hands cut off any Indian who did not fill a three-month quota.
>
> Before returning to Spain from his second voyage in 1495, Columbus went on a massive slave raid. He used dogs to round up 1500 Arawak men, women and children and imprisoned them in guarded animal pens. The best 500 were chosen for the long journey back; only 300 survived the voyage to Spain, where they soon died from cold, disease and abuse.
>
> What Columbus initiated in the Bahamas, Cortez continued . . . in Mexico, Pizzaro . . . in Brazil and the English in Massachusetts.

But mostly I concentrated on the current situation in the United States, as in the following article that I wrote for the *Los Angeles Times*, entitled "Hungering for the Real U.S. Issues."*

> Now that the Soviet Union has collapsed, what are we going to do about the United States? Will we accept the propaganda that "our system is triumphant" and should be established all over the world, with the U.S. as Superpower? Or will we admit that our system has failed too, depriving millions of their basic human rights, from food, housing, health care and jobs to a safe and healthy environment and realistic participation in the decisions that affect their lives? During the period in which the Soviet Union was falling apart, the U.S. had a doubling of billionaires and of

*September 30, 1992.

the homeless. Shall we pretend that the children of billionaires and the children of the homeless are "born equal" and that this is a democracy? More U.S. children die every year for reasons related to poverty than the total number of U.S. combat deaths in the entire Vietnam War. And in the United States, the rate of Black incarceration is six times that of whites. Do Blacks have a proclivity for criminality in their genes? Or is the economy, culture and system of "justice" criminally racist?

At one level of their consciousness most people know these realities—and more! Public discontent is far greater now than in the Sixties. But because it embraces more issues than when civil rights and anti-Vietnam War dominated public demonstrations, not everyone goes to the same city on the same day to shout the same slogans. This makes it easier for the media to claim that "the days of social revolt are over." Nonetheless, the volcano that the military-corporate elite is so fearfully sitting on is bound to erupt, one way or another, just as the Soviet volcano did.

One of our purposes in fasting is to encourage the development of a nonviolent movement that will have the power of a volcano without its mindless destructiveness. I am re-dedicating myself to principles that Martin Luther King Jr. articulated in the last few months of his life [principles that made him so dangerous to the power elite that elements within it arranged for his assassination]*

> For years I labored with the idea of reforming the existing institutions. . . , a little change here, a little change there. Now I feel quite differently. I think you've got to have a reconstruction of the entire society, a revolution of values.

> We can't have a system where some people live in superfluous, inordinate wealth, while others live in abject, deadening poverty. From now on, our movement must take on basic class issues between the privileged and the underprivileged.

*The words in brackets were omitted by the *Los Angeles Times*.

> The evils of capitalism are as real as the evils of militarism and evils of racism.
>
> We . . . must work out programs to bring the social change movements through from their early and now inadequate protest phase to a stage of massive, active, nonviolent resistance to the evils of the modern system.

King called for imaginative experiments in new forms of human relatedness based on respect for the dignity and ultimate sanctity of every human being, regardless of race, age, sex, sexual orientation, abilities, skills and whatever mistakes or crimes that anyone may have committed. Even crimes? Some of society's victims do terrible things that are deplorable even though they harm far fewer people than the crimes of our present society and its rulers. But as Judge David Bazelon has written: "Society should be as alarmed by the silent misery of those who accept their plight as it is by the violence of those who do not."

And *The New Yorker* wrote concerning the recent riots in Los Angeles: "But what, as a nation, did we really expect? The residents of our inner cities have for many years now been unable to lay claim to our sense of common humanity and simple decency. On what basis can we expect to suddenly lay claim to theirs?"

Martin Luther King once said to me: "We don't have to like everyone, but we won't solve our problems if we don't love them." While fasting, my colleagues and I will attempt to spell out some of the concrete steps through which we think that these principles—and that love—can be implemented. But the task will require the combined trial-and-error efforts of many hearts, minds and lives, with many experiments in our own lives and communities and in the overall society. As I once heard a wise person say, "If you tell me that what I propose will take a thousand years to accomplish, that's all the more reason for starting this afternoon."

A COUPLE OF YEARS AGO I GAVE UP READING A SERIES OF ARTICLES BY DAVE DELLINGER ON HIS TRIP TO CUBA BECAUSE HE'D OBVIOUSLY BEEN BRAINWASHED. LAST YEAR IN HAVANA I ASKED MR. DELLINGER IF I COULD TAKE A SECOND LOOK AT THOSE ARTICLES. IT TURNS OUT I WAS THE ONE WHO'D BEEN BRAINWASHED. I DON'T KNOW HOW TO KEEP FROM BEING BRAIN-WASHED —
BUT LIBERATION TAKEN ONCE A MONTH IS A DAMNED GOOD ANTIDOTE.
JULES FEIFFER

Index

Index